Evangelical Christian Responses to Islam

Also Available from Bloomsbury:

American Evangelicals, by Ashlee Quosigk
The Christian Encounter with Muhammad, by Charles Tieszen
The New Apostolic Reformation, Trump, and Evangelical Politics, by Damon T. Berry

Evangelical Christian Responses to Islam

A Contemporary Overview

Richard McCallum

BLOOMSBURY ACADEMIC
LONDON • NEW YORK • OXFORD • NEW DELHI • SYDNEY

BLOOMSBURY ACADEMIC
Bloomsbury Publishing Plc, 50 Bedford Square, London, WC1B 3DP, UK
Bloomsbury Publishing Inc, 1359 Broadway, New York, NY 10018, USA
Bloomsbury Publishing Ireland, 29 Earlsfort Terrace, Dublin 2, D02 AY28, Ireland

BLOOMSBURY, BLOOMSBURY ACADEMIC and the Diana logo are trademarks of
Bloomsbury Publishing Plc

First published in Great Britain 2024
Paperback edition published 2025

Copyright © Richard McCallum, 2024

Richard McCallum has asserted his right under the Copyright, Designs and Patents Act, 1988, to be identified as Author of this work.

For legal purposes the Acknowledgements on p. xii constitute an extension of this copyright page.

Cover images: Moon over cross of church © Image Source/Getty;
crescent moon © Todd Ryburn Photography/Getty

All rights reserved. No part of this publication may be: i) reproduced or transmitted in any form, electronic or mechanical, including photocopying, recording or by means of any information storage or retrieval system without prior permission in writing from the publishers; or ii) used or reproduced in any way for the training, development or operation of artificial intelligence (AI) technologies, including generative AI technologies. The rights holders expressly reserve this publication from the text and data mining exception as per Article 4(3) of the Digital Single Market Directive (EU) 2019/790.

Bloomsbury Publishing Plc does not have any control over, or responsibility for, any third-party websites referred to or in this book. All internet addresses given in this book were correct at the time of going to press. The author and publisher regret any inconvenience caused if addresses have changed or sites have ceased to exist, but can accept no responsibility for any such changes.

A catalogue record for this book is available from the British Library.

Library of Congress Cataloging-in-Publication Data
Names: McCallum, Richard (Sociologist of religion), author.
Title: Evangelical Christian responses to Islam : a contemporary overview / Richard McCallum.
Description: London ; New York : Bloomsbury Academic, 2024. |
Includes bibliographical references and index.
Identifiers: LCCN 2023027690 (print) | LCCN 2023027691 (ebook) |
ISBN 9781350418219 (hb) | ISBN 9781350418257 (paperback) |
ISBN 9781350418226 (epdf) | ISBN 9781350418233 (ebook)
Subjects: LCSH: Christianity and other religions–Islam. |
Islam–Relations–Christianity. | Evangelicalism.
Classification: LCC BP172 .M377 2024 (print) | LCC BP172 (ebook) |
DDC 261.2/7–dc23/eng/20230810
LC record available at https://lccn.loc.gov/2023027690
LC ebook record available at https://lccn.loc.gov/2023027691

ISBN: HB: 978-1-3504-1821-9
PB: 978-1-3504-1825-7
ePDF: 978-1-3504-1822-6
eBook: 978-1-3504-1823-3

Typeset by Newgen KnowledgeWorks Pvt. Ltd., Chennai, India

For product safety related questions contact productsafety@bloomsbury.com.

To find out more about our authors and books visit www.bloomsbury.com
and sign up for our newsletters.

For Laurel and Herbie

Contents

List of tables	ix
Foreword *Philip Lewis*	x
Acknowledgements	xii
Note on the text	xiii
List of abbreviations	xiv
Introduction: Evangelicals responding to Islam	1

Part 1 A micro-public sphere

1	Public spheres	15
2	Typologies of encounter	33

Part 2 Evangelicals talking among themselves

3	Allah	49
4	Muhammad	65
5	Qur'an and Hadith	77
6	Sharia	91
7	Islamization	103
8	Persecution	119
9	Violence	135
10	Israel-Palestine	151
11	So Islam is …	167

Part 3 Evangelicals engaging with Muslims

12	Talking strategies	181
13	Mission strategies	193

| 14 | Types of Evangelical response | 207 |

Conclusion: The Evangelical micro-public sphere on Islam   211

Notes   227
References   251
Index of public sphere participants and organizations   277
Index of topics   283

Tables

2.1	Closed and open views of Islam	34
14.1	Motivations for Evangelical attitudes and actions	208
14.2	How Evangelicals view Islam	208
14.3	How Evangelicals view Muslims	208
14.4	Evangelical approaches to Islam and Muslims	208

Foreword

Philip Lewis

For today's cultured despisers of religion, Muslims and Evangelical Protestants tend to attract most odium. This is perhaps unsurprising since sociologists of religion noticed more than twenty years ago that these two groups were in the vanguard of a global resurgence of religion, in part a reaction to secular modernity. Scorn and contempt for such religiosity easily translate into an essentialist reading of both traditions, whereby they are reduced to some unchanging essence and pathologized. This can generate fear and disable people from living well with religious diversity, the reality for an ever-increasing number of societies.

This study of global Evangelical responses to Islam and Muslims, in the twenty years since 9/11, provides an invaluable contribution to religious literacy, a precondition for healthy and robust debate in argumentative, Western democracies – a priority, not least for politicians, policymakers and the media. After reading this book, the diversity and deep differences among the Evangelical Protestants documented cannot but subvert lazy caricatures.

Specialists will appreciate its conceptual sophistication, the general reader its illuminating contextualization of occasionally arcane issues. Evangelical Protestants will learn that fear of Islam goes back to Ottoman military expansion at the time of the Reformation. However, nineteenth-century colonialism brought Evangelicals into direct encounter with Islam and Muslims and generated serious engagement with Islamic texts and Muslim communities.

Evangelical Christians today build on these earlier foundations when they debate a range of contentious, theological, historical and socio-political issues regarding Islamic belief and practice. These range from whether they worship the same God as Muslims; what to make of Muhamad; Islam's scriptures – Qur'an and Hadith; the Sharia and worries about the extent of Islamization of Western societies; persecution of Christian minorities in Muslim-majority states; and the resurgence of violent extremism. These issues comprise the heart of the present work, where the complete spectrum from confrontational to conciliatory views is clearly laid out. Each chapter concludes with a discussion which judiciously summarizes the implications of such different perspectives, especially for constructive encounter and mission, themes dealt with in the final section of the book.

Although it does not ignore the digital world, the focus is the books written in English by two hundred Evangelicals, some acknowledged scholars of Islam, working in about a dozen countries. Most of the authors are men from America, Britain or Australia. However, Evangelicals from the Middle East and Africa are finding their voice, along with a growing minority of women. Indeed, some of the most illuminating and profound contributions to the debates are being made by Arab and African voices. Cumulatively, these works comprise an 'Evangelical micro-public sphere' – McCallum's coinage drawing on the work of Habermas, Fraser and others identifying voices and texts that coalesce around a topic or issue of concern in public discourse.

There are views here which will be uncongenial to liberals of all persuasions, religious or secular. The chapter on Israel-Palestine shows the dangers of allowing Christian Zionism and eccentric readings of biblical prophecy to become the lens through which Islam is interpreted. At the same time, Evangelicals are increasingly active in inter-faith encounter, peacemaking, humanitarian aid and efforts to challenge fellow believers locked into suspicion and polemic.

The author has a nice line in irony. For example, if some Evangelicals in the West are not sure about using the term 'Allah' for God, Christians in Malaysia agitate to *continue* using 'Allah', despite government attempts to prohibit such usage. Muslims and Evangelicals alike may be weary of caricatured misrepresentations of them by sections of the Western media; yet both draw on such media stereotypes when writing of the other.

While the book is about Evangelical responses to Islamic belief and practice, rather than primarily a book about Islam, its judicious commentary on a range of contested issues is a good way into many such issues which Muslims themselves are now also debating and about which they are often equally divided. Let us hope Muslim scholars will be challenged to write an equally candid and insightful study of Muslim attitudes to Christianity, or at least different branches of Christianity.

It is not too much to say that the future peace of our diverse societies will turn on the extent to which institutional spaces exist to enable informed debates on a range of contentious issues, religious and secular, fed by the proliferation of such micro-public spheres.

Dr Philip Lewis' first book on British Islam appeared in 1994, and his most recent, *British Muslims, New Directions in Islamic Thought, Creativity and Activism* (2018), was co-authored with Sadek Hamid, a British Muslim scholar.

Acknowledgements

This book was a long time in the making, and there are more colleagues, friends and family than I have space to thank for their help, support and encouragement. Special thanks go to Grace, my doctoral supervisor, who, a long time ago now, was willing to take on someone with such an 'eclectic academic background' and was consistently patient and encouraging. I am also very grateful to the trustees of the Solomon Academic Trust, which operates the Centre for Muslim-Christian Studies Oxford, for allowing me a three-month writing leave at the end of 2022 without which this book would never have been finished. The leave was made possible with the financial support of the Spalding Memorial Educational Trust along with family and friends who contributed to a JustGiving campaign. Thank you! My greatest gratitude goes to my wonderful wife, Heather, who throughout has supported and encouraged me with patience, love, endless cups of tea and hours of proofreading. I would not want to have done it without you.

Note on the text

A full index of participants in the Evangelical public sphere which forms the focus of this work can be found at the end of the book. On first mention in the text, the participant is briefly described in a phrase, although space does not allow for fuller biographies. Where participants have their own blogs or websites, these are footnoted throughout. More biographical details of authors and their bibliographies can be found at www.christianresponsestoislam.com.

Full books, edited volumes and book chapters authored by primary sources are cited in separate reference sections at the end of the book, as are journal, magazine and website articles written by the various participants. However, all secondary sources are noted in the endnotes. This is to make it clear for the reader when they are reading the words of the Evangelicals themselves who are taking part in the public sphere. It is also to create a useful reference section for those researching primary Evangelical responses to Islam.

Commonly anglicized Arabic terms such as Qur'an, Sharia, Sunnah and ulama that appear in the *OED* have not been transliterated or italicized and appear using the *OED* spelling and capitalization. However, terms that are not in the *OED* appear in italics and have been fully transliterated according to the *International Journal of Middle East Studies* system.

All quotations from the Qur'an are taken from Muhammad Abdel Haleem's 2005 translation, *The Qur'an* (Oxford: Oxford University Press).

Note that AD (anno domini) is used for years in preference to CE (common era). This system of counting is not 'common' to all cultures, and to suggest so is more egregious than to admit its culturally bound origin. Other civilizations, including Muslims (AH – Anno Hegirae), have their own systems for numbering the years.

Where electronic books have been consulted, KL in citations denotes Kindle Location.

All weblinks in the endnotes and reference section were accessed on 22 May 2023 unless otherwise stated.

Abbreviations

ACW	A Common Word between Us and You
ABTS	Arab Baptist Theological Seminary, Beirut
APPG	All-Party Parliamentary Group
BMB	Believer from a Muslim background
FGM	Female genital mutilation
FoRB	Freedom of religion and belief
IM	Insider Movement
OED	*Oxford English Dictionary*
PCI	Peace Catalyst International
RZIM	Ravi Zacharias International Ministries
SR	Scriptural Reasoning
UDHR	Universal Declaration of Human Rights
VOM	Voice of the Martyrs
WCC	World Council of Churches
WEA	World Evangelical Alliance

Introduction: Evangelicals responding to Islam

9/11

Tuesday, 11 September 2001. It rocked the world, not least Evangelical Christians. For many of them, it was 'the day that changed everything' (Wallis, 2013: 133). Apparently, 'it was the day truth died' (Garlow, 2005: 84). It was a 'hinge of history' (Garrison, 2014: 20), an 'epoch-making event [which] blew the lid off the boiling pot of relations between the Islamic East and the Christian West' (Kuhn, 2009: 49). It was 'the official beginning of the "clash" of civilizations' (W. Wagner, 2012: 15). 'Everyone remembers where they were … in a hotel lobby in Atlanta' (Price, 2001: 7), 'in Peshawar, Pakistan, two blocks from the Taliban hospital … [because] the BBC had just reported that a plane had flown into the World Trade Center' (Woodberry, 2011: 32).[1] Until then, Americans had 'felt protected by large oceans and distance, but 9/11 and the events that followed smashed that sense of security and safety' (Jabbour, 2008: 24). Fear was unleashed, along with 'a flood of Christian publishing on Islam and terrorism', much of it by Evangelical Christians and much of it filled with shocked clichés and doom-laden soundbites.[2]

Some was written before the dust even settled. 'When officials are through counting the dead from the terrorist attacks, the number of civilian fatalities alone will likely more than double the death toll at Pearl Harbor' (MacArthur, 2001: 6). A whole new world, a whole new abyss, was opening up, particularly for American Christians, some of whom felt they were 'learning a great deal that we didn't know about Islam's past and present. And frankly, the picture that emerges isn't very pretty' (Hitchcock, 2002: 1). Evangelicals reacted with disgust to reports of Arab Muslims cheering America's pain on the streets of the Middle East. Even in Europe 'it was reckoned in some newspapers of that time that some 35 per cent of British Muslims praised God for the destruction brought to America in the bombings of 9/11 and would support suicide bombers in their work of jihad' (Goldsmith, 2009: 51). Islamic identity was being strengthened among a younger generation of Muslims who were more religious than their parents and acutely conscious of, and loyal to, the umma, the worldwide body of Muslims. This was a 'trans-national identity above their own national identities and nations' (R. Sookhdeo, 2004: 125). Muslims were even reported as 'openly saying that the twenty-first century belongs to Islam' (Larson, 2012: 88).

Interest in Islam exploded. Along with others, Christians wanted to know more about this new manifestation of an old enemy. One lecturer reported that at Fuller

Seminary he taught '100 more students than usual' in his classes on Islam following 9/11. It also fuelled a new interest in Evangelical mission to Muslims, and apparently there was 'a 26 per cent increase between 2005 and 2010 in the number of missionaries working in Muslim-majority countries' (Woodberry, 2011). Indeed, there were reports of huge numbers of Muslims – thousands, tens of thousands, even hundreds of thousands – leaving Islam and turning to Christianity (T. Green, 2011: 101n1).

These were not the only responses. The United States was 'a nation traumatized by 9/11 and its terror attacks … easily manipulated into military and covert engagements in the name of post-9/11 national security' (Gushee, 2013: 3). When President George W. Bush, a self-professed Evangelical, announced his 'crusade, this war on terrorism' and unleashed 'shock and awe' on the nations of the Middle East, many Evangelicals cheered (Bush, 2001b). They believed that 'the next World War ha[d] already started' against 'the Islamofascists' (Evans, 2007: 5). This seemed later to be proven true when young Muslims around the world travelled to join the caliphate of the apocalyptic ISIS army which had emerged on the battlefields of Iraq (Dyer and Tobey, 2015). The End Times clock was ticking (Intrater, 2011).

However, not all agreed. One writer was 'most worried about how the U.S. government would respond' and was aghast at the 'the war on terror' (Wallis, 2013: 134). Another argued that in some ways 'the terrorists won on 9/11. Terror laid hold of the American soul and, under the guise of strength, America weakened its grip on its fundamental values' (Harper, 2013: 12). For another Evangelical, 9/11 'changed [his] life' and 'acted as a trigger', launching him into a new 'grace response to Muslims' (Bell, 2006, 133, 38). Along with him, others noted the shock that many Muslims themselves experienced at 9/11. These Evangelicals understood that this was not just a battle between Islam and the West, but it was also a battle for the 'souls and minds of Muslims' (Jabbour, 2008: 84). They sympathized with Muslims who were struggling to come to terms with the phenomenon of global terrorism, believing that 'Islam stands at the crossroads' of modernity and violent obscurantism (Riddell and Cotterell, 2003: 216).

Some of these texts were written much later after time for reflection. Some were well considered, thoroughly researched and very helpful. Many more were impulsive, ill-informed and frankly unhelpful. This book is the story of the response of Evangelical Christians around the world not just to 9/11 but also to Islam and Muslims more generally in the first two decades of the twenty-first century. As far as possible, through a textual study, it allows them to tell the story in their own words and in doing so tries to build a picture of a 'micro-public sphere' engaging in rational debate as Evangelicals wrestle with these difficult issues. It is an attempt to map how Evangelicals think about Islam and how they relate to Muslims, and it finds that stereotypes may be unreliable. Evangelical responses to Islam are complex and deeply divided.

A brief history

Evangelicals trace their roots back to the sixteenth-century Protestant Reformation, a period during which the Muslim Ottoman Empire was at its zenith and its armies were threatening Europe, having conquered the Balkans and laid siege to Vienna.

With the medieval Crusades still a memory, fear, isolation and hostility were the dominant characteristics of European Christian responses to Muslims at the time. For John Calvin (1509–1564), an Ottoman invasion of Europe would have been 'the end of Christianity as a power to be reckoned with'.[3] For Martin Luther (1483–1546) the Turks were a judgement from God and constituted one of the three great enemies of God along with the Pope and the Devil.[4] The views of these Reformers endured. 'Once images are firmly rooted in the collective memory of a community, they die hard.'[5] So it was that much subsequent Protestant writing followed the polemical tradition of the medieval and Reformation periods. The development of Evangelical thought on Islam is particularly closely connected with the literature of the Protestant missionary movement which arose in the late eighteenth century. Islam was no longer a threat at this time, but was still to be confronted. Thus, the apologetics of Henry Martyn (1781–1812), the polemics of Karl Pfander (1803–1865), the criticism of Samuel Zwemer (1867–1952), along with the more appreciative approach of Temple Gairdner (1873–1928), all represent different strands running through that movement. Hugh Goddard suggests that Gairdner's more irenic approach had the greater influence within denominational missionary societies, but that it was Zwemer's confrontational approach that was dominant among most Evangelicals.[6] In either case, the common thread was the general expectation – increasing with the confidence engendered by colonial expansion – that Islam would decline and Muslims must be converted to Christianity. This optimism reached its zenith with the Edinburgh Missionary Conference of 1910 with its goal of world evangelization within a generation.[7]

Jane Idleman Smith, however, notes an irony here.[8] The success of the resulting global missionary effort to plant churches led to the foundation of the World Council of Churches (WCC) in 1948, an organization which today is held in deep suspicion by many Evangelicals wary of ecumenism and a tendency to liberalization. During the same period, there was a crisis of confidence among Evangelicals engaged in mission to Muslims. Elaine Sharkey, for instance, recounts how, in Egypt, meagre fruit from the effort expended among Muslims caused a reappraisal of the missionary enterprise within Protestant agencies.[9] The decline of colonial power and the rise of Arab nationalism, coupled with a growing appreciation of Islam, caused some missionaries to move away from seeking conversions towards helping 'to make Muslims better Muslims'.[10] To many Evangelicals, this, along with developments at the WCC, smacked of accommodation and led to a 'growing divide between [those] in favour of dialogue and those who [were] not'.[11] Since that time, a dialogical approach has been favoured by liberal mainstream Protestants, but has been treated with scepticism by conservative Evangelicals. Against the backdrop of 9/11, the 'war on terror' and the decimation of the Christian population in parts of the Middle East at the hands of Muslim extremists, this debate has been reignited.

Defining the Evangelicals

Building on the above history, this book is all about Evangelical responses to Islam in the context of the post-9/11 world. However, it is by no means clear what the word 'Evangelical' may mean or who the 'Evangelicals' may be. It is a contested term with doubtful currency. Certainly, Evangelicals are Christians, that is, evangelical Christians. Unusually, in this book, the word 'Evangelical' is capitalized throughout to mirror the capitalization of the word 'Muslim' as the word 'Christian' has generally not been inserted after it. So, the capital letter serves to remind of this parallel. It is not to suggest that evangelicalism is a religion in its own right or even that it is separate from other Christian traditions. It remains very much a tradition within historical Christianity. Indeed, Evangelicals are found in all of the Protestant denominations. It should also be noted that the authors discussed in this book think of themselves as 'Christians' and do not usually explicitly address their comments to other 'Evangelicals'. Rather, they are speaking about and addressing Christians more broadly without thought to denomination or tradition. So, in the discussion that follows, I refer to those speaking and writing as Evangelicals, but often to their audience as Christians.

The roots of the word 'Evangelical' lie in the Greek word *euangelion*, meaning 'gospel' or 'good news'. Simply put, Evangelicals are 'people of the Gospel' (Guinness, 2010: 166). Or, as Karl Barth had it, 'Evangelical means informed by the Gospel of Jesus Christ, as heard afresh in the sixteenth-century Reformation by a direct return to Holy Scripture'.[12] Certainly there is a strong sense of historical rootedness with various other authors mentioning the Puritans, the Wesleyan revival of the eighteenth century and the social activism of the later Clapham Sect as all being the forebears of today's Evangelicals.

There are geographical and denominational considerations. While, on the European mainland, the term *Evangelisch* is denominational and associated mainly with the Lutheran Church, globally the term carries no denominational association but is normally viewed as a subset of Protestantism cutting across denominational boundaries. Thus, Evangelicals may be Anglican, Baptist, Free Church, Pentecostal, Reformed and a host of other Protestant denominational labels, including 'non-denominational'. Denominational allegiances may also be fluid – even outside of Protestantism. For instance, Bishop Michael Nazir-Ali moved from Anglicanism to Catholicism in 2021, yet remains closely connected to Evangelicals, and Egyptian Coptic priest Zakaria Botross is held by some Evangelicals to be one of their own (see Robinson and Botross, 2008). In the Global South, evangelicalism is often expressed in a more charismatic form, even where it is not part of a formal Pentecostal denomination, such as the Western-based Assemblies of God, Four Square or Elim. In Africa, new apostolic movements, such as the Redeemed Christian Church of God (RCCG) based in Nigeria, are highly charismatic, and evangelicalism might include some of the African indigenous churches with all the attendant concerns around syncretism with traditional African practices and heterogenous theology.[13]

With such global diversity, no attempt will be made in this book to define evangelicalism too prescriptively. Many have attempted to do so, and their descriptions and definitions have value.[14] Some are concerned with theological descriptions, others are historical or sociological, and still others are a blend. John Stackhouse takes Bebbington's well-known 'quadrilateral' of *conversionism*, *activism*, *crucicentrism* and *biblicism* and adds to them *transdenominationalism* along with *orthodoxy* (right belief), *orthopathy* (right feeling) and *orthopraxy* (right practice), although 'right' according to him is not so clear.[15] Rather than a particular definition, the approach taken here is that the Evangelicals in this book are included because they recognize one another as being in the same family. They talk to one another, write about each other and attack one another because it seems to matter. It is a sibling camaraderie – and rivalry. If someone from another Christian tradition writes or says something about Islam, it does not seem to matter as much as that *this* person has said it, because *this* is family. These are fellow travellers who at some point have converted to Protestant Christianity, who take the Bible seriously and engage in mission. There is 'the connectedness of a family grouping',[16] and they are taking part in what will be called the same 'public sphere'.

Of course, there will be people in this book whom some think should be excluded from the family. They will feel that those people do not (or no longer) represent an Evangelical view on Islam, and their very inclusion here will affirm their worst fears that the movement is being irrevocably diluted. At the same time, there will be others included in this book who do not appreciate the label Evangelical and would prefer to exclude themselves.[17] One of the phenomena within evangelicalism in recent decades has been people moving away from the word because of its unwelcome associations with, for instance, 'right-wing US politics, an arrogant loudmouth who refuses to listen to other people's opinions ... or "happy-clappy" simpletons'.[18] Many in this book would probably prefer to simply call themselves 'Christian'. Others might term themselves, or label others, as 'post-Evangelical', signifying a moving away from their Evangelical roots. This might especially apply to those sometimes associated with the Emergent Church.[19] Others, in order to clarify their connection to evangelicalism, might modify the label in some way. The meanings of 'Conservative Evangelical', 'Open Evangelical' and 'Liberal Evangelical' are clear enough. Other labels are more enigmatic, whether it is simply 'Followers of Christ' or 'Red Letter Christians'.[20]

Yet, for all the lack of clarity surrounding the term, there are good reasons for exploring Evangelical responses to Islam. Firstly, Evangelicals, including Pentecostals, form the largest and fastest growing section of the Christian church worldwide. This might not be so evident in the West, but is increasingly true in the Global South, which is the demographic centre of gravity for Christianity and from whence some see *The Next Christendom* coming.[21] Secondly, the strong Evangelical commitment to revealed truth, while not identical, mirrors the similar conviction of orthodox Muslims – especially Salafis – who often respect Christians who hold strongly to their scriptures, even while not appreciating their evangelizing activities.[22] Thirdly, this shared commitment to proselytism – evangelism and *daʿwa* (invitation or calling) respectively – is exactly what brings Evangelicals and Muslims into conflict and makes coexistence challenging for these two vibrant faith communities. Finally, Peter Berger at the end of the twentieth century saw both Islam and Evangelical Protestantism – especially in its Pentecostal form – as evidence of the global resurgence of religion, describing them as 'reactive counter-formations' to the challenges of secular modernity.[23] The two communities have shared concerns about secularism while at the same time harbouring mutual suspicion and stirring competition. This makes the encounter all the more intriguing.

Previous research

Despite these incentives, little has been written on the Evangelical encounter with Islam. A lot has been written about the history and practice of Christian-Muslim relations, but little of it specifically references Evangelicals. For instance, the 2008 edited volume *Christian Responses to Islam* has no chapter dedicated to the topic.[24] At the same time, much has been written about Evangelicals, the majority of it in the North American context, yet little of it relevant to the encounter with Islam. Islam appears once in a footnote in Michael Lindsay's *Faith in the Halls of Power* and not at all in David Swartz's *Moral Minority* despite his mentioning some of the progressive American Evangelicals featured in this book.[25] Other books are too dated for post-9/11 Islam to be an issue.[26]

There are four book-length treatments related to the main topic of this book, all of them focused exclusively on the United States. Thomas Kidd's 2009 book *American Christians and Islam* provides an excellent overview of Evangelical texts and attitudes in the American context. His historical survey covers up to the year 2007, and the later chapters are particularly relevant to this study. In common with others, Kidd notes a great increase in Christian publishing on Islam and terrorism since 9/11, and being himself 'a practising Christian', he is concerned that too much of it has 'cultivated sensationalized ideas about Islam and the Prophet Muhammad at the expense of charitable understanding'.[27] Many of the books written have 'essentialized and stereotyped Muslims out of pain, anger and fear'.[28] He finds that American Evangelical 'discussions of Islam have historically revolved around several key themes: the desire to see Muslims convert to Christianity; the fascination with missionary work among Muslims; the mixing of political policy and theology as it relates to the Muslim world (and Israel); and the insertion of Islam into eschatological schemes'.[29] Within these he focuses on three particular genres of writing: stories of mission to Muslims, books about Islam as part of the Last Days, and biographies of Muslim converts to Christianity. The majority of the authors he mentions also feature in this book.

Walter Ratliff's 2011 *Christians and Muslims at the Epicenter: How the Sept. 11th Attacks Shook and Transformed American Evangelicalism* is more journalistic in nature but nonetheless valuable. Again, Ratliff believes that the 9/11 tragedy marked a definite shift in American Evangelical responses to Islam. Those events 'not only shook the overall American sense of security and isolation from terrorism, it also revealed new fault lines in the Evangelical religious landscape'.[30] Whereas before 9/11 the major threat to the faith was seen to be secular humanism, that shifted to include Islam.[31] However, Ratliff found that the rift did 'not always follow traditional denominational boundaries'. Rather it left Evangelicals of all backgrounds walking 'a line between militant opposition and constructive engagement' with Islam.[32]

Amit Bhatia's 2017 *Engaging Muslims and Islam: Lessons for 21st-Century American Evangelicals* also includes some textual analysis, and along with an in-depth description of Evangelical theologies of religions, he engages with the work of Colin Chapman who is a major participant in the discussions featured below. The author himself 'serve[s] at a ministry that reaches out to Muslims', and his main contribution is an empirical qualitative study based in four Chicago churches in which he interviews forty grassroots Evangelicals, their leaders and an Evangelical ministry working with new arrivals in America, many of whom are Muslims.[33] While the grassroots are not a focus of this study, his findings concerning the influences on Evangelicals in the public sphere are important. He finds that many of those interviewed are primarily influenced by the secular media and that 'as long as popular Evangelical writers focus on the negative aspects of Islam without presenting a sound framework within which to interpret these aspects, they will greatly hamper accurate knowledge of religious others and will influence the perspectives, attitudes, and practices of American Evangelicals' in a detrimental way.'[34]

The most recent work has been done by Ashlee Quosigk, herself an Evangelical, who also conducted qualitative research among American Evangelical leaders and congregations. In *American Evangelicals: Conflicted on Islam* (2021), she found that, contrary to the stereotypes, 'Evangelicals are actually complex in their theological, moral, and political attitudes about Islam', and their perceptions of Islam range from the idea that it is 'inspired by the devil' to 'those who greatly admire Islam'.[35] She constructs a typology for these responses and identifies several genres of Evangelical writing on Islam, adding 'terrorism literature' and 'critiquing literature' to the three identified by Kidd above (see Chapter 2). In her fieldwork questions, Quosigk then focused on the conflict over Islam among Evangelicals, attitudes to the Qur'an and Muhammad, as well as issues in inter-faith dialogue. Links are made between her findings and the views of authors and practitioners in relevant places in this book.

In a second 2021 book, *One Faith No Longer*, co-authored with George Yancey and drawing on both quantitative and interview data, Quosigk explores the divisions in American evangelicalism more broadly and wonders whether the split in the movement is irreparable. Using the relationship with Islam as a special case, they find that conservative Evangelicals are 'theologically rigid' and yet still tend to see Christian progressives as being part of their 'in-group' with Muslims being one of their main 'out-groups'.[36] On the other hand, they find that progressive Evangelicals focus more on social justice than theology and tend to see conservatives as their 'out-group' and themselves as 'more closely aligned with Muslims than with conservative Christians'.[37] This is indicative of other divisions between conservatives and progressives, and they suggest that as 'the United States has become a socially and politically polarized culture ... it is reasonable that Christianity in the United States would be shaped by this polarization'.[38] As this research is based mainly on empirical fieldwork in the United States rather than textual studies, it is difficult to draw a direct link between these findings and the views of those featured in this book. However, there are certainly echoes of this rift in the global Evangelical community. For instance, Bebbington also sees an increasing polarization within evangelicalism between conservative Evangelicals who embrace a 'logo-centric modernity' and charismatics and open Evangelicals who display 'a postmodern delight in variety, authenticity and relevance to felt needs'.[39]

Along with these book-length treatments, some articles and book chapters written in the American context are of relevance here. Richard Cimino finds 'Evangelical books and articles that have been published' since 9/11 reflect increased antagonism towards Islam. He analyses books written before and after 9/11 and identifies four broad genres.

'Apologetic' writing displays a 'distinctively anti-Islamic thrust'. 'Prophetic' writing sees 'Islam as a player in the End Times' and has only 'in the last decade assumed a central role in biblical prophecy' interpretation. This is closely related to 'charismatic spiritual warfare literature' which demonizes Islam. Finally, Cimino does find that a minority of Evangelicals, motivated by a desire to evangelize Muslims, take a softer 'contextualist' approach which is more affirming of Muslim culture.[40]

José Casanova corroborates Cimino's findings. He believes that 9/11 exacerbated a pre-existing, 'mainly Protestant, native backlash against Islam'. He identifies three main sources of the 'new anti-Muslim evangelical discourse': 'militant pre-millennial Zionism' which sees all Muslim countries as enemies of Israel (see Chapter 10); the 'missionary competition between Muslims and Christians' which leads to the 'evangelical frustration of being unable to preach openly the gospel of Jesus Christ in Muslim countries' (see Chapter 13); and lastly support for the global 'war on terror' which some Evangelical leaders have characterized as a crusade against 'an essentially violent Islam' (see Chapter 9).[41] Similarly, Dennis Hoover, in company with Quosigk, reminds us that American evangelicalism is not a monolith and embraces a variety of responses. He makes this clear through a quantitative analysis of articles appearing in two American Christian magazines, *Christianity Today* and *World*, which 'did not suggest a gathering storm across *all* of evangelicalism'.[42]

Finally, two unpublished pieces of research in the US context are worthy of mention. First, Michal Meulenberg's doctoral dissertation submitted to Fuller Theological Seminary focused on the 'favorable and unfavorable attitudes American Evangelicals have had both historically and today about Islam and Muslims'. Alongside a review of Evangelical books written since 9/11, which has some overlap with the present volume, she gathered survey data to which she applied various theories around Reasoned Action to explain the connection between Evangelical attitudes and behaviour.[43] Secondly, a research team from Multi-faith Matters explored why some American Evangelical churches engage in 'neighborly forms of multi-faith encounters'. They tested theories from social psychology, particularly around the Contact Hypothesis, and found that indeed those churches that risked contact 'worked through their fears and theological assumptions and engaged "the other"' – including Muslims.[44]

Outside of the United States, Andrew Atherstone, an Evangelical scholar, 'focuses predominantly on British sources' to complement Kidd's findings. He finds similar Evangelical genres of writing and expands them to include 'missionary exemplars, apologetics and disputation, concerns to unveil "the true face of Islam", prophetic predictions of the End Times, and Christian converts from Islam'.[45] He too observes that Evangelicals are 'sharply divided among themselves in their understanding of Islam's multiple identities, and the opportunities or threats that Islam and Islamism present to the Christian church', but goes on to note that the large number of Muslim-background converts from the Global South are beginning to 'alter the balance of the debate'.[46] This is something that this book begins to address, although much more needs to be done. In his overview of 'ecumenical Christian responses to Islam in Britain', Michael Ipgrave presents three hostile Evangelical approaches towards Islam represented by British Bible teacher David Pawson (d. 2020), Patrick Sookhdeo and the website *Answering Islam*, which again all feature in this book.[47] In the same edited volume, Barbara

Mitchell explores the denominational response to Islam of the Church of England and mentions three Anglican Evangelicals – Philip Lewis, Michael Nazir-Ali and Kenneth Cragg. Lewis, a former Anglican inter-faith advisor, writes as an academic, not as an Evangelical, and even co-writes with a Muslim.[48] His sociological approach to Islam in Britain has been very important in the field and has influenced a younger generation of British Evangelicals.[49] However, as his work is non-confessional, it only features in this book as a secondary source. Nazir-Ali, an Anglican bishop, author and academic, writes more self-consciously as a Christian, and his work features prominently. Cragg (1913–2012), also an Anglican bishop, author and intellectual, was a colossus in the field of Christian-Muslim relations, writing over sixty books in a career spanning six decades. Rather revealing her own opinion of Evangelicals, Mitchell notes that 'despite his evangelical upbringing, Cragg always asked deep theological questions and was not satisfied with simplistic answers'.[50] Certainly, his books are deeply theological, and Cragg is widely recognized as being 'very influential among a generation of Christians across all denominations'.[51] Nicholas Wood, a Baptist academic, has compared and contrasted Cragg's oeuvre with that of Lesslie Newbigin (1909–1998), another influential British bishop. He finds that, while Cragg in his work emphasizes the continuity between Christianity and Islam, Newbigin emphasizes the *dis*continuity (Wood, 2009). This later becomes an important theme in the discussion of contextualization and Insider Movements (see Chapter 13). Kidd too notes Cragg's influence among Evangelicals and yet 'his suspicion of evangelical missionary tactics'.[52] While reference will be made to some of Cragg's post-2000 publications, the majority of his best-known work was firmly rooted in the twentieth century as was Newbigin's. So, despite the enduring influence of both these men, especially on the older generation of authors below, their works do not feature greatly in this study.

Also in the UK, Greg Smith has conducted some of the only quantitative research among Evangelicals. He finds, as elsewhere, that there are mixed attitudes and 'tension in the British evangelical community' concerning Islam. For instance, only 16 per cent agree that Muslims and Christians worship the same God, but 59 per cent 'admire Muslims' devotion to prayer'. Despite this, Smith finds that 'Evangelicals in the UK do not entirely conform to the stereotype of a conservative evangelicalism that is in alliance with a nationalistic "religious right" that is portrayed as the norm in the United States and some other parts of the world'.[53] This again points to complexity.

Less research has been done in other parts of the world, and the Global South is particularly underexplored. However, African scholars are beginning to address this in their context, and some have published works on Christian responses to Islam (e.g. Azumah and Sanneh, 2013). For instance, Matthews Ojo has published on the responses of Pentecostals in Nigeria.[54] Akintunde Akinade writes as an academic and as a Nigerian Christian who significantly has spent time living in Muslim Qatar. While outlining the complex history of Christian-Muslim relationships in Nigeria and noting the Pentecostal demonization of Islam and commitment to mission work there, he himself believes that 'both Christians and Muslims can contribute to conflict resolution, peacemaking, and nation building in contemporary Nigeria' (Akinade, 2014: x–xi).

Finally, back in the European context, mention should be made of *Sharing Lives*, a short book published on a Christian label by Bert de Ruiter,[55] a missionary among Muslims in Europe, who, in encouraging Christians to overcome their fear of Muslims, analyses several of the books which will be encountered below (de Ruiter, 2010). As he writes for a Christian audience, he will be referenced as a participant in the Evangelical public sphere. However, where the other authors mentioned above write as academics for an academic audience, rather than as Christians for a Christian audience, their works are noted as secondary rather than primary sources.

The author

I too write as a Christian whose faith and family roots lie in the Evangelical tradition. Before engaging in academic research, I was involved in church leadership, and I remain active in my local church. Yet, in company with some of those above, I have reservations about the stereotypes attached to the Evangelical label today. Having taught in Tunisia for several years, I have many Muslim friends and colleagues and am on occasion embarrassed by Evangelical statements and extremes with respect to Islam. My experiences among both Evangelicals and Muslims definitely inform my writing. However, this book is intended for an academic audience, although my hope is that practitioners and leaders involved in the Christian-Muslim encounter will also find much of benefit here. I do not seek to pronounce judgement on different Evangelical responses and attitudes, although my views inevitably emerge in the discussion section at the end of each chapter. Rather, my aim in writing is to give academics – Christians, especially Evangelicals, and Muslims too, should they choose to listen in – an insight into the discourse within the Evangelical public sphere as it wrestles with issues related to Islam.

The book

As should have become clear, there is no previous academic book-length treatment of *global* Evangelical responses to Islam. To plug the gap, this book provides an overview of the full range of responses to Islam by those who may be considered to be in some way Evangelical, who are publicly commenting on Islam. The very fact of gathering these views together provides for the first time a comprehensive global map of Evangelical thought on Islam. Of course, it is not exhaustive. I am sure to have missed texts and authors, some of them potentially important. While lamentable, this is not deliberate. No one volume could capture all the texts produced by such a fast-moving, vibrant public sphere. Neither does it exhaust all the important issues and topics that the Evangelical encounter with Islam raises. Much more could be said about convert care, gender, racism and the environment, for instance. In particular, the book does not deal with questions of Christian theology and Muslim objections to it. Rather the focus is on Evangelical responses to Islamic belief and practice. Another significant limitation is that this volume includes only English-language texts and takes no account of the many, undoubtedly rich, texts produced in other languages. A particular omission is those produced in Arabic and other languages proximal to the Muslim-majority world, although several authors in this volume publish in more than one language, including Arabic. The limitation is entirely my own linguistic ability and does not imply that non-English contributions are less important. That said, the majority of the transnational discourse in this public sphere has English as its lingua franca. Furthermore, while the aspiration is for the book to be global, in reality its geographical centre of gravity is the Western English-speaking world, particularly North America, Britain and Australia, along with many English-speaking contributions from the Middle East and Africa. Sadly, Asia outside of the Middle East is less well represented. Again, this is due to my own limitations. Finally, it should be noted again that the great majority of the texts featured here were published post–11 September 2001 up to and including 2022. There are a few exceptions for authors who were particularly influential in the twentieth century, such as Cragg and Newbigin, and significant books which were republished in the twenty-first century. As befits a vibrant public sphere, texts and books are constantly being published, and this book will soon become a work of history, a snapshot in time. However, despite this, it will remain relevant as a map of Evangelical thought on Islam and in time might serve in comparative and longitudinal studies.

Neither is this work a thorough review of individual books or authors. Much more could be said about each individual book that has been published, many of which deserve deeper exploration. Likewise, each author and practitioner has a fascinating history, unique motivations and more to say than can be captured in this book. This in some ways may be unsatisfying, and at times the reader may wish more was said about a particular author or book. However, this work is thematic and brings together a range of quotations from different authors to illustrate the spectrum of views around various issues and strategies. The bringing together of so many texts, references and authors is designed to create a resource for those researching, teaching and practically engaging in Christian-Muslim relations with a special interest in the Evangelical tradition. I have tried to include as many full-length books authored by Evangelicals as possible as well as to balance the number of quotations from them, although inevitably some books and authors are more influential than others, which is reflected in the number of quotations from each one. That said, the texts and quotations have been chosen to illustrate particular arguments rather than to highlight the approach or position of particular participants, and I have not labelled individuals according to their approach, although the reader will quickly get a feel for who takes up the various positions.[56]

Part 1 provides the theoretical backdrop for the book. Chapter 1 presents the concept of a 'micro-public sphere' based on the work of Jürgen Habermas and his critics and considers why it might be a useful framework for exploring the texts generated globally by Evangelicals responding to Islam. It looks at the participants whose work will be analysed, the types of texts they produce and the issues they deal with. Chapter 2 then looks at some typologies which have been proposed to describe these responses and some of the variables that influence them based on politics, social context, experience and theology. Part 2 features nine chapters looking at key theological, historical and sociopolitical issues and questions which Evangelicals are grappling with in regard to Islam. Not included here are the diverse debates among Muslims themselves, as rich as those are, nor their responses to Christian views. Rather, the focus is solely on Evangelical responses to elements of Islamic belief and practice. In every case, the full range of response is illustrated with quotations from primary texts, and there are only occasional references to secondary material. Each chapter concludes with a short discussion of the key takeaways and likely future implications of the various positions. These attitudes obviously have an impact on the approaches and strategies which Evangelicals adopt when encountering and engaging with Muslims, which are the focus of Part 3. Chapter 12 explores how Evangelicals engage in evangelism and talk with Muslims, including the vexed questions of whether dialogue is productive and whether aggressive polemics are desirable alongside an apologetic defence of the faith. Chapter 13 extends these concerns to the international, cross-cultural mission of Evangelicals to Muslims in Muslim-majority contexts. Of particular interest here are the acceptability of what are known as Insider Movements and the risk of syncretism between the two faiths feared by some. Chapter 14 then graphically presents the factors, approaches and responses seen throughout the book in a series of dyads or spectra which it uses to construct a set of descriptions which depict the various Evangelical responses to Islam exhibited in this public sphere. Finally, the Conclusion gathers up these observations and summarizes what has been discovered before going on to discuss some key issues not previously mentioned. The book concludes by discussing what this Evangelical public sphere can teach the wider public sphere debating these issues surrounding Islam and asks whether global evangelicalism is at a crossroads in its response to Islam.

Part 1

A micro-public sphere

1

Public spheres

A best-selling book, a magazine article, comments at the bottom of a blog, a conference speech or even a coffee shop discussion group, all of these may be part of 'a public sphere'. The public sphere is all about discussion, debate and opinion formation. It is a dynamic, active, participative concept drawing people together, eliciting views and taking positions. We use the phrase a lot. But what do we mean by it? Within the fields of sociology and political philosophy, the concept of the public sphere has come to mean more than just 'in public' or the 'public domain' or the 'public realm'. It is not physical or geographical in the way that 'public space' may be. The closest to a synonym is probably the 'public square' which carries echoes of the Athenian *agora* (marketplace) as a place of public debate.

The idea of a public sphere is closely associated with the work of Jürgen Habermas, a German political philosopher and sociologist, whose work has been highly influential in thinking about the philosophical basis of political democracy. He developed the public sphere as an ideal construct for thinking about deliberative democracy. However, it is also useful as an analytical framework for looking at the network of people and texts that grow up around certain issues within society. Using Habermas's theory, this chapter explores the background to the concept of the public sphere and its connection with democracy and rational debate. It imagines the existence of many small, micro-public spheres that together form a global network of spheres making up broader transnational macro-public spheres.[1] These spheres form around issues and ideas of concern or interest to ordinary citizens as opposed to political leaders and state actors. While religion was sidelined in the early development of these concepts, it has become increasingly salient in a world 'as furiously religious as ever'.[2] As seen in the Introduction, no religions today are more 'furious' than Evangelicals and Muslims. So, the chapter goes on to propose the idea of an Evangelical micro-public sphere which has coalesced around the topic of Islam and Muslims and is engaged in rational debate through the exchange of texts in various media as it seeks to influence opinion within its own community and the broader society. There will be discussion of the various types of texts that will be encountered throughout this book followed by a presentation of the types of participants and some examples of this sphere in action.

Habermas and the public sphere

Habermas's early thinking on the public sphere appeared in his 1962 *The Structural Transformation of the Public Sphere*, which traces the rise of the middle class in eighteenth-century Europe with the aim of identifying an ideal model for public debate and opinion formation.[3] Habermas starts by considering the Greek idea of the *polis* (city or public), which met representatively in the *agora* in Athens as an *ekklesia* (gathering of citizens). This latter word has particular resonance for this book as *ekklesia* is the Greek word that the New Testament uses to describe God's people, that is, 'the church'. This might immediately be suggestive of the overlap between the ideas of a public sphere and intra-religious discourse.

However, it was the rise of trade from the thirteenth century, through the development of printing in the fifteenth century, culminating in the appearance of daily journals in the seventeenth century that provided 'the elements of a new social order'.[4] According to Habermas, in the eighteenth century, social circles emerged among businessmen who began to discuss trade and labour. These circles met together in the new coffee houses that sprang up around Europe and of which there were as many as 3,000 in London alone. Newsletters and journals began to circulate, which included opinion and comment, uncensored by the state authorities, and evolved into such well-known titles as *The Spectator* and *The Guardian*. These circles expanded from the coffee shops into libraries, reading rooms and reading societies as books became more widely available and accessible to the general public, thus breaking the monopoly of the state and church on learning.

For Habermas these circles together formed the 'public sphere' which enabled rational debate of issues of public concern and became representative of 'public opinion'. Importantly, this was a sphere independent of and uncensored by the state, which Habermas sees, along with the economy, as being the 'system'. This system world is differentiated from what he calls the 'lifeworld', which is made up of civil society, the public sphere and private individuals.[5] In this model, the public sphere, which is discursive, and civil society, which is associational, are distinct yet overlapping. So, Charles Taylor sees the public sphere as a 'dimension of civil society' and describes it as 'a common space in which the members of society are deemed to meet through a variety of media: print, electronic and also face-to-face encounters; to discuss matters of common interest; and thus to be able to form a common mind about these'.[6]

To put it another way, the public sphere is 'a zone of mediation between the state and the private individual' concerned with discourse, debate and negotiation for the purpose of public opinion formation.[7] So, for example, churches, mosques and charities are considered part of civil society, while the debates that are generated by individuals within these associations form the public sphere.

Habermas suggests that the eighteenth-century bourgeois circles were inclusive and accessible to all. This, of course, is a rather dubious claim, ignoring as it does barriers of education, class and not least gender, and there has been no shortage of critics. Craig Calhoun points out that it was a sphere 'oriented not just toward defence of civil society against the state but also toward the maintenance of a system of domination within civil society' whereby the bourgeoisie protected their own economic interests.[8] In other words, it was self-interested and unrepresentative. Furthermore, Nancy Fraser notes that it was also not the only public sphere at the time. There were other competing public spheres with other priorities centred around nationalists, elite women and the working class. Indeed, according to her, the bourgeois public sphere 'deliberately sought to block broader participation' from these other groups.[9] These are all criticisms which Habermas now accepts, acknowledging that 'it is wrong to speak of one single public' and admitting the marginalization of women and the existence of parallel public spheres 'interlocked' with his proposed public sphere.[10]

Habermas goes on in his book to describe what he saw as the 'fall of the public sphere' in succeeding centuries. He saw various reasons for this, including the way that states colonized civil society. However, his sharpest criticism is reserved for the rise of the mass media which he believes to have transformed the public sphere from 'a culture-debating public into a culture-consuming public ... The sounding board of an educated stratum tutored in the public use of reason has been shattered; the public is split apart into minorities of specialists who put their reason to use non-publicly and the great mass of consumers whose receptiveness is public but uncritical'.[11] The newspapers, which started out as a means of disseminating information and opinion, became, in the nineteenth century, commercial interests concerned with profit and the agendas of their powerful owners. Even worse, television and radio turned debate into entertainment, and 'critical publicity [was] supplanted by manipulative publicity'.[12] Such is the strength of Habermas's criticism of today's mass media that Goode accuses him of 'technophobia and ... a logocentric antipathy towards the audio-visual media'.[13]

Counterpublics and micro-public spheres

Following her critique of Habermas's work, Fraser proposes a modification of the theory whereby she envisages a multiplicity of publics which she calls 'subaltern counterpublics', defined as 'parallel discursive arenas where members of subordinated social groups invent and circulate counterdiscourses to formulate oppositional interpretations of their identities, interests, and needs'.[14] This multiplicity of publics ensures that marginal voices are heard and remain part of a larger public sphere in which all contribute to debates on matters of universal concern. Of course, some of these counterpublics are stronger than others in the sense that they are more closely connected to the power of the state and/or the economy. Others remain relatively weak without the power to enact any of their deliberations, having only recourse to the normal avenues available in a democratic society. Furthermore, Fraser later points out that initial conceptions of the public sphere were Western-centric and bound to the idea of the nation-state.[15] The participants in a public sphere were imagined to be the citizens of one nation engaged in discussing issues of domestic importance. However, in a globalized, interconnected world, public spheres are bound to become transnational. Borders are porous. International media, the internet and migration all enable discursive interaction across national boundaries.

The above criticisms notwithstanding, the literature around the public sphere has grown and explored new avenues. One such avenue is what have been called 'micro-public spheres'.[16] Gerard Hauser imagines these as a 'montage of publics' all engaged in 'vernacular discourse' on 'matters of mutual interest' trying, where possible, 'to reach a common judgement about them'.[17] He describes them as a 'lattice of spheres', or 'nested spheres', linked together at various nodes. This sort of theorizing leads Michael Warner to suggest that these micro-public spheres may be a useful analytical tool for understanding the various debates taking place within society. For him, 'publics are essentially intertextual, frameworks for understanding texts against an organized background of the circulation of other texts, all interwoven not just by citational references but by the incorporation of a reflexive circulatory field in the mode of address and consumption'.[18] In other words, these micro-public spheres are generating a body of texts that engage and critique one another. For that to happen, three elements are required. There has to be an *issue* of common concern, *participants* engaged in discussing it, and *texts* circulating through different media.

These spheres have no fixed membership. They are not associations. Rather, they have 'permeable boundaries', and participants may well be strangers, although they might come to know one another in the course of their interaction within the sphere.[19] Individuals may participate in several different spheres simultaneously, according to their interests and concerns. This means that micro-public spheres may overlap and intersect in various ways. Discussions in one sphere might inform the discussions in another, as will be seen below. Neither are these spheres permanent. Many micro-public spheres are ephemeral, quickly forming and dissolving as the contexts and issues change. As one issue is resolved, another takes its place. As issues change, participants come and go depending on their interest in the topic of concern. Other spheres may be longer-lived, as is the case with the sphere in this book.

Religion, rationality and the public sphere

Although, in his original description of the public sphere, Habermas ignored religion, in more recent years he has accepted the need for the religious voice to be heard. Of course, a public sphere can exist whether or not it is heard outside of its own confines. Indeed, many spheres operate in exactly that way, forming their own echo chamber. However, part of the argument of this book is that a micro-public sphere such as this should both be heard in public and be opened to engagement with other spheres and to outside critique.

With regard to religion and public life, philosopher John Rawls proposes the pragmatic concept of 'public reason', which is an outworking of what he calls a citizen's 'duty of civility'.[20] This is the duty, particularly of those in public life, to explain the reasons for their political positions, including those inspired by their religious convictions. According to Rawls, these reasons have to be couched in a way accessible to all, and so religious language should necessarily be excluded. Religious communities may hold their own comprehensive doctrines of truth, but only as 'long as those doctrines are consistent with a democratic polity', and they 'translate' all their public communication into non-religious language.[21]

In a seminal article concerning 'Religion in the Public Sphere', Habermas accepts much of Rawls's thinking on the use of public reason.[22] However, he suggests that requiring faith communities to translate all their communications places an unfair burden on them, which might exclude them from the political process – an undesirable outcome. He feels that a liberal democracy needs the input of not just one but multiple religious voices. Indeed, they may contain 'key resources', 'moral intuitions' and even 'possible truth content' which could benefit the whole community.[23] So, both sides, the secular and the religious, need to be prepared to listen to and learn from each other. This requires the willingness not only of religious citizens to adjust and translate for a secular audience, but also of secular-minded citizens to do the hard work of listening. In his view, this will lead to 'complementary learning'.[24]

Roger Trigg also feels that 'religious voices must be heard in the public life of every country'.[25] This is not just so that society can benefit from any available intrinsic truth, but because it is also better for religion to be out in the open. 'Suggesting that reasons grounded in religion should not be advanced on the public stage merely protects religion, and the public behaviour inevitably flowing from it, from public scrutiny and rational debate'.[26] In other words, religious voices need to be included in public debate in order to prevent the darker side of religions from developing unchallenged. This suggests that 'rational debate' in the public sphere is not only oriented towards 'understanding' but is also 'instrumental'.[27] That is to say that rationality not only demands an internal logic and coherence but also entails a 'strategic purpose' to reach a desired goal. Of course, what that goal is and its impact on the common good are clearly subjective, and it is quite possible for two opposing arguments to both be rational. Indeed, this is the root of debate and disagreement in all public spheres, and Evangelicals are no exception.

An Evangelical micro-public sphere responding to Islam

Public spheres inevitably form in all societies and within all religious groupings. The first use of the phrase 'Evangelical Christian public sphere' appears in the literature in a 2001 journal article, 'The Square of Intimate Citizenship', describing it as a 'multiple, hierarchically layered and contested public sphere'.[28] Interestingly, while this phrase has not since gained traction in Christian contexts, the phrase 'the Muslim public sphere' has. So, for instance, chapters in Salvatore and Eickelman's volume *Public Islam and the Common Good* trace the formation of public opinion in the illiterate culture of nineteenth-century Ottoman coffeehouses, look at the rise of printed material for the masses in the same period and examine the religious public sphere that was formed in opposition to the colonial power in India.[29] Maybe this is part of an endeavour to show that there is no inherent contradiction between Islam and democracy, although 'the popularization of the public sphere does not inevitably translate into liberal pluralism'.[30] Whatever the case, these works and others show that the concept of the public sphere does have utility in discussing the sorts of religious discourse to which we now turn.

Based on the above theorizing, this book proposes that there is a transnational Evangelical micro-public sphere which is concerned with responding to Islam and

Muslims. It is a long-standing sphere with a rich history of interaction that has generated texts since the dawn of modern missions to Muslims in the nineteenth century. In proposing an Evangelical micro-public sphere, I am not trying to organize it, nor control it, nor define who is in or who is out. I am not criticizing its existence. It is partly an analytical device to capture the discourse that is taking place among a broad range of Evangelicals with respect to Islam. It is a way to imagine how their deliberations proceed, who is engaging at different times and what the collective memory generated may be. In short, it is a way of building a map of Evangelical thought concerning Islam.

At the same time, this study is a concrete example of what the theorists above have been proposing. This is an active, vibrant micro-public sphere that has generated a large number of texts among a relatively small number of actors that can be described in a treatment of this length. It serves as a model for studies of other counterpublics in other fields and, I hope, suggests ways of presenting and analysing such material.

Finally, it is an opportunity for outsiders to listen in on the deliberations of a micro-public sphere. Are there things to be learned from the discussions Evangelicals are having about Islam and their relationships with Muslims? Are there critiques, advice or interventions that can come from outside which would strengthen and enhance this sphere? Are there ways in which others could engage in similar, even intersecting, debates in fruitful ways?

Obviously, I do not suggest that this is the only Christian sphere responding to Islam. There are other Christian micro-public spheres that form within denominations or other traditions of Christianity. Roman Catholic engagement in the topic is extensive, and, indeed, it forms an overlapping sphere as some of those active in the Evangelical sphere are also engaged in discussions with Catholics. There are broader ecumenical spheres that bring a wide variety of Christians together, and there are spheres that bring Christians, Muslims and others together in what might be termed an 'inter-faith micro-public sphere'. Again, these interlock with the Evangelical sphere, and their deliberations, texts and reports inform or sometimes stimulate debate within that sphere. Some of the participants in the Evangelical sphere also participate in other spheres that are not concerned with Islam per se, but in which the topics and issues inform the discussions about Islam. This is often the case with theological circles or those looking at specific sociopolitical issues. Where participants are active in more than one sphere or where texts are publicly available, these spheres too interlock and inform one another.

Unsurprisingly, all of these spheres are international by nature, and the Evangelical sphere concerned with Islam is certainly a transnational sphere. While much of the discussion has historically taken place in English and the texts have largely been generated in Western contexts, this is changing. This study focuses exclusively on English-language texts. However, it is certain that other texts are significant and could well be brought into the conversation where there is linguistic competence or where translations are available. These include Arabic texts, and over thirty of the participants in the public sphere mentioned below are Arabs, although the majority are living in the West and write mainly in English. Along with these Arab voices, there are more than half a dozen black Africans, residing in Africa and the West in roughly equal numbers;

a dozen Asians, mainly living in the West; together with another dozen Christian voices from Iranian, Turkish and Jewish backgrounds.

Influence is another important theme within a public sphere. Some within this sphere are influential because of their knowledge and expertise with regard to Islam. Education and qualifications still carry weight in the public sphere. However, background and experience also command significant respect, especially for those who have spent many years living in Muslim-majority contexts or interacting with Muslims. Likewise, authors from previous generations can remain influential in a public sphere. Although no systematic attempt is made to trace this intergenerational influence, occasional reference will be made to those, such as Cragg (d. 2012), whose main body of work was in the twentieth century but who continued to write into the new millennium. He published over sixty books in his lifetime, many, but not all, related to Islam, and, as already mentioned, he had a profound impact on the older generation of today's Evangelical public sphere. His books are still widely read, and some of his twenty-first-century works are included below.

Others are influential because of their organizational or denominational positions. However, while they are influential within their own institution, they may not carry such influence outside of it. As Jonathan Oloyede, a convert from Islam and now a Black British church leader, puts it: 'When I step out of my black Pentecostal community I step into a different world where I am not always recognized and don't have the same authority or profile to speak out. I am nobody in this world.'[31] He is, however, still part of the Evangelical public sphere, although in that sphere his influence resides only in the force of his arguments and not in any institutional position. Of course, there is a danger that influence may become overbearing and coercive, but it can also be highly informative and enriching, something that outsiders could also benefit from.

Issues

The first requirement for a micro-public sphere is a topic or issue of mutual concern around which the participants coalesce. These citizens generate debate in response to certain events which creates publicity.[32] It is clear in this case that the issue is Islam and Muslims. Evangelicals and Pentecostals, maybe more than other branches of Christianity, are interested in and concerned about Muslims. They engage in significant missionary effort to convert Muslims, causing much angst in those communities. Furthermore, some Evangelicals feel threatened by Muslims, who are now present in previously Christian societies in greater numbers than ever before. So, there is a lot to talk about and a lot to debate as the participants seek to influence their own constituencies as well as more general public opinion.[33]

While the overarching issue for the sphere is Islam, certain events spark subtopics within the sphere. So, Part 2 breaks down the debate within the public sphere into smaller topics. It seeks to focus on some of the most difficult discussions Evangelicals are having among themselves related to Islam and Muslims. It is not claimed that they are the only topics or that there are no other equally important topics. Some are theological or religious, and others are sociopolitical, but together they illustrate the range of subtopics that stimulate debate within this micro-public sphere.

However, before proceeding to the issues – which are the main focus of this book – it is necessary to paint a picture of the participants and the texts they catalyse, which together constitute this micro-public sphere. These people interact with one another, sometimes as representatives of churches, denominations or agencies, but more often as private individuals concerned with Islam. According to Fraser's description, they are part of a 'subordinated social group' (Evangelicals) who 'invent and circulate counterdiscourses' (books, articles, video, blogs) to 'formulate oppositional interpretations of their identities, interests, and needs'.[34] These latter are, indeed, often expressed in strong disagreement with one another as well as with Muslims, who, of course, form their own counterpublics.

Participants and voices

The second element of a public sphere is its *participants*. There is no fixed membership. Nobody decides who belongs or who should be expelled. The sphere exists because people are exchanging texts; and as long as someone participates, is in some way Evangelical and produces texts on Islam, then they are de facto a participant in this Evangelical public sphere. Some are long-standing contributors; others are young, new entrants into the arena; some are influential; others less so; some are only part of it for a fleeting moment and are never heard from again; others remain resolutely apart.

Notwithstanding the fact that the key participants all self-identify as, are identified as or associate with Evangelicals, it is clear that there is something of a blurred boundary between an *Evangelical* public sphere as such and a wider, more inclusive *Christian* public sphere. As noted in the Introduction, some participants may object to being labelled Evangelicals. Others may feel that people have been missed who should rightly be included, or that the very concept is too limiting. No study of this kind can create perfect categories. Each individual participates as an autonomous actor, but inevitably brings an agenda which may well be influenced by organizational allegiances or vocation. Different participants meet at conferences, organizational gatherings, speaking engagements and so on, but there is no external requirement to do so. Indeed, some never meet, being separated by geography, circumstance or ideology.

This is not surprising as we have already seen that this is a transnational public sphere and includes voices from different nations and ethnic backgrounds, including those who have converted from Islam. The voices are, of course, gendered, although, as will become clear, female voices are a minority in this public sphere, at least when it comes to publishing. The two dozen female participants below are responsible for around just 10 per cent of the books included in the bibliography. There are now initiatives afoot to rectify this disparity and make sure that female Evangelical voices are heard in the public sphere. For instance, the Angelina Noble Centre exists 'to encourage, support and facilitate women cross-cultural workers … in research projects and higher degree research in cross-cultural missions'.[35] When Women Speak is a network which recognizes that women are 'surprisingly under-represented in the development of mission and missiologies, in publishing and teaching' and aims to 'give attention to the place of women's voices where Christianity, Islam and missiology meet'.[36] Naturally, Christian women have been particularly concerned about understanding and relating to Muslim women and have published several books on the topic (Adeney, 2002; Dale, Hine and Walker, 2018; F. Love and Eckheart, 2000; R. Sookhdeo, 2004). Other female authors have published on broader topics related to Islam (Glaser, 2016; Jardim, 2014; Reisacher, 2017b; Taber, 2009; Womack, 2020). This is obviously not an exhaustive list, and other books will be found in the bibliography and throughout the book. This does, however, illustrate that the female voice is present in the public sphere and will become increasingly important in the years to come.

Some of the voices in this public sphere are professional practitioners. This is their life's work. They are highly informed specialists who have spent their whole careers working with Muslims or in Christian-Muslim relations. For other high-profile participants, who may or may not be well informed, Muslims are just one interest or concern among many. Yet, due to their public roles, they still make important interventions in this public sphere and are often more influential than the 'professionals' – much to those individuals' frustration. All of these are seeking to influence the grassroots of their communities and also the wider public sphere. The degree to which they are successful in that endeavour is beyond the scope of this study, although it seems likely that, despite their better efforts, many ordinary Evangelicals, and certainly the wider public, are still mainly influenced by mainstream media and society-wide attitudes to Islam and Muslims.[37]

The following sections mention some of the general profiles of the contributors who will feature prominently in discussions in Parts 2 and 3. The inclusion of names at this point is in no way exhaustive and does not suggest that these voices are more important than others, although many of the more prolific authors are included. At this stage they are merely examples. Furthermore, their mention as an example under one type does not mean they might not also exhibit characteristics of other types.

Specialists and practitioners

Among the specialist voices in the Evangelical micro-public sphere on Islam are many who have lived and worked cross-culturally in Muslim contexts in the Muslim-majority world. They have worked in churches, education and mission agencies, may still be on the field or have sometimes become significant in the public sphere *after* returning to their home countries. Specialists with cross-cultural mission experience include Joseph Cumming, Warren Larson, Carl Medearis, Phil Parshall and Evelyne Reisacher in the United States; Steve Bell, Colin Chapman, Ida Glaser and Bill Musk in the UK; and Moyra Dale, Cathy Hine, Bernie Power and Stuart Robinson in Australia. Others have spent time living in areas of high Muslim population in the West, maybe combined with shorter periods in Muslim-majority contexts, such as Phil Rawlings and Andrew Smith.

Those who come from Christian backgrounds in Muslim-majority contexts are also influential voices in this public sphere. They speak the language and share much background with Muslim cultures. George Houssney, Fouad Masri and Nabeel Jabbour are all Arab Christians, originally from Lebanon, who now live and work in the United States. Chawkat Moucarry is a Christian Syrian living and writing in France. Martin Accad (Lebanon), Munther Isaac (West Bank) and Imed Shahadeh (Jordan) are examples of those who still live in their home countries engaging with the issues, although this is easier in some countries than others where censorship or security is a problem.

The final group with significant experience in Muslim-majority contexts are those who have converted to Christianity from Muslim backgrounds, such as Mark Gabriel, Nabeel Qureshi and Sam Solomon. These individuals play a particularly important role in the public sphere. They are seen by many as experts due to their considerable knowledge of Islam and experience of being Muslims. They may speak Arabic or other languages as natives and have sometimes memorized the Qur'an. However, they do not all take the same approach to their former religion, often depending on their experience and context, as will be seen in Chapter 2.

Some of these converts, such as Abdu Murray, founder of Embrace the Truth, live or write under pseudonyms due to the threats on their lives as they are considered by some Muslims to be apostates or traitors (see Chapter 8).[38] They are not the only ones to use pseudonyms or be cautious about using their own names in published writing. For instance, Stafford Allen, Warwick Farah and Nik Ripken are pen names, used due to security concerns or because of their past missionary activity. As Jack Smith (pseudonym) says, 'perceived insults to Islam's messenger … are frequently followed by some type of violent retaliation by Muslims, which necessitates the concealment of one's identity' (2011: KL428).

For some of the specialists within the public sphere, their principal engagement with questions of Islam is within academia or education in the fields of Islamic studies, theology, missiology or the social sciences. Some have particular specialisms within the field; for instance, Keith Small (d. 2018) was an expert on early qur'anic manuscripts; Mark Anderson focuses on qur'anic studies; and Martin Whittingham researches Muslim views of the Bible. Other specialists are activists in some way. Patrick Sookhdeo, one of the most prolific authors in this sphere who has written over a dozen books on Islam, founded the Barnabas Fund with his wife Rosemary, herself an author with at least four titles to her name.[39] This Christian agency supports persecuted Christians around the world, but has a particular focus on Muslim contexts. In the United States, Joshua Lingel founded i2Ministries to 'mobilize, equip, and energize believers to reach Muslims with the Gospel' and runs training programmes.[40] Jay Smith is a polemical debater and founder of Pfander Films.[41] Some have a particular geographical or interest focus. For instance, Gary Burge, Chapman, Pawson and Stephen Sizer all write about the Israel-Palestine issue, although not always linked to Islam.

Finally, there are, of course, participants who span multiple categories. John Azumah, for example, is a Ghanian academic from a Muslim background, who founded The Sanneh Institute and writes on African Islam, among other things. Furthermore, Nazir-Ali comes from a mixed Christian-Muslim family background in Pakistan; was a bishop in the Church of England; founded OXTRAD, an NGO supporting the church under pressure; and is widely recognized as a scholar of Islam.[42]

Non-specialists

Other contributors to the Evangelical micro-public sphere are not specialists in Islam, but rather it is a side concern or one interest among many. This does not mean to say that they are uninformed, but are rather less informed than the specialists and may rely on other participants in the sphere, or even the media, for their information. In the US context, high-profile conservative Evangelical leaders – such as Franklin Graham, son of world-renowned evangelist Billy Graham; Jerry Falwell (d. 2007), Baptist pastor and televangelist; and Pat Robertson (d. 2023), media mogul, Southern Baptist minister and one-time Republican presidential candidate – have all made inflammatory statements about Islam. At the same time, well-known open Evangelicals such as Brian McLaren, Tony Campolo and Jim Wallis have all had more positive things to say. In the UK, the Anglican archbishop Justin Welby,[43] seen as being Evangelical, has made a few limited comments about Islam. Lord Carey, a former archbishop, and Baroness Cox are both influential Evangelicals in the House of Lords who have either written or spoken about Islam. Even some American presidents, known to be Evangelicals, have contributed to this public sphere, as will be seen.

Alongside these high-profile figures, there is no shortage of Evangelical church leaders and pastors who have written on Islam, particularly in the United States. They do so alongside their church ministry, maybe motivated by pastoral concern for their congregations as well as for Muslims. Examples are legion, including James Garlow, James Greear and John Piper. Garlow, a former megachurch pastor in California, provides a particularly interesting case for the study of a public sphere as, according to the author, an e-mail he had sent to a pastor friend went viral and then by popular demand was turned into a book, thus contributing to the public sphere (2005: 5). Others, such as Bob Roberts and Rick Warren, engage with Muslims or inter-faith relations, but have not specifically written about their work. There are also mainstream Evangelical theologians who have engaged in discussions around Islam, such as Don Carson, Timothy George and Timothy Tennent, who are all associated with Evangelical seminaries. Finally, there are several participants whose main focus is Christian apologetics. As part of their general concern to defend and explain the Christian faith, they engage with Islam and sometimes debate Muslims. Amy Orr-Ewing, Daniel Janosik, James White, David Wood and Ravi Zacharias (d. 2020) are all examples of this type of approach.[44]

Texts and media

The third and final of the three elements of a public sphere is texts. Warner sees a public sphere as 'the social space created by the reflexive circulation of discourse' consisting of 'the concatenation of texts through time'.[45] Certainly, there is a great reservoir of texts generated by Evangelicals on the topic of Islam, many of them since the turn of the century and the events of 9/11. They represent a great number of different opinions and approaches. Many of them are reflexive in the sense that they consciously respond to and critique others within the sphere, sometimes in very sharp, direct ways.

The main focus of this book is on the medium of published books, including edited volumes and book chapters. However, texts have also been collected from Evangelical journals, magazines and websites, although no claim is made to comprehensive coverage.[46] It references over 250 full books authored by Evangelicals and mainly published since 2001 that deal with some aspect of Islam. Some are short and written for a popular audience without footnotes, indexes and detailed referencing (P. Sookhdeo, 2010b; Nazir-Ali, 2002). Others are in excess of three hundred pages, fully referenced and written for a more specialist readership (Durie, 2018; Accad, 2019).

Along with the single-author books, there are more than twenty Evangelical edited volumes, sometimes edited by someone well known within the sphere (Reisacher, 2012b; Azumah and Riddell, 2013). These volumes are occasionally collated to address a particular issue or topic. For instance, there are volumes on Insider Movements and contextualization (Lingel, Morton and Nikides, 2012; Talman and Travis, 2016) and on law and human rights (Claydon, 2009). Often they are the output from a conference (Dale, Hine and Walker, 2018; Greenlee, 2006). Some volumes include chapters from those well regarded and experienced in this micro-public sphere. Others contain texts from younger participants or those less well known. These latter volumes provide an opportunity for those from a variety of contexts, countries and cultures who might not otherwise have the chance to publish (Azumah and Sanneh, 2013). This especially includes voices from Islamic contexts (Accad and Andrews, 2020). Most of these edited volumes collect texts from similar viewpoints. However, a few deliberately collect texts from divergent viewpoints in order to bring the authors into dialogue with one another (Bell and Chapman, 2011). A few might even include both Christian and Muslim voices (Crowther et al., 2017).

Individual book chapters sometimes come from volumes on other topics edited by Evangelicals (Anyabwile, 2011). However, sometimes they come from collections written under the auspices of other traditions, but which include Evangelical voices. Chapters from the Building Bridges series would be examples of this, whereby Evangelicals have been invited to attend the annual seminar convened by Georgetown University bringing together Christian and Muslim scholars (Azumah, 2008a). In these cases, their voices are heard alongside those from other traditions. Other individual book chapters are taken from full books written by single Evangelical authors where Islam is just one interest among many (Campolo and Claiborne, 2012: chapter 7; Tennent, 2007: chapters 2 and 8). Indeed, it might not even take up a whole chapter, in which case it becomes a passing – although, maybe, important – reference to Islam in a larger body of work (Welby, 2018: 79–83).

One final book type is the coursebook or study guide. Evangelicals frequently put together training courses or produce study guides usually giving a general overview of Islam or encouraging Christians to engage in relationship or evangelism with Muslims. There are numerous examples, such as *Friendship First* (Bell, 2011), *Bridges Study Book* (Crescent Project, n.d.), *Christian Apologetics to Islam* (Lingel, 2016a, 2016b) or *Unveiled* (Barnabas Fund, 2011b).

The majority of these books are published by Christian publishers. However, some, especially those of a more academic nature, are distributed by secular publishers, while others are self-published – either for ease of process or to avoid peer review. Some authors and ministries even have their own labels. For instance, Patrick and Rosemary Sookhdeo have published over twenty books between them through their US-based label Isaac Publishing.[47] Many more texts on Islam are published by Evangelicals in magazines, newspapers and specialist journals. Although less than a hundred are referenced in this book where the comments are particularly pertinent, it is clear that the total number of articles published runs into the hundreds, even the thousands. Some of these publications are Evangelical, such as *Christianity Today* and the *Christian Post* in the United States; *Christianity*, the *Church of England Newspaper* and *Evangelicals Now* in the UK; or *Eternity News* in Australia. Others are more ecumenical with a wider readership, such as *Christian Century* or the *Church Times*.

Other publications are akin to journals and have a more narrowly defined audience, although they are widely read in this Evangelical micro-public sphere. For instance, the *International Bulletin of Missionary Research*, the *International Journal of Frontier Missiology* and *Evangelical Missions Quarterly* have been key sites of debate and discussion about Islam between various factions within the sphere. Other journals may appeal more to one or another group within the sphere. For instance, the *Journal of Biblical Missiology* is more conservative and only features articles written by those of that persuasion. Many Evangelical organizations also publish their own magazines or newsletters which often contain opinion and comment about Islam.

Of course, Evangelical voices are occasionally heard via secular media. So, for instance, in 2005, a British magazine, *The Spectator*, published a letter written by Patrick Sookhdeo titled 'The Myth of Moderate Islam'; and in 2019, *Newsweek* published an opinion piece by David Garrison, a Southern Baptist missiologist, titled 'Why More Muslims Are Turning to Jesus'. Evangelicals have also appeared on mainstream television both as commentators and as the subject of documentaries.

It is worth remembering that almost all of these publications are available online, and many of the books and edited volumes are also available as e-books. This is a reminder that the public sphere has undergone a radical transformation since the internet became a widely available public utility in the 1990s – significantly just a few short years before the events of 9/11 in 2001. Evangelicals, along with the rest of the world, no longer rely on paper publications, cassettes, VHS videos and in-person conferences.[48] Websites, podcasts, online forums and Zoom conferences have revolutionized not just how Evangelicals can spread the gospel but also how they discuss and debate among themselves.

This book does not deal rigorously with texts and debate on the internet. For instance, it does not engage with the ubiquitous comment sections on websites or online discussion forums which generate a multitude of responses to posts from Christians, Muslims and many whose identity it is impossible to verify. Just one such instance illustrates both the significance of the medium and the impossibility of capturing the discourse in a meaningful way. In 2012, Brian McLaren,[49] a public theologian and leader in the Emergent Church movement, posted a blog on CNN which was sympathetic towards Muslims (McLaren, 2012a). It provoked over 8,000 responses, some more pertinent than others, and with affirmation and vitriol in equal measure. However, the book does include occasional online references of interest, especially from websites belonging to Evangelical organizations that publish articles or resources about Islam. These are a major source of texts in the modern public sphere and have particular potential for impact as they are normally made available without the need for a paid subscription. Examples include the Zwemer Center for Muslim Studies, the Arthur Jeffrey Centre for the Study of Islam at Melbourne School of Theology, and Fuller Studio.[50] Other websites exist solely for the purpose of engaging in debates on Christian-Muslim themes, such as *Answering Islam* and *Debate.org.uk*, both of which have hundreds of articles defending Christianity and attacking Islam.[51] Personal blogs are another rich source of texts disseminating views on a vast array of topics. Many of the participants and organizations in the Evangelical micro-public sphere have their own blog sites, including Bell, Durie and Kuhn.[52] These blogs sometimes invite comment which again opens up discussion within the sphere. Where participants have their own websites or blogs, these are included in the endnotes.

YouTube and similar sites utilize a very different form of media. Video has become extremely important in today's public sphere. It appeals to those who do not ordinarily engage with written texts but are interested to engage audio-visually. Groups such as Pfander Films post videos, often of debates with Muslims or documentary material, and under each post, there will be a textual description or even transcripts.[53] This can then attract tens or even hundreds of comments and reactions by both Christians and Muslims agreeing or disagreeing with the post. There is a plethora of other video material online, ranging from workshops, talks and courses to documentaries (e.g. Crescent Project and One Truth Project).[54] One website, the *Forum of Christian Leaders*, hosts a wide variety of videos to equip Evangelical leaders around the globe, including a whole section on Islam.[55] Video is rather more difficult to analyse than written texts and is not a major focus of this study, although some relevant examples are given. Its importance, however, should not be underestimated, and it deserves a study of its own. There are also some innovative attempts to combine various media. This is often the case with the courses mentioned above which have both study guides and videos or DVDs sometimes linked to websites. Likewise, books by Garrison (2014) and Moyra Dale (d. 2022) (2021), an Australian ethnographer and educator, have their own associated webpages with links and resources.[56]

Text genres

All of the above media types are featured in the pages below with the emphasis being on published writing. They all, however, exhibit a range of genres adopting different tones and approaches. Some of these have already been introduced in the Introduction through the work of Kidd, Quosigk and Atherstone. However, together with those identified by these authors, which are incorporated here, more genres in Evangelical writing will be noted in this study, including:

1. *Academic*, scholarly works, both articles and book length, that deal in great specialist depth with focused topics, sometimes resulting from doctoral or postdoctoral research (Accad, 2019; Cumming, 2012; Kuhn, 2019; Small, 2011; Tavassoli, 2011; Whittingham, 2021).[57]
2. *General books* on Islam written by Evangelicals from a confessional viewpoint, explaining Islam to a Christian audience (Azumah, 2008b; Chapman, 2007b; Chedid, 2004; Nazir-Ali, 2002; R. Sookhdeo, 2019). These often explain the basic beliefs and practices of Islam.

3. Books on *specific Islam-related topics* such as the Qur'an (Anderson, 2016b; Cragg, 2005; Nickel, 2020), Muslim women (Dale, 2021; Mallouhi, 2004; Robinson, 2017), violence and terrorism (Musk, 2003a; Orr-Ewing and Orr-Ewing, 2002; D. Richardson, 2003) or Sufi and folk Islam (Musk, 2003b; Collins, 2021; Parshall, 2006).
4. Books on the *encounter, dialogue and theology* between Christians and Muslims (Accad, 2019; Bell, 2006; Glaser, 2016; Houssney, 2010; Jabbour, 2008; Moucarry, 2001; Riddell, 2004; Shehadeh, 2020).
5. *Comparisons* between Christianity and Islam (Gauss, 2009; Goldmann, 2008; Morton, 2011; Shenk, 2003; Sproul and Saleeb, 2003; Zaka and Coleman, 2006).
6. *How to share your faith* advice for ordinary Christians evangelizing their friends and neighbours (S. Allen, 2016; Chatrath, 2011; Maurer, 2008; Shumack, 2011).
7. *Apologetics* both answering and explaining how to answer questions that Muslims ask Christians (Hicham, 2008; Gilchrist, 2009; Nickel, 2016; Scott, 2011).
8. *Polemical* writing that claims to expose 'real Islam' or poses questions for Muslims to answer about their faith (Caner and Caner, 2003; Malone, 2002; Peltola and Dieppe, 2022).
9. Books by *former Muslims* which often also claim to expose Islam (Gabriel, 2007; Solomon and Al-Maqdisi, 2010) although not always (Chandler, 2007).
10. *Warning of the threat* of Islam and the dangers of Islamization in the West (Cox and Marks, 2006; Pilcrow Press, 2007; Robinson, 2003; W. Wagner, 2012; Youssef, 2017).
11. Books on *eschatology*, the role of Islam in Israel and the End Times or the Mahdi as the Antichrist (Evans, 2007; Hunt, 2005; J. Richardson, 2015; Stice, 2005).
12. Books about *human rights* and the situation of Christians in Muslim-majority contexts (Durie, 2009c; Claydon, 2009; P. Sookhdeo, 2009b).
13. *Self-critical* books which reflect on the shortcomings of Christian engagement with Muslims (Camp, 2016; Gushee, 2013; R. Love, 2017).
14. *Muslim conversion stories*, sometimes from extreme backgrounds or with significant personal sacrifice (Husnain, 2016; Qureshi, 2014; Saada and Merrill, 2008; H. Shah, 2010; Yousef and Brackin, 2010).
15. *Missiology* discussing effective practices in mission to Muslims and including a lot on contextualization (Garrison, 2014; Reisacher, 2016; Woodberry, 2008).
16. *Missionary biographies*, stories of both modern-day missionaries to Muslims (Brother Andrew and Janssen, 2004; Haile and Shenk, 2011; Livingstone, 2014; Pieh Jones, 2019) and older stories rewritten to inspire a new generation (Rockness, 2003).

The examples given for each genre above are by no means exhaustive, and many more will be found in the pages below. The bibliography of Evangelical authors does, however, contain a fairly comprehensive list of books published by participants in this sphere between 2001 and 2022.

The Evangelical micro-public sphere in action

While many, maybe even the majority, of the participants above are aware of each other and some will have met in person, this is by no means universally true. Any micro-public sphere will inevitably include those who are strangers to one another. That said, while it never convenes in totality, various segments of this public sphere do meet together and have direct interaction from time to time. While this more often than not takes place between those who are of like disposition, maybe belonging to the same domination or working in the same agency, this is not always the case. Some events and networks seek to bring together those who do not necessarily agree with each other.

As a case in point, Bridging the Divide describes itself as a global 'network of biblically faithful scholar-practitioners building bridges among workers and believers in Muslim contexts', meeting several times between 2011 and 2018. Many of the reports and resource documents on its website illustrate that these participants hold divergent opinions and are engaged in a rational debate on difficult issues in the field.[58] Christian Responses to Islam in Britain (CRIB) is another 'ongoing attempt to establish a network of Evangelical Christians in the UK who will recognize and support each other' and estimates that 'over 80% of Evangelical Christians involved in Muslim ministry in the UK would be happy to be part of CRIB' (Knell, 2014: 102–3). The network meets biannually, and there are often robust debates about difficult issues among those who disagree. The Coalition of Christian Ministries to Muslims in North America (COMMA) plays a similar role there.[59] These networks, including the Network of Ministries to Muslims in Europe (NMME), which is affiliated to the European Evangelical Alliance (EEA), also seek to 'equip local churches and ministries to engage in cross cultural ministry to Muslims'.[60] In addition to these established networks, large international conferences convened by organizations such as the Lausanne Movement or the World Evangelical Alliance (WEA) have tracks for those engaging with Muslims. Finally, specialist centres such as The Sanneh Institute in Ghana organize conferences which attract Evangelicals, albeit alongside those of other traditions, including Muslims.[61]

One particularly significant conference was organized in response to 'A Common Word between Us and You' (henceforth ACW), an open letter published in 2007 and signed by 138 prominent Muslim scholars around the world. It was addressed to named and unnamed Christian church leaders worldwide, and the authors suggested that the shared fundamentals of Islam and Christianity are the unity of God and love – both love of God and love of neighbour. They went on to invite Christians to come together with Muslims on this common ground for the sake of world peace.[62] Over three hundred prominent Christians, including many well-known Evangelicals, signed a welcoming response authored by the Yale Divinity School under the leadership of Yale theologian Miroslav Volf (Attridge et al., 2007).[63] Many of them attended the subsequent conference held at Yale in 2008. This all drew sharp criticism from other Evangelicals suspicious of Muslim motives and generated a wealth of texts (e.g. Solomon and Al-Maqdisi, 2009a; Barnabas Fund, 2008a; Durie, 2008a) (see Chapter 3).

An exchange of texts in 2017–18 provides another example of the micro-public sphere in action. In May 2017, Colin Chapman, an Anglican clergyman and author who had spent many years in the Middle East, posted an article on *Fulcrum*, the website of a network of Evangelical Anglicans, titled 'Christian Responses to Islamism and Violence in the Name of Islam'. Australian Mark Durie, another ordained Anglican and academic, posted a strong response on the website generating an exchange that went on until October of that year (Chapman, 2017b). The following year, Jenny Taylor,[64] a Christian journalist and founder of Lapido Media,[65] wrote an article in a Christian journal again attacking Chapman's views, drawing on Durie's critiques (J. Taylor, 2018). This prompted Chapman, together with Azumah, to write a reply rebutting Taylor's article (Chapman and Azumah, 2018). These are all very direct, reactive texts which are explored further in Chapter 9.

One final example of how a public sphere seeks to mobilize support within its public came in 2012 when the *Journal of Biblical Missiology* launched an online petition to garner support against various agencies involved in what they felt to be harmful Bible translations (see Chapter 13).[66] Despite over 15,000 people signing the petition and WEA publishing translation guidelines in 2016, the dispute rumbles on.[67]

These examples illustrate well the visceral nature of the discourse in the Evangelical public sphere on Islam. These are no mere academic debates. They matter. The participants feel them deeply. For many of them, they concern their life's work, their sense of vocation. It is not surprising that temperatures run high and disagreements are sharp. As Nicholas Adams says of religious public spheres, participants need 'to risk upsetting each other if [they] are to work together. This displays not a desire to disturb, but a willingness to share what matters most deeply'. This is true of both inter-faith and intra-faith spheres as in this case. After all, 'the public sphere will not be merely an arena of discussion and compromise; it is also potentially a zone of transformation and conversion. That makes it risky and sometimes dangerous'.[68]

That sense of risk and conflict will certainly be on display in the overview of issues discussed in Part 2. However, before turning to those debates, the next chapter looks at how the above participants and their responses may fit into the various typologies that have been constructed to describe inter-faith engagement.

2

Typologies of encounter

Evangelical Christians Take Aim at Islam[1]
Seeing Islam as 'Evil' Faith, Evangelicals Seek Converts[2]
Most White Evangelicals Don't Believe Muslims Belong in America[3]

These headlines in the secular and Christian press could be replicated many times over. There is a general impression that Evangelicals, especially in America, are opposed to Muslims or even worse. This seems to be borne out by incendiary statements made by high-profile Evangelical leaders. However, this is not necessarily always the case. There are many Evangelicals who have warm relationships with Muslims and are happy to live and work together with them. They are much more conciliatory in their public statements about Islam, but, of course, do not usually make the headlines. An exception was a video by Bob Roberts,[4] an American megachurch pastor, who sought to counter the reasons 'Why Evangelicals Hate Muslims' (2019) and explained how he once took an imam duck-shooting. It was much quoted online.

Given these divergent examples, it is not surprising that the Evangelical public sphere exhibits a range of responses to Muslims. This chapter discusses ways of describing these different approaches by introducing various typologies that have been developed, some in the context of Christian-Muslim relations and others more broadly in inter-faith relations and social science. Where these typologies have been proposed by Evangelicals, it will be pointed out. Other typologies have been suggested by academics in the field who may or may not have Christian convictions. The chapter then goes on to an initial exploration of the underlying causes of these different responses which range from the political through contextual and experiential factors to theological differences.

Typologies

In Part 2 it will quickly become obvious that Evangelicals fall along a spectrum when it comes to their approach to Islam. This is not a new discovery. Previous empirical and text-based research has demonstrated a basic tension between negative and positive responses to Islam.[5] Clinton Bennett describes the poles of this spectrum as either a 'confrontational' approach, characterized by 'polemic, diatribe and debate', or a 'conciliatory' approach, characterized by 'dialogue' and 'bridge building'. He suggests that 'although conciliation has a long history, confrontation has dominated both sides'.[6] Most of the typologies below reflect this basic tension. For instance, Martin Accad,[7] a Lebanese Evangelical academic and activist based at the Arab Baptist Theological Seminary in Beirut (ABTS), proposes a couple of typologies. The first is similar to Clinton's and labels these polarized Christian tendencies as the 'Islam-antagonistic' and the 'Islam-friendly' approaches (Accad, 2011: 182).[8] Greg Smith, a researcher who has worked with the UK Evangelical Alliance, couches a similar dyad in terms of the 'Crusader' and 'Missionary' views tracing it back to the days of St Francis and the twelfth-century crusades.[9] These opposing tendencies have created a rift within the Evangelical public sphere today in their approaches to Islam, which many observers have noted. For instance, Joseph Cumming,[10] a former missionary, pastor and Yale academic, is

> concerned that in American Evangelicalism today and, to a lesser extent, Evangelicalism around the world, there is a split developing between two camps. One is the camp that has been influenced by people who advocate peacemaking, but who do not talk much about witness to Muslims. The other camp is the people who are denouncing the evils of Islam, and who are promoting fear of Muslims. (2013: 49)

This stark opposition is a very simple and much-used tool and is reminiscent of the model presented by a well-known 1997 report on Islamophobia in the UK authored by the Runnymede Trust, titled 'Islamophobia: A Challenge for Us All' (Table 2.1). It described 'open' and 'closed' views of Islam held by non-Muslims which mirror Clinton's conciliatory and confrontational approaches. It unpacks these positions to explain how Islam is being viewed by people at the two poles. The first set of dyads represents how Islam is seen by non-Muslims. While those with 'open views' accept that Islam is diverse and that Muslims genuinely want to engage in Western societies, those with 'closed views' tend to essentialize Islam as a monolith and view Muslims as being insincere, detached and subversive. This latter group does not see any blame

Table 2.1 Closed and open views of Islam

	Open view	Closed view
Islam seen as	Diverse	Monolithic
	Interacting	Separate
	Different	Inferior
	Partner	Enemy
	Sincere	Manipulative
Self-criticism of the West is	Considered	Rejected
Discrimination of Muslims is:	Criticized	Defended
Islamophobia is seen as	Problematic	Natural

Source: Adapted from *Islamophobia: A Challenge for Us All* (London: Runnymede Trust, 1997), 5.

attached to the West in world affairs and defends discrimination against Muslims as being necessary for self-preservation.

The final dyad in this table points to the controversy that was to unfold around the concept of Islamophobia itself. While many, including some Evangelicals, see anti-Muslim prejudice and hatred of Muslims as serious justice issues to be resolved, others feel they are inevitable as they see Islam as a threat and being incompatible with Western culture. The term continues to be highly controversial among Evangelicals, especially in the UK. The original definition of Islamophobia as 'dread or hatred of Islam – and, therefore, fear or dislike of all or most Muslims' was expanded in a twentieth-anniversary report to focus on 'anti-Muslim racism'.[11] This was an idea picked up in the UK context by an All Party Parliamentary Group (APPG) which defined Islamophobia as 'rooted in racism and [as] a type of racism that targets expressions of Muslimness or perceived Muslimness'.[12] This caused concern among some Evangelicals who saw it as 'a well-meant statement … flawed in that it conflates "race", "culture" and "religion" … which potentially shuts down discussion about controversial issues, which are arguably cultural' (Bell, 2021).[13] There were also concerns of a hidden agenda on the part of Muslims.

The original report clearly stated that 'it is not intrinsically phobic or prejudiced to disagree with or to disapprove of Muslim beliefs, laws or practices'.[14] Similarly, the APPG report says, 'The aim of establishing a working definition of Islamophobia has neither been motivated by, nor is intended to curtail free speech or criticism of Islam as a religion.'[15] However, some Evangelicals feel that 'the concept of Islamophobia has been used in recent years as a way of shielding Islam and Muslims from criticism' (P. Sookhdeo, 2008a: 201). Tim Dieppe of Christian Concern, a UK Christian lobby group, agrees and says, 'It appears that the authors of the [APPG] report do want to silence criticism of Islam or of Muhammad and that they consider that such criticism should be called Islamophobic even if it is rooted in Islamic teaching. This is therefore a flagrant attempt to curtail free speech.' He goes on to suggest that such definitions make people afraid to critically evaluate Islam, a concern which he labels 'Islamophobiaphobia' (Dieppe, 2019b: 31–3).

Islamophobia is clearly an important issue for many societies around the world, including Europe and North America, and much has been written.[16] Writing in the US context, Catholic scholar Jordan Duffner offers her own definition of Islamophobia as being 'the prejudice and discrimination that targets people based on their perceived association with Islam and Muslims'.[17] Taken alone, this definition helpfully focuses the attention on Muslims as people, rather than on Islam as a religious system. In Europe, Evangelical de Ruiter (2010: chapter 2) has written about Islamophobia and various Christian responses to it. Certainly, the idea of Islamophobia and the various claims and counterclaims surrounding it form an important backdrop to all of the discourse within this Evangelical micro-public sphere, especially in Western contexts. It is obviously part of a wider debate taking place in a much larger sphere to which Evangelicals are contributing. For instance, Dieppe's piece above was included in an anthology produced by Civitas, a civil society think tank. It is also worth noting that there were Christians on the panel that produced the original Runnymede Trust, including at least one Evangelical. So, this is clearly an example where the Evangelical micro-public sphere intersects with a broader societal public sphere.

While the opposing pairs in the original Runneymede report provide useful diagnostic categories, they do not necessarily mean that Evangelical views of Islam amount to Islamophobia or anti-Muslim hatred. Concern, alarm, fear and hatred, while often very closely related, need to be carefully distinguished. Nonetheless, these dyads along with those of Bennett and Accad are used as shorthand throughout this book along with other dyads, including confrontational/conciliatory, critical/affirming, combative/irenic, hawkish/dovish, hard/soft and so on.[18]

The world, of course, is not black and white. A dyad gets us only so far, and Peter Berger reminds us that there is important middle ground. He presents a simple typology for thinking about religious reaction to pluralism, which he defines as 'a situation in which different ethnic or religious groups co-exist under conditions of civic peace and interact with each other socially'. 'Fundamentalists' on the right 'attempt to restore or create anew a taken-for-granted body of beliefs and values' shared by the whole of society. 'Relativists' on the left abandon any commitment to an objective truth and celebrate anything and everything. He sees either extreme as 'bad for civility' and as making 'civil discourse impossible' – fundamentalism because it 'produces irresolvable conflict', and relativism because it 'precludes the moral condemnation of virtually anything at all'. Rather, Berger observes that most people 'gravitate toward a more reasonable middle ground'.[19]

Recent work by Quosigk in the United States has shown this to be the case with respect to attitudes towards Muslims. While she found that Evangelical leaders tended to polarized positions, the grassroots tended to be less extreme and were more centrist, having what she calls 'a moderate hybrid identity'.[20] She concludes that 'Evangelicals appear to be divided among themselves about how much engagement is appropriate and how important it is to protect orthodoxy'.[21] Quosigk finds an explanation for Evangelical behaviour in Hunter's 'culture wars' theory, which pits those of an 'orthodox' disposition against those who are more 'progressive'.[22] Preferring the term 'traditional' to orthodox, with its connotation of acceptable correctness, she proposes a spectrum of her own for Evangelical views on Islam, ranging from 'traditional' on the right, through hybrid identities ('traditional-progressive' and 'progressive-traditional') to 'progressive' on the left. This is a helpful reminder that, while the authors and influencers quoted in this book are often at polarized ends of the spectrum, many ordinary Evangelicals, depending on their context, occupy a more agnostic – even confused – middle ground, lacking the specialist knowledge to make a judgement unless convinced and persuaded by the experts. There are also, of course, experts who tend towards this middle ground and emphasize the importance of a variety of approaches to Islam, as will be seen.

Finally, there is Accad's (2012) second typology which he calls the 'SEKAP' spectrum. P and A on the right represent polemics and apologetics (see Chapter 12). The 'existential' E-type is a pragmatic accommodation of others and focuses on living together well. However, the extreme left 'syncretistic' S-type goes rather further than an appreciation of pluralism to embrace both faiths as being of equal truth, equating to Berger's 'relativism'. The middle K-position in this model is the arcanely named 'kerygmatic' approach, taken from the New Testament Greek word *kerugma*, meaning proclamation. Accad claims this as a 'suprareligious approach' in which 'God is seen to be above any religious system' and the focus is on God's action towards the world 'in Christ'. Thus, the Christian is proclaiming the Good News, but without tribal labels.

Accad even provides a diagnostic tool, the 'Test of Attitude to Islam and Muslims', for people to determine where they are on the spectrum (Accad, 2012: 44–7). His categories are not static, discrete categories which define a person and their views. Rather, they are approaches, or even tools, that may be used at different times, in different places, with different people. So, Accad explains that he 'would favour a combination of E and K in a public setting, where the tackling of issues (E) is crucial and more likely to be fruitful'. However, in private settings, he 'would favour a combination of K and A, the apologetic approach often serving to clarify certain deep-rooted misunderstandings that Muslims have about Christ and the Bible'. He says, 'I find myself leaning toward E in conversation with Muslim religious leaders, and more toward A in conversation with less prominent Muslims' (Accad, 2012: 43). This is an important observation on the Evangelical, or indeed any, micro-public sphere. Responses, attitudes and approaches are not static. Participants deploy different tactics in different situations, and, as will be seen, people's opinions and approaches evolve over time for various reasons.

All such models are a useful but limited shorthand to describe what we observe happening among Evangelicals with respect to their responses to Islam and Muslims. They are only descriptions and are not designed to be prescriptive or limiting. The reality is always more diverse and messier, and the middle ground remains critically important. Even so, in this book, it is the conciliatory/affirming/open and confrontational/critical/closed poles which set the frame for the discussion, as 'the extremes almost always define the terms of reflection and debate'.[23]

Conceiving of these poles as either positive or negative, however, is problematic. Firstly, it depends on one's own viewpoint as to whether one judges these attitudes and approaches to be helpful or detrimental. Secondly, there are times in any relationship when conciliatory peacemaking is required and yet other times when there needs to be the freedom to confront and respectfully disagree, a point alluded to by different Evangelicals below, many of whom look for some sort of middle ground. Models and typologies can help us understand one another better. When they become limiting or are used in negative ways, then they cease to be helpful. The intention in presenting the above models is that they should help Evangelicals themselves, and others interested in Christian-Muslim relationships, understand the different attitudes and responses and thus develop better approaches towards Islam and Muslims.

While these poles and models are useful descriptive labels, what is more interesting is to consider *why* these positions have developed and *how* the attitudes have formed among Evangelicals. The various spectra reflect ideas and opinions not only about Islam and Muslims but also other important factors such as politics, social context, experience and theology. The following discussion begins to situate some of the voices within the Evangelical public sphere and considers what might be important for different participants.

Underlying causes

Politics

The political domain is a classic example of a spectrum of opinions, views and approaches, usually extending from right to left. The right is associated with conservative values, maintaining traditions and preserving institutions. The left meanwhile favours liberal values, progressive reform and breaking down hierarchies. In their more extreme forms, the right wing tends to be nationalist, even fascist, and the left can be socialist, even revolutionary. While Muslim politicians may be found on both sides, of course, and individual Christians of either persuasion may be more or less open in their views of Muslims, there tends to be more angst about Islam among those on the right than among those on the left, especially for those with strong nationalist or patriotic feelings. So, within the Evangelical public sphere, we may expect political views to have an influence on a participant's approach to Islam and Muslims. Those on the right, the left and the centre will react in ways that line up with their political persuasions.

These political views are expressed differently in different places, and in some countries, other political factors are important, not least communal politics between Muslims and Christians in non-Western contexts. Where Christians are a minority, they may see their best chances of self-preservation lying with a non-Islamist party, however autocratic the ruler may be. For instance, Christians in Syria have generally supported Assad's minority Alawite regime against the Islamist opposition. The same has been true in Egypt where Christians have viewed the El-Sisi regime more favourably than they might otherwise have done since the removal of the Muslim Brotherhood government in 2013–14. In Nigeria and other countries where the communities are more comparable in number, political support might run along religious or even ethnic, tribal lines. In Lebanon it is even more complex, as some culturally Christian parties are in alliance with Muslim parties, although the sands of Lebanese politics are constantly shifting. Evangelicals in these contexts engage in politics at different levels. For instance, Sami Awad, a peace activist and founder of the Holy Land Trust, has stood in West Bank elections.[24] In Lebanon, Accad is the director of Action Research Associates, an initiative 'bringing together political and religious voices', seeking to facilitate 'dialogue and collaboration between political actors of various allegiances'.[25] In the US context, political allegiance has been particularly pronounced in recent decades. Evangelicals have often been associated with the 'Christian Right'. Leaders such as Robertson, Falwell and John Hagee, another American pastor and televangelist, all lean politically to the right, have been closely associated with the Republican movement and have made highly critical public comments about Islam. On the other side, Jim Wallis, the founder of Sojourners,[26] and Tony Campolo,[27] a former spiritual adviser to Democratic president Bill Clinton, have both written conciliatory words regarding Muslims and espouse left-leaning politics. These are again all examples of how the Evangelical micro-public sphere interacts with the wider political sphere.

In the West, there are particular areas of political policy which have implications for Muslims and their relationship with the West. The first of these is immigration and resulting social pluralism. Generally speaking, those on the right want to limit immigration, seeing it as a threat to their way of life, and those on the left are more relaxed, seeing it as a justice issue. Data seem to suggest that Evangelicals are not uniform in their approach. A majority of white Evangelicals in the United States supported President Trump's 2017 ban on Muslim immigration, with a strong correlation with those registered as Republicans.[28] In the UK, however, a majority of Evangelicals voted to remain in Europe during the 2016 Brexit referendum, a position associated with being supportive of the freedom of movement.[29] Of course, the causes, benefits, drawbacks and solutions to migration are complex. Matthew Kaemingk,[30] a theologian at Fuller Theological Seminary, discusses immigration and observes that it is not so simple as saying one side is right and the other is wrong. 'Muslim immigration presents very real and very deep cultural and political challenges to the Western status quo [and] nationalists are absolutely right to call leftists to account.' However, he goes on to say that Christians can 'passionately defend [Muslims'] rights and can even praise their many contributions to the common good' (2018: 3, 19).

Evangelicals may have other reasons to be positive about migration. For instance, David Cashin of Columbia International University believes that current patterns of Muslim migration to the West are 'the best chance we've had in human history to share the love of Christ with Muslims'.[31] Accad sees the movement in a slightly different light. The fact that 'Muslims today are an integral part of virtually every society in the world' offers an opportunity for 'cross-fertilization' and mutual learning so that Christians and Muslims do not 'perpetuate the mistakes of the past' (2019: 103–4). Similarly, Steve Bell, an author and former missionary, believes 'Muslims are here in the purposes of God' and muses whether 'God has allowed the influx of God-fearing Muslims at precisely the time when European societies are walking away from the Judeo-Christian principles, in favour of godless secularism. Muslims are among us for a reason' (2006: 142).

Secondly, foreign policy, particularly in the Middle East, has been another issue which has divided Evangelicals along political lines. Some Evangelicals have been very supportive of American and British military interventions in Afghanistan, Iraq and Syria (e.g. P. Sookhdeo, 2007: 435). Indeed, some such as Sookhdeo have acted as advisors to Western armed forces.[32] Mike Evans, an American Evangelical author and journalist, warns that 'the next World War has already started, and we are right in the middle of it. America needs to have the same resolve in dismantling the terrorists' worldwide network'. He complains that 'the liberal Left remains firmly committed to the agenda of appeasement and apathy' rather than military action (2007: 5, 184). Others have been much more critical of these policies and see them as having led to needless confrontation and loss of life. British church leader and social activist Steve Chalke, in his book *Radical*, cites the number of casualties in Afghanistan and Pakistan and the resulting impact of the West's 'War on Terror' as evidence that when it comes to violence and military retaliation, 'the same old approach will always yield the same old outcomes' (2016: 10). Dave Andrews,[33] an Australian Baptist and former missionary to India, also rehearses the casualty statistics from Afghanistan and Iraq, lamenting 'the same old story' of reliance on warfare. He is critical of Western policies, and especially of those who support violence in God's name (2015: 23).

Thirdly, the engagement of Muslims in national politics and domestic policies has been another point of controversy. Some Evangelicals in the United States, such as Representative for Idaho Bill Sali, an Evangelical, were concerned when the first Muslim, Keith Ellisen, was elected to Congress in 2006.[34] As of 2021, there were three Muslim representatives in Congress but no senators.[35] One of these, Congresswoman

Ilhan Omar, incurred the wrath of right-wing politicians and Christian news sites when she was deemed to have played down the significance of the events of 9/11. She was also labelled anti-Semitic for her opposition to US policies towards Israel.[36] Other Western countries have rather more Muslim representatives in their parliaments. Following the 2019 elections in the UK, there were twenty-six Muslim MPs in the British Parliament and twenty-four peers in the House of Lords.[37] In Australia in 2022, two Muslims were appointed as federal ministers for the first time.[38] While this is undoubtedly a problem for some, there are occasions when Evangelicals applaud the work of Muslim MPs, such as in Britain when MP Khalid Mahmood spoke against the APPG definition of Islamophobia (Dieppe, 2019a).

Finally, there are, of course, political issues directly concerning Islam and the accommodation of Muslim communities in Western societies, which some on the political right see as leading to 'Islamization' (see Chapter 7). However, the above examples should suffice to demonstrate that Evangelical responses to Islam and Muslims are diverse and very often reflect political opinions. In the West, those Evangelicals who lean towards left-wing, liberal or libertarian politics tend to support the freedom of movement and the rights and independence of migrant communities, including Muslims. Those who lean towards right-wing, conservative or nationalist politics tend to favour strong controls on immigration, assimilation of communities and restrictions on the religious freedoms of non-Christians. In non-Western contexts, Evangelicals will have other concerns, particularly where community identity politics are strong. These differing views inevitably have a profound impact on attitudes towards Muslims.

Social context

The question of context is important not only for politics. Evangelical responses to Islam and Muslims will also be affected by geography, economics, environmental factors and local history. It is one thing to encounter middle-class Muslims in a leafy suburb; it is another to encounter Muslim vigilantes on the streets of a Muslim-dominated, inner-city neighbourhood. The historical harmony between Christians and Muslims in places such as Syria and Ethiopia has given way more recently to suspicion, segregation and even open conflict. The experience of Christians in northern Nigeria living in Muslim-majority states that have imposed the Sharia cannot be compared to an academic discussion of religious law in a Western university.

The first decades of the twenty-first century have certainly seen big changes in the contexts in which Christians and Muslims encounter one another. The Middle East has become a war zone between Western armies and groups branded as Muslim terrorists, with local Christian–Muslim relationships often as collateral damage. The economic and cultural influence of Wahhabi Islam in Africa and Asia has upset settled patterns of historical friendship. Demographic growth, migration and the impact of climate change have turned parts of West and East Africa into flashpoints of violence between Muslim and Christian communities competing for power, land and resources. Moreover, the rise of populist nationalism in many European and American countries has fuelled fear, xenophobia and anti-Muslim sentiment.

Experience

These sorts of contexts go a long way towards determining the experiences that Evangelicals and Muslims have of one another. Accad suggests that the reactions Christians have towards Muslims are 'instinctive and experiential [rather] than carefully thought out'. They grow out of 'bad experiences with Muslims', on the one hand, or 'positive encounters with Muslims', on the other (Accad, 2011: 182). For instance, Shirin Taber, an American Evangelical from a mixed Iranian-Catholic background, writes warmly about her relationships with Muslims and says, 'Not all Muslims are the same, and my experience among Muslims has been mainly positive' (2009: 79).

On the other hand, some Evangelicals have no experience at all and do not even know a Muslim, meaning their attitudes and opinions are built entirely second hand via the media, political debate or Christian commentators. This has consequences. In the United States, 'research has shown that those who know Muslims in their communities tend to hold more positive views and are more likely to see commonalities between their two faiths'. However, this research also shows that only 35 per cent of Evangelicals in the United States, and 44 per cent of Protestants in total, know a Muslim personally. Predictably, these groups (Evangelicals are included within the Protestant label) also exhibit the highest levels of fear and criticism of Muslims.[39]

Others have observed this when looking at the backgrounds of Evangelical authors such as those featured in this book. Cumming identifies two categories of Christian books that came onto the market following 9/11. 'One category advocated loving Muslims, building bridges and relationships, practicing hospitality, and reaching out with the love of Christ. The other category screamed that Muslims are a threat, that Islam is a threat, and that we have to defend ourselves against Muslims.' He goes on to conclude:

> If you look at the authors of those books, the authors who speak about love are those who have lived and worked among Muslims, perhaps for decades, as my wife and I lived in North Africa for fifteen years. These authors have learned Muslims' languages, been in Muslims' homes, had Muslims in their homes, and shared meals with them. The authors who promote bigotry and fear are people who do not have Muslim friends or experience with Muslims. (2013: 49)

This may be overstating the case, but it is certainly true that open authors such as Chapman, Bell, Musk, Rick Love and Shenk had spent many years living in Muslim countries. Others, such as Accad, Shehadeh and Azumah, are native residents in those countries. Whereas leaders such as Garlow, Southern Baptist pastor Jerry Vines[40] and world-renowned missiologist Don Richardson (d. 2018), for example, have not had prolonged exposure to a Muslim-majority context and have all written or spoken combatively about Islam. This seems to suggest that there may be a correlation between time spent in Muslim company and more peaceable attitudes and approaches. However, there are plenty of exceptions. Jay Smith lived in West Africa before moving to London and engaging in polemical debate. Australian Stuart Robinson,[41] a Baptist pastor, worked among Muslims in South Asia, and compatriot Durie did fieldwork in the Aceh province of Indonesia, yet they both take more hawkish approaches to Islam. Finally, Moucarry and Michael Youssef,[42] an Egyptian-American megachurch pastor, were both born into Arab Christian families – in Syria and Egypt, respectively – before leaving their homelands in early life to study in the West. Moucarry's writing on Islam, however, is much gentler and more sympathetic than Youssef's, suggesting that there are more complex, personal dynamics at work.

This leaves one other very special type of experience. Those who have converted from Islam to Christianity are variously known as 'Muslim Background Believers' (MBB), 'Believers from a Muslim Background' (BMB) or sometimes just 'ex-Muslim Christians'. Not all converts become Evangelicals, of course. For instance, Lamin Sanneh, a Gambian scholar widely respected and referenced by Evangelicals, became a Roman Catholic. However, many are, and they have a very particular experience of Islam from the inside. This gives them a special place in the Evangelical community, not just as living proof that Muslims can and do become Christians but often as 'authorities' on Islam. However, there is by no means conformity among these BMBs on what Islam is or on how Christians should respond to Islam. It varies depending on the context they have come from, their experience during the process of leaving Islam and their ongoing relationship with their family and former community.

Kidd observes that 'angered by the perceived deceptions of their former religion, and by the rough treatment received from Muslims following their conversion, Christian converts have often supplied … inflammatory characterizations of Islam'.[43] He uses brothers Ergun and Emir Caner as an example. They apparently converted to Christianity after moving from Turkey to the United States; both rose to senior positions in Evangelical seminaries; and they wrote the widely read *Unveiling Islam: An Insider's Look at Muslim Life and Beliefs* (2003), which according to Kidd 'depicts Islam as an aggressive religion of violence'.[44] However, their story claiming involvement in Muslim extremism has now been discredited.[45] Other converts who participate in the micro-public sphere also present very negative views of Islam. Mark Gabriel,[46] a former Egyptian imam who studied at Al Azhar University in Cairo, wrote *Islam and Terrorism*, which, according to Kidd, again paints violent jihad as 'true Islam'.[47] Gabriel gives a harrowing account of being tortured by the Egyptian authorities when he began his journey away from Islam and survived an attempted murder. These experiences must certainly affect his view of Islam (2002: 7–17; also 2007). Mosab Hassan Yousef,[48] a former Hamas militant, wrote the popular book *Son of Hamas* (2010), expressing similar views as do Walid Shoebat's books (2005, 2008). Shoebat also claims to have been a terrorist and has been a popular speaker in the United States, but, like the Caners, his story has been cast into doubt.[49] Sam Solomon, an author and advisor to Christian Concern in the UK, is another convert from Islam, as is Abdul Saleeb (pseudonym), co-author of *The Dark Side of Islam* (2003), and Sookhdeo also reports being from a partially Muslim background. Traumas such as those experienced by some of these converts have a lasting impact and must surely impact the victims' views of their former religion. Converts need reassurance that their sacrifice has been worthwhile.

This can come in the form of positive affirmation from their new community, but can also come from discrediting their old community.

Whatever the truth of their stories may be, it is not surprising that such individuals carry a great deal of authority when speaking about their former faith. Some received an Islamic education and went on to Islamic universities. Others belonged to Islamic organizations and were zealous for Islam. They speak their native language fluently and can quote the Qur'an and other Islamic texts in Arabic, which carries great weight with a non-specialist Christian audience eager to understand Islam and the roots of the world's problems today. These people inevitably come across as experts, and it is difficult to contradict them. This is not at all to say that these people do not have genuine insights to share about Islam, but it can be confusing when others, also with a wealth of experience, take a different approach.

Certainly not all Muslim converts are so negative about their former Muslim communities, although they may on occasion have critical things to say about Islam. In the African context, Azumah still has cordial relationships within his mixed Muslim-Christian family, having himself been brought up as a Muslim. Azumah was a student of Sanneh, another former Muslim who wrote respectfully on Islam and culture as well as theology. Mazhar Mallouhi, a Syrian author, is a former Muslim who is a remarkable example of someone who was rejected by his family, with his uncle even trying to murder him, yet has maintained a positive affection for his birth religion and community (Chandler, 2007: 26). He even controversially continues to refer to himself as a Muslim, much to some Evangelicals' disapproval (see Chapter 13).

Others have also been mistreated by Muslims and yet overcame the experience and went on to build friendships with Muslims and be involved in peacemaking. For instance, the story of *The Imam and the Pastor*, made into a popular film, is a powerful example of how two individuals in Nigeria overcame their violent enmity to make peace with one another. One was pastor James Wuye, an Assemblies of God Pentecostal pastor, who got involved in a militia and had his arm chopped off by a Muslim mob before he became involved in reconciliation (Akinade, 2014: 166–7). Cumming too recounts having 'close friends who were tortured with electric shocks and beatings, and other friends who have been murdered by Islamist militants'. He personally has been beaten by Islamist 'lynch mobs on more than one occasion' (Cumming 2019). Yet he remains open and irenic in his engagement with Muslims.

It would be too simplistic to say that those converts who were mistreated and persecuted by their Muslim families and community have a combative relationship with Islam, whereas those who had an easier transition and who maintain a positive relationship with their families do not. Interestingly, even Christians from Muslim-majority contexts exhibit a similar disparity. For instance, we have already seen the contrast between Moucarry and Youssef above. Likewise, Lebanese writers Accad and Jabbour both take a more open approach to Islam than has George Houssney, a Christian Arab evangelist, also originally from Lebanon. This all suggests that, while negative experiences must surely have an impact, the underlying reasons for the different approaches are again complex and unique to each individual.

Theology

Some of these differences may surely be found in natural disposition, social conditioning and particularly church environment. One important variant is the Christian denomination the participant belongs to. Evangelicals are found in every Protestant denomination, yet there are no easy correlations between denomination and attitudes towards Islam. For instance, many of the Evangelical Anglicans within the Church of England take a dialogical, engaged approach with Muslims. However, Durie is also Anglican, yet is rather more polemical. Missionary David Shenk (d. 2023) was a Mennonite pacifist with a warm relationship with Muslims, but Jay Smith, also a Mennonite, is more combative. Albert Mohler[50] and John Piper[51] are both Baptist pastors who are suspicious of Islam, while Accad and Munayer are also Baptists but much more irenic. Finally, Pentecostals are often known for their spiritual warfare approach to Islam, but Cumming and Volf are both Pentecostals who are dovish in their engagement, although London-based Elim pastor Colin Dye is more hawkish.

More significant probably is the stand they take on the 'theology of religions'. How do Christians – and any person of faith – explain the existence of other religions? What is the source of those religions? Are they good or bad? What will be the eternal destiny of those from other religions? Such questions are key to determining Evangelicals' attitudes towards Islam and Muslims.

The best-known theological model for representing one's views on other religions is the three-fold paradigm developed by Alan Race.[52] He labels Christians as either *exclusivist*, *inclusivist* or *pluralist*. The basis of this categorization is soteriological, that is, who will be 'saved' or go to heaven in the next life? This is a key concern for many of the Evangelicals mentioned in this book. Exclusivists hold that only those who have explicitly heard and accepted the gospel of Christ will be saved. At the other end of the spectrum, pluralists take a relativist stance and see all religions as being equally true and therefore equally valid paths to salvation. Inclusivists take a middle position which holds to the objective truth of Christianity, and yet suggests that God may save some outside of the Christian church because of the work of Christ.

Race's typology has, of course, been criticized – as are all typologies – for being too simplistic and for focusing too narrowly on salvation (e.g. A. Smith, 2018: 18). These critiques notwithstanding, the application of Race's model to Christian-Muslim relations is obvious. Almost by definition, the majority of the Evangelicals in this book would not espouse a pluralist view, although some post-Evangelicals are moving in that direction. Otherwise, there would be no need for evangelism or conversion and no critique of theology apart from where it may be intolerant or impinge on shared lives. All of the participants in this public sphere hold these things as central tenets to some degree. The majority would adopt an exclusivist position which draws a clear distinction between Christians and Muslims. Evangelism and conversion are imperative, potentially causing tension between Christians and Muslims. This view has the great benefit of being very clear. The lines are drawn in black and white, and the mission is compelling. Other Evangelicals in this book tend towards an inclusivist position. Indeed, Christopher Lamb calls Cragg 'one of the elder statesmen of inclusivism' which he describes as being 'boldly hospitable to other faiths and ready to learn from them, but secure in the Christian home from which such hospitality is offered'.[53] Other Evangelicals at least find themselves at the inclusivist end of the exclusivist position. They still hope, as does Cragg, that Muslims will convert and even see seeds of that hope in the Qur'an or Muslim thinking. However, they also hope that God in his mercy will be at work in Muslim lives even without them becoming explicitly Christian. This makes the situation much less clear. Evangelicals of this persuasion may be more predisposed towards partnership and cooperation with Muslims while leaving the issue of conversion up to God.

Typologies such as those seen in this chapter help us understand the different responses to Islam that we see in the Evangelical public sphere. As we move to look at various issues in Part 2, some of these types and labels will be referred to. However, no attempt will be made to categorize different individual writers, thinkers or leaders according to the above typologies. This would be unhelpful, divisive and invidious as people do not usually like to be labelled. It would also be difficult to do so and might give the impression that these categories are static. This is not necessarily the case. While different quotations illustrate a particular approach or position, people may change over time or have different views according to context or a specific topic.

Part 2

Evangelicals talking among themselves

3

Allah

The first issue to be examined is, in many ways, the most fundamental of all. Who is Allah according to Evangelicals? To put it another way, 'do Christians and Muslims worship the same God?' Answers to this question in the Evangelical public sphere set the tone for all other issues and ultimately decide the question as to what Evangelicals believe Islam is (Chapter 11). It is a question that has come to the fore since the events of 9/11 with new force (Volf, 2012: vii). Cumming reports that, in sixteen years prior to that date, no American Christian ever asked him this question, but 'suddenly on September 11, 2001 everything changed … Suddenly one chief question was on everyone's lips' (2019: 218). Since that time, other smaller events have reignited the question and, on each occasion, generated a flurry of texts and debate within the public sphere.

In 2003, US President George W. Bush commented to a reporter that he believed Muslims and Christians worship the same God. The remark sparked a furore.[1] Chuck Baldwin,[2] an American pastor and radio broadcaster, immediately labelled the president a 'universalist' and an 'apostate' and warned that 'his erroneous remarks portend much evil' (Baldwin 2007). In 2007, ACW (see Chapter 2) also sparked fierce debate. Some Evangelicals seemed to accept the premise of ACW that the same loving God was in view in both religions (Volf, bin Muhammad and Yarrington, 2010: 51–6; Andrews, 2015: 78). This drew sharp criticism from other Evangelicals who disagreed and were suspicious of Muslim motives, believing that theological distinctives were being compromised (e.g. Solomon and Al-Maqdisi, 2009a; Barnabas Fund, 2008a; Durie, 2008a). Then in 2015, Larycia Hawkins, an associate professor at the conservative Evangelical Wheaton College in Illinois, donned a hijab in solidarity with Muslims because, according to her, 'we worship the same God'. She was dismissed by the seminary, not for wearing a hijab but for her theological statement. Again, this event drew comment, debate and disagreement among Evangelicals, even including some in the Middle East who were quoted in American Christian media.[3] Finally, during the whole of this period, there was an ongoing legal battle in Malaysia where Christians had been banned by the Muslim government from using the word Allah in their Bibles and publications.[4] Ironically, while some Christians in the West were agitating against using the word Allah, Christians in Southeast Asia were fighting to be allowed to continue using it, again stimulating comment in the public sphere (Tennent, 2007: 45–6; Morey, 2002a).

All of these are excellent examples of events which happen around a particular question, provoking reaction among Evangelicals, generating texts which circulate for debate and opinion formation in the public sphere. So, this chapter serves as a case study of the Evangelical micro-public sphere as it debates the question of whether Muslims and Christians worship the same God. It explores the question as a subtopic of the sphere's main issue and gives an overview of the types of texts and media deployed in the discussion. It gives a first opportunity to see the range of responses among the sphere's participants as they give differing answers to the question and interact with one another's texts. Finally, the chapter explores the types of arguments and reasoning deployed across the different texts. Many of these patterns and tropes will then repeat in later chapters as successive questions are explored.

Allah: An issue within an issue

The first element for a public sphere to form is an issue of concern, and if the main issue for this Evangelical micro-public sphere is Islam, then the questions around the identity and nature of Allah form one of the most important 'sub-issues'. It is a natural, fundamental question to ask, and yet it does not permit an easy answer. Elie Haddad, president of the Arab Baptist Theological Seminary in Beirut, says, 'I think it's absolutely the wrong question to ask. That's why we can only get a wrong answer.'[5] Chapman (2007c) agrees and suggests it is akin to asking a man whether he has stopped beating his wife. Others suggest reformulating the question or breaking it down into more specific questions. One of the most prevalent of these, although not less complex, becomes the book title *Is the Father of Jesus the God of Muhammad?* (George, 2002; also used by Tennent, 2007: chapter 2). Alternatively, Arab theologian Imed Shehadeh, founder of the Jordanian Evangelical Theological Seminary, poses it as whether 'the God of Absolute Oneness is the same as the God of Oneness in Trinity' (2020: 92).

Nonetheless, most Evangelicals accept its importance. Musk calls it the 'big question' (2005: 59). Timothy Tennent,[6] president of Asbury Theological Seminary, sees it as a 'life-or-death question' because the salvation of Muslims depends on it (2007: 47). Bell thinks that 'it is a critical question because how you answer it will determine everything else about your response to Muslims … whether you take an apologetic or a polemic approach … look for similarities or the contrasts. If Allah is not the God of the Bible, it blows Muslims and Christians totally apart' (2011: 82–3). If the stakes are high for evangelism, according to some, they are even higher for theology and, indeed, by implication, for the future of Evangelicalism. So, Mohler (2015) warns that 'the cost of getting this question wrong is the loss of the Gospel'.

However, this theological question is being asked against the backdrop of global events. As Cumming reflects on his experience described above, he suggests that 'what changed [post-9/11] was the social and political context in which Christians think theologically about Islam' (2019: 218). This lends the question added jeopardy. Volf goes as far as to say that 'Muslims and Christians will be able to live at peace with one another … [only if they] turn out to have a "common God"' (2011: 8–9). This view has been much criticized by those wondering how we are then to explain intra-religious violence between, for instance, Protestant and Catholic, or Sunni and Shia (e.g. Power, n.d.).

Texts about Allah

Along with an issue, a public sphere requires texts. Already in the above discussion, we have seen a variety of media employed to transmit texts in this debate: complete books, book chapters, journal articles, news reports, blogs, websites and even a conference workshop. More will follow. Half a dozen or so books have been published on this question by Evangelicals, and only one of them, Volf's 2011 book *Allah: A Christian Response*, gives an unequivocal affirmative answer. Two books that take a more intermediate stance believe the answer is both 'yes' and 'no' but needs to be qualified (George, 2002; Shehadeh, 2020). Other books give a categorical negative answer (Andy Bannister, 2021; Durie, 2013; Moshay, 2008; Solomon and Debs, 2016).[7] One further significant full-length treatment, edited by two Evangelicals from Liberty University in Virginia, presents four different Christian views on the question, including two by Evangelicals, along with two ministry responses by other Evangelicals (Campbell and Gnanakan, 2019).

Authors also include significant chapters on this issue in their books on broader topics, such as Accad (2019: chapter 3 – 'God in Christian-Muslim Dialogue'). Two of the most detailed chapter overviews laying out the arguments come from Musk (2005: chapter 4 – 'And Who Exactly Is God?') and Tennent (2007: chapter 2 – 'Theology: Is the Father of Jesus the God of Muhammad?'), although they arrive at rather different conclusions. Despite the title of Qureshi's *No God but One: Allah or Jesus?* (2016b), the book only contains one section on this question titled '*Tawhid* or the Trinity? Two Different Gods'. Other authors include passing references to this debate in their books.

Added to these, there have been plenty of articles published in journals and magazines. *Christian Century* published a series of five articles by three Christians, a Muslim and a Jew responding to Bush's comment above. These included one by veteran missionary and Fuller Theological Seminary professor Dudley Woodberry, and another by Sanneh. Along with these published texts, there is extensive material on the internet, especially on apologetic websites, although they have more articles in defence of the Trinity than texts discussing this question. Video on the topic is also ubiquitous on the internet. For instance, Jay Smith's video 'Is Allah God?' (2006) on the Pfander YouTube channel is a trenchant rebuttal of sameness.

Participants and their views

The final requisite for a public sphere is participants and their various answers to this question, which range from 'yes' to 'no' with not a few choosing to answer 'yes and no'. Not all the participants are so committal in their response as Smith. For instance, Matthew Stone, a Messianic Jew who had at one time converted to Islam,[8] is 'not taking sides on the issue' (M. Stone, n.d.), and Sanneh in his *Christian Century* article states no personal position.[9] Others merely presume a common starting point for talking about God without explicitly addressing the question. For instance, McLaren accepts that Muhammad 'came to believe that this one true and living God was the same God who had been revealed to Adam, Noah, Abraham, Moses and Jesus' (2012b: 90). Missionary David Goldmann uses the word 'God' referring to both religions, notes the 'common beliefs' and goes on to contrast the 'essence and attributes' (2008: 29–35).

However, other Evangelicals make it explicit that they believe the answer to the question to be a resounding 'yes'. Cragg is, maybe, the best example of this as the whole of his work is based on this assumption. In his very first book, first published in 1956 and still in print and influential today, he makes it clear that Christians and Muslims are 'obviously referring to the same being … To suppose otherwise would be confusing … [although] the differences [are] undoubtedly real … far-reaching and must be patiently studied' (2000: 30). We have already seen Bell's opinion above and Volf's book-length defence in which he suggests that there are 'similarly sufficient descriptions' of God in the two faiths to warrant this conclusion (Volf, 2011: 96). Shenk believes that a negative answer to this question is a 'Christian distortion about Allah', and he strongly dissociates from it (2014: 117). Musk too largely accepts the premise but, with many below, suggests that 'our role as Christians needs to be one of accepting to use the term Allah and seeking to fill it with biblical meaning' (2005: 147; also Azumah, 2008b: 139; Medearis, 2008: 30–1).

Several Evangelicals point out that Muslims themselves believe it is the same God. 'Nothing in the Qur'an suggests that Muhammad ever believed that Jews and Christians, "the People of the Book", were worshipping a different God' (Chapman, 2007b: 264). Qur'anic passages supporting this include Q.29.46 and Q.42.15 (Peters, n.d.). Arab Christians also use the word 'Allah' for God, and so Accad says, 'Living in a Muslim-majority country, neither I nor my Muslim friends had ever thought of asking each other this question. Allah was the word I had used to address God in Arabic since my childhood' (2019: 75). Syrian Arab Moucarry likewise leans in this direction and thinks that 'the convergence between God's biblical and Islamic "portraits" suggests that Christians and Muslims do worship the same God though they do not know him in the same way' (2022: 168). Not all Arab Christians agree, and Azar Ajaj (2016), president of the Nazareth Evangelical College, explains that 'for an Arab Christian to use the word "Allah" does not imply any specific theological congruence between our respective understandings of God'.

However, the largest number of Evangelicals who are well disposed towards Muslims agree with Ida Glaser – a Christian Bible scholar and author from a Jewish background – that 'this can be a misleading question, as it expects an answer of either "Yes" or "No". However, it needs an answer of both "Yes" and "No"' (2016: 17). For some this is a 'mostly yes' position as 'it is logically impossible for there to be two different "one Gods" who are *both* the only creator of the universe and only judge of the world. There *can* be only one such God' (Cumming, 2019: original emphasis). This would seem to be the case for many who agree with Musk's position above (Chapman, 2007b: 266; Moucarry, 2022: 169; Shehadeh, 2020).

Others lean towards 'yes but mainly no' for theological reasons. American theologian Timothy George in his book-length treatment says, 'The answer to this question is surely both yes and no. Yes, in the sense that the Father of Jesus is the only God there is … but the answer to the question is also no, for Muslim theology rejects the fatherhood of God, the deity of Jesus Christ, and the personhood of the Holy Spirit' (2002: 69). Tennent (2007) takes a similar position, and Woodberry writes that 'as monotheists we both refer to the One and only Creator God, but what we understand about the character and actions of God are significantly different' (2004: 37).

Another group of Evangelicals, however, are adamant that the answer is 'no' (e.g. Caner and Caner, 2003; Pawson, 2003: 108). Mohler insists that 'there is no way to remain faithful to Scripture and the gospel and then claim that Christians and Muslims worship the same God' (Mohler 2015). Jay Smith in his video (2006) says, 'Is Allah God? Absolutely not!', and commenting on the Wheaton row, Graham declared that Muslims 'clearly do not worship the same God'.[10]

Andy Bannister,[11] director of the Solas Centre for Public Christianity, in his book (2021) compares the concept of God in the two religions and decides that two different Gods are in view. Durie comes to the same conclusion that 'despite significant similarities, there is no family resemblance. Some features from the face of the God of the Bible may have been glued onto Muhammad's Allah, but the heart of the matter is that Allah and YHWH share no DNA. They are not the same God' (2013: 160).[12] Finally, Solomon and Debs' book is written specifically to refute Volf's idea of sameness and 'sufficient similarity' as well as to make it 'clear to any objective observer that the Allah of Islam has no resemblance whatsoever to the Lord God of the Bible' (2016: 23).

These Evangelicals sometimes even accuse Muslims of not believing it is the same God. Robert Morey (d. 2019), an American pastor and apologist, insists that 'the Muslim god "Allah" is not the same God that Christians worship. The vast majority of Muslims know this to be true. This is why they call Christians "infidels" and persecute them. Those Muslims in the West who claim otherwise, do so as an evangelistic tool to convert ignorant and unwary Westerners to Islam' (2002a: 67). Solomon and Debs also suspect claims of sameness by Muslims, as in the ACW letter, of being 'a veiled threat' to get Christians to conform to Islamic conceptions of oneness (2016: 195).

Azumah notes this possibility but, in the African context at least, says it is Christian pastors who tend to hold the negative position. Ordinary believers tend to be more affirming (Azumah, 2008b: 139). This confirms a similar tendency noticed by Quosigk among American Evangelicals.[13] These sorts of negative views are criticized by Moucarry who says, 'My experience suggests that many Christians (including Arab Christians) who take this negative view of God in Islam have not taken much time to understand the faith of their Muslim neighbours. They have little meaningful interaction if any with Muslim people' (2007: 88).

This spectrum, from an affirming view of Islam (yes) through middle-ground ambiguity (yes/no) to a critical response (no), will become familiar throughout this book, and, indeed, many of the protagonists will reappear at similar points on this spectrum with regard to other questions.

Interaction in the public sphere

We have already seen that these Evangelicals are interacting and responding to one another's texts in the public sphere. Sometimes this is in a positive affirming sense. McLaren draws on Volf's work and calls his book 'an extremely important contribution to the subject of Christian identity in a multi-faith world' (2012b: chapter 2, n13). Musk references Moucarry and borrows a diagram from Chapman (Musk, 2005: 138–9). Tennent favourably refers to George's book and engages with the series of articles in *Christian Century* (2007: 26). Accad briefly summarizes the books by Volf, George and Shehadeh before developing his own views (2019: 78–9).

Other times the interaction is more critical, such as Dan Brown's critique of George's 2002 book which highlights both the positives and the perceived negatives (2004: 81–4). This was particularly the case with Volf's 2011 book. Some welcomed Volf's desire to approach Muslims positively, but still questioned many of his arguments and saw his work as unwarrantedly positive (Moucarry, 2011a; Shehadeh, 2011). Others were highly critical, and at least four books were written largely to rebut Volf (Andy Bannister, 2021; Durie, 2013; Qureshi, 2016b; Solomon and Debs, 2016). He is criticized for misunderstanding the concept of love in Islam; omitting the question of salvation; and ignoring Islam's attitude to religion and state, including the mistreatment of Christians in Muslim contexts (see especially chapter 16 of Durie, 2013). Bernie Power,[14] an Australian speaker and author, concludes that some of Volf's reasoning is 'disingenuous' and that he 'appears to have sacrificed the quest for theological truth on the altar of political correctness' (Power, n.d.). Durie has another theory, asking whether 'Volf's blind spots are manifestations of cognitive dissonance which is itself driven by fear of the very conflict he seeks to avoid' (2013: 139). This is a good example of a very sharp, very personal debate within the micro-public sphere.

Arguments concerning Allah

While some of the responses are reactive, even knee jerk, the majority are rational, considered and well expressed – whether or not one agrees with them. That does not mean to say that they are always logical, convincing or popular. The participants draw on a wide range of academic disciplines in answering this question including linguistics, history, philosophy, theology, epistemology, phenomenology and missiology. Indeed, several of the authors self-consciously construct their articles and arguments under some of these headings. For instance:

- Tennent (2007) – etymology, ontology, (implicitly) theology, evangelistic and pastoral
- Musk (2005) – history, philology, theology, missiology
- Johnston (2002) – philology, culture/language, theology, practice

The debate is too wide to capture all the detail and nuance in this short chapter, but the following gives some indication of the main arguments under the various headings with some examples.

Linguistic

Etymology, philology, semantics, translation and onomastics (the origin of proper names) appear frequently as linguistic arguments around this topic. Almost all writers explore the etymology of the word 'Allah' agreeing that it existed before Islam. They recognize its roots in earlier Semitic languages, especially in Hebrew words for God such as 'El' and 'Elohim'. Some of them then suggest that it is a loan word from Aramaic and Syriac and so is not native to Arabic (Tennent, 2007: 29). Some see evidence for Christian usage of the word before Islamic times, although it is uncertain when the Bible was first translated into Arabic (Musk, 2005: 128).[15] Others find the explanation within the Arabic language itself and suggest that it was a contraction of the Arabic for *al-ilah* (the god) (Medearis, 2008: 30; Glaser, 2016: 17). Others reject this notion as being an unlikely, non-standard Arabic contraction (R. Brown, 2012: 169).

When it comes to the use of the word today, everyone acknowledges that Arab Christians have no other word to use for God and that it is used in all Arabic translations of the Bible (Shehadeh, 2020: 97). This is not necessarily the case with Christian communities in other Muslim-language contexts. Musk points out that in Persian contexts the word *khudā* is used for God (2005: 140), and Chatrath mentions the use of *tanri* in Turkish (2011: 102). So Glaser advises Christians to use the word Allah when talking to Muslims in Arabic or other Muslim languages and use God in English, and then to discuss what God is like rather than arguing about what to call him (2016: 18). In fact, Shehadeh warns it is 'incorrect to use the word "Allah" in English to refer to the God of Islam, as if "Allah" and "God" were different beings' (2004: 25).

However, other Evangelicals disagree and feel very strongly that the name is important. They argue that Allah is not just a word for God, but, for Muslims, it is a proper noun, an Arabic name that he had even before creation (Geisler and Saleeb, 2002: 14; Shamoun, 2002: 61). Similarly, Jay Smith (2006) argues that he has searched the Bible for the name Allah, and the Qur'an and other Islamic texts for the name Yahweh but could not find them. He wonders why Muhammad did not use the name Yahweh if he was a true prophet and finds it 'unfortunate today that translators use the word [Allah]', boldly stating that 'sooner or later we're gonna have to change that because that is not … the God of the Bible'.[16] As a Bible translator, however, Kenneth Thomas (2001) would disagree. He recommends that translators stick with the traditional name used by the Christian community in the host country. Shenk too points out that while Muslims have always brought their Arabic name for God into new contexts, Christian missionaries 'seek for a local name for God' and then fill it with new meaning (2014: 118–20).

Historical

Some of the discussions above hinge around historical uses of the word Allah, which depend on the situation in Arabia in the seventh century. Authors discuss the Kaaba and the idols that were worshipped there prior to Islam. They also look at the use of the word Allah in pre-Islamic poetry and in personal names, such as Abdallah (the servant of Allah), the name of Muhammad's father (Shehadeh, 2004: 21). For some, these all point to the possibility that Allah was the name for 'the supreme high God' prior to Islam (Nazir-Ali, 2002: 2), which Muhammad then used to talk of the one creator God, much as Shenk's missionaries above.

Others reject the legitimacy of this argument and attempt to use history in highly polemical ways. Youssef confidently associates Allah with the Canaanite god Baal and claims that is why the crescent moon is an Islamic symbol (2015: 69). Robertson (2003) names Allah's precursor as 'Hubal, the Moon God of Mecca'. However, Rick Brown, a Bible scholar and mission strategist, strongly refutes this connection with a moon god, arguing that the crescent was 'a symbol imposed by the Ottoman Turks for political reasons' (2006: 80). Dan Brown, author and director of the Institute for the Study of Religion in the Middle East, concurs and suggests that such authors display 'a stunning ignorance of Islam and of history' (2004: 74–5). This does not stop Peter Wagner (d. 2016), a well-known American prayer leader and founder of Global Harvest Ministries, declaring that 'Allah is the proper name of a spirit being … Make no mistake about it, Allah is not the Creator, he is a creature' (P. Wagner, 2002). This raises the question of whether there can, indeed, be more than one god-being.

Philosophical

Some of the arguments put forward in this debate are therefore necessarily more philosophical in nature. Several authors discuss ontology and whether the being referred to is one and the same, or whether there are two beings in view. All agree that there can logically only be one Creator. This is the One whom Islamic philosophy describes as the 'uncaused Cause of all that exists' (Shehadeh, 2004: 22). So, many authors suggest that at least the subject referred to is the same in both cases. The question then comes – using a grammatical concept – as to whether the predicate is equivalent. Are the descriptions of that being the same?

One simple method used by several writers to determine this is analogical reasoning. Bannister humorously compares the investigation into the identity of God with the board game *Cluedo* (2021: 34). More seriously, Peter Cotterell (d. 2021), a former missionary and Bible college principle, develops an analogy of a table. Two people each have a table and believe it to be the same table, but then discover that it has different colours, different numbers of legs and different shapes. Can it still be the same table? The different predicates prove that the subjects must be different. This is a rather limited analogy as it involves a visible, inanimate object (Cotterell, 2006: 41).

A rather more subtle analogy, although still inanimate, is offered by Chapman and arrives at a different conclusion. He imagines two countries, one where the sun always shines and another where the sun is always obscured by cloud. Yet it is the same sun. He suggests that, if we assume two different planets such as the sun and moon, then this is 'likely to make communication between Christians and Muslims extremely difficult, if not impossible' (2007b: 265). This is not a problem for some, however. For instance, they point to the first commandment (Ex. 20.3) to suggest that the Bible itself accepts that there may be other gods (e.g. Morey, 2002a: 62).

Several writers develop a more complex analogy by imagining two people talking about an old friend (Andy Bannister, 2021; McDermott, 2019; Piper, 2013; Power, 2012).[17] In Piper's version, two people are reminiscing about a mutual friend from school days, but disagree over his description. Finally, they get out the photobook only to discover that they have been talking about two different people. They look nothing like each other. Duncan Peters, an Evangelical minister in the Free Church of Scotland, counters this analogy in a response to Bannister's book, imagining that he meets someone who knew Einstein. 'My knowledge of the man and his work is extremely limited. I know a little about him but never knew him. However, if his friend and I refer to Albert Einstein, it is one and the same [person] we refer to, even though our knowledge of him varies widely' (Peters, n.d.; see also Peters, 2022).

A final example yields another dynamic example of interaction in the Evangelical micro-public sphere. Durie (2010) proffers the analogy of a counterfeit bank note, an idea also used by Bannister (2021), which Durie borrows from an earlier booklet.[18] It is not enough, he argues, for a counterfeit note to look similar. To be accepted as legal tender, it has to be identical. Volf later quotes Durie's analogy in his book and takes him to task for emphasizing 'difference' over 'commonality'. He favours what he calls an approach of 'sufficient similarity' (Volf, 2011: 89–94), an idea strongly rejected by his critics (e.g. Solomon and Debs, 2016: 30). In a later edition of his book, Durie then accuses Volf of 'misrepresenting' him and restates the case for his analogy (2013: 83).

Jon Hoover, a Mennonite minister and academic, acknowledges that 'analogies are never completely adequate to the task' (2005: 295). So, others focus more on comparing God's character and essential nature. Cumming takes a deep dive into Islamic philosophical thought on God's essence and attributes and finds that the two faiths are, maybe, 'much closer to one another than is commonly supposed' (2012: 145). Musk too finds much in common when comparing the ninety-nine Beautiful Names of Allah in Islam (2005: 136), and George agrees, saying: 'Rightly understood, as they can be from the perspective of biblical faith, all ninety-nine of the Beautiful Names of God in Islam are beautiful for Christians as well' (2002: 72). Accad notes that the eastern church has historically favoured apophatic (negative) rather than kataphatic (positive) descriptions of God (2019: 105). Most writers, however, employ positive attributes, and several produce tables that compare the descriptions of God in the two faiths. Goldmann (2008: 29–35), Scot and Abdulhaq (2009: 130) and Rosemary Sookhdeo (2005: 107–9) all create charts to compare the nature and character of God, or Yahweh and Allah, in the two religions. These comparisons lead Shehadeh to speak for many Evangelicals when he says, 'The adherents of both Absolute Oneness and Oneness in Trinity may speak of the same subject, "God", but they ascribe different attributes to him to the point that it seems the two sides are speaking about two completely different subjects' (2020: 102).

Stone explores this further because 'as a philosopher' he knows that he has to 'be aware of [his] assumptions'. He breaks the main question down into six further sub-questions, the final one being, 'how many true attributes of God must one accept to believe in the true God? How many false attributes of God can someone accept without failing to believe in the true God?' (M. Stone, n.d.). This is akin to the ancient 'Ship of Theseus' conundrum; how many planks can be replaced in a ship, and it remains the same ship? This sort of impasse prompts Hoover to propose 'a shift in focus from the ontology ... to the history of God's interaction with humankind' as a way of breaking the deadlock (2005: 295). This requires a shift to theological reasoning.

Theological

The story of God's interaction with humankind and his self-revelation is a theological question. This is the real ground zero for Evangelical debate on Allah. We have already seen the reformulation of the question as 'is the God of Muhammad the Father of Jesus?' (George, 2002). This is a fully theological question that can only be answered by argument from revelation. For instance, Sandra Teplinsky, a Messianic Jew and president of Light of Zion Ministries,[19] draws a stark contrast. 'The Islamist Allah does not resemble the divine personality of the Creator portrayed in Scripture. The nature and attributes of the two differ dramatically. Moved by the power of love, Father God offers the sacrifice of His Son on our behalf. Moved by the love of power, Allah orders the sacrifice of his followers' sons on his own behalf' (2013: 134). As convert, Abdu Murray puts it: 'While the common ground for Christians and Muslims is their shared conviction that God is the greatest possible being, Islam and the gospel clash in their understanding of how God is great and what makes him great. The paradox is that the most important point of agreement is also the greatest point of departure between the two faiths' (2014: 166).

If there is substantial agreement on some of God's attributes, the key difference is centred on 'the deity of Jesus Christ' (McDermott, 2019). It is here that Muslims inevitably part company with Christians. Power (2012) reports using the Apostles' Creed as a theological test to demonstrate to Muslims that they worship a different God. This highlights the incarnation which is crucial, as it is from Jesus that Evangelicals get their image of God. As Campolo puts it, 'From churches and theologians, I get conflicting images of God. It's only when I view Jesus in the red letters of the Bible [i.e. words spoken by Jesus] that I am able to say, "Ah, here's a clear image of God. God is like Jesus!"' (2012: 56). Piper (2013) says, 'I don't care how many attributes line up between your god and my God. Jesus says you can't be worshipping the Father if you are rejecting him [Jesus]. And that is the approach I think we should take with all Muslims'.

Closely related to the concept of the incarnation is the doctrine of the Trinity. All Evangelical writers are careful to point out that Christians worship only one God, but it is a 'Oneness in Trinity' rather than the 'Absolute Oneness' of Islam (Shehadeh, 2020: 92). This is a perennial topic of debate between Christians and Muslims and too vast to cover in detail in this short section. However, for many Evangelicals, if Muslims do not accept the Trinity, then they are talking about a different God. Shehadeh sees an evolution in the Islamic denial of the Trinity beginning with misunderstandings that Christians also reject. It began with a 'rejection by the qur'anic suras of an erroneous concept of the Trinity' (that Mary was one of the three, for instance) and went on in modern times to reject that 'God is composed of parts' (also a heresy for Christians), which 'finally led Absolute Oneness to an explicit and unwavering denial of the true doctrine of the Trinity' (Shehadeh 2020: 101). Yet, this is not a doctrine which Evangelicals shrink back from or are embarrassed about. It is central to their faith. The Trinity is 'not a problem to be solved but rather a beauty to be discovered' (Shehadeh, 2020: 14). George believes that 'we Christians need to revisit the doctrine of the Trinity, not only for apologetic purposes, but also to rekindle our love and devotion to the one true God' (2002: 56). So, several authors include a chapter or section with advice on how to talk about the Trinity to Muslims (e.g. Masri, 2014: chapter 9; Shumack, 2014: chapter 4; Scott, 2011: chapter 5).

However, the Muslim rejection of the Trinity is not enough to persuade some Evangelicals who accept that Christians and Muslims are worshipping the same God. For them, the Jews, who also deny the Trinity, are a case in point. David Johnston, an academic at the University of Pennsylvania, remains 'unconvinced that the God of the Qur'an is any different from the God of the Old Testament. If we say Jews worship the same God as we do, then we must logically grant Muslims the same "privilege"' (2002: 12). It is interesting that almost all Evangelicals do agree that Christians and Jews worship the same God, although not all see it as a proof in the Muslim context (e.g. McDermott, 2019). However, it is important to note that a few dissent from this view. American Baptist Jerry Walls,[20] a philosophy professor, declares that 'Jews do not worship the same God as Christians for essentially the same reasons that Muslims do not' (2019: 160). That is, they do not believe in the Trinity and the deity of Christ. Volf points out that the reverse is also true and 'for the most part, Jews do not think they worship the same God as Christians do' (2012: ix).

A further theological argument concerns the knowability and love of God. Based on the incarnation and the doctrine of the Trinity, Evangelicals strongly believe that it is possible for humans to live in relationship with God, but do not see this concept in Islamic theology. 'While Christians aspire to fellowship and intimacy with God, Muslims have no such hope – or even the expectation that such a hope is possible' (Houssney, 2010: 85). Some ask, 'Where in the Qur'an does it say that Allah loves everyone? The answer is: *nowhere*' (Peltola and Dieppe, 2022: 36, original emphasis). So, many make a contrast between a God of love in Christianity and a God of power in Islam (e.g. P. Sookhdeo, 2009a: 116), and this was a main contention around the publication of ACW. For instance, the Barnabas Fund, closely associated with Sookhdeo, asserted that 'in Islam the focus is on submission, so love is never more than one of many secondary themes. Modern Muslim apologists in the West sometimes assert that God is a God of love. This is not a concept which traditional orthodox Islam would accept but appears to be a modern stance of adaptation to the environment they find themselves in' (2008b: i–ii).

Not all Evangelicals see it quite as starkly. They point out the diversity in the Islamic tradition and find love to be a strong theme in Sufi writing and poetry. Ted Collins (a pen name) recalls 'being told as a young man preparing to serve in the Muslim world that Muslims know about judgement but not about salvation … [and that] "there is no love in Islam"'. However, he goes on to quote a popular Sufi hymn which says: 'If you love Muhammad, you must love everyone, for his light is truly inside everyone. He is the mercy sent to everyone. Only through love can we all be one'. Such examples cause Collins to suggest that 'the outlook of Sufis is significantly different from that described in typical Christian books about Islam' (2021: 14, 16). Dan Brown likewise feels that the binaries set up by some Evangelicals are unfair. For instance, he critiques George's 2002 book for a lack of understanding of Islamic theology and suggests that 'many of the theological dichotomies [George] sets up collapse under the weight of the sheer complexity, sophistication and variety of the Islamic theological tradition' (2004: 83). Added to this theological diversity, there are Muslims who report a different experience, as will be seen in the discussion of phenomenology below.

However, before that, one final aspect of theology in the discussion of God is worthy of mention and is rather more political in nature. Campolo poses the question 'how often do we create an image of God that serves the interest of our own ethnocentric values and prejudices?' (2012: 56). Cumming believes that this could be happening in this debate and that Evangelicals are in danger of 'henotheism', that is, elevating their tribal god to be the most important among other gods. 'We do not want God to belong equally to all humankind. We want God to be our God. We want God to be loyal to our group. We want God to reassure us that our group is right.' Maybe echoing Volf's concerns about world peace, Cumming sees this as a heresy 'with the blood of millions on its hands' (2019: 219). Azumah sees a similar problem in the African context. 'We need a theology that takes seriously and wrestles with the African reality of religious pluralism, a refocus from the present inherited henotheism (the "our God" versus "their God" mentality) to true monotheism, a belief in the one true God who knows no partiality' (2013b: 61).

Phenomenological

It goes without saying that much of the preceding argument, regardless of where participants are on the spectrum, relies largely on a faith-based epistemology. Evangelicals base their beliefs and judgements on the Bible and what they believe God has revealed of himself. They pit this against what they think Muslims should believe based on their understanding of the Islamic texts. However, there are other routes of enquiry into this question, including phenomenology.

So, some Evangelicals are interested in what people actually experience. We have already seen that, growing up, Accad assumed it was the same God and he now believes that, rather than being intellectual, this question is 'a far more subjective matter' and suggests that 'we each have a different mental image of the recipient of our worship' (2019: 75, 104). This leads some to recommend that 'before we begin to ask whether Christians and Muslims worship the same God, we ask if it is possible for any two of us to have the same image of the same God' (Campolo and Claiborne, 2012: 56; see also Volf, 2011: 96). Cumming points out that Christians differ on various topics concerning God's nature, and, indeed, he himself feels that his 'own personal understanding of God in this area has changed over time, so that if differing perspectives in this area mean worshiping different gods, then [he] was worshiping a different god ten years ago' (2019: 211).

The experience of converts seems particularly important at this point. Most Evangelicals accept that the majority of Muslim converts to Christianity report feeling that they are still seeking to worship the same God. Even Durie admits that converts 'do not consider themselves to have exchanged gods, but rather to have revised their understanding of Allah' (2013: 149). Allen is one of the few to demur and reports that all the converts 'who have had a deep experience of God have felt the need to make a break with Islam and its God' (2016: 59). Cumming, however, claims to have known thousands of such converts and 'can count on one hand those who believe they worshiped a different, false god before coming to know Christ'. Those in that small category, he suggests, have 'lived in the West and experienced pressure from Christians to emphasize the chasm between Islam and Christianity' (Cumming 2019: 217). Convert writers such as Caner, Gabriel and Solomon might all fit this category as they all refuse to equate Allah with God. Nabeel Qureshi (d. 2017), a Pakistani-American convert from a Ahmadiyya background, certainly reports changing his view over time. 'For years after leaving Islam and accepting Jesus as Lord, [he] believed that Muslims worshiped the same God as Christians' but he then changed and became confident that 'Muslims and Christians do not worship the same God' (Qureshi, 2015). These different experiences demonstrate what Musk calls the 'delicate dynamics of "continuity" and "discontinuity"' which is a theme of much Evangelical debate (2005: 144).

When it comes to what Muslims experience, most Evangelicals presume that Muslims do not experience the relationship with God mentioned above. However, several people, including Peters, claim to know Muslims who 'speak of having a relationship with Allah or at least desiring to have one. Muslims speak to Allah in prayer' (Peters, n.d.). Cumming (2019) confirms this and reports knowing Muslims, particularly Sufis, who 'see God as immanent, approachable, and covenantally loving, and they find support for this in the Qur'an'. Evangelicals certainly differ in their understanding of such experiences.

Missiological

Finally, the question of Allah's identity is clearly an important factor when it comes to evangelism and mission. Some Evangelicals argue strongly that it is an advantage to presume we have the same God in view. Johnston contends that 'if my opening statement is, "You and I believe in a different God", we have already lost a precious bridge to [the Muslim's] heart' (2002: 13). Likewise, Peters says, 'how much better to start with the truth Muslims already have about God and use this to build a bridge for communicating Biblical teaching about God' (Peters, n.d.). Others see it as a grave error to 'rely on apparent commonalities', which is doing 'great damage' to Christian mission (Solomon and Debs, 2016: 198). That said, no Evangelicals report making this their opening statement when meeting a Muslim. As Ajaj (2016) says, 'We as Arab Christians do not seek to inflame emotions and relationships between the communities by aggressively highlighting our differences at every turn'. These divergent views are clearly reflected in the various strategies that are adopted in approaching Muslims, which will be discussed in Chapters 12 and 13.

Discussion: On the same page?

The question of Allah's identity is clearly a controversial and divisive one among Evangelicals. As many Evangelicals do, it is probably wise to break the question down and unpack it into a series of more focused questions. What is the story told about God in the two faiths? In what ways are the two descriptions of God similar or dissimilar? What have different traditions within each faith said about God? Who is the individual Christian or Muslim concerned seeking to worship? What is their experience of that worship? Of course, even the framing of these questions can be controversial, but it behoves the seriousness of the topic to explore it with thoroughness and deep reflection. The answers to them, however, usually fall along preexisting fault lines.

In terms of the Evangelical relationship with Muslims, this question is not uppermost in most Muslims' minds as they presume the answer to be 'yes', albeit with the proviso that they see Christians as having seriously distorted the true understanding of God. So, if Evangelicals are not leading with this question, as appears to be the case for most who actually engage with Muslims, then it may not provoke the sorts of problems between Evangelicals and Muslims that later issues do.

At a geopolitical level, it has been suggested by Volf that world peace depends on Christians and Muslims agreeing that they worship the same God (2011: 8–9). This seems to promise too much. The intra-faith conflicts raging throughout history and in various parts of the world today give the lie to the felicity of sharing a deity. Heterodox worship of the same God clearly stirs violent emotions which can lead to war. Moreover, it has to be hoped that world peace can be maintained without this sort of religious agreement, or else what hope is there for coexistence between the monotheistic religions and other civilizations with different gods or no gods? It may be more accurate to say that worshipping different gods could be a factor in *causing* war – as opposed to securing peace. Certainly, if Christian and Muslim henotheistic, tribal attitudes continue to develop and find expression in the political realm, as happens from time to time, then the likelihood of conflict increases.

However, at interpersonal and theological levels, the consequences of this question are, maybe, more profound. At the extreme end, if an Evangelical views a Muslim as a devil-worshipper, then it is hard to imagine a relationship being established. Fear will reign, undermining the Evangelical instinct to share the gospel with Muslims and stymying what is sometimes called 'friendship evangelism' (see Chapter 12). Of course, not all Evangelicals approve of such friendship in any case and prefer a more adversarial approach to engaging with Muslims, as will be seen. However, it also frustrates a quest for the common good. If a whole community is seen as following a foreign god, then it becomes a lot more difficult to see what there is in common and where shared interests lie.

There is also the question of how this issue affects the Christian community. Do different Christians themselves, even within the same tradition, worship the same God as one another? If the 'counterfeit note' test is applied, then apparently even the smallest discrepancy in the description of God between Christians would result in them believing in different gods. Christian denominations would be unreconcilable, as indeed they often are. This is because despite a perfect reproduction of a bank note with all the genuine materials, if not made by an authorized mint, then that bank note would not be legal tender. This suggests that it is *who* is making the note (or describing God) as much as the note (or description) itself which is decisive in this argument.

Theologically, black and white is easier. It is the safe option. Once Evangelicals admit that Christians and Muslims are referring to the same God, then they are in some sense 'on the same page'. This immediately begs the question of how much on that page Muslims may share with Christians. Does God accept Muslim worship, however misguided or misinformed it may be? Does God hear 'their' prayers, as he hears 'ours'? Does he sometimes answer them? It also raises questions about conversion and continuity. How much of former Muslim practice and experience can converts carry over with them into their new lives? These are the sorts of questions that concern the Evangelicals answering the Allah question with a resounding 'no'. For them, admitting that Christians and Muslims worship the same God presages the slippery slope to a watering-down of the gospel, pluralism and, ultimately, the end of the Evangelical gospel mission.

There is no doubt that different pages are easier. 'Our God is not their god'. No mixing, no compromise, no fuzzy boundaries. Grey is more challenging.

4

Muhammad

While the question of whether Muslims and Christians worship the same God is a foundational theological issue, the person and life of Muhammad are often the touchstone issues that set the tone for Christian-Muslim engagement. Muslims are passionate about the honour of their prophet, as riots following the publication of the infamous Danish cartoons in 2005 demonstrated. This has not stopped some Evangelicals publicly insulting him. However, while negative Evangelical statements about Muhammad have hit the headlines in recent years, less is heard about those seeking to build a positive assessment of his character and ministry.

Certainly, his character has been maligned, his ministry denigrated and his example vilified by those Evangelicals who take a combative approach towards Islam, and he is frequently compared unfavourably with Jesus. Others are sceptical of the traditional Islamic telling of Muhammad's history and wonder whether he ever even existed. At the same time, as will be seen, there are those who take a more respectful, even positive view of the 'Prophet of Islam'. Unsurprisingly, the boundaries among these Evangelical voices fall in similar places to the previous chapter. Those who do not accept that Christians and Muslims worship the same God tend to see Muhammad as an imposter and a false prophet. Those who see a continuity between Allah and the God of the Bible are more likely to have, or at least attempt, a positive assessment of his life and work.

Muslim reverence for Muhammad

Evangelicals for the most part are fully aware of how central and important the person of Muhammad is to Muslims. Mike Kuhn,[1] an American missionary and educator, realizes that 'for Muslims, Muhammad is much more than a prophet or teacher. He is the epitome of manhood, the moral role model for all people and all times' (2009: 201). His example is what Muslims call the Sunnah and is to be followed by all Muslims. Glaser begins a chapter on Muhammad with reference to *Be Careful with Muhammad!* written by Muslim philosopher Shabbir Akhtar (d. 2023) which 'explains to non-Muslim readers why Muslims were so offended by Salman Rushdie's portrayal of their beloved prophet in his book *The Satanic Verses*' (2016: 211).[2] Sookhdeo notices that in Islam, although Muhammad is just the 'human channel for God's revelation', in practice 'Muhammad's figure towers over Islam, not just as its founder, but as the "perfect man"

… considered infallible, free from sin, and serves as the supreme example whom all Muslims are obliged to emulate' (2009a: 19).

This causes some Evangelicals to question just how far the reverence for Muhammad goes (Moucarry, 2022: 23). Azumah notes that, while there is no suggestion of a divine nature, 'God is always coupled with Muhammad' in Islam and he is traditionally given 201 titles compared to the ninety-nine names of God (2008b: 21). He is also popularly seen as an intercessor, and Cragg observes that 'whatever orthodox theology might say about the possibility of his "mediation" with Allah, popular Muslim piety has no doubts' (2001: 126). In fact, such is the devotion on the part of some Sufi Muslims that Chapman reports they 'believe that Muhammad existed in heaven before he was born', although not all Muslims would agree with this (2007b: 86).[3] Scott also notices the devotion of Sufi Muslims and quotes a Sufi poem 'in praise of the best of creation' and gently muses that 'if an idol is someone or something which replaces the one true God as the reason for the way we live, then it is hard not to see Muhammad as an idol' (2021: 63). So, while Evangelicals acknowledge Muslim sentiments and love of Muhammad, they also suspect them of concealing a depth of veneration which borders on attributing to him a sort of divine status which goes beyond the claim that he is merely a human prophet. Solomon and Debs make this explicit in what they describe as the Islamic 'doctrine of the Finality of Muhammad' in which 'he is in absolute charge over humankind and its affairs, jointly with Allah', suggesting that this 'tight association between Muhammad and Allah might sound like *shirk*' (i.e. the sin of associating something with Allah) (2016: 169–71).

Negative Evangelical assessments of Muhammad

Such awareness of this importance and devotion, however, has not stopped some Evangelicals being highly derogatory and insulting about Muhammad. Denigration of Muhammad has a long history in Christian writing. In the eighth century, John of Damascus ridiculed him for writing 'many ridiculous books', making legal provision for polygamy and committing adultery.[4] In the sixteenth century, Calvin described Muhammad as one of the 'two horns of the anti-Christ', the other being the Pope, and Luther claimed that Christians were 'fighting that the Turk may not put his devilish filth and the blasphemous Muhammad in the place of our dear Lord, Jesus Christ'.[5] So it is, maybe, no surprise that this tradition lives on.

Today his moral character is frequently attacked by some Evangelicals, especially in relation to his attitude to women, his multiple wives, his marriage to Aisha at a young age and his taking his adopted son's wife, Zaynab, to be his own wife (e.g. J. White, 2013: 36–45; Peltola and Dieppe, 2022: 63). One of the highest-profile attacks was by Vines who, following the events of 9/11, infamously called Muhammad a 'demon-possessed paedophile'.[6] While this was extreme, it is not uncommon. Don Richardson uses the same word and describes the houris of the Qur'an as 'a host of virgins' who will 'forever satisfy' the sexual cravings of Muslim martyrs in what he calls a 'heavenly brothel'.[7] He goes on to make lurid claims about Muhammad's own sex life (2003: 75). Other Evangelicals make similarly negative assessments and quote specific verses in the Qur'an and Hadith which they believe demonstrate that Muhammad saw women as 'deficient in intelligence and religious devotion, ... as a possession – along with gold, silver, horses and cattle – ... [to be] used like a field' and even as devils (Scot and Abdulhaq, 2009: 121).

Other Evangelicals are sharply critical of these sorts of accusations and those that follow, finding them abhorrent and unhelpful, as indeed all Muslims must do. For instance, Dan Brown criticizes this sort of 'unveiling' of Islam as the 'prevailing cliché' among Evangelical leaders in the twenty-first century (2004: 69). In *Unveiling the Truth about Islam: Too Many Christian Books Miss the Mark* (2006), Warren Larson,[8] a former director of the Zwemer Center, calls it 'unfair' and believes that Richardson's supposedly 'fact-based commentary' makes 'unfair assumptions'. On the issue of polygamy, plenty of authors point out that 'biblical heroes from Abraham to David were polygamous, too, and even in the Christian Roman Empire polygamy was widely practised for many centuries' (McLaren, 2012b: chapter 11, n9).

Muhammad's engagement in warfare and violence is another major area of criticism (see Chapter 9). In similar fashion to Vines above, Falwell told CBS News in 2002 that 'Muhammad was a terrorist', which led to protests, riots and death threats in some parts of the world.[9] Many authors recount the number of battles that Muhammad was personally involved in, often referring to Ibn Ishaq's biography (or *sīra*) of *The Life of Muhammad*.[10] They point to the many Hadith traditions recorded in Bukhari's *Book of Jihad* and contemporary Muslim biographical works such as Martin Lings's *Muhammad: His Life Based on the Earliest Sources* (2006). The story of the beheading of the men of the Banu Qurayza tribe comes in for particular opprobrium. Sahaja Carimokam devotes a whole chapter to it and points out that 'between six hundred and nine hundred boys and men were brutally murdered' with the consent of Muhammad (2010: 372; see also Peltola and Dieppe, 2022: 53).[11] Cotterell, in a biography of Muhammad largely based on early Muslim accounts, suggests that after the move to Medina his was 'a very violent life' and that in Islam 'a clear trajectory of violence developed that had its origins in Muhammad' (2011: 161). Gabriel calls this the 'uncensored version' of Muhammad's story, which he believes Muslims often filter out from the traditional narrative for a Western audience (2007: 129). Carimokam sees some academics as being complicit in this filtering process:

> The tragedy of modern historical critical writings on Islam in the late twentieth century is that they tend to sanitize the Islamic texts. They produce a sanitized version of an already sanitized version of history. In other words, they produce propaganda. We would invite anyone to compare Karen Armstrong's *Life of Muhammad* with Ibn Ishaq's history (which is supposedly her source) to see how this works. Not surprisingly, her book is sold on Islamist propaganda web sites. (2010: 11)

Overall, for many Evangelicals, Muhammad's involvement in warfare 'casts a bleak question mark' over the assessment of Muhammad as an 'exemplar, the perfect example' (Riddell and Cotterell, 2003: 30). Nonetheless, as is discussed further in Chapter 9, some Evangelicals, while not at all condoning violence, are willing to listen to the Muslim rationale for Muhammad's actions. Kuhn points out that 'Muslims are generally offended when [Muhammad's engagement in warfare] is referred to and uphold Muhammad's activities as a necessary measure taken for the good of mankind in establishing Islam' (2009: 201).

Finally, there are Evangelicals who call into question Muhammad's motivation and inspiration. Anees Zaka, an American Presbyterian with Middle Eastern background, and co-author Diane Coleman believe that 'the picture that emerges from biographical data, *even from Muslim scholars*, is not flattering ... Muhammad was, at his core, ambitious and deliberate. The claim to prophethood, based on periodic seizure-like episodes, gave him status and authority among the Arab people' (2004: 54, original emphasis). They suggest that Muhammad was ill and claim that 'recent studies [by] a Turkish neurologist ... demonstrate very convincingly that the underlying physiological source of Muhammad's experiences was the combined effect of hydrocephalus and epilepsy' (2004: 34).

Others more bluntly assign Muhammad's supernatural experience to demonic causes. The Caner brothers point out that at first Muhammad himself was worried that he was 'possessed by an evil spirt or jinn', and the 'uncontrollable convulsions' recorded in Islamic tradition combined with 'his mental state' make him untrustworthy (2003: 42–4). Pawson also refers to Muhammad's trances and seizures and suggests that 'it is not hard to see an "unearthly" force behind it' (2003: 83). This is reminiscent of suggestions by some of the reformers that Muhammad was an Antichrist.[12]

Contrasting Muhammad and Jesus

Even for those who tend to be more sympathetic towards Islam, Muhammad's role and character can present a challenge. After all, many of the above accusations are based on the Islamic traditions themselves. So, some Evangelicals settle for a degree of ambiguity. Cotterell believes that 'Muhammad was a remarkable man, with a breathtaking range of gifts' and in his writing tries to walk a path between 'damning and belittling Muhammad from sheer prejudice', on the one hand, and 'sanitising and canonising him from an opposite prejudice', on the other (2011: 2). Glaser too wants to 'honour Muhammad as we would honour any human being made in the image of God, and ... appreciate all that is good about him' but recognizes that he does 'function as what is called, in 1 John 2.18–27, "an antichrist". Insofar as an antichrist "denies the Father and the Son" (1 John 2.22), Muhammad can be said to be one'. However, she notes that 'on the other hand, Muhammad does not easily fit some other aspects of the "antichrist" description' (2016: 227).

For many Evangelicals, much depends on a comparison with the person and character of Jesus, although some would say they 'cannot be *compared* with one another, but must be *contrasted*' (Cotterell, 2011: 156, original emphasis). Bannister says that, even in the Qur'an, 'Jesus stands out, head and shoulders above every other qur'anic prophet. He is born miraculously of a virgin. He performs a galaxy of miracles, in both childhood and adulthood; no other prophet (certainly not Muhammad) did anything like them' (2021: 139). Several authors provide tables comparing the two men's character and teaching (e.g. Goldmann, 2008: 21; Scot and Abdulhaq, 2009: 100), and there are two book-length treatments of the topic. First, Gabriel finds 'some amazing parallels, such as the fact both men were prophesied over as children, both had cousins who introduced them to the public, both were rejected by their hometowns, and both were assisted by twelve disciples' (2004: viii). Thereafter, the descriptions diverge as he looks at their miracles, teaching on war and love and their respective attitudes towards women, among other things. Second, Power (2016c) looks at all the same categories and expands them to reflect on theological themes around Christology, the sinlessness of Jesus and the Trinity. He finishes by contrasting their deaths and the significance of this for faith. All the authors highlight that in both traditions Jesus is still alive in heaven, while Muhammad is dead.

A few of the contrasts are rather more polemical in tone. American author James Gauss contrasts the 'good fruit' he sees from the biblical prophets with the 'extremely bad fruit' from Muhammad, who led people to 'accept false and satanic teaching that led them to oppress and kill their neighbours; rape women and children; pillage and destroy whole communities and cause havoc wherever they went' (2009: 84). An even more scathing, pejorative contrast comes again from Richardson, who says, 'Jesus raised the dead; Muhammad killed the living. Jesus healed the sick; Mohammad harmed the healthy. Jesus released the oppressed; Muhammad enslaved the free. Jesus sanctified earth with that which is heavenly; Muhammad sullied mankind's understanding of heaven with the earthly' (2003: 81).

Unsurprisingly, such statements are extremely inflammatory and upsetting to Muslims. Most Evangelicals are more circumspect, although the best that a lot of authors can say is that Muhammad was 'a man of his day, deeply influenced by the mores and traditions of seventh-century Arabia. It's when those mores and traditions are made specifically normative for all cultures and all times that conflict is sure to result' (J. White, 2013: 37).

The historical Muhammad

While those above use the traditional Islamic narrative to attack Muhammad, other Evangelicals doubt its very historicity. Drawing on the work of revisionist scholars, they suggest that Islam was a religious system created after the seventh-century Arab expansion for the purposes of empire building and to call into question the very existence of a man called Muhammad.[13] Jay Smith, in particular, has pursued this idea, and many of the over 500 videos on the Pfander Films YouTube channel address this sort of issue.[14] He believes that, while the traditional Muslim narrative is based on sources written in later centuries, there is evidence from the seventh century itself that the original *qibla* (direction of prayer) was towards Petra in modern-day Jordan (not Jerusalem and then Mecca); that coins prove that the first Islamic inscriptions do not appear until the end of that century; and that the early qur'anic *qirāāt* (variant readings) were predominantly of dialects from further north than Mecca, a city for which, he says, there is no record before the middle of the eighth century. Summing up, he claims that Muhammad 'doesn't appear until the eighth century, and much too far north, and takes his real form under the auspices of the Abbasids', proving that 'the Islam practiced today is nothing more than an Abbasid creation, redacted back to the seventh century, proving that they have the wrong book, the wrong man, and the wrong place!' (J. Smith, 2020).

However, most Evangelical authors note the historical uncertainties and then proceed on the basis of the traditional Islamic narrative. For instance, James White,[15] an American apologist, suggests that 'it is difficult to conceive of a scenario where a narrative this complex could be fabricated, [yet] the fact remains: Most Muslims accept a story that is not nearly as foundationally certain as they think it is' (2013: 20). Mark Anderson,[16] a Canadian Evangelical lecturer, believes 'the preponderance of the evidence points to Mecca as Islam's true birthplace' (Anderson n.d.).

Dan Brown sees the question relationally, pointing out that 'if I actually want to interact with Muslim friends, revisionist scholarship is unlikely to help my relationship building efforts. Is it not more charitable to engage, as much as possible, with what my friend actually thinks about the origins of Islam rather than summarily dismissing it as myth?' (2020a: 184). Given the lack of sources attesting to early Islamic history from outside the early Muslim community, Brown suggests that agnosticism and humility are, maybe, the best approaches and to admit that we just do not know.

Others suggest that there is a difference between the 'Muhammad of history' and the 'Muhammad of faith' – but for rather different purposes than the revisionists. For instance, Accad suggests that 'by largely dismissing the historical reliability of the classical Muslim portrait of Muhammad, we have also debunked the legitimacy of using that portrait for polemical purposes'. He assumes that Muhammad was indeed the founder of Islam and the author of the Qur'an, but suggests that, maybe, he belonged to a 'syncretistic Judeo-Christian sect' in Arabia or that later writers added to his work, thus distorting his original message (Accad, 2020: 305, 303). He finds himself 'personally unable to accept the traditional narrative about Islam's prophet at historical face value in a way that permits [him] to use it as a polemical tool in [his] perception of Muhammad' (Accad, 2019: 321).

Of course, it would still be perfectly possible to attack the classical Muslim image of Muhammad in order to undermine faith, even if it was ahistorical. However, Accad is exploring ways in which Christians could have a more positive approach to Muhammad and wonders whether 'the Muhammad of history, reframed in the way suggested in this contribution, can thus fit the profile of the Muhammad of faith for Muslims who are willing to lay aside for a time their venerable exegetical traditions for the sake of dialogue and the common good' (2020: 305). However, this still leaves the question of Muhammad's prophethood.

The prophethood of Muhammad

Some Christians from other traditions have been willing to accede to Muslim claims that Muhammad was a true prophet. For instance, Roman Catholic theologian Hans Küng was willing to make this affirmation.[17] However, for Evangelicals and more conservative Christians, this has been a red line they cannot cross, much to Muslim disappointment. They would agree with Sookhdeo that Muhammad 'cannot be accepted as a prophet because his message contradicts biblical teaching and because Christ was the final revelation of God to humankind' (2010b: 9). This leads Azumah to conclude that 'for Muslims to demand that Christians acknowledge Mohammed as a prophet is like Christians demanding that Muslims accept Jesus as the son of God and God incarnate. These demands are asking partners in dialogue to commit confessional suicide!' (2008b: 146).

So, how should Christians interpret what Muhammad was doing if he was not a prophet, on the one hand, or demon-possessed, on the other? Glaser suggests that he was 'proclaiming a reformed monotheistic faith that we could call "Judaic" in that it has a measure of continuity with the Judaic roots of Judaism and Christianity … [but] outside the flow of covenant history'. She offers the northern Israelite king Jeroboam in the Old Testament as an analogy as he 'set up worship outside Jerusalem and a kingship outside the Davidic covenant in order to keep the people under his rule' (Glaser, 2020: 325, 329). Accad explores a different approach and suggests that Muhammad started well and then went off course:

> If as Christians we may not feel comfortable either with the idea that God sent a messenger with a new message after Christ, or that he changed his mind in the process of his guidance of that prophet, we will then retain the possibility that Muhammad set out with one mission and mandate, which may perhaps even have been inspired by God, but that he later shifted course for utilitarian political purposes. (2020: 301)

Shehadeh supports this argument arguing that 'Muhammad began with the one and only true God, Allah … but then he departed from the biblical portrayal of God's nature, which later affected all other doctrines of Islam' (2004: 25).

Positive Evangelical assessments of Muhammad

The rejection of his prophethood does not stop some Evangelicals seeking to be more affirming of Muhammad than some of the highly polemical statements about him above. Glaser suggests that 'we need to work out as positive and realistic an assessment of Muhammad as possible' (2000b: 47) and seeks to do this alongside several other authors in the second part of an edited volume dedicated to developing a 'biblical understanding' of *The Religious Other* (Accad and Andrews, 2020). Power is more positive than most. In his book on the Hadith, he compares Muhammad to the prophet Moses and highlights characteristics such as his obedience to the law, bravery, generosity, care of others, humanity, humility, forgiveness and tolerance. He illustrates each of these points with examples from the Hadith and argues that 'it is possible, from a Christian perspective, to affirm some of what Islam teaches' about Muhammad (2016b: 53).

American missiologist Evelyne Reisacher (d. 2019) mentions him as an example of generosity and hospitality, as well as someone who was interested in and cared for creation (2016: 95, 126). Cotterell acknowledges that, despite the 'undeniable negatives', Muhammad was a poet, a forceful personality, a lateral thinker, a military strategist, and any one of his achievements should command respect from the historian (2011: 9, 159). Moucarry goes as far as to say that Muhammad's 'victory brought many peoples to worship the Creator God as the one and only God', although he warns that a Christian cannot agree with the Muslim *shahada* (witness or profession) that Muhammad was the 'Apostle of God' without 'dismissing their own faith' (2001: 264). Fouad Masri,[18] the founder of the Crescent Project, agrees that Muhammad 'taught the worship of one God … and actually released the Arabs from paganism'. He encourages his readers that it is good to 'acknowledge some of his triumphs' as 'this can actually be a great conduit to deepen the conversation with your friend'. He adds to the positive list that 'Muhammad stopped the practice of infanticide … gave more rights to women, … taught that men and women are equal in the sight of God … and abolished idols and destroyed them' (2014: 96–7). McLaren suggests that at least some of the negative aspects of Muhammad's story were, maybe, a result of how Christians were behaving at the time. Perhaps Muhammad might not have turned to the use of force had Roman Christianity not already gone in that direction under Emperor Constantine. This allows McLaren to 'interpret Mohammed's choices and convictions in a more sympathetic light', as, after all, 'Mohammad's message included deep love and respect for Jesus as a great prophet' (2012b: 90, 90n7). Perhaps the most positive Evangelical voice has been Cragg's, and Marshall points out that 'it is widely assumed that [Cragg] calls on Christians to recognize Muhammad as a prophet'. However, although Cragg encourages a 'sympathetic understanding', Marshall concludes that there is 'no point at which Cragg unequivocally affirms that Christians can or should regard Muhammad as a prophet'.[19]

Finally, Dan Brown takes a step back and suggests that any Evangelical with a confidence in the sovereign purposes of God 'must affirm that God raised up Muhammad, that God brought power and prosperity to Muslim empires, that God has preserved Islamic civilization, and that he did all of this for his purposes'. This leaves Brown free to evaluate and appreciate 'both the good and the bad' in Muhammad's legacy (2004: 79).

Is Muhammad's coming prophesied in the Bible?

This may be of some comfort to Muslims, but ultimately will not be enough. They feel that Christians should at least see Muhammad as a prophet in the same way that they revere Jesus as a prophet. Moreover, many Muslims believe that Jesus predicted the coming of Muhammad in the Bible, but that Christians deny, conceal or refuse to believe this. In the Qur'an, it is reported that 'Jesus, son of Mary, said, "Children of Israel, I am sent to you by God, confirming the Torah that came before me and bringing good news of a messenger to follow me whose name will be Ahmad"' (Q.61.6).[20]

There is a long history of various claims being made to support this idea, and Moucarry points out that 'all Muslim theologians seek to interpret biblical texts in a way that makes them agree with the qur'anic message'. He goes on to explain that, using the New Testament verses (Jn 14.16 and 16.7) concerning the coming of the Holy Spirit, some Muslims 'argue that the Greek word *parakleetos* may very well have replaced a very similar Greek word, namely *periklytos*, which translated into Arabic, could mean "one who is worthy of praise", that is Muhammad'. Moucarry, however, believes that 'Jesus clearly identified the Paraclete as the Holy Spirit whom he would imminently send' (2022: 125–6). Shenk concurs, stating that 'there are at least 5,000 ancient manuscripts of the New Testament. All of these manuscripts, with no exception, assert that Jesus promised the Counsellor would come and that the Counsellor is the Holy Spirit … We encourage our Muslim friends likewise to respect the trustworthiness of the biblical account concerning the Holy Spirit' (2014: 116–17).

'What do you think of Muhammad?'

This still leaves Evangelicals to answer the question, often posed by Muslims, as to what they think of Muhammad. In seeking to answer this question, several Evangelicals in recent years have repeated the words of the Nestorian Patriarch Timothy (d. 823) to the effect that Muhammad 'walked in the path of the prophets' (Woodberry, 2007: 27; see also Glaser, 2016: 228). However, they are careful to point out that such ancient Christian Syriac authors were 'only speaking of the alignment of Muhammad's monotheistic and moral teachings with ancient biblical prophets of Israel' (Yousif, 2020: 161). As British author Mark Beaumont puts it, 'Muhammad may have been a prophet like Hosea and Amos, but he was not an apostle like John or Paul' who proclaimed Jesus (2018: 41).

This does not mean that Muhammad did not at times say things that are true. Some Evangelicals are willing to allow that, wherever Muhammad spoke truth about God, he was in some sense being prophetic. 'Truth, after all, is truth, wherever it is found' (Musk, 2005: 83), and 'Christians need to be careful not to dismiss any truth in Islam or any evidence of God's grace at work in the life of Muslims' (Moucarry, 2001: 271).[21] This opens up the way for some Evangelicals to see Muhammad as a bridge for Muslims to think about Jesus and the gospel. For instance, Tennent says:

> As Christians we strongly reject any notion of prophetic infallibility for Muhammad. We categorically reject any doctrine that posits that Muhammad is the final 'seal' of the preceding prophets. Nevertheless, I am still prepared to hail the emergence of early Arabian monotheism as a positive development, a potential *preparatio evangelica*, which may yet serve as a bridge for Islamic peoples to cross over and receive the Christian gospel. In short, despite our differences, Christians need not speak disparagingly about Muhammad or Islam. (2007: 44)

Accad takes this a little further and suggests that, while the term prophet would 'be more than what the Bible could allow', Muhammad may be seen as a messenger of sorts. He says, 'I stretch the theological boundaries of my thesis to the possibility of affirming that Muhammad, as a messenger and proclaimer of the God of the Judeo-Christian tradition, may function as a bridge to Christ' (2019: 339).

Musk, Tennent, Accad and others are quoted in a 2014 article which was published in the *International Journal of Frontier Missiology* and posed the question 'Is Muhammad also among the Prophets?' The article argued for a positive assessment of Muhammad and for 'expanding constricted categories of prophethood to allow Christians to entertain the possibility of Muhammad being other than a false prophet' (Talman, 2014: 185). The article provoked a series of responses over the following years, which ranged from positive welcome, through cautious critique, to outright rejection and accusation of Christian duplicity and deception (Accad, 2014; Azumah, 2016; Ibrahim, 2015a, 2015b).

For those who reject these attempts at an affirmative assessment of Muhammad, even referring to him as 'Prophet Muhammad' is problematic. When Christians at Yale – many of them from Evangelical backgrounds – used this honorific in their response to ACW, they were criticized by those Evangelicals who felt they were going too far in accommodating Muslim views of Muhammad (e.g. Dye's preface in Solomon and Al-Maqdisi, 2009a: 11). Azumah suggests 'prophet of Islam' as a more neutral title and the extent to which he could go (2008b: 146). Musk (2005) is one of the few who is prepared to use 'Prophet Muhammad' in his writing.

Others seek to avoid answering the question altogether and choose to remain agnostic. Rather, they recommend changing the topic of conversation and avoiding speaking of Muhammad. Shenk says that, rather than talking about Muhammad, he prefers instead a 'Messiah-centred response' (2014: 58). George Bristow, an American academic based in Turkey, takes a similar line and suggests that 'respectfully confessing my belief in the uniqueness and finality of Jesus is the best answer to the question of what I think of Muhammad' (2020: 322).

Discussion: Speaking freely

The inability of Evangelicals – and most other Christians – to accept Muhammad as a prophet in the full sense will, undoubtedly, continue to disappoint Muslims, who would hope for a much more positive assessment. They might, in the first instance, appreciate those Evangelicals above who do emphasize the positive aspects of Muhammad's ministry. However, it might often be a case of damning with faint praise, especially if it turns out the motivation is to co-opt Muhammad as some sort of signpost to the Christian gospel.

Speaking of Muhammad, more than any other issue in this section, raises important questions about the limits of free speech in a liberal society and how a public sphere moderates its language. At the very least, Muslims will continue to demand that others do not publicly insult or denigrate Muhammad. On the other hand, there are certain to be Evangelicals who continue to insist on their right to speak freely about Muhammad. But where are the limits? Akhtar believes strongly that 'absolute and unrestricted freedom of speech is morally a non-starter'. He wants 'a minimal level of respect for the Prophet of Islam', which would 'enable cohesion and harmony in societies that aspire to being mature democracies that can effectively manage internal dissent'.[22] This seems very reasonable. However, agreeing what constitutes 'a minimal level of respect' might still prove difficult.

While some of the more extreme statements above are gratuitously offensive and may well fall foul of Western laws against inciting hatred, others may quite properly belong to a serious discussion in which some may 'dissent' in their interpretation of historical texts and narratives. For instance, it is not hateful for someone to say that they do not believe Muhammad to be a prophet. So, is it hateful if they say he was a *false* prophet? It is factual to point out that Aisha was Muhammad's child-bride, but when does it become unacceptable to debate the morality of the age at which Muhammad consummated that marriage? Muhammad undoubtedly went to war, but can there be 'mature' debate about whether this was legitimate force or excessive violence without giving or taking of offence?

There are already concerns about overbearing political correctness and restrictions on free speech. For instance, Evangelicals such as Australian author Tony Payne (2012: 121) point to the 2004 case in Australia in which the Islamic Council of Victoria took Daniel Scot and Danny Nalliah of Catch the Fire Ministries to court for allegedly inciting hatred and vilifying Muhammad while teaching Christians about Islam. The pair argued that they were merely drawing on the traditional Muslim accounts of Muhammad's life. That did not stop them being initially found guilty, before eventually being acquitted in 2005 after a legal battle. These Evangelicals would argue that freedoms have already been eroded too far in response to concerns about Islamophobia. Others even argue, as will be seen in the next chapter, that it is the Islamic texts themselves which should be censored for inciting hatred.

It seems unlikely that criminal law will ultimately be able satisfactorily to police the boundaries of free speech. Much will depend on public spheres moderating their own speech and persuading one another as to what the limits, and thus benefits, should be. Muslim spheres, of course, will need to do likewise, and Muslims should certainly not turn to violence to vent their grievances, not least because this fatally defeats their purpose in Western eyes. They must remain within the law, whether in the West or in Muslim-majority countries. However, Evangelicals and others in the wider public, particularly where they have cultural power, should beware of causing offence which inflames emotions and forecloses conversation. Robust discussion and debate must, and certainly will, take place, but it should do so in a spirit of respect and honesty.

Evangelicals might also reflect on what might ultimately best serve their cause. A small number of Muslims, perhaps already disaffected with Islam, may respond positively to negative critiques of Muhammad. It is unlikely that the majority of Muslims will give Evangelical arguments – and indeed the Christian gospel – a hearing if they feel they are being disrespected and their prophet is being slandered. There would seem to be a much better chance of a fruitful, rational debate if temperatures were cooler and assessments of Muhammad more nuanced.

5

Qur'an and Hadith

Unsurprisingly, Evangelical attitudes to the Qur'an closely follow those towards Muhammad as outlined in the previous chapter. In Islam, Muhammad is not the author of the Qur'an. The Qur'an is presumed to be God's unmediated word passed to Muhammad verbatim by the Angel Gabriel. However, Muhammad is so closely associated with the Qur'an that any attack on the book is considered an attack on the prophet. It is holy, and any desecration, insult or even criticism can provoke an angry response. Once again, this has not stopped some Evangelicals speaking of it in extremely derogatory terms, and the responses fall into familiar patterns. Confrontationists see it as an entirely negative book that is not fit to be read, except for purposes of argumentation and 'exposure'. The more affirming are willing to engage with it as a serious text and even find elements of Christian truth in it.

Almost of equal importance for many Muslims are the Hadith. These are large collections of the various traditions of all that Muhammad is believed to have said and done during his lifetime and contain the Sunnah or practice of the prophet. They were compiled many years and generations after his death and are a vast ocean of texts that deal with everything from the mundane, through religious practice, to affairs of state. They are often a source of contention among Muslims, and different sects, such as the Sunnis, Shia and Ibadis, have different collections. The majority of Evangelicals who engage with the Hadith see it as problematic, although a few do attempt to use it in positive engagement with Muslims.

Evangelicals and the Qur'an

In the same way that few Muslims have ever read the Bible, few Evangelicals have ever read the Qur'an beyond, maybe, a few isolated verses. Most agree that it is not an easy book for non-Muslims to read as it has little narrative and is very different in style to much of the Bible. What Evangelicals believe they know of it comes second hand, usually from Western critics, Christian commentators or the media. Fewer Evangelicals will ever have read a Muslim explanation of the Qur'an or seriously listened to a Muslim talking about the Qur'an. At the same time, there is a general belief that 'few Muslims have actually read what the Qur'an says in a language they understand' (Allen, 2022: 70). Allen notes that, even among Arabic speakers, many 'seem to be very unfamiliar with all but a few passages ... [and] the emphasis is on learning by heart and recitation, not on understanding'. Noting that ordinary Muslims are reticent to read and interpret the text for themselves, he suggests that 'we must do everything we can to encourage our Muslim friends to read the Qur'an' and ask questions of it in order to 'render it accountable' (2016: 233–4). This is because for most Muslims 'the truth of the Qur'an and Sunnah is *self evident*' (Shumack, 2011: 20, original emphasis). It exists in the same way that creation does, unquestioned. This assumption does not sit comfortably with Evangelicals.

Yet, as with Muhammad, Evangelicals are aware of the strong Muslim emotions concerning the Qur'an, although again that does not stop some of them attacking it. Musk observes that 'scripture is dangerous stuff. Assessments of the Qur'an by Christians stretch far across a continuum, with people at one extreme viewing it as from the devil with folk at the other extreme accepting it as validly God's Word' (2005: 34). No one in this review would go as far to say that it was sent down from heaven. Rather, Muhammad is always presumed to have played a major role in its compilation – if he had any role at all.

Negative assessments of the Qur'an

At the confrontational end of the spectrum, the Evangelicals who vilify Muhammad also condemn the content of the Qur'an. In a pamphlet (2005), Stephen Green, the leader of Christian Voice, a small UK lobby group, declares that the Qur'an is 'more intolerant, racist, punitive and violent than Hitler's *Mein Kampf*. Don Richardson also compares it to *Mein Kampf* and mines it for war verses and accuses Muhammad of 'pretending to quote God verbatim' to serve his own purposes (2003: 60). Such polemical views led to a widely publicized Qur'an-burning in 2012 by Terry Jones, the previously unknown maverick pastor of a very small independent Evangelical church in Florida. His actions led to Muslim riots in some parts of the world, but they were condemned by most other Evangelicals, including WEA (2012). There were also reports of Qur'an desecrations at Guantanamo Bay, a detention camp associated – in the Muslim mind at least – with Evangelicals.[1]

Without taking such extreme physical action, other Evangelicals call into question the source and inspiration of the Qur'an. We saw above how some see Muhammad as having been mentally ill or even demon-possessed. Darrell Pack (2014),[2] an American who once pastored a church in Casablanca, describes the qur'anic account of Jesus as a 'demonic deception'. Gauss puts it equally bluntly. 'The scriptures and message of [the Bible and the Qur'an] are fundamentally and spiritually diametrically opposed to each other. The Qur'an's message is one of darkness, oppression, and death. The message of the Bible is one of light, freedom and life.' He goes on to suggest that 'Muhammad's wisdom and knowledge were often confused, ignorant, and erroneous. He often had his historical facts wrong and frequently contradicted himself and the revelations he claimed to have received from Allah ... . [The Qur'an was] complete fabrication inspired by satanic sources' (Gauss, 2009: 37, 63).

The Caner brothers present a more mixed, but no more flattering, picture. They reckon that 'Muhammad oscillated between revelations from Satan and Allah. The most famous of these visions resulted in the so-called "Satanic Verses"' (2003: 44). These verses were made famous by Salman Rushdie's 1988 novel of that name and refer to an incident surrounding the reported revelation of the qur'anic verses in Sura 53.19–20. In traditional Islamic biographies by Ibn Ishaq and al-Tabari, Muhammad initially received a positive statement about the three goddesses *al-Lāt*, *al-ʿUzzā* and *Manāt*, which would have appeased local tribal leaders.[3] It was later revealed to him that he had been deceived by Satan, and these verses were not included in the Qur'an. Although the historicity and interpretation of these traditions is controversial among Muslims, the story is often picked up by Evangelical writers (e.g. Peltola and Dieppe, 2022: 98–9). From his experience in debates, White observes that these accounts have 'become an embarrassment to modern Muslim apologists … and for Christians, whether or not this incident took place is very relevant to our evaluation of Muhammad's claims' (2013: 26, 29).

Human sources

For others, the source of Muhammad's words in the Qur'an is rather more mundane and human. After all, it has long been known that many of the stories and events in the Qur'an can be found in previous writings, especially the Bible, the Jewish Talmud and Midrash or the gnostic gospels.[4] Various authors trace these borrowings, and White points out that the idea that these stories were merely 'legends of the ancients' being repeated was a frequent accusation recorded in the Qur'an itself (2013: 229–47). In a detailed study, Bannister finds that the 'Qur'an makes extensive use of older religious material, stories, and traditions that predate the origins of Islam', much of it passed on in an oral context (2014: abstract). Durie does an in-depth study of these links between the Qur'an and other scriptures, but finds a 'paradox' in the 'Qur'an's knowledge' and yet 'ignorance about the Bible'. He concludes that there is no continuity between the Bible and the Qur'an as 'the Qur'an, did not arise by a process of organic development out of Christianity, Judaism or a form of Jewish Christianity. Instead, the Qur'an is the outcome of a uniquely creative process … and marches to the beat of its own theological drum' (Durie, 2018: 254, 256, 260). In other words, the Qur'an was designed to give its own message.

The doubt over the historicity of the traditional Muslim narrative about Muhammad, discussed in the previous chapter, also raises questions about the origins of the Qur'an. This leads some Evangelicals to suggest that the Qur'an was written later during the Arab expansion for ulterior motives. For instance, one book says that 'recent research shows that Muhammad probably had nothing to do with the Qur'an' (Peltola and Dieppe, 2022: 77). Similarly, Pfander Centre for Apologetics, associated with Jay Smith, believes that the version of the Qur'an extant today is only 1,200 years old, leaving a '150-year gap' from the seventh to ninth centuries (Pfander, n.d.).

History of the text

Dan Brown, however, believes that 'a preponderance of evidence, especially radiocarbon dating of manuscript leaves, now suggests that consonantal texts of the

Qur'an were circulating by the 650s' (2020a: 177). This would fit, of course, with the Muslim chronology, although debate over dating continues. Issa Diab, a Lebanese scholar, concurs and accepts that the finding of the Birmingham Qur'an Manuscript in 2015 'confirms that at least some portions of the Qur'an were written close to the lifetime of Prophet Muhammad' (2020: 228).

That does not mean to say that the Qur'an as it exists today is an exact, unchanged version of some original. So, some Evangelicals are doing research into the origins of the Qur'an and particularly investigating the Muslim claim that today's Qur'an has been unaltered since its first delivery. These works are not necessarily antagonistic in nature but seek to lay out the evidence from the manuscripts. Early Islamic sources make it clear that there were early variants, and Chapman recounts the story of how the early Muslims sought to standardize the text (2007b: 89–91). Daniel Brubaker, a scholar, textual critic and 'believing Christian with a high view of scripture',[5] has done a lot of research into the earliest existing manuscripts and fragments and examined twenty examples of *Corrections in Early Qur'ān Manuscripts*, which suggest 'a greater degree of perceived flexibility of the Qur'an text in its early centuries' than is usually admitted (2019: 9). Small did similar research on both the Qur'an *and* the Bible. He concluded that, because Muslims' efforts have been directed towards 'establishing and promoting one version of the text at the expense of others, … it can be confidently asserted that the original text of the New Testament has been transmitted more accurately than that of the original forms of the Qur'an' (2009: 78; see also Small, 2011). Diab explains the large amount of analysis done on ancient manuscripts found in Sana'a, Yemen, in 1965. These 'palimpsests' have the modern text written on top of an earlier text, and he gives tabulated examples of over a hundred variations between the two. He concludes that there are 'gaps in the theory asserting that the qur'anic text remained unaltered, though the changes it underwent were slight' in the time between Muhammad's reported revelations and the first compilation (Diab, 2020: 228–40). While this type of research is rigorous and scholarly, it has been used by some polemical Evangelicals, such as Smith, to bolster their arguments concerning the historicity of Islam and the claims made for the Qur'an, as some of the video titles on Pfander Films YouTube channel make clear: 'Huge problems if the Qur'an isn't Perfectly Preserved!', 'Historical errors prove the Qur'an is made by man!', 'Why are there over 30 different Arabic Qur'ans?'[6]

These issues coupled with the uncritical nature of much traditional Islamic scholarship mean that many Evangelicals believe that 'Muslims generally have been very reluctant to ask critical questions about the origins of the Qur'an' (Chapman, 2007b: 165). Indeed, 'most Muslims refuse to countenance any kind of historical, contextual, archaeological or literary analysis of their holy book, so the Qur'an is rarely given the same rigorous scholarly treatment as the Bible gets' (P. Sookhdeo, 2008a: 18).

Books on the Qur'an

However, many Evangelicals feel that attempting to undermine the historical Muslim position in this way is not conducive to good relations or to evangelism. Most start by accepting the significance of the Qur'an to Muslims and then engage with it in some way. Several books have been written to help Christians understand the

Qur'an, including some by those from Muslim backgrounds who have a particular understanding of the role of the text in Muslim life. For instance, former Muslim Mateen Elass,[7] an Arab Reformed theologian, wrote *Understanding the Koran: A Quick Christian Guide to the Muslim Holy Book* (2004), which explains why it is so important to Muslims and tells stories of how they take offence if it is mistreated. He unpacks various themes in the Qur'an from a Christian perspective, including Allah, Jesus, paradise and jihad. Another BMB, Steven Masood (2012),[8] a convert from a Pakistani Ahmadi background, wrote a book comparing the reliability of the Qur'an with that of the Bible.

Alongside these 'entry level' books, an increasing number of Evangelical academics are producing scholarly works on the Qur'an from a Christian confessional viewpoint. Durie's 2018 book *The Qur'an and Its Biblical Reflexes*, mentioned above, is detailed in rejecting any continuity between the religion of the Qur'an and Christian theology. Anderson's 2016 book *The Qur'an in Context* seeks a middle path between polemical rejection and pluralist acceptance. The author explains, 'I take their scripture seriously and have no interest whatsoever in mocking it. I aim to highlight the Qur'an's uniqueness and do not wish to belittle the Muslim prophet or present the Qur'an as a "copy" of anything.' While studying the Qur'an critically, his goal is 'to respond "Christianly", with both grace and truth', although he is concerned with 'the Qur'an's [re]sacralization of violence and its apparent criticism that the biblical text has been seriously corrupted'. He also argues that by his 'mix of flattering and unflattering attention to Jesus, the qur'anic author deftly marginalizes him while seeming to revere him' (Anderson, 2016b: 4, 305).

The Quran with Christian Commentary, written by Gordon Nickel (2020), a Canadian Evangelical scholar, also goes into great depth and reproduces the text of the Qur'an with a commentary underneath that addresses issues which the Qur'an raises about Christians and Christian theology. The commentary is interspersed with short articles dealing with frequent qur'anic objections concerning topics such as the Son of God, the crucifixion and tampering with scripture. He treats the Qur'an as a work of literature and does not necessarily accept Islamic reports of its traditional origin and chronology. He does, however, recognize the long history of different Muslim interpretations of many parts of the Qur'an. With rather less academic pedigree, David Hungerford (d. 2019), an American surgeon, also produced an annotated text with Muslim co-author Safi Kaskas. It has over three thousand references to the Bible in footnotes beneath the qur'anic text and seeks to build a bridge between the two reading communities. However, there is no attempt at critical assessment of those links as to whether the referents or theology underlying the two texts are consistent (Kaskas and Hungerford, 2016).[9]

Finally, Cragg has probably engaged more deeply with the Qur'an, and certainly over a longer period of time, than any other Evangelical writer and thinker. Several of his books deal principally with the Qur'an, including two later books written since the millennium – *Muhammad in the Qur'an* (2001) and *The Qur'an and the West* (2005). These reflect on concepts such as the pre-existence of the Qur'an, an important topic in the history of Islamic philosophy; the significance of the claim to Muhammad being illiterate (*ummī*); and the 'divinely liable politics' of the Qur'an (Cragg, 2005: 155).

Unlike some others, his approach is mainly to focus on what he sees as common ground, and it has been suggested that Cragg 'accepted the validity of the Qur'an as a word from God that must be respected within its religious community' but with shortcomings that the Christian will want to address.[10]

Reading the Qur'an

Whether such books are helping the ordinary Evangelical to read the Qur'an would be difficult to ascertain. White argues that the Qur'an is a challenging book for the non-specialist to read as it jumps 'back and forth between periods of Muhammad's life, and in this way, obtaining a meaningful background and context is next to impossible'. He suggests that 'the best possibility for reading it in the fairest and most accurate way' is to read it chronologically and gives a possible order of suras, or qur'anic chapters, to follow (2013: 52), as does Anderson (2016a).

However, not all Evangelicals would agree with this approach. Although he does read the Qur'an in English, Shenk says:

> I grieve, as do Muslims, when Christians take an English interpretation of the Qur'an and determine that they have come to understand the meaning of this scripture. To understand the meaning, there is only one acceptable and wise way; that is to ask the Muslim ulama to explain the Qur'an to those of us who are not Muslim. This is urgent. It is not wise or appropriate to claim we have come to understand the Qur'an unless we have submitted to the rugged disciplines of study and consensus that Muslims believe are necessary to understand the Qur'an's message. (2014: 121–2)

This might also apply to teaching in the classroom. Rather than Christian teachers and lecturers giving their own opinions on the Qur'an, Accad recommends that 'when teaching Islam in Christian institutions, it should be minimum courtesy that Christian professors teach their students to read and understand the Qur'an according to the hermeneutical principles that Muslims use to approach it' (2019: 65). Himself a Christian Arab, he relates the chastening experience of having spoken to a group of Muslims quoting the Qur'an only to have a Muslim sheikh say, 'although we appreciate your amicable approach, it is arrogant on your part to claim the right to interpret our Holy Text. Only our trained ulama (religious scholars) are permitted to do this, in line with the legitimate principles of our tradition' (Accad, 2019: 35). This, of course, requires a measure of trust in Muslim scholars, which many Evangelicals simply do not have (see the discussion of *taqīya* in Chapter 11).

Apart from Evangelical specialists such as those mentioned in this chapter who are reading the Qur'an for academic or polemical purposes, there is a small but increasing number of Evangelicals who read it as part of a Scriptural Reasoning (SR) group. This is a practice whereby Christians, Muslims and often Jews too read their texts together and are 'encouraged to be both self-critical and deeply rooted in their commitment to their own particular faith in search of a common language with which to understand and engage with difference' (Jardim, 2014: 4).[11] This is an approach which many

Evangelicals are comfortable with as it does not require them to relinquish uniqueness or ignore difficult topics.

Interpreting the Qur'an

These issues of hermeneutics – of who has the right to interpret the Qur'an and the diversity of those interpretations, even within the Muslim community – are important for some Evangelicals. Glaser reckons that 'like so many other books, even the Bible, [the Qur'an] can be used for good or for evil, for peace or for violence, to seek truth or to propagate falsehood. The key question for Christians is not how we should categorize the Qur'an, but whether we can use it for good, for peace and for truth' (2016: 209). This also applies to Muslims, of course, and different Muslims have different ways of interpreting their text. Musk recognizes that a literal reading of any religious text can cause problems. He warns Christians against literal, fundamentalist interpretations of the Bible, which he feels sometimes fuel anti-Muslim policies, particularly in America. But he also challenges Muslims to consider the need to reinterpret their texts and insists that 'traditional methods for interpreting the Qur'an must be subject to careful and reasoned evaluation' to avoid extremism (2008: 59).

Muslims use different methods to interpret and decide the meaning and application of their texts, which some Evangelicals are well aware of. One is the principle of abrogation, or *al-nāsikh wal-mansūkh* (the replacing and the replaced), which is often foregrounded by those Evangelicals who mention interpretation at all. This is the principle whereby discrepancies in the revealed text are resolved by concluding that later revelations abrogate or supersede earlier revelations. The Qur'an was revealed to Muhammad over a period of twenty-three years. During that period, his situation and that of his followers changed significantly, and so too did the tone and content of the revelations he received. This principle is uncontroversial, being used by Muslim jurists to explain obvious contradictions in the Qur'an and to decide legal matters.[12] However, some Evangelical authors present abrogation as the *only* hermeneutical method used by Muslims (e.g. Gabriel, 2002: 30; P. Sookhdeo, 2007: 54). Focusing exclusively on this interpretive principle has implications, especially when it comes to explaining the violence of extremist Muslims who often draw on it (see Chapter 9).

There are, however, other interpretive principles which Muslims use, such as *asbāb al nuzūl* (the occasions of revelation). This refers to the efforts by Muslims to understand when, where and why a particular verse was revealed which 'give clues by which to "read" the passages concerned' (Cragg, 2005: 163). Chapman believes that it is, maybe, the most important principle of interpretation as 'Muslims have always tried to interpret verses of the Qur'an by studying them in their original context' (2007b: 93). Accad is another Evangelical who takes this sort of contextual interpretation seriously and suggests that among Muslims it has been the 'single most important principle in classical qur'anic *tafsīr*' (2019: 47). *Tafsīr* means exegesis, and, just as with the Bible, many commentaries on the Qur'an have been written over the years. An untrained Muslim will rarely try to interpret the Qur'an for themselves. Rather, they refer to the *tafsīr* of a respected scholar. They might even memorize a *tafsīr*. For instance, Dale in her study of women in Syria noted that in the mosque, 'after the Qur'an was committed to memory, the women were encouraged to memorize the *tafsīr* (commentary) of influential Syrian scholar Ibn Kathir (1301–1373), reinforcing a conservative view of Islam, the Qur'an and history' (2018: 79).

So, Accad suggests that, rather than going straight to the Qur'an to understand different Muslim views, Christians should 'adopt the Islamic method in using the tradition in qur'anic exegesis, even if we reach unconventional conclusions'. In his discussion of topics such as Jesus and the Bible, he looks for *tafsīr* sources that would provide 'hermeneutical keys to break the deadlock' in centuries of Christian-Muslim misunderstandings (2019: 57, 70). However, this does not seem to resolve the hermeneutical problem. It merely removes it one step. Christians may still be accused of being unreliable interpreters – just this time – of the *tafsīr* rather than the Qur'an.

Accad goes on to mention a third hermeneutical principle referred to as *al-'āmm wa al-khāṣṣ* (the universal and the particular) by which Muslim scholars moderate between the two principles above (2019: 55). If there is doubt over the context or the chronology, then they will take the interpretation that seems to be the more universal principle within Islam. This often allows moderate scholars to counter the extremists' abrogation-based interpretations by citing what they consider to be more general, irenic principles. However, other Evangelicals are suspicious of this method and suspect that Muslims are deliberately trying to sanitize their texts for a Western audience. There are frequent accusations of selective interpretation, especially by those who see the qur'anic trajectory as being towards violence. For instance, British peer Caroline Cox and her co-author, educationalist John Marks, suggest that 'cherry pickers are those who select a few verses from the Qur'an or selected hadith and emphasize these at the expense of the totality of the verses and the sunna ... Such people may be sincere. But they may also be disingenuous or even deliberately deceptive'. They insist that 'ironically, the most straightforward expositions of the Qur'an and the Sunnah are often those given by the Islamists whose brutal clarity is in stark contrast to the evasiveness of many cherry pickers' (2006: 193–5). Gabriel likewise accuses Muslims – through either 'wishful thinking' or 'deception' – of presenting 'nice Islam' in the West by using only the early Meccan suras which 'sound more like Christianity than Islam' (2003: 51–5).

In contrast, irenic Evangelicals feel that Muslims have to be allowed to interpret their own texts. Azumah is 'of the opinion that the Qur'an is made for Muslims and not Muslims for the Qur'an. Muslims have the power ... to reinterpret the Qur'an in terms that fit with contemporary realities' (2008b: 99). So Shenk says, 'I lean on Muslim writers and imams for my understandings of Islam and interpretation of the Qur'an' (2014: 121).

Using the Qur'an

Finally, it is important to remember that, however academic or sympathetic, Evangelical authors very often have an evangelistic goal in writing about the Qur'an. In his book *Christian Exegesis of the Qur'an*, Scott Bridger, an American professor of global studies and world religions, examines how Christians living under Islam in the East have historically read and used the Qur'an. His goal is the apologetic defence of the Christian faith and to 'subvert the Qur'an' (2015: 33). White, already quoted above, writes in similar vein in *What Every Christian Needs to Know about the Qur'an*, which also has both apologetic and polemic intent. White believes that 'accurate knowledge of the Qur'an can help open doors' for Christians to introduce Muslims to Jesus (2013: 16). Similarly, Raouf (d. 2015) and Carol Ghattas, Baptist missionaries, wrote *A Christian Guide to the Qur'an* (2009) with the subtitle *Building Bridges in Muslim Evangelism*.

There are also evangelistic strategies built around using the Qur'an as an entry point for talking with Muslims about the gospel. One of the earliest was the CAMEL method developed by an American Southern Baptist missionary (Greeson, 2010). It focuses on Sura 3 in the Qur'an which talks about the birth of Jesus (Q.3.42–55) and suggests that Christians point out to Muslims that, according to the Qur'an, Jesus was 'Chosen', announced by 'Angels', performed 'Miracles' and offers 'Eternal Life', hence the mnemonic. This use of the Qur'an is controversial. When the *New York Times* published an article reporting how Ergun Caner had called this method 'deceitful' and questioned the integrity of its proponents, it provided another example of how an Evangelical conversation can burst into the wider public sphere.[13] These accusations notwithstanding, Larson notes that the 'Camel Method has been successful' in Bangladesh, but not always in other places and is certainly 'not the panacea' for converting Muslims (2012: 92).

Evangelicals and the Hadith

After the Qur'an, the Hadith are the most important collections of texts in Islam and are closely related to matters of interpretation and *tafsīr*. However, while many Evangelicals are aware of their importance, fewer have ever read or know anything about them, leading Power to wonder that 'surprisingly, little attention has been paid to … the Hadith' (2016b: ix). That said, most standard Evangelical introductions to Islam will include a small section on the Hadith, sometimes combined with the Qur'an and the Sunnah (e.g. Chapman, 2007b: chapter 9; Azumah, 2008b: chapter 5). Peter Riddell, an Australian lecturer and academic, sees the Hadith, along with the Qur'an and the Sharia, as part of the 'glue' that 'binds Muslims together' (2004: 210). Indeed, Sookhdeo suggests that 'for most Muslims, Hadith are seen as divinely inspired … [and] in practice often take precedence over the literal qur'anic statements, as they explain and interpret the Qur'an's sometimes obscure meaning and are heavily used to establish legal rulings' (2007: 48, 66). Power thinks that the reason for this is that 'the Qur'an has only 6,200 verses and remarkably little legal or practical detail. If Islam is to fulfil its claim to be an all-encompassing rule of life for all Muslims at all times, a significant volume of extra material is needed to cover every possible situation … . The Hadith provides this service' (2016b: 239).

Hadith and law

To illustrate this dependence on the Hadith, Moucarry provides a list of 'Islamic beliefs and laws based on the Hadith' for which the Qur'an provides insufficient support, including the five canonical prayers, circumcision and the death penalty for apostasy (2001: 55). In his large volumes *Understanding Islamic Theology* (2013) and *Understanding Living Islam* (2020), Sookhdeo goes into even more detail and draws heavily on the Hadith to illustrate the origins of different Muslim beliefs and practices. He explores the various collections and classification of the Hadith and the development of the 'science of hadith'. He quotes many hadiths and explains his understanding of how they impact the formulation of the Sharia. He, along with other Evangelical writers, is suspicious of the Hadith and sees them as a cause of many problems. Several authors, for instance, point out that there is no death penalty for apostasy in the Qur'an, although that penalty appears in the Hadith and subsequent jurisprudence (P. Sookhdeo, 2009b; Chapman, 2007b: 310–12). This issue will be discussed in more detail in Chapter 8. Another instance where the Hadith seem to take precedence over the Qur'an is the question of the punishment for adultery. Musk explains how a verse in the Qur'an (Q.24.2) prescribing a hundred lashes is seen as being abrogated by hadiths prescribing stoning.[14] For Musk, this raises significant questions about how Muslims can be certain of their text and 'suggests that not all is transparent in traditional Muslim claims concerning the original content of the qur'ānic texts' (2008: 51).

Problems with the Hadith

These concerns are not only issues of law. Musk believes that the Hadith are a part of keeping Muslims, 'and especially Arabs', focused on the past. He points out that

> the penultimate book of al-Bukhari's collection of *ḥadīth* deals with 'holding fast to the Qur'an and the tradition' … . That golden age is romanticised and made perfect. It provides a vision with which no current government can compete … . For Arabs, copying the past is a positive aim. 'Innovation' is a bad word. Arabs will rather patiently wait for old times to renew themselves. There is a genuine suspicion about new ways. They are oriented towards the past, in complete contrast with Westerners who are oriented towards the future. (2004: 145)

The Hadith are also seen by some as an obstacle to building relationships with Muslims and to their integration into society. For instance, Sookhdeo warns that 'Christians may be puzzled or bewildered by the apparently capricious way in which Muslims relate to them'. He quotes a hadith which says 'do not greet the Jews and Christians' to explain why some Muslims will not greet Christians (2009a: 76).[15] The Caners also give scenarios where a Christian may unwittingly give offence to a Muslim by using the left hand, serving forbidden seafood or baking with lard. They make the point that these 'idiosyncratic cultural rules are actually in the Hadith and Sunnah' (2003: 95).

They also wonder why there are scientific claims in the Hadith that are clearly false. They give examples of unscientific cures and spurious facts and say 'one should not mock ancient health cures, but if Islam holds to infallibility of its sacred texts, the Hadith presents Muslims with a quandary' (Caner and Caner, 2003: 100). Phil Parshall, an American missionary and author, has a chapter on medicinal claims in the Hadith, including the healing efficacy of cumin, flies and camel's urine. He notes that even Maurice Bucaille, 'a French medical doctor who converted to Islam' and defended the accuracy of the 'science' found in the Qur'an, was 'forced to equivocate on a few of the Traditions that run counter to scientific realities' (Parshall, 2002: 13: chapter 20).

Opportunities in the Hadith

However, some Evangelicals realize that 'it is possible to find both positive and negative material on almost any topic' in the Hadith (Dale, 2021: 73). In addition to gaining an understanding of Islamic interpretation and the formulation of legal principles, they believe that the Hadith can help Christians understand Muslims and even be a bridge for sharing the gospel. Parshall, quoted above, wrote one of the few recent Evangelical books entirely devoted to the Hadith. *Inside the Community* was published first in 1994 and then republished in 2002 in response to 9/11 as *Understanding Muslim Teachings and Traditions: A Guide for Christians*. He collects together Bukhari hadiths related to both theological topics such as the Qur'an, salvation, Muhammad, miracles and Jesus, and more practical topics such as women, food and medicine. During his two readings through the '4,705 pages' of al-Bukhari's Hadith, he found them 'eminently readable', and they produced reactions ranging from laughter through perplexity to horror (Parshall, 2002: 14–15). His aim in writing was to facilitate 'a contemporary understanding of the inner workings of Islam as a system and of Muslims as a people', although he also notes that most Muslims have never read the Hadith. Rather 'their information is filtered to them through their Islamic teachers and oral traditions' (Parshall, 2002: 11–12).

Over twenty years later, Power (2016b) wrote another such volume titled *Engaging Islamic Traditions*. He too draws almost exclusively from Bukhari's collections with the purpose of, as the subtitle suggests, *using the Hadith in Christian ministry to Muslims*. He quotes from the Hadith and the Bible to show that there are places where there is 'concord' in areas such as the life of Muhammad, the treatment of women and some theology and ethics. In other areas where there is less convergence, such as the character of God, the nature of humankind, forgiveness, the inadequacy of works and the cross, he seeks 'connections', arguing that where the Hadith are 'moving in the same or a similar direction … they contain within them the seeds of something more'. In this way they may be 'springboards for Muslims to approach the truth' because 'the glimpses of truth found in the Hadith may point Muslims to the full-orbed revelation found in Holy Scripture … the Hadith could be one of the stepping-stones in this process' (Power 2016b: 107, 109, 48). Power followed this volume with a second, *Challenging Islamic Traditions* (2016a), which offers a more critical analysis of the Hadith pointing out internal inconsistencies and problems from a Christian perspective.

The need for modernization

By and large, Evangelicals see the Hadith as a major obstacle for those Muslims wishing to modernize and integrate Islam into Western life. Some authors challenge Muslims to rethink the status of the Hadith. For instance, Riddell boldly states that 'it is time for some of the Hadith materials to be downgraded in importance' (2004: 201). In order for this to happen, he and Cotterell suggest that 'the way forward for Islam seems to lie in accepting for the Qur'an and Hadith a hermeneutic, a system of interpretation, that will allow their *meaning*, intended by Muhammad for specific situations in the seventh century and not for unimagined situations 1,300 years later, to be interpreted for the modern world by identifying the present *significance*' (2003: 214, original emphasis).

Some go much further and see the Qur'an and the Hadith as hate speech and want to see them banned altogether. For instance, they point to negative Qur'an and Hadith passages about Jews that are seen as being antisemitic.[16] Christian Voice (2005) urged their supporters to 'report Islamic Bookshops for selling the Quran and Hadith, which, if they aren't hate speech, nothing is'.

Evangelicals are aware that some Muslims are already engaged in the difficult and controversial work of reform and reinterpretation. For instance, Kuhn says:

> We readily admit that we, as Christians, are not the authoritative interpreters of the Qur'an. At the same time, we note that Islamists throughout the world are forging their strategy based on these ancient texts as well as the example of the prophet Muhammad and the caliphs. While their interpretation of the texts may be flawed, we are compelled to admit the force of their argument and appeal to more moderate Muslims to supply a more accurate reading of the textual sources. (2009: 208)

Sookhdeo also points out that 'some progressive Muslim reformers are trying to change traditional understanding of Qur'an and Hadith. Some are willing to use Western academic tools of textual criticism in examining the Muslim scriptures ... [However], they face charges of apostasy and blasphemy as well as threats of violence and death, so many have emigrated to the West' (2013: 36).

At the end of the day, most Evangelicals find themselves unable to accept the Qur'an as a divinely given scripture, and the Hadith as an authoritative guide for life today. But they do recognize their centrality to Muslim faith. Indeed, many make the comparison that in Christian thought, Jesus is the eternal Word of God made flesh; in Muslim thought, the Qur'an is the Word of God made book (Azumah, 2008b: 50; Chapman, 2007b: 88; Elass, 2004: chapter 3). A second parallel is sometimes drawn between the Christian gospels and the Hadith. The reasoning goes that the gospels are eyewitness accounts written in human language by those who knew Jesus and then passed on that others might believe (1 Jn 1.1–3). Similarly, the Hadith report to be eyewitness accounts of Muhammad's life and sayings. So, it could be argued that 'the Christian idea [of revelation] is analogous to the concept of Hadith in Islam: true, divinely protected from error and expressing the mind and will of the Almighty, but not direct revelation from the mouth of God. Hence, the gospel of Matthew, to a Muslim, at best seems a mishmash of Hadith and revelation' (P. Sookhdeo, 2013: 148). Even so, most Evangelicals 'conclude from the discrepancies between the teaching of the Bible and the Qur'an, particularly on what they say about Jesus Christ, that the latter is simply not the word of God' (Moucarry, 2001: 264).

Brown suggests a way forward for the Christian reader that combines respect with integrity. He suggests 'we call them classics … [and] take these texts seriously, treat them with a certain cultural reverence, and expect to learn important lessons from them', as we may do with Plato or Shakespeare. This 'assigns them a kind of authority, though not ultimate authority' (Brown 2020b: 268).

Discussion: Rigorous reading

All religious public spheres have texts that they consider sacred in some way. How they interpret, teach and publicize those texts will continue to have a great impact, both within their own spheres and also in wider society. As religions claiming to possess divinely revealed texts of universal relevance, this will be particularly important for both Islam and Christianity. There will always be those within any religious public sphere who hold to literalist interpretations of their texts. How others in the public sphere, both the elite participants and the grassroots audience, respond is crucial for the health of societies at large.

One vital step is to ensure that *both* communities publicly read and exegete *all* of their scriptures without selectivity. In an interesting study, historian Philip Jenkins discovered that for Christians, at least, this is not always the case. Difficult Old Testament passages are often allegorized, and many of the major church lectionaries, the lists of verses for the public reading of scripture, 'eliminate much of what is unpalatable'. This means that 'over the three-year cycle [the congregation] would hear just a small and unrepresentative selection of the controversial books', thus avoiding violent verses in, for instance, Deuteronomy, Joshua and 1 Samuel.[17] However, it is extremely important that Christians read these difficult texts and explain to themselves, and to a listening public, how it is that God commands violence in the Old Testament and yet does not in the New. Chronology alone is not a sufficient explanation to deter those who, for instance, may see in the book of Joshua a model for the treatment of Palestinians today (see Chapter 10). Evangelicals, as long as they believe that both the New and Old Testaments are divinely inspired, need to explain clearly how those revelations are to be understood and applied today.

Muslims need to do the same. Of course, there are differences in practice. While the whole of the Qur'an will certainly be recited in mosques, it will be done in Arabic without all the listeners necessarily understanding. It is then left to a religious scholar to choose and expound certain passages. It would be preferable if the text could also be read in the vernacular alongside the Arabic original. Rational arguments need to be made to explain how the difficult passages in both the Qur'an and the Hadith can be understood and applied today. Of course, many are attempting to do this, and it is important that the whole Muslim public sphere and the wider general sphere make space to hear their debates. This should ensure that all the various exegetical traditions within Islam are heard.

For both traditions, it is important that Muslims, Christians and academics should be free to engage in the rigorous examination of physical manuscripts, textual histories and interpretative traditions without charges of 'Orientalism'.[18] This term usually refers to what is seen as the politically motivated and hegemonic academic writings about Islam of previous generations which continues today. Orientalism stereotypes and demonizes what it sees as a monolithic Islam, allowing for no diversity of Muslims. However, this must never be confused with rigorous critical work that honestly poses difficult questions about texts and histories and seeks satisfactory answers to them. Complaints of Orientalism must not foreclose legitimate, genuine enquiry. Rather, such rigorous academic work should help inform discussions both within the Christian and Muslim public spheres as well as for the wider public.

In addition to this academic endeavour, it is healthy for the two communities to read their scriptures together. In a way, of course, this is done in adversarial debate, as will be seen in Chapter 12. However, such discourses are often heated and ill-tempered. It need not be the only way. For example, the practice of SR, mentioned above, is another way of reading scripture together, and there is a growing literature describing its benefits for the wider public sphere.[19] Evangelicals, with their focus on reading scripture and interpreting it for themselves, may find SR particularly agreeable. Muslims, who are more used to an authority figure interpreting scripture for them, often find it more difficult at the outset, but then frequently embrace it as a helpful exercise.[20] Here too, difficult scriptures and sensitive topics should not be ignored. However, when SR is practised in a spirit of respectful inquiry, seeking to understand one another's interpretative process, it is likely to produce more light than heat and holds much hope for all public spheres.

6

Sharia

The previous chapters have focused essentially on theological and religious issues, which are matters of belief, conviction and historical narrative. There is, however, a close connection between Islamic texts, especially the Hadith, law and the way Muslim societies organize themselves. So, as we now turn to look at Evangelical responses to the Sharia, the issues become much more sharply sociopolitical. Law colours relations between communities and largely determines freedoms and rights. It is inextricably linked to questions of power and politics. Of course, law in Muslim contexts is a much wider topic than just the Sharia. Muslim states have always passed other laws, incorporated other legal codes, often colonial, and have had 'an uneasy relationship with Islamic jurists'.[1] However, this is not often noted by Evangelical authors, whose focus is usually solely on Sharia.

This chapter looks at Evangelical concerns surrounding the Sharia in both the West and in places where Christians are living as minorities under Muslim-majority rule. It looks at the degree to which Evangelicals believe the Sharia may or may not be compatible with Western legal codes and their concerns over the extent to which the desire of Muslims to be governed by the Sharia is practicable or desirable in the West. This immediately gives rise to the question of how all religious sensibilities should be regarded under Western law. While none of the authors is impressed by or supportive of the Sharia as a whole, some are inclined to view the creation of space for religious conviction and practice as an important principle in a free society that Christians too want to benefit from. Others are adamant that no space should be given for the Sharia, seeing it as the thin end of a wedge leading to the unwelcome Islamization of societies (see Chapter 7).

The law and salvation

Despite their sociopolitical concerns, the first objection Evangelicals have to the Sharia is actually theological. Law is not natural territory for Evangelicals.[2] The New Testament reinterpretation of the Mosaic law and the Protestant emphasis on 'sola fide', justification by faith alone, create a suspicion of law in the Evangelical mind. Chapman thinks that 'Christians will no doubt find it hard to understand why we need to give attention to law, since the concept of law seems foreign to Christians who are taught that salvation is by faith, not by works' (2007b: 107).

In contrast, Islam is seen as 'a religion of law, rituals and duties … a total way of life, an all-encompassing religious, social and political system' (P. Sookhdeo, 2009b: 15). Even Accad suggests that 'the defining feature of Islam is the field of law' (2019: 43). So, it is common to hear Evangelicals contrast Islam as a religion of 'law' and 'works' with Christianity as a religion of 'love' and 'grace' (e.g. Azumah, 2005). There is a concern that Islam leads people back into slavery to the law. For example, Samy Tanagho, an Egyptian-background Christian who works as an evangelist with the Salvation Army in the United States, in his book *Glad News! God Loves You My Muslim Friend* says, 'Obedience to the law can never bring salvation. The law merely shows the sinner that he is guilty before God. The law demands perfect obedience, but man is not capable of perfection because sin makes us fallible. Under the law we are condemned' (2003: 114). Evangelicals see the idea of Islamic law as 'Allah offering a self-help programme' or 'good advice', not 'good news' (Bannister, 2021: 111, 121). The answer for Evangelicals is not law but a saviour figure. Daniel Janosik,[3] an American apologist, says, 'Christians do not follow a mere code, but they follow a person, the Lord Jesus Christ' (2019: 140).

Glaser also recognizes that the Sharia 'cannot save people', but is mindful that, nonetheless, 'law is very important in the Bible', showing people how to do good, warning of wrong and being 'part of God's way of dealing with evil'. She points out that 'Muslims themselves recognize that they cannot keep [the law] perfectly but must hope for God's mercy', and she sees a positive – although ultimately insufficient – aspect to the Muslim emphasis on law. 'We need more than the law, but not less than the law. The presence of Muslims can be a reminder of that' (2016: 248–52; see also Glaser, 2020a). A further concern, noted by Glaser and others, is that in Islam 'God has revealed not so much his character as his will' (Musk, 2003a: 210). His will or pattern or path is laid out in the Sharia, whereas in the Bible, God encounters people and has revealed himself, principally through the incarnation of Jesus. Thus, the Sharia obscures God's character. For these Evangelicals, this has direct consequences for social life and the norms in the following sections.

Evangelical concerns over Sharia

As with the topics of previous chapters, Evangelicals are well aware of how important and central the Sharia is to the life of the majority of Muslims. Azumah acknowledges that it is broader than just law. 'The Sharia is more than stoning of adulterous women and cutting off limbs as often portrayed in the media. It is the very fabric of Muslim religious expression. The Sharia has to do with every aspect of Muslim life – personal, family and communal. Christians have to appreciate this fact' (2005: 249). Indeed, Muslims themselves see it as 'totalistic'.[4] However, most Evangelicals are also convinced that religious law is no more successful in regulating social behaviour than it is in achieving eternal salvation. Several of them remark on the similarity between the Sharia and the Halakha, or Jewish law (e.g. Bell, 2006: 73; Moucarry, 2022: 20). For instance, Aaron Taylor, an American missionary and *Sojourners* blogger, points out that 'Israel arguably had the best set of laws under the sun during the Old Testament era and what was the result? The result was prophet after prophet rebuking the people for their idolatry, violence, lust for material possessions, and their oppression of the poor'. He suggests that Muslims who think that theocracy and the Sharia are the answer will be disappointed. 'Theocracy was tried once and it turned out to be a big fat failure' (Taylor 2009: KL259). This makes Evangelicals all the more concerned about attempts to introduce the Sharia, particularly with regard to certain groups of people. Chapman observes that 'in traditional Islamic law there are three fundamental inequalities: between Muslims and non-Muslims; between men and women; and between slaves and free men and women' (2007b: 168). This suggests that the Sharia does not offer adequate protection of rights for the individual, women, slaves, non-Muslims and even for some Muslims.

The individual

Firstly, many Evangelicals are concerned that the rights of the individual are not respected under the Sharia. Azumah suggests that 'Muslims are not impressed by arguments that appeal to human rights' (2008b: 131). Such rights are often regarded as being secular and so contrary to God's law. Inequality is not seen as being a problem. In fact, it is the norm as 'traditionally Sharia operates on the basis of inequality between men and women and between Muslims and non-Muslims' (Nazir-Ali, 2008b). The root cause suggested for this by some Evangelicals is the Islamic view of God and humanity. In contrast to the biblical teaching that humans are made in the image of God (Gen. 1.27), in Islam an 'absolutely transcendent God leaves no space for the individual as a free moral being' (P. Sookhdeo, 2009b: 50). If humans are not in God's image, then they can be devalued, and the Muslim community and its interests become more important than the individual.

Women

The issues facing women under the Sharia cause a special concern for Evangelicals – and others – advocating equal rights. Gabriel lists the various ways in which he believes men and women are not treated equally in the Qur'an, including men having four wives (Q.4.3); a man's right to divorce (Q.2.22); a woman inheriting half the share of her brothers (Q.4.11); men being over women (Q.4.34); women staying at home (Q.33.33); and a husband being permitted to beat his wife (Q.4.34) (2002: 42–3). These sorts of examples are picked up by other authors such as Rosemary Sookhdeo, although she does acknowledge that, in the context of their time, the Qur'an's rules and Muhammad's example were an improvement on existing mores. While she accepts that, maybe, equality for women was being sought, she argues that 'this theoretical equality has not been seen in practice'. Rather 'Islam is a man's world', and when Sharia is applied, 'it is the women and the girls who pay the price' (R. Sookhdeo, 2004: 37, 127). Robinson agrees arguing that 'within countries where Islamic law predominates, [women] are mostly silenced in public spaces and rendered effectively invisible by the clothing they are obliged to wear. They are frequently condemned to suffer abuse and indignity through male mouthpieces who determine their roles and outcomes' (2017: KL236). Furthermore, Solomon (2009) accuses the Sharia of sanctioning physical abuse against women based on Sura 4.34. He claims that 'this is continuously denied [by Muslims] both out of embarrassment and being in conflict with the civilized world so it is toned down'. He then goes further by laying the blame for honour killings – which disproportionately affect women – at the door of the Sharia.[5] Most Evangelical writers on mission to Muslims deal with the topic of honour and shame in some way, but most do not usually connect it so directly to the Sharia, seeing it more as a cultural phenomenon (see, for instance, Dale, 2021: chapter 5; Musk, 2003b).

The Sharia is also seen as allowing, or at least not condemning, the practice of female circumcision or female genital mutilation (FGM) (Janosik, 2019: 139). Evangelicals universally condemn FGM, as do many Muslims. However, by no means all Islamic jurists reject it, and so opinion is divided within the Muslim community (see Durie, 2009c: 74–8; Robinson, 2017: chapter 2). Dale explains that 'rulings differ with the various schools of Islamic law', and for one it is a 'duty', for two it is 'advised' and for another it is 'commendable' (2021: 304). This leaves many Evangelicals concerned, even for young Muslim girls living in the West, although some recognize that 'Muslims leaders have spoken out to condemn the practice as un-Islamic' (R. Sookhdeo, 2004: 93). Other Evangelicals also believe that 'FGM is not strictly speaking an Islamic custom. It is practiced in many non-Islamic societies, and Arabs practiced it long before the birth of Islam' (Moucarry, 2022: 44). Dale notes that it is even practised by a 'number of African Christian communities' (2021: 304).

As usual, there are other more positive voices reflecting on women under the Sharia. Bassma Dabbour Jaballah, a Canadian-Tunisian BMB, recognizes that while women have always been 'discriminated against', there are 'strong, intellectual women within Islam'. With increasing calls for 'literal application of Sharia, many Muslim women are no longer remaining silent' (2018: 55). Miriam Adeney, an American anthropologist and missiologist, warns against seeing Muslim women as 'passive and submissive' and failing to see the 'strengths and beauties' in Muslim culture with regard to women (2002: 19–20). Dale mentions examples of this, including Sisters in Islam in Malaysia which has 'worked to improve the lives and experiences of women, within the framework of Islam and existing Shariah court laws' (2021: 258). Finally, Reisacher points out that not all Muslim women are negative about the Sharia, which is not in any case static, meaning that the treatment of women tends to change depending on the political context and who is interpreting the rules. That said, she 'does not mean Christians should keep silent if they see abuse of women's rights in Muslim laws' (2012a: 84).

Slavery

It is not just women, however. Evangelical authors have many other concerns about individual rights under the Sharia. Several authors look at the issue of slavery. Azumah believes that slavery is justified in classical Muslim thinking. He traces the history of Arab slave-trading in Africa which was driven by 'religious, racial and ideological frameworks' and was 'contrary to conventional theories of a humane Muslim slavery,

... as cruel and harsh as any other slave system' (2001: 232–3). He points out that Muhammad himself had slaves, and when slavery was finally formally abolished in Muslim states, it was not for religious reasons. Rather, it was pressure from Europe, which was resented by many of the Muslim slave traders who lost their livelihoods.

Charlotte Thorneycroft, a criminal law barrister who has worked for the Lawyers' Christian Fellowship in the UK, observes that 'although no Muslim nation today officially sanctions slavery, it remains a part of Shariah law and therefore a part of Islamic culture' (2013: 109). Cox and Marks concur and suggest that, from the time of Muhammad onwards, slavery 'became deeply entrenched in Muslim culture and practice'. They point to various qur'anic passages condoning slavery (Q.16.71) and concubinage (Q.4.3, Q.33.50) and trace the history of slavery in Muslim contexts through history, including the capture of white slaves in North Africa by the Barbary corsairs. They also give eyewitness accounts and case studies of modern-day slavery by Muslims, which Cox has collected in Sudan (2006: 181, 63–73).

Non-Muslims

Other categories of people deemed to be at risk under the Sharia and mentioned by Evangelical writers are Christian minorities living under Muslim majorities, other non-Muslims, converts leaving Islam and Muslims who do not wish to live under the Sharia. Thorneycroft concedes that actual practice is better than the Sharia stipulation, which is often not adhered to, but still sees the Sharia as problematic. She says, 'Most modern Muslim states have granted non-Muslims citizenship on a par with Muslims, although some have retained the bar on intermarriage, and reserve the position of head of state for Muslims. However, the rules of Shariah regarding non-Muslims remain theoretically in place and therefore pose a constant threat if they are re-invoked' (2013: 104).

The case of Christians and converts will be looked at in more detail in Chapter 8, but suffice to say at this point that the situation of Christian minorities in Muslim-majority contexts is one of the greatest concerns and complaints Western Evangelicals have with regard to Islam and the Sharia. Carimokam puts it strongly when he says, 'Sharia law at its core is religious apartheid, the separate and unequal treatment of people based on their religious beliefs. Neither Muhammad nor his law is the perfect exemplar for the twenty-first century' (2010: 540). Azumah even goes as far as to say that for Christians in minority contexts 'supporting the sharia, which explicitly denies them the right to freely proclaim their faith and many other issues central to their belief, amounts to signing their confessional death warrant' (2008b: 138).

Muslims

Finally, Muslims themselves are also seen by some Evangelicals to be in danger from the Sharia. Abdallah Bahri, a Christian minister in Australia who converted from Islam, points out that 'Koranic teaching and Islamic law are not known by every Muslim, and not all Muslims believe in these laws, nor do they all seek to be obedient to them' (2009: 189). For these Muslims, the imposition of such laws can be deeply problematic. Indeed, many Muslims relocate to the West precisely looking for freedom from regimes that practise Sharia, the Iranian case since the 1979 revolution being a notable example.[6] This was one of the main reasons why a proposed Sharia arbitration tribunal in Canada was abandoned. Elizabeth Kendal,[7] an Australian analyst and advocate who has worked for WEA, writes about the case and observes that there was a fear among Muslims that such a move would disadvantage them. She believes that '*Sharia* law divides Muslims, as it radicalizes some while repelling others. Islamists use *Sharia* as a tool to advance their own power, firstly to control Muslims, then society as a whole' (2009a: 195).

Universal Declaration of Human Rights

Such concerns lead several authors to contrast the Sharia with the Universal Declaration of Human Rights (UDHR) adopted by the UN in 1948, 'an ideal comparator when looking at the compatibility of Shariah with the principles of human rights law' (Thorneycroft, 2013: 97). Evangelical authors see the rights and freedoms guaranteed by the UDHR as deriving from Christian principles. They 'depend on the Judaeo-Christian view that men and women have been created in God's image' and 'they cannot flourish' without this understanding (Nazir-Ali, 2008c: 3, 5). They are concerned that, in their view, the Sharia does not appear to be able to uphold the same values.

Kendal notes that historically 'Muslims were so resistant to the UDHR, primarily because of its articles on religious freedom, that they formulated their own declaration of human rights, the "Cairo Declaration on Human Rights in Islam" (CDHRI)'. She points out that the rights and freedoms granted in the CDHRI, written in 1990, are all, in fact, subject to two important clauses: 'All the rights and freedoms stipulated in this Declaration are subject to the Islamic Shari'ah' (Article 24) and 'The Islamic Shari'ah is the only source of reference for the explanation or clarification of any of the articles of this Declaration' (Article 25). She points out obvious drawbacks with this, particularly in relation to a Muslim choosing 'to change his/her religion or belief', which is forbidden under the Sharia (Kendal, 2009b: 84–6).[8] In similar fashion, Thorneycroft compares the UDHR with another document, the 1981 Universal Islamic Declaration of Human Rights (UIDHR). She is concerned that subtle differences in the Arabic and English versions of the UIDHR give a false impression. For instance, 'saying that Shariah will be applied equally [in the Arabic version] is not the same as saying all individuals are equal [in the English], as Shariah does not treat all individuals as equal' (Thorneycroft, 2013: 101). This discrepancy in translation has been noticed by others such as Chapman (2007b: 168).

Geographical trends

There is a perception among Evangelicals that the introduction of Sharia is increasing globally, regardless of whether or not Muslims form the majority or minority in a society. Musk suggests that 'it is one of the marks of change in many Muslim nations today that

Islamic law (the *sharīʿa*) is being increasingly applied' (2003a: 237). Durie observes that 'all around the world, *Sharia* law is very much on the rise. In the past 50 years, virtually every Muslim state has taken steps, however small, towards re-implementing it' (2009a: 153). Even in the West, some feel that the Sharia is encroaching and is a mark of looming Islamization (see Chapter 7).

However, some see it differently. Ziya Meral,[9] a researcher and advisor, points out that 'of some forty-four Muslim-majority nations, only a handful use aspects of *sharīʿa* law in their legal systems', and even the most conservative, such as Saudi Arabia, show 'increasing signs of modernization' (2011: 130). Johnston notes that there are 'intense debates' in Muslim societies about the role of the Sharia. He draws on Gallup polling data from over forty Muslim-majority countries to say that, while most Muslims want Sharia to play some juridical role, 'only in Jordan, Egypt, Pakistan, Afghanistan, and Bangladesh, did the majority of respondents want "*Sharia* as the 'only source' of legislation". Elsewhere the majority favoured Shariʿa as "a" source of legislation'. This equivocality was reinforced by the fact that 'the great majority of those who want Shariʿa applied also want women to have equal rights' (David Johnston, 2012: 60).[10] Furthermore, in places where Muslims are a minority, Bahri believes that ultimately the vast majority of Muslims want to live in peace and on equal terms and 'know it is not in their interest to actively pursue [Sharia]' (2009: 190).

As far back as 2001, Azumah was concerned about developments in Nigeria, and subsequent events only confirmed his fears. He believes that

> the recent clamour and unilateral declarations and implementation of Shariʿah in a number of Northern Nigerian states ... are concrete evidence of conservative revivalism in modern sub-Saharan Africa. ... Despite the repeated claims that the Shariʿah in Northern Nigerian states has nothing to do with non-Muslims, there are already clear signs that ... the Shariʿah institutionalizes and sanctions not only discrimination along religious lines but that it is set to impose Islamic value systems and legal codes on non-Muslims. (2001: 194, 202)

He recognizes the importance of the Sharia for African Muslims who reject secular democracy as a Western Christian imposition and are trying to 'insulate themselves from the effects of globalization and Westernization'. They see it as 'part of their history and thus of their identity ... [and as] essential for the rediscovery of and reinstatement of "Africa's glorious Islamic past"'. However, although many Christian responses are ill-informed and fuelled by prejudiced 'knee-jerk reactions and defensive arguments', there are issues of human rights, and 'as far as Christians are concerned, signing onto classical formulations of the Shariʿah is equivalent to agreeing to religious and sociopolitical subjugation by Muslims' (Azumah, 2008b: 70–4).

His concerns are backed up by others. A 2016 report on the situation in Nigeria by Open Doors, titled *Crushed but Not Defeated*, found that 'the introduction of enhanced Sharia in 12 northern states in 2000 [had] increased discrimination against Christians' (2016: 12). However, Muslims are not immune. Durie relates the 2001 case of Amina Lawal, a Muslim woman in a northern Nigerian state who came to international prominence when she was sentenced to death by stoning for adultery. The sentence was later overturned, but Durie suggests that it will be hard for Muslims to modernize such laws. 'The clear grounds for stoning adulterers in Muhammad's example and teaching need to be thoroughly acknowledged and dealt with, if conservative Muslims are to remove this sentence from the Islamic *Sharia*.' He predicts that the incompatibility between the Sharia and human rights will 'surely prove to be one of the most persistent, difficult and divisive questions of the twenty-first century' (2009a: 153–4).

However, whatever the situation of Muslims and Christian minorities living under the Sharia in Africa and elsewhere, the loudest complaint among many Evangelicals in the West is that some in Muslim communities are agitating for Sharia provision in their own nations. This is often felt to be part of a wider 'conspiracy of Islamization' (see Chapter 7). Indeed, Europe is seen as being quite far along the road to Islamic domination in the eyes of some observers in North America and Australia, including in the legal domain. In a small booklet, Robinson points out that by 2009 there were eighty-five Sharia courts operating in Britain, apparently '17 times more than authorities anticipated' (2010: 22). David Claydon, an Australian Anglican minister who was at one time the international director of the Lausanne Committee for World Evangelism, edited a volume, *Islam, Human Rights and Public Policy* (2009), and chose to include a chapter on 'Eurabia' by the well-known American critic of Islam, Daniel Pipes.[11] Pipes admits that it is difficult to predict future trends, but suggests that it is possible that Europe will soon be dominated by Muslims or that there will at least have to be a conflict to prevent it. The general tenor of all the contributors is that Sharia is a growing problem around the world.

There is concern in the UK too. An anonymously authored 2007 booklet, published by the Pilcrow Press and titled *The Islamisation of Britain and What Must Be Done to Prevent It*, expresses concern over a range of issues, including the increasing presence of Sharia courts in the UK. This is also a theme in a 2011 booklet written by Sookhdeo for the Barnabas Fund, called *The Slippery Slope*. He warns of a 'parallel legal system for settling disputes among Muslims' and argues that whereas Jewish courts have operated for many years 'within national law', 'sharia represents an alternative to national law' (P. Sookhdeo, 2011b: 23). Nazir-Ali too has expressed concern. He acknowledges that 'we must expect that Muslims will seek to influence public policy in accordance with the teaching of Islam' but insists that 'the autonomy of the public law must be upheld' and that Islamic councils and tribunals should be carefully monitored (2012: 73–4).

In the US context, Pack self-published *The Shari'ah Bomb: How Islamic Law Can Destroy American Freedom* (2013). Janosik also asks whether 'Sharia is compatible with the U.S. Constitution' and finds that, while Muslims are 'able to fit in with American lifestyles', Sharia is 'incompatible with democracy since non-Muslims are not equal with Muslims' under it (2019: 131–3).

This illustrates well how many Evangelicals fear that any accommodation to the Sharia will be the thin end of the wedge, an Islamic takeover or Islamization by stealth. Bahri observes that 'once a few *Sharia*-based laws are implemented, there is pressure for more to be introduced' (2009: 183), and others are concerned that, through all these small changes and constant challenges, 'the host society becomes indifferent to the religious, social and political tactics used to establish a totality of Islamic rule under *Shariah*' (Solomon and Al-Maqdisi, 2009b: 77).

This raises the difficult question of the degree to which Muslims as minorities should be allowed to live according to Sharia principles in the face of the above concerns about Sharia courts or tribunals in the West. For instance, Sookhdeo, while insisting that a state should never impose the Sharia on its citizens, does recognize that it might be 'adhered to voluntarily' (2008a: 222). Julian Rivers, a British Christian expert on law and religion, discusses some of the problems that can be created, for instance, by Islamic marriages (*nikāḥ*) which are unregistered with the civil authorities. They can leave a partner, usually the wife, at a serious disadvantage with no recourse to civil law. It is also a route to '*de facto* polygamous marriage' as they are seen as 'non-marriages' by the state allowing a man to 'co-habit' with as many women as he likes. He observes that 'shari'a councils actually offer a partial remedy' to the problems and abuses arising by requiring divorcing husbands to provide financial support (2017: 146–9).[12] Tanya Walker, former dean of the Oxford Centre for Christian Apologetics, is not so convinced and warns that 'calls for the recognition of Shari'a councils in Britain … should be viewed with caution' if 'the abuse of women within patriarchal settings' is to be avoided (2017: 202, 187).

Such issues are clearly complicated, as then-Archbishop of Canterbury Rowan Williams found out in 2008 when he made an ill-judged comment in the media about Sharia being 'unavoidable' in Britain.[13] Maybe cautioned by his experience, the next, rather more Evangelical archbishop, Justin Welby, chose to make his position on the Sharia clear. In his 2018 book, *Reimagining Britain*, he wrote that 'the system of Sharia is both complex and sophisticated, with clear demarcations between civil law and criminal law'. However, the 'Sharia, which has a powerful and ancient cultural narrative of its own, deeply embedded in a system of faith and understanding of God, and thus especially powerful in forming identity, cannot become part of another narrative' (Welby, 2018: 81–2).

Support for Muslim modernizers

As mentioned before, some Evangelicals recognize and acknowledge that Muslims interpret the Sharia in different ways and that there are some who want to modernize it (Nazir-Ali, 2006: 150). For instance, Johnston compares two unlikely Muslims – Hasan al-Hudaybi, a member of the Egyptian Muslim Brotherhood, and Abdolkarim Soroush, an Iranian philosopher – who share similar views with different end points. Both believe that 'past formulations of Islamic law are no longer binding, because the sacred texts (Qur'an and Sunnah) have to be interpreted by people and made to apply to changing socio-political environments … It is people who determine its meaning and decide on its application within the changing circumstances of their societies' (David Johnston, 2012: 59). For the Muslim Brotherhood, this works out in 'Salafi Reformism', which sees the Sharia as a path to be followed by the whole of a society, but for Soroush, it points towards a more pluralist society.

Several Evangelicals acknowledge the work of Sudanese scholar Mahmoud Taha who taught that much of the Sharia is based on the later Medinan revelations, whereas the earlier Meccan principles were 'the ideal and the more original' but 'could not be implemented in all their openness' during Muhammad's lifetime due to human weakness (Musk, 2008: 74; see also Accad, 2020: 74).[14] However, Taha was eventually executed by the Sudanese regime for heresy in 1985, and today, Abdullahi an-Naʿim, his disciple, is based in the United States. He is also quoted by some Evangelicals, and Douglas Johnston, founder of the International Center for Religion and Diplomacy, thinks that, despite being 'branded as a heretic (a label he wears with some pride), Naʿim is attracting a notable following among young Muslims in Malaysia and Indonesia' (2013: 55).[15]

Thomas Johnson, a special envoy for the WEA, describes another modernist Muslim approach promoted by Nahdlatul Ulama, a large Indonesia Muslim organization. Johnson explains that 'humanitarian Islam is distinguished from some other types of Islam by the way it applies the term Sharia to eternal norms, not to specific, contingent civil laws or criminal punishments'. He believes that

> such a definition of sharia, if followed by the global Muslim movement, would undermine most reasons for Islamophobia, since it would shift the discussion of the religious ethics of public life away from, for example, the proper way to execute blasphemers and toward a principled discussion of what human goods are primary and what types of religious and civil laws would protect those human goods. (2021: 22, 4)

Others are less sanguine about the Muslim modernizers' chances and feel that 'these ideas seem to have little resonance across the Muslim world' (Cox and Marks, 2006: 196). Azumah too remains wary. 'It is not out of sheer spite or fear of Islam and Muslims that Evangelical Christians find it difficult to support the implementation of the Shariʿa in its entirety, especially in a pluralistic context such as Africa.' There are 'existential implications' (2005: 249).

Chapman is one of the few Evangelicals to point out the failings of Western legal systems. He admits that the Christian record has not always been good with regard to rights and equalities, especially for women (2007b: 182). There have been periods in history where Christian-orientated laws have been applied extremely harshly. Even today many states in the United States practise capital punishment for which some find sanction in the Old Testament. Moreover, the failings and injustices in Muslim-majority countries may not always be due to the Sharia or foundational texts. As Chapman puts it:

> When we look at many countries today which describe themselves as 'Islamic' and claim to be following Islamic law, we don't always see the kind of ideal society that Muslims believe can be created by Islam. There may be many reasons for the state of these societies, so it wouldn't be fair to blame 'Islam' for everything that we see. We can't help feeling, however, that the Islamic diagnosis of the human condition is too optimistic because law, the prophetic model and living in an Islamic community are incapable of dealing adequately with the root of the brokenness of individuals and societies. (2008: 23)

Discussion: Legal futures

For Evangelicals, this root is sin. The strong Evangelical belief in human sinfulness and inability to match up to God's perfection means that no system of law, however well it serves society, would ever be sufficient for eschatological salvation. Neither will it ensure the common good. While several authors admit the parallels between the Sharia and Old Testament Mosaic law, for Evangelicals, first and foremost, people need a saviour to rescue them so that their hearts are changed and they are then empowered to keep the law – both religious and civil. This inside-out process is the very opposite of the imposition of an external law which hopes to operate from the outside in.

It would be fair to say that none of the Evangelical authors reviewed for this chapter was positive about the Sharia. Where Sharia is applied, either partially or in full, whether in Muslim-majority settings or in places where non-Muslims form a significant portion of the population, it is seen as being discriminatory and incompatible with Western laws and freedoms. Women; slaves, including migrant workers; dissident Muslims; and apostates are seen as being at particular risk. The Evangelical commitment to justice and individual freedom, stemming from a strong belief that humans are made in the image of God, means that many will continue to advocate on behalf of those suffering discrimination under the Sharia, as will be seen in Chapter 8. However, any modernization or reform of the Sharia will, of course, have to be a process conducted by the Muslim community. It will require a reassessment of the Hadith and so be extremely controversial. Therefore, it is doubtful that vocal, public, Evangelical support for the modernizers would help their cause in the eyes of more traditionally minded Muslims, among whom Evangelical stock is low. That said, Evangelicals will want to lend personal support to individuals wherever they can make a difference.

At the same time, this commitment to the freedom of religious choice in Muslim contexts will pose a quandary for Evangelicals thinking about the Sharia in Western contexts. Evangelicals often complain about the impact of Western laws on their own consciences in matters of abortion, sexuality, bioethics and free speech. If they want the law to accommodate the Evangelical conscience, then what about the Muslim conscience? Some Evangelicals will doubtless want to put further restrictions around Sharia councils and Muslim family practice in the West. Others may be willing to be more pragmatic, recognizing a shared interest and advocating for Muslim freedoms provided they do not break existing laws or international standards of human rights.

In all cases above, arguments to secular audiences will best be made on the basis of reason, human rights and international law. While religious arguments may provide 'key resources', 'moral intuitions' and lead to 'complementary learning' where secular powers are willing to engage,[16] there will be an onus on Christians – and Muslims – to persuade using rational arguments based on the common good. In doing this, Evangelicals will continue to point out that Christian thought and principles had a significant influence on the Enlightenment process that led to the formulation of the above standards. They will also argue that evolutionary humanism cannot provide a sufficient underpinning for law and society while explaining why Christian concepts of sanctity of life, marriage and honesty encourage the common good.

In encounters with many – particularly non-Western – Muslims, however, rational or philosophical arguments will carry little weight. In this case, Christians and Muslims would do better to have a theologically informed conversation drawing on understandings of God's mercy and justice in both traditions. Even so, in all likelihood, the Sharia will remain a contentious issue between Evangelicals and Muslims both in the West and globally. In the next chapter, we see how the Sharia and Muslim traditions are important in forming Muslim identity and how Evangelicals may feel threatened by any perceived process of Islamization in their societies.

7

Islamization

For any religious community, their laws and regulations are not solely about theology and divine command. They are also about identity, boundaries and security. Human beings inevitably form themselves into groups, tribes or gangs based on ethnicity, geography, clan, interest, occupation, politics, age or, in this case, religion. To create a sense of community, they establish boundaries in order to know who is in and who is out. In the religious case, these boundaries not only run between religions but also mark out intra-faith distinctions between Orthodox, Catholic and Protestant, Sunni and Shia, practising and nominal, and so on. Such boundaries keep the faithful within, and others without. In that sense, they are like the geographical boundaries which tribes use to mark out their territory. Straying outside of the borders is unwise and potentially dangerous as it may involve an encounter with the members of other tribes hostile to one's own. In their turn, trespassers are challenged and should enter only by invitation. It is, maybe, these sorts of dangers which lead Volf to suggest that 'the future of our world will depend on how we deal with identity and difference'.[1]

As Vishanoff points out, 'Human beings have long occupied themselves with erecting what we call religious boundaries between themselves and others.' He suggests that 'almost any kind of difference can be used as a boundary' and lists 'practices, doctrines, symbols, institutions, sacred texts, sacred spaces … lineage, race, ethnicity, nationality, language, culture and geography'.[2] For example, we have seen in Chapter 3 that identifying Allah as a rival god to Yahweh creates an important boundary for some Evangelicals, separating them from Muslims and even from other Christians who disagree with them. Belief in the death and resurrection of Jesus – and the denial of them in the Qur'an – forms another central identity marker for Evangelicals. Furthermore, Yancey and Quosigk point to the theological and political beliefs that underlie the rift between conservative and progressive Christians when it comes to seeing not just Muslims but one another as 'out-groups'.[3]

These unseen boundaries between religious communities are often reinforced by more visible markers. Arguably, part of the purpose of religious law is to create and maintain these symbols and markers that ensure that adherents of different religious tribes remain distinct from one another. That is not to say that the adherents intend these signs and practices to prevent contact and integration, but it is an inevitable outcome and is part of how societies have emerged and kept themselves distinct and separate. This chapter focuses on Evangelical reaction to just some of these visible markers, including food, language and audible signals, buildings, clothing, objects and religious symbols. It then briefly considers how these are linked to territorial boundaries and the construction of 'parallel lives'.[4] It ends on one of the galvanizing issues in the Evangelical public sphere – the idea that there is a subversive process of Islamization under way in the West and elsewhere.

Identity and symbols

Thabiti Anyabwile,[5] a former Muslim and now Black American church pastor, believes that Islam is not mainly a theology or an institution but is 'primarily an identity' (2011: 89). So, perhaps, part of what troubles Evangelicals about Muslims may be their identity markers. Islam is a very visible religion, and many Muslims self-consciously create distinctiveness. When Evangelicals react to Muslims, they are reacting not only to their theological and legal differences but also to the sheer publicness of their faith – especially in the West today. Consequently, this chapter is more Western-focused than are other chapters. While Christianity in the West has become increasingly private since the Enlightenment, this has not been so with Islam. Indeed, the de-privatization of religion in the West today is largely down to the obvious presence of Islam.[6]

Of course, Muslims are not alone in this. Sikh turbans, Jewish ringlets and Buddhist saffron robes are equally conspicuous in the West, although often confused with Muslim attire, sometimes with disastrous consequences.[7] In comparison, Christians, including Evangelicals, have few identity markers, apart from maybe 'good works' (Mt. 5.16). The situation is often very different in non-Western parts of the world, especially where Christians have lived alongside Muslims for many centuries. Here Christians may well have visible identity markers of their own, as will be noted below. Could it be in the West, however, that the lack of visible Christian symbolism – compared to the obvious public Muslim display – makes Evangelicals feel weak or uneasy? After all, how does the community recognize people of Christian faith? How do they know whether Christians are present in numbers or not? How do members of the Evangelical community recognize one another? It is normally just not possible to tell practising Christians from their fellow citizens by their appearance.

Food laws

Food laws are a classic case of how religious law may be used to define boundaries and prevent socializing – and thus assimilation – between different tribes. In fact, the 'symbolic significance associated with the preparation and sharing of food make foreign food restrictions ideally suited for a separatist agenda'.[8] That does not mean that all Muslims who want to eat halal food, or abstain from alcohol, are separatists, but it does signal difference and potentially makes integration more difficult.

The proliferation of halal food in the West is of great concern to some Evangelicals. Sookhdeo believes that the halal system is a deliberate attempt at the creation of an Islamic consciousness which at the very least is divisive, as it stops Muslims from visiting the homes of non-Muslims (2006: 73). He points out that the global market for halal products is worth $2 trillion, exerting a strong economic influence on food exporters and restaurant chains (P. Sookhdeo, 2011a: 52). There is also concern that, in some areas of the UK, halal food is becoming a monopoly and forcing the unwanted 'adoption of a form of religious ritualism in Britain', thus marking territory as Muslim (Pilcrow Press, 2007: 27). This is particularly the case when halal food is routinely served to all, regardless of faith, in various institutions. Solomon sees this trend in a very negative light, believing it to be part of a Muslim strategy (*tamkīn*) of strengthening or empowering their position in society. He points out that the Qur'an permits Muslims to eat the meat of Christians (Q.5:3), but suggests that imams and scholars 'choose to overlook it deliberately' in order to demand halal food in hospitals, schools and prisons (Solomon and Al-Maqdisi, 2009b: 40, 75). This point has not gone unnoticed by Christian Concern in the UK (2010).

On the contrary, other Evangelicals see the accommodation of halal requirements in an entirely different light. Carl Medearis,[9] an American author and speaker who has lived in the Middle East, simply says that 'halal food is tasty and good for you' and points out the importance of sharing food in 'winning people's trust and their hearts' (2012: KL447). Wallis recounts how one church in America hosted a halal barbecue to welcome Muslims to the neighbourhood (2013: 138). These Evangelicals see permitting or providing halal food as extending generous, thoughtful Christian hospitality. Others clearly believe it to be a naïve capitulation to Islamic demands.

Language

Language is another potent identity marker. Whether it is a tribal language in Africa, the language of migrants to the inner cities of the West or the formal religious language of texts and rituals, language can embrace, exclude, protect and identify. One of the most important educational requirements in any immigrant community is that children should learn the language of their parents' homeland. Furthermore, there is a desire for their children to learn religious languages. So, in many countries in Europe and North America, it is common for Muslim children to attend mosque schools after regular school finishes to learn Arabic, Urdu or other languages of religious and cultural importance. The most important of these for the Muslim community is qur'anic Arabic. Children learn to recite the Qur'an from a young age, even if Arabic is not their mother tongue.

This is indicative of the central importance of Arabic to Islam. Musk believes that for Islam 'its Arab identity outweighs its embrace of other cultures and languages' (2005: 163). Arabic then acts as a centripetal force drawing Muslims together. Interestingly, this is in contrast to the historical translation of the Bible into other languages, which has been a centrifugal force driving outward missional expansion and cultural adaptation.[10] At its best, this produces fabulous variety and diversity within the Christian community. However, it does mean that there is no unifying language. Christians in the West today do not usually greet one another in Hebrew, or quote verses to one another in *koiné* Greek.[11] It is not uncommon for Christians to use an occasional 'hallelujah', 'praise the Lord' or 'bless you', but nowhere near the degree to which Muslims use religious language in everyday life. Regardless of their mother tongue, all Muslims embrace Arabic for prayer, reciting (although not necessarily understanding) the Qur'an and for a whole range of social formulae. Arabic is almost always used in all settings for greetings, blessings and invocations. 'Salaam', 'mashallah' and 'eid mubarak' are commonly heard in Muslims communities on the lips of Arab and non-Arab Muslims alike, including on Western streets.

This is another strong identity marker and flows over into normal English usage, which for some Evangelicals is problematic. For instance, Barnabas Fund believes that

> the increased use of Arabic/Islamic words and phrases in contemporary English expresses the growing influence of Islamic religion and culture in the English-speaking West. It encourages users to accept Islamic thought patterns and definitions of reality, religion and politics and thus makes them better disposed towards the claims of Islam. As a result, they will be more inclined to support Muslim demands for a privileged status, or even in some cases to convert to Islam. (2011a: ii)

Others are worried that a failure to use English in the West keeps Muslims separated. Nazir-Ali (2008a) observes that, in Britain, 'living as separate communities, continuing to communicate in their own languages and having minimum need for building healthy relationships with the majority' is a real problem. This is not the case to such a degree in the United States, where Muslim arrivals have typically had better English due to higher immigration criteria. However, even there, people's names linguistically create a sense of community identity, and it is often possible to identify a person's Muslim background by their name, although it tells you nothing about the nature of their religious practice.

Prayer call

Along with language, another audible identity marker in Muslim community life is the adhan (call to prayer). It is sometimes likened to church bells summoning the faithful to prayer, but for a lot of Evangelicals, it is more than this. A Christian Concern article (2021) explains that 'church bells carry no effectual message apart from their innocuous tintinnabulation', whereas the adhan has 'a clear and divisive message to it. It is a statement of faith, carrying an explicit and direct message of religious superiority'. Sookhdeo agrees and sees the adhan as 'a public statement of Islamic faith … inviting non-Muslims to pray in the mosque and thereby in effect to convert to Islam' (2011b: 34). While occasionally a Western Evangelical might countenance a once-weekly-publicly-broadcast call to prayer in a predominantly Muslim area, most are very opposed to the idea. Indeed, the article cited above recounts a successful legal action taken by Evangelicals in London to stop the broadcast in the borough of Newham. In an earlier case, Nazir-Ali opposed another Anglican bishop who was supporting a request for such a broadcast in Oxford. He believes that the adhan can contribute to 'no-go areas' and points out that 'such amplification was unknown throughout most of history and its use raises all sorts of questions about noise levels and whether non-Muslims wish to be told the creed of a particular faith five times a day on the loudspeaker'.[12]

One Evangelical puts the adhan in a more positive light and recalls how, when he was living in Egypt, there was a mosque loudspeaker mounted on the roof of their apartment. He decided that rather than complain about it, he would use it as a reminder to himself to pray (Jabbour, 2008: 53). Accad even admits his nostalgia and happy memories of the adhan growing up in Beirut (2019: 104). For most Evangelicals, however, the adhan in the context of a Muslim-majority community is a very different thing to an adhan in the West.

Mosques

Other identity markers are visible, not least among them the mosque. The proliferation of purpose-built mosques in the West excites strong feelings among Evangelicals. Many would agree that 'in a free society, adherents of different faiths should have the right to set up their own places of worship', as long as they show sensitivity and do not allow the mosques to become the centres of segregated communities (Riddell, 2004: 183). Nonetheless, many Evangelicals have a gnawing sense of injustice that Christians are not granted the same rights in some Muslim-majority countries, especially Saudi Arabia where church buildings are not permitted (Musk, 2003a: 239). This concern for reciprocity leads Sookhdeo to wonder whether there could be 'an argument for trying somehow to negotiate for reciprocal permission for Christian minorities in Muslim contexts before allowing Muslim minorities in the West to build as many mosques as they want' (2009a: 84). Gauss asks, 'What do you think the chances might be of America establishing Christian or Jewish schools, institutions and churches or synagogues in Muslim countries? Absolutely none!' (2009: 321). Solomon and Maqdisi even challenge the Saudi signatories of ACW to 'petition their government for the building of churches for the Christians in Saudi Arabia as evidence of their neighborly care for those Christians in their esteemed country' (2009a: 23). However, for some, a demand for reciprocity is not the right approach (see Chapter 8). Roberts says, 'Saudi Arabia isn't my standard. We can and should set the tone, not just around the world, but right here at home' (2013: 91).

Aside from issues of reciprocity, many Evangelicals are alarmed at the sheer size and number of mosques as well as their strategic location and role. Hal Lindsey,[13] an American author and End Times watcher, makes the unsubstantiated, inaccurate, alarmist claim that in England there are now 'more active mosques than churches' (2002: 6). Writing in 2005, Garlow notes the 'shocking statistic' that 'the number of mosques in the United States has increased 25% in the last five years' (2005: 11). In the UK, while appreciating the 'renowned British tolerance' which allows Muslims to build mosques, some are concerned about 'the growth in the number of mosques' even if there are still many more churches (Pilcrow Press, 2007: 20). Belteshazzar and Abednego, in their booklet *The Mosque and Its Role in Society*, emphasize their conviction that Muslims deliberately build these mosques to be bigger and grander than all other surrounding buildings, particularly churches. They believe that 'such edifices are to prove a point more than [their] actual usage or need' and suggest that 'soon in almost all major British cities the mosques will be the biggest most spectacular buildings' (2006: 23, 37).[14] In other words, in these Evangelicals' opinions, mosques are deliberately built by Muslims as identity-forming symbols.

The foreign funding of mosques is another source of concern. This is particularly the case when the money comes from political or religious sources in Saudi Arabia, Iran or Turkey (P. Sookhdeo, 2008a: 219; W. Wagner, 2012: 99). For instance, in the United States, Gauss warns that the Saudis are 'the biggest exporters of their form of radical Islam (known as Wahhabism) to the West, including the United States. In the United States and throughout Europe they fund the building of mosques from which vehement hatred of the West is preached' (2009: 320). Evangelical author Christopher Catherwood concurs saying that the 'Wahhabi-Hanbali school of interpretation has lots of money, all stemming from the very considerable coffers of the Saudi kingdom. Need a new mosque, complete with an imam? Your Saudi friends will pay!' (2003: 137).

A few take a negative view of *all* mosques. Sookhdeo suggests that 'in Muslim thinking, mosques function as bridgeheads in the struggle to overcome unbelief in territory that is not under Islamic rule and bring it under the authority of Islam. So, Muslims build mosques to widen their geographical sphere of influence and rule' (2011b: 34). In their booklet, Belteshazzar and Abednego stress their understanding that a mosque is not just a religious centre but also a political centre for the Islamization of society, and a military centre from which jihad is launched (2006: 16). In doing this, it is supposed, Muslims are following Muhammad's example, for whom the mosque was 'where he planned his war strategy, held court and received tribal leaders. It was like the Pentagon, the White House and the Supreme Court all in one place. The Islamic world was ruled from the mosque' (Gabriel, 2002: 98).

In contrast to these negative views of the mosque and its role, some see them in more positive light. Kaemingk quotes research to show that, in the American context, it is not Muslims within mosques who have become radicalized. Rather, it is those who are 'disconnected' from the mosques and their attendant communities. He suggests that mosques and other Muslim community spaces 'are actually critical to national security' and 'play a critical role in protecting, nurturing, maturing and extending their [attendees'] Islamic vision of the good life in America' (2018: 279, 281). Wallis tells a story of how a church in Memphis, Tennessee, positively welcomed the building of a new mosque next to its site, even allowing Muslims to pray in their church building while it was being built. He reports that 'the Muslim leaders were astonished … It had not occurred to them that they might be welcomed'. He goes on to tell how 'a group of Muslim men in Kashmir' were so impacted when they heard this story that it caused them to rethink their attitude towards Christians, and one even went to clean the local church in his village. They phoned the pastor and said, 'We are now trying to be good neighbours, too. Pastor, tell your congregation we do not hate them, we love them, and for the rest of our lives we are going to take care of that little church' (Wallis, 2013: 139).

However, in 2017, the Southern Baptists' International Mission Board (IMB) in the United States had to backtrack, and its president, David Platt, had to resign after it supported an Islamic society's legal battle to build a mosque in New Jersey. IMB was accused by its supporters of losing focus on its mission to evangelize and plant churches.[15] Other high-profile mosque building projects have also run into opposition. The most controversial mosque project in the UK was the attempt by the Tablighi Jamaat (TJ) to build a 'mega-mosque' reportedly to accommodate 40,000 worshippers next to the site of the 2012 London Olympics complex.[16] There was an outcry among

Evangelicals, as well as the popular press, against such a large mosque being built in such a prestigious location. The vigorous opposition was led by Evangelical Alan Craig, a local politician then with the Christian People's Alliance Party, with support from Christian Concern, Christian Voice and Jay Smith (2008a), among others.[17] The affair became even more contentious when a building belonging to Kingsway International Christian Centre, the largest church in the UK at the time, was knocked down to make way for the Olympic site, and the church was then refused planning permission to rebuild in the same area (Craig, 2008). In the US context, 'the so-called "Ground Zero Mosque" in New York has also been labelled a mega-mosque'.[18] The original proposal in 2010 to build a mosque near the site of the 9/11 attack on the World Trade Center provoked considerable 'verbal sparring' among Evangelicals (Anyabwile, 2011: 82), most of whom were against the idea, considering it to be disrespectful to the victims and handing a victory to Muslim extremists. 'Even the center's originally proposed name, "the Cordoba House", evoked the Islamic conquest of Spain' (Houssney, 2010: 39). Not all agreed with this assessment, and Wallis saw it as an opportunity to work with the planners – moderate Muslims with whom Wallis felt he could 'work together as peacemakers' (2013: 140).[19]

Other Evangelicals, however, consider this sort of welcome naïve. Increased mosque-building in the West comes at a time when more and more church buildings, particularly in Europe, are closing. Some of these churches are bought by Muslims and turned into mosques and Islamic centres. Although not his view, Musk paints a vivid picture. 'For some Christians ... every church converted into a mosque or every school authority giving in to Muslim parents' demands concerning codes of dress is a defeat before Satan's onslaught' (2003a: 239). Inner-city areas are particularly prone to church buildings becoming mosques. High Muslim population coupled with white flight and declining Christian practice mean that in many places, Christian denominations have found it unsustainable to keep large buildings open for small congregations.[20] Some fear that this could happen in the United States too. Garlow warns that 'if the Evangelical church does not "step up to the plate" many of America's church buildings, within half a century, will have crescent moons on their steeples rather than crosses. (Lest you scoff, there are several former predominantly Christian countries who said, "It will never happen to us". But it did.)' (2005: 84).

Clothing

Another more personal visible identity marker, mentioned in the quotations above, is clothing – and one might include men's beards.[21] A man with a long beard and shaved top lip, wearing a prayer cap and a long white tunic looks like a Muslim. Even more familiar – and contentious – is the clothing worn by Muslim women, be it a hijab, niqab or the all-encompassing burqa. Evangelicals have, with others, frequently expressed concern over the increased prevalence of such dress on Western streets. This is partly fuelled by a concern that it may be an oppressive custom that denigrates women, although oftentimes it is the woman's choice. The veil is also a reminder of the gender segregation enforced in some cultures which runs counter to Western norms. However, Islamic dress is also seen as being a politically motivated statement.

For instance, Sookhdeo believes that 'some modern Muslim women in the West are adopting the strictest version as a way of asserting their Muslim identity' (2008b: 97). In the American context, Anyabwile agrees and says that 'the adorning of veils is as much about *sharia* and its legal requirements as it is about culture. Protecting the wearing of veils begins the process of extending other *sharia*-inspired practices in Western societies' (2011: 94). Others suggest that there is a deliberate progression in a community from wearing the hijab to wearing the niqab, thus signifying increasing Muslim dominance (Solomon and Al-Maqdisi, 2009b: 76).

Again, not all Evangelical writers are so concerned. Larson (2005) recognizes that for Muslim women, wearing the hijab creates a sense of 'sisterhood' that the church has failed to provide. Nazir-Ali likens the burqa to a nun's habit and other religious dress in the Middle East and sees it more as a mark of modesty (2002: 58). Many are aware that the covering is a contested practice even within the Muslim community itself (Riddell, 2010). However, the fact remains that clothing is a very visible marker of identity for which there is little Christian equivalent, at least in the West. In some Evangelical traditions, women might still cover their hair in worship meetings, and outlying groups such as the Amish are very visibly different in their clothing and lifestyle. Organizations such as the Salvation Army, Church Army and Jesus Army wear uniforms, and the occasional more extrovert Evangelical might wear a 'Not Ashamed' t-shirt.[22] However, they are very much the exception.

Religious objects

Muslims may have other symbolic objects such as the *misbaha*, or prayer beads, which they use in dhikr (remembrance of God). There are also various amulets and charms that might be warn as part of 'Folk Islam' (see Chapter 11), although these are not identity markers. In this department, Christians may be more visible. Some Christian traditions have similar objects such as the Catholic prayer beads or the Orthodox prayer rope which can function as visible identity markers when carried publicly. However, such things are rarely used by Evangelicals. More recently, some Evangelicals have started wearing wristbands with cryptic mnemonics such as WWJD (What Would Jesus Do), or Jewish jewellery featuring the Star of David and Hebrew inscriptions, although this would be confusing to outsiders.

However, one ancient symbol still in public use today is the *ichthus*, the fish, which is a mnemonic in Greek for 'Jesus Christ, God's son, saviour'.[23] A simple fish sign was employed as a secret symbol during times of persecution in the early church. This symbol is still widely in use, even among Evangelicals, from lapel pins to bumper stickers and is a low-key way of signalling identity. Some Muslims have noticed this, and in a dark twist, bumper stickers appeared in Cairo featuring Muslim sharks chasing Christian fish.[24]

Another visible symbol is the tattoo. A 2019 report found that religious tattoos have become 'all the rage among growing segments of Evangelical youth culture' in America as a way of 'demonstrating one's identity'. The most common tattoos feature the cross, but many are also verses of scripture. The report's authors point out that 'for centuries, Egyptian Christians (Copts) have set themselves apart from Muslims by getting a small cross tattoo, typically on their right wrist. The Coptic cross tattoo works like an entry badge to get into Christian churches and Christian schools in a country where religious tensions can spur violence'.[25] These tattoos now operate in a similar way among some Western Evangelical youth, although not to differentiate them from Muslims. However, Muslims may not be too impressed with Christian tattoos. For most Muslims, tattoos are considered forbidden, and the idea that one might take a holy symbol or verses of scripture into the bathroom on one's body could be shocking.

Of course, it is not surprising that the cross is the most popular symbol chosen for tattoos. The cross has historically been the preeminent Christian symbol and been worn by Christians and displayed in churches for centuries. However, the cross can be problematic as an identity marker. After all, it is an extremely common item of jewellery. Many people who seemingly have no connection with Christianity or the church wear a cross round their neck. This creates an immediate confusion. Not all those who wear a cross are practising Christians. More serious is the history of the cross itself as a symbol. Since the time tradition records that the Roman emperor Constantine saw a vision of the cross and heard the command to conquer, the symbol of the cross has become confused with political power and military prowess. Crosses have appeared on the shields and cloaks of Christendom's warriors. During the Crusades, 'to take up the cross' was literally interpreted as meaning to sew the cross on one's garment prior to leaving for battle (Glaser, 2010: 10). Moreover, many national flags, including those of Scandinavia and the UK's constituent countries, feature a cross, perhaps usurping its spiritual significance for the nationalist cause.

It seems that the cross as a symbol of faith does not always say what Christians, including Evangelicals, might intend it to say to those outside of the Church. Muslims, Jews and Eastern Christians are frequently reminded of the Crusades – a word derived from the Latin *crux*, meaning cross.[26] Shenk notes that 'tragically the cross maintains its crusader legacy for most Muslims and reminds them of war against Muslims' (2019, 231). This leads Joseph Cumming to lament that

> Satan's greatest masterpiece was the Crusades. Why? Is it because the Crusades were the worst atrocity that ever happened in history? I think Hitler was worse. Stalin was worse. Pol Pot was worse. What is so horrible about the crusades is that it was done under the symbol of the cross, that Satan succeeded in distorting the very heart of the Christian faith. (2008: 322)

This suggests that if Evangelicals want to use the cross as a marker of their identity, they might need to work hard to convince some communities of its spiritual message.

Territory

As suggested above, all these symbols and identity markers have a potent connection to the marking of territory. Buildings, soundscapes, clothing, food laws and language along with rituals, initiation ceremonies and public worship, which are not considered here, all contribute to giving identity not just to people but also to a geographical area.

The concern among some Evangelicals is that these markers suggest that Muslims arriving in Western cities are deliberately creating parallel communities, separate associations and segregated education, all leading to the Islamization of Western societies.[27] These Evangelicals, in company with commentators in other public spheres, fear that Europe, and Britain in particular, is rapidly becoming Islamized, with the United States in future danger.[28]

Parallel communities

According to these Evangelicals, Muslims are deliberately making *hijra* (migration) to the West and are a Trojan Horse. They posit this on Muhammad's migration from Mecca to Medina in 622 AD to form his new political community, suspecting that 'migration is an obligatory duty on Muslims for the enhancement and the advance of Islam', intimately connected with jihad. In which case, 'the first foundational principle for the creation of a successfully visible Islamic society is to be *separate* and *distinct*' (Solomon and Al-Maqdisi, 2009b: 8, 18, original emphasis). All the above identity markers help bring this about. Sookhdeo warns that 'migrant Muslim communities in the West are constantly engaged in sacralising new areas', starting with buying private homes close together effectively creating 'Muslim enclaves'. Then they move into the public sphere with marches, changing place names and building mosques. Once built, a mosque 'can never be given up or demolished' as it has become part of sacred territory. He goes on to warn church ministers against allowing Muslims to pray in their church buildings, lest these too be claimed as sacred Islamic space. All this results in non-Muslims being 'squeezed out of some Muslim-majority areas by various devices' (P. Sookhdeo, 2008a: 52–3). So, plenty of Evangelicals are critical of government policies on immigration. Nazir-Ali points out that both British-style multiculturalism and French-style assimilation have resulted in young Muslims feeling alienated (2006: 163). In a volume exploring 'Faith and Power', co-edited with Newbigin and Sanneh (2005), Jenny Taylor shares her concern that the weakness of Western governments and the growth of multiculturalism has allowed 'the emergence, with state collusion, of discrete territories where vastly different norms prevail, shut off and sometimes resentful, a breeding ground for ferment and a target for hostility' (2005: 107).

Even Chapman recognizes that this territoriality has been a historical trend and says that 'bringing land under the control of Islam and keeping it within Islam has always been a very fundamental goal for Muslims who know anything of their history' (2007b: 85). Azumah observes a similar trend in Africa:

> The unashamedly public face of Islam (the minarets, call to prayer, veiling of women etc) makes the tendency to colonise space very high in Islam. Even in places where there are only a few Muslims one cannot miss them. One can see, feel and breathe Islam! … Their motivation is to announce the Islamic presence and lay claim to the public space for posterity. (2008b: 11)

However, he also sees Christians and white Westerners as contributing to this phenomenon as Christians tend to 'retreat from the public space by vacating or avoiding

Muslim suburbs and communities ... [thus] conceding the public space to Muslims'.[29] Richard Sudworth, who is secretary for inter-religious affairs to the Archbishop of Canterbury, agrees, seeing 'the drift of Christians from poorer communities into affluent suburbs' as a potential abandonment of the church's mission. He has 'a sneaking feeling that some Christians would prefer a *cordon sanitaire* of Christianity in Britain, a place which didn't have to deal with the messiness of turbans, veils and gurus', thus leaving ethnic minority communities isolated (2007: 147, 158). Bell too identifies the problem of white flight and is more sympathetic to isolated Muslim communities who are after all 'ordinary human beings'. He can understand 'why these immigrants preferred to live in clan ghettos in the UK ... [as] it safeguarded their identity and gave mutual support' (Bell, 2006: 11–12). Similarly, Nazir-Ali admits that Islamophobia has played a role in increasing this 'ghettoization' by creating fear (2002: 74), although in later writing he has been critical of 'a worldwide resurgence of the ideology of Islamic extremism' which has helped 'alienate young [Muslims] from the nation in which they were growing up' and turned 'already separate communities into "no-go" areas where adherence to this ideology has become a mark of acceptability' (Nazir-Ali, 2008a). His comments about no-go areas created a furore in the British media and among his fellow bishops.[30]

Associations

As part of the settlement of any migrant community, new associations and institutions are formed. This has naturally been the case for Muslims in the West, but again some Evangelicals are suspicious of their motives. Sookhdeo in his 'handbook on British Islam', titled *Faith, Power and Territory*, lists a raft of Muslim institutions in Britain, including charitable, financial, legal, media and educational associations along with their attendant 'umbrella organizations', such the Muslim Council of Britain (MCB) and the Mosques and Imams' National Advisory Board (MINAB) (2008a: chapters 6–12). He later did the same in the US context (Sookhdeo, 2011a: chapter 3). He suspects that these institutions 'vary their discourse to suit different audiences', their real intentions only being 'made known in what they say to fellow-Muslims'. For instance, in the UK, he accuses Muslim lobby groups of lobbying 'mainstream society ... to place Islam and Muslims beyond criticism, which would be tantamount to achieving a privileged status in comparison with all other British communities' (P. Sookhdeo, 2008a: 133, 202). Others suspect the Council on American-Islamic Relations (CAIR) and the Islamic Society of North America (ISNA) of having similar agendas (e.g. Youssef, 2015: 21).

Some of these associations, such as the madrasas, are educational, and there is concern that Muslims are engaged in trying to segregate education. Gauss thinks that the Saudis are the 'major backers of madrassahs [*sic*] in the United States and other Western countries – schools that teach the most radical form of Islam' (2009: 320). This is often linked to violent radicalization in the Evangelical mind, although conservative Saudi expressions of Islam are not necessarily violent. Others feel that Muslims receive preferential treatment within the state school system. For instance, in one case, Garlow claims that 'the New York City Public Schools administration now allows Muslim children to be excused from classes to go to a state-funded classroom for their daily prayers. Christian children are forbidden to pray or conduct Bible studies in the same schools' (2005: 85). In some places, catchment areas are predominantly Muslim, and in the UK, the state is funding some Muslim faith schools, creating fears that 'such schools will increase segregation of Muslim young people from mainstream society as well as potentially be a source of radicalism' (P. Sookhdeo, 2008a: 181).[31]

Islamization

For all these reasons, many Evangelicals fear that there is a conspiracy under way in Western societies. This involves Muslims deliberately coming to the West, then seeking the 'Islamization' of these non-Muslim-majority societies. This is all part of 'Islam's plan for world domination' (D. Richardson, 2003: 160), and they point to sub-Saharan Africa, Malaysia and Indonesia as historical examples of places which they believe were gradually overrun or Islamized by Muslim immigration and *da'wa* ('invitation', i.e. proselytization) (Solomon and Al-Maqdisi, 2009b: 85–8; see also P. Sookhdeo, 2014a). The presumed strategy is 'to infiltrate the educational, academic, and economic systems as well as the power centres and political lobbies in order to impact them in favor of Islam'. This 'works especially well in societies that harbor relatively large Muslim societies' (Zeidan, 2003: 97). In a similar vein, 'where direct military confrontation is inadvisable' for conquest, Robinson suggests that Muslims rely on 'propaganda', 'political processes', 'social engineering', 'demographic change', and he adds 'terrorism' to the list (2003: 216–18). In the United States, Garlow believes that American Christians 'incorrectly assume that Islam is "merely a religion". They often fail to see the multifaceted nature of this religious-legal-military-political force'. He goes on to suggest that 'Americans would do well to recognize that some Muslim immigrants have come to the US to convert America and believe that America needs to be rescued by Islamic solutions to its moral failure' (Garlow, 2005: 56, 59).

This is certainly not a new concern. G. K. Chesterton's 1914 novel *The Flying Inn*, a story of Islam taking over the UK and banning alcohol sales, only reflects European concerns dating back to the Ottoman incursions into Europe during the sixteenth and seventeenth centuries. So, it is not surprising that fears of Islamization and warnings of a 'threat' have constituted a whole genre of Evangelical writing and speaking on Islam in the first two decades of the twenty-first century. For instance, American William Wagner,[32] former missionary and vice president of the Southern Baptist Convention, explains *How Islam Plans to Change the World*. He invokes the imagery of an Arab proverb that 'if the camel once gets his nose in the tent, his body will soon follow', and he warns of a four-fold 'loose strategy' that Muslims have involving *da'wa*, jihad, mosque building and immigration (W. Wagner, 2012: 16, 43–4). A short anonymous booklet, *The Islamization of Britain: And What Must Be Done to Prevent It* (2007), details suspected Muslim incursion in the realms of Western commerce, finance, law, culture and politics. The same concern exists in other countries. Abdullah Al-Araby, a pseudonym meaning the Arab servant of God, produced an early Evangelical book, endorsed by Gabriel and Morey, on *The Islamization of America* (2003) and the needed 'Christian response'. American Rick Joyner leads the Morning Star prophetic ministry as well as the Oak Initiative.³³ In 2010, he spoke out, as did others, against the proposed building of the mosque at Ground Zero in New York and warned of the 'Threat of Islam to America' (Joyner, 2010). Wagner claims that in London over 600 mosques have been built since 1960, and whereas 'a mere thirty years ago there was only one mosque in Bethlehem [Palestine], today there are eighty-nine' (2012: 96, 104). Robinson cites Saudi-funded mosque building in sub-Saharan Africa and the power of Islamic financial institutions (2010: 20).

Associated with this, the Muslim push for the accommodation and incorporation of Islamic finance, focused on the Sharia's ban on interest, is another statement of Islamic identity in the West. Sookhdeo in a full-length book concludes that 'shariʻa finance is part of a wider agenda of jihad, in accordance with the vision of Islamist ideologists of the overthrow of non-Islamic systems and the establishment of a pan-Islamic caliphate that will rule the earth' (2008b: 39).

Again, Evangelicals complain of an imbalance and a lack of reciprocity in the demand for religious and cultural accommodation. Zacharias notes 'how difficult Islamic countries make it for those of other faiths living among them, but how demanding Islam can be of the American culture to provide it unlimited freedom'. His message is that Western Evangelicals need to mobilize to protect their nations from the danger of Islamization. 'One is entitled to freedom, but one is not free from the responsibility to protect the nation's right to exist on the terms that made it great in the first place. Culture is dangerous when it is used to hijack the basic ethos of a nation' (Zacharias, 2002: 104).

De Ruiter observes that 'the presence of Islam in Europe forces Christians to deal with the issue of identity and diversity' and wonders whether 'one's fear of Islam is a fear of losing one's identity' (2010: 58). However, although the trope of Islamization is very common among Western Evangelicals, by no means all Evangelicals are so afraid or negative. While agreeing that Islam is 'radically subversive of Western political order wherever, in any diaspora, an Islam of classic mind-set is present', Cragg footnotes that 'happily, innumerable diaspora Muslims de facto give the lie to this charge that their presence is subversive'. He feels that 'they seek – and deserve – to be trusted' (2005: 159n5). Deanna Womack, an American Presbyterian minister and academic, believes that 'some media outlets mistakenly suggest that immigration and rising diversity threatens America's Christian majority. In reality, Christians will make up the majority of the US population for the foreseeable future' (2020: 12). Bell too is sanguine and sees that 'Muslim fertility rates are dropping noticeably in Europe' and affirms that 'Christians do not need to fear Islamic take-over in the UK'. After all God is sovereign, and the presence of so many Muslims in the West 'cannot be a mistake or God is not sovereign. It is God who is steering human history to His appointed end' (Bell 2008).

Discussion: A(n) (un)civil public square?

This chapter has thrown up several areas which Evangelicals need to consider carefully. Firstly, one of the great ironies surrounding concerns over parallel communities which do not integrate with the host culture is that Western expatriates during the colonial era frequently did not integrate into the colonies, but rather set up compounds to insulate themselves from 'the natives'. With admittedly many notable exceptions, they did not bother to learn the languages, saw no need to adapt to the host cultures and kept themselves to themselves. Of course, the power dynamic was very different but, maybe, no less concerning for all that. The colonists were there to control, exploit and bend the hosts to their will. Some now fear that Muslims might be doing the same thing in their day.

In fact, the compound is a useful image. A compound has a clear boundary, maybe even a physical fence, much like the identity markers we have seen above. It is very clear who the in-group is and who the out-group is.[34] The fence is there precisely to keep the out-group out. Indeed, many Evangelicals are now using the ideas of Paul Hiebert to talk about whether churches should be 'centred sets' or 'bounded sets'.[35] Is a boundary – guarded by formal membership or statements of faith, maybe – necessary, or is it sufficient for people or members to be heading towards the central truth? This shows that the idea of identity and boundaries is very much alive in Evangelical minds and will be seen again in Chapter 13 when we consider the identities of those Muslims who choose to convert to Christianity.

Secondly, the discussion raises the issue of what Evangelicals think a plural society should look like. Newbigin, one of the most widely respected and frequently quoted Evangelical thinkers on society, believed that 'a Christian must welcome plurality but reject pluralism'.[36] Many different images are used to represent this dilemma. Is society a 'melting pot', in which everyone loses their distinctives to become part of the national dish, or a mosaic 'patchwork quilt', in which everyone is alongside but separate and distinct, or a 'fruit salad', in which the individual parts remain distinguishable but are more integrated? We have seen critiques of multiculturalism and how, at least in its British forms, it has overemphasized celebrating cultural (and religious) difference to the exclusion of shared values, integration and good judgement. Os Guinness, an Evangelical author and social critic, repudiates such multicultural relativism, believing it leads to 'the evils of complacency'. Something more robust is required as 'there are rights that require defending, evils that must be resisted, and interferences into the affairs of others that are morally justifiable' (Guinness 2010: 178).

This raises the question of faith in the public square more generally. Many Evangelicals understand that Islam is not just a religion but also a way of life, which usually includes a vision for civil society and for government. In response, some Western Evangelicals hanker for a Christendom model in which the church had considerable temporal power in a religious monopoly. Others, in seeking to protect society from Islam, or any other coercive religion, favour a strict secularity which removes religion from public life. Guinness rejects both these extremes and argues that 'the Evangelical choice is for a civil public square – a vision of public life in which citizens of all faiths are free to enter and engage the public square on the basis of their faith, but within a framework of what is agreed to be just and free for other faiths too' (2010: 178). The key here is coming to agreement across different cultures, worldviews and ideologies on what is just.

Thirdly, such agreements need to be reached in the knowledge that there are Muslims who *do* have plans for *da'wa* and the Islamization of Western societies. At the same time, many other Muslims are naturally keen for more accommodation of their religion and will, by their very lifestyles and engagement in the community, influence culture more generally. So, Evangelicals and others should not be naïve while not succumbing to fear, scapegoating and conspiracy theories. Rather, Evangelicals should be all the more committed to embodying their own calling as salt and light in society (Matt. 5.13–16).

Lastly, this calling should be not least evident in caring for Muslims. This chapter has mainly considered the case of Muslim minorities in Western contexts. Doubtless, many of these Muslims feel powerless, marginalized and abused. Certainly, there has been a sad litany of unprovoked attacks against innocent Muslims on Western streets, especially following the events of 9/11. Christians should be vocal and active in combatting such abuse.[37] Yet, many Evangelicals see these Western Muslims as powerful actors, cynically benefitting from Western liberal freedoms and rights, guided and resourced by conniving Muslims from outside. In their estimation, these Muslims do not need protection against Islamophobia (see Chapter 2) but rather need to be restrained. This is in what they see as a stark contrast to the lack of rights and freedoms available to Christian minorities living in Muslim-majority contexts, the focus of the next chapter.

8

Persecution

Arguably no problem is more damaging to the image of Islam in the minds of Western Evangelicals than the pressure and disadvantage experienced by Christian minorities and converts in Muslim-majority contexts around the world. Indeed, De Ruiter identifies it as one of the major 'fear-raising factors' among Evangelicals (2010: 44). Two high-profile cases illustrate the problem. Asia Bibi, an illiterate Pakistani Catholic farm worker, was arrested and charged with blasphemy in 2009. Subsequently sentenced to death for supposedly insulting Muhammad during a dispute with a Muslim neighbour over a drinking cup, her case received international attention and raised concerns over the implementation and abuse of blasphemy laws in Pakistan (Bibi, 2020). The long legal trial process was punctuated by the assassinations of Salman Taseer and Shahbaz Bhatti, politicians who dared defend her, along with death threats against the trial judges from Muslim clerics. Bibi was finally released in 2019 after international pressure and relocated to Canada.[1]

In a second example, Abdul Rahman, an Afghan Muslim who had converted to Christianity, was sentenced to death in Afghanistan in 2006. The trial judge reportedly stated that 'the Prophet Muhammad has said several times that those who convert from Islam should be killed if they refuse to come back'. He went on to add that 'Islam is a religion of peace, tolerance, kindness and integrity. That is why we have told him if he regrets what he did, then we will forgive him.'[2] Rahman too was finally released, again after international pressure.

These stories illustrate just two of the concerns – blasphemy and apostasy laws – troubling Evangelicals with regard to freedoms for Christians – and others – living under Islamic jurisdiction. Along with the usual authors and commentators in the Evangelical public sphere, there are many Evangelical advocacy groups dedicated to supporting the 'suffering church' or 'the church under pressure'.[3] They maintain websites, produce monthly magazines, circulate newsletters asking for prayer, raise petitions and speak in churches. Their publications carry a litany of disturbing stories of how Christians are suffering for their faith around the world today, and, although some of the agencies were originally started because of Christian persecution under communism behind the Iron Curtain and in China, Muslim contexts now feature prominently, albeit with a rising number concerning Hindu extremism in India.

Before looking at some of the arguments, it is worth noting that there is perhaps less disagreement among Evangelicals over the issues surrounding the persecution of Christian minorities than any other topic in this book. It is something that is demonstrably happening.[4] It is hard for Evangelicals to ignore the suffering of other members of the Christian family. The stories speak for themselves and are backed up by media reports and academic research. How it should be reported and what can be done to support the freedom of religion and belief (FoRB) is not so easy.

Evangelical reports of persecution

The World Evangelical Alliance (WEA) has held an 'International Day of Prayer for the Persecuted Church' since 1996, and its secretary general, Thomas Schirrmacher,[5] insists that 'the part of the Church which is free of persecution, cannot ignore the large numbers of Christians under severe persecution and even threat of death, but must act'. At the same time, he is aware that claims about the extent of Christian persecution provoke a reaction from the media and others who feel 'it disparages other religions or means that their persecution is less evil' (Schirrmacher, 2018: 16, 137).

Open Doors is an example of an Evangelical advocacy group that is trying to act and 'support persecuted Christians worldwide'.[6] It is well known among Evangelicals, partly due to the life and writings of its founder, Brother Andrew (d. 2022), who was known as 'God's Smuggler'.[7] As part of its awareness-raising programme, it publishes what it calls a 'World Watch List' listing the top fifty countries where 'following Jesus costs the most'.[8] Of the countries on the list in 2022, over thirty were Muslim-majority countries, several of which, including Afghanistan (1), Pakistan (8), Iran (9) and Saudi Arabia (11), incorporate the Sharia into their legal systems (Chapter 6).

The Barnabas Fund is another advocacy group which works to 'provide hope and aid for the persecuted Church', and while dealing with persecution in Hindu, Buddhist and secular countries, it takes a particularly keen interest in Islamic situations.[9] It has in the past produced a similar index to that of Open Doors, called the 'Convert Danger Index', published in its bimonthly magazine called *Barnabas Aid*, which catalogues stories of Christians under pressure in many parts of the world and frequently highlights the Muslim case, often illustrated with articles about different aspects of Islam.[10] Barnabas Fund's founder, Patrick Sookhdeo, has also published several books relating to Christian persecution (2009b, 2019, 2002).

Many other Evangelical advocacy groups feature in this chapter, which looks at the different causes Evangelical writers and agencies identify as impacting the treatment of Christians in Muslim contexts. These include the historical *dhimmi* status of minorities, the Pact of 'Umar, Muslim extremism and ethnic cleansing, restrictions on church building, blasphemy laws, the ban on proselytizing Muslims, laws governing apostasy and conversion away from Islam, and geopolitical realities. They all raise questions as to how Evangelicals should respond to the situation of their co-religionists living among Muslims.

Perceived causes

The *dhimma* and Pact of 'Umar

For some Evangelical writers, these issues date back to Muhammad's lifetime and the early days of Islamic expansion. Zaka and Coleman paint a picture of how in his early life Muhammad 'greatly admired both Jews and Christians' but then, according to them, later 'became more critical … referring to them as infidels' (2004: 33, 9). Riddell and Cotterell record how 'Muhammad is said to have offered [these] people three options: conversion to Islam, submission to Islamic rule or death' and see in this the beginning of the *dhimmi* system (2003: 73). A *dhimmi* refers to Jews, Christians and certain others who lived under the *dhimma* (covenant of protection) of the Muslim authorities in return for paying the *jizya* tax and accepting certain restrictions on their property, activities and freedom.[11]

For some minorities, the new rulers may not have been as bad as the previous Byzantine Christian rulers. 'All the Muslim conquests did was to substitute one kind of oppression for another, and for all intents and purposes Islamic oppression was less obnoxious to them than to be harassed by the church and state authorities' (Catherwood, 2003: 67; see also Riddell and Cotterell, 2003: 90). Nonetheless, rather more Evangelical writers take a negative view of the *dhimmi* regulations. Azumah questions why Christians would need 'protection' in the first place:

> Some Muslims have always tried to reassure non-Muslims that as *dhimmis* under an Islamic System, they have nothing to fear. However, leaving aside the obvious debilitating and discriminatory aspects of the sharia regarding the *dhimmis*, the meaning of the term itself, 'protected persons', is not only condescending and patronising but also implies hostility and therefore arouses suspicion. (2001: 201; see also Merkley, 2001: 112)

Others see in the system the seeds of a psychological 'complex' they refer to as 'dhimmitude', which is typified by servile attitudes caused by socio-religious disadvantage (e.g. Scot and Abdulhaq, 2009: 71–3; Durie, 2009c).[12] Drawing on the work of Bat Ye'or, as several of these writers do, Don Richardson explains that after the initial Arab expansion, 'fewer and fewer Jews and Christians were forced to convert to Islam, because those left unconverted could be subjected to unconscionable extortion'. This amounted to 'a strategy of milking Jews and Christians' (2003: 153–4). Durie also argues that the *jizya* was much more punitive than often suggested by Muslims today. He claims that at times it was the equivalent of one to three months wages compared to the 2.5 per cent *zakat* tax paid by Sunni Muslims, equivalent to, maybe, only one week's wages (2009c: 167–8). Scot and Abdulhaq have an even higher figure. Quoting a hadith, they claim that at one time for the Jews of Khaybar, 'Muhammad charged 50% of their income' (2009: 72).[13]

In time, after the death of Muhammad, a document appeared called the Pact of 'Umar, which is often attributed to the second caliph of that name.[14] In it a group of unknown Christians agree to certain restrictions being placed on them by their Muslim overlords. Many Evangelical authors rehearse the conditions the Christian party promised to abide by (see, for instance, Chapman, 2007b: 329; Scot and Abdulhaq, 2009: 72; W. Wagner, 2012: 133). Durie summarizes them as restrictions on conversion, marriage, worship and practice of faith, opposition to Muslims, critiquing Islam, the exercise of authority, housing, public appearance, status and behaviour. There was also a demand that *dhimmis* should render assistance and loyalty to Muslims (Durie, 2009c: 141–6). Nazir-Ali, while recognizing some improvements over previous systems, is concerned that such regulations introduced 'innovations, such as the wearing of special dress by the *dhimmis* and the ritual humiliations that they had to face in their daily life' (2012: 65).

The Barnabas Fund is particularly concerned about the legacy of the *dhimmi* system and the Pact of 'Umar today and, in a study guide on Islam, points out that today 'just as in the early days of Islam, most Christians in Muslim countries are not treated as equal citizens. The kind of problems and pressure they face vary from country to country. But many of the restrictions they suffer are like the sharia rules for *dhimmis*'. It goes on to comment that 'it is sad that Christians sometimes convert to Islam to escape the pressures on them in Muslim countries' (Barnabas Fund, 2011b: 67).

Muslim extremists and ethnic cleansing

Other agencies are more sparing in their contemporary use of the term *dhimmi*. For instance, Open Doors usually employs it only in the context of extremism in the Middle East, such as when it reported the savage ISIS ultimatum to non-Muslims, mimicking the historical options mentioned above: 'We offer them three choices: Islam, the *dhimmi* contract, and if they refuse this they have nothing but the sword.'[15] Rather, in a commentary in the *Open Doors* magazine in 2016, it explained that the World Watch List, described above, shows that 'Islamic extremism' – and not Islam in general – 'is by far the most common driver of persecution'.[16] Likewise, Schirrmacher believes that fundamentalism and religious nationalism are the top two causes of 'increasingly limiting religious freedom'. He notes that 'the main culprits are predominantly not governments or people groups. Rather, it is above all violent, fundamentalist movements, which in most cases fight against the governments of their countries of origin', although he makes exceptions for the regimes in Iran, Saudi Arabia and Pakistan (Schirrmacher, 2018: 142–3).

For instance, many non-Muslims were killed by ISIS, a non-government militia, in Iraq and Syria, and these events were widely reported by the media around the world. Moreover, similar threats have been noted in other parts of the world where Muslim extremists are active. In an article for *Christianity* magazine in the UK, Evangelical Johnnie Moore, a two-time presidential appointee to the United States Commission for International Religious Freedom, highlights 'Africa's Silent Genocide' with 'radicalized Fulani militants in the Middle Belt [of Nigeria] increasingly appropriating the terrorist tactics of Boko Haram and IS [Islamic State] as they torture Christians and their communities'. Quoting Nigerian sources, he reports that 'thousands of churches have been torched, scores of children slaughtered, countless women enslaved, pastors have been beheaded and Christian homes have been set ablaze … and the victims are mainly Christian' (Moore, 2021: 33, 5; see also Moore and Cooper, 2020).

Other publications mentioned in this chapter frequently report on such atrocities. For Schirrmacher, they are reminiscent of the massacres of Armenian and Assyrian Christians at the hands of the Muslim Ottomans in the early twentieth century. In a WEA publication, he warns that today there is still 'constant ethnic cleansing carried out by Islamic states against Christian peoples (for example in southern Sudan)'. Referencing the exodus of Christians from the Middle East following the Second Gulf War and the rise of ISIS, he goes on to speculate that 'if the developments seen over the prior years continue, [the Islamic world] will perhaps soon be Christian-free, with the exception of Southeast Asia' (Schirrmacher, 2018: 102, 144). Sookhdeo similarly wonders if 'the rapid Christian exodus in response to the radical Islam and Islamist violence of our day means that these countries too may soon be emptied of all Christian witness' (2019: 67). Finally, Kendal does not hesitate to claim that 'genocide is unfolding in the ancient Christian heartland' of the Middle East. The innocuous title of her book, *After Saturday Comes Sunday*, references an apparently 'popular Arab war cry' which has the chilling meaning of 'as sure as Saturday (the day of Jewish worship) is followed by Sunday (the day of Christian worship), first we'll kill the Jews, then we'll kill the Christians'.[17] The carefully researched book details the decline of both communities in their historical homeland and describes the brutal atrocities perpetrated against them following the Western intervention in Iraq, decrying the silence of Western Christians who have failed to speak out in their support (Kendal, 2016: KL157).[18]

Blasphemy laws and freedom of conscience

Another serious issue for Evangelicals is the use of blasphemy laws to discriminate against and punish Christian and other minorities. Pakistan has seen a particularly high incidence of such cases, and in 2021, International Christian Concern (ICC) produced a special report titled *The Voiceless Victims of Pakistan's Blasphemy Laws*. It recounts the story of Asia Bibi, mentioned above, and details over twenty other personal stories of how 'members of Pakistan's religious minority communities are disproportionately accused and punished under the country's blasphemy laws' which are often 'widely abused to settle personal scores and incite religious hatred' (Stark, 2021: 1).

Another group, Release International, has also been 'calling for many years for the repeal of Pakistan's blasphemy laws, which fuel religious hatred and are often used to target minorities'.[19] They frequently send out stories in e-mails about Christians charged with blasphemy and, in 2016, started an online petition 'to abolish blasphemy laws in Pakistan'.[20] Nazir-Ali suggests that if this is to happen, 'the only real solution is to find resources in Islamic tradition itself to question the very basis of the law and thus to lead to its repeal' (2012: 63). However, ICC cautions that, while 'it would be ideal if Pakistan's blasphemy laws were repealed altogether, publicly advocating for this action is likely to anger religious fundamentalists and worsen the condition of those still in prison'. In the meantime, ICC recommends 'quiet, consistent, and specific advocacy on behalf of each individual' and makes recommendations on how this should be done (Stark, 2021: 5).

Release International also campaigns for the release of prisoners of conscience, including Christians. Many of these are held in prisons in Muslim contexts, and for each prisoner, Release International publishes a 'Prisoner Profile' appealing for prayer and asking people to write letters of support. One such high-profile prisoner was the Christian former governor of Jakarta, Indonesia, Basuki Tjahaja Purnama (known as 'Ahok'), who in 2017 was 'imprisoned for blasphemy in a politically-motivated campaign and sentenced to two years in prison'.[21] Voice of the Martyrs (VOM) also publishes 'Prisoner Alerts' to raise awareness and mobilize prayer.[22]

Restrictions on Evangelism

The plight of some of these prisoners illustrates the concern these organizations have over the restrictions on Christians evangelizing Muslims. For instance, according to VOM, Abraham Ben Moses, 'a well-known former Muslim and Christian apologist in Indonesia', is in prison for blasphemy, although his real crime is being 'active in Internet evangelism and debates with Muslim groups'.[23] He was filmed apparently speaking with a taxi driver about Muhammad and inviting the driver to convert to Christianity, which led to a large Islamic organization filing a complaint, leading to his arrest.

Sookhdeo sees all these things as part of a vicious spiral of historical Muslim discrimination against Christian and other minorities which continues to this day:

> The subjugation of Christians by Muslims is a phenomenon repeated around the world from C7th to C21st. Effectively there is a cycle in which discriminatory laws reinforce discriminatory attitudes, which in turn lead to calls for more discriminatory laws. Unlike Christianity, Islam has no teaching about loving your enemies nor that all human beings are of equal worth. So, there is nothing to break the cycle unless Islam itself can be reformed in line with modern concepts of human rights and religious liberty. (2010a: 51)

Even though the Ottomans formally abandoned the *dhimmi* laws in the nineteenth century, Durie warns that 'today they are making a comeback as part of the worldwide shari'a revival' (2009b: 32), and he quotes examples from Afghanistan, Pakistan, Egypt, Malaysia, Nigeria and Iran (2009c: chapter 8). Even where *dhimmi* laws are not formally part of national laws, there are reports of individual Islamic preachers 'invoking the teaching to inspire violent mob attacks on minorities in Indonesia, Northern Nigeria and Pakistan' (Azumah and Bahri, 2009: 145).

Some Evangelicals recognize that there are Muslims working to improve the situation for Christian minorities. For instance, Evangelical leaders Roberts and Rick Love (d. 2019), former director of the Frontiers mission agency, attended a 2016 consultation hosted by the Moroccan government and the Forum for Promoting Peace in Muslim Societies, which resulted in the signing of the Marrakesh Declaration.[24] This document is a call for the protection of 'the rights of religious minorities in predominantly Muslim majority communities' and draws on the Constitution of Medina, an agreement that Muhammad is reported to have made with the people of Medina, including non-Muslims, after his migration there in 622 AD. Many Christian leaders received the document warmly. For instance, Love called it a 'game changer' although cautioning 'it is too early to determine the actual impact this declaration will have'.²⁵ Interestingly, Nazir-Ali had presciently suggested in 2012 that the Constitution of Medina might serve 'as a model for polities in Muslim countries in which non-Muslims play an equal part as citizens rather than dhimmis' (2012: 66). Others were more sceptical. Riddell (2016) felt the new document 'avoids hard questions' and suggested it was 'naive to accept the positive words of the Marrakesh Declaration without scrutinising the very document which the declaration declares to be its foundation stone ... [as the Constitution of Medina] still assumes that Islam predominates, and that all matters of significance and dispute shall be resolved within an Islamic framework'.

Ban on apostasy

The biggest concern for most Evangelicals is what happens when a Muslim leaves Islam to become a Christian. By definition, this is a deliberate goal for Evangelicals and so becomes a touchstone issue for them, and there is no shortage of accounts and testimonies, such as the twenty-three stories told in *Why We Left Islam* (Crimp and Richardson, 2008). However, many Evangelical authors point out that all the Sharia law schools still criminalize leaving Islam, which is termed 'apostasy' (*ridda*), and that the punishment for a male apostate is death. Moreover, there is still strong support for such a law in some parts of the world.²⁶ This means that in many places Islam is in effect 'a one-way door' (Azumah, 2006: 21; also Bell, 2006: 47). Riddell believes that 'conversion represents one of the greatest obstacles in Christian-Muslim interaction in the modern world. This should not be swept under the carpet, as it were. Indeed, it cries out for sensitive discussion' (2004: 178). Evangelical writers as far apart as Volf and Sookhdeo agree that 'the laws against apostasy must go' (Volf, 2011: 234), as 'the only hope for real freedom of religion within Islam lies in the abolition of all penalties for apostasy and permission for those who want to leave Islam to do so' (P. Sookhdeo, 2009b: 100).

Most Evangelical advocacy groups publish reports of those leaving Islam being either imprisoned or threatened with death. For instance, Elam Ministries, which exists to 'strengthen and expand the church in the Iran region and beyond', keeps a list of those in prison in Iran and those recently released.²⁷ It notes that 'the threat of an apostasy conviction hangs over converts from Islam, which, for men, would result in the death penalty if applied' and tells the story of Youcef Nadarkhani, one such convert sentenced to death, who was later acquitted, although he continued to be harassed and rearrested.²⁸ Indeed, a 116-page report from CSW²⁹ on the 'experiences of apostates from Islam', titled *No Place to Call Home*, notes that such sentences are rarely carried out 'due to international sensitivities' but that discrimination continues (Meral, 2008: 47). The report detailed the constitutional situation in all Muslim-majority countries and found that while only 'Sudan and Malaysia have codified laws which stipulate capital punishment for apostasy', other countries such as Saudi Arabi, Mauritania and Iran rely on Sharia for their law and so, therefore, by implication, do have the death penalty. Where such laws do not exist, other laws are used to harass and punish apostates. The report lists some examples such as 'harming national unity' in Iran and Egypt; blasphemy in Pakistan; 'shaking the faith of a Muslim' in Algeria; and 'reviling Islam' and 'insulting Turkishness' in Turkey (Meral, 2008: 48–9). Finally, quite apart from the legal dimension, there is huge social pressure against apostasy. Families and whole communities will often shun those who renounce Islam. In extreme cases, apostates are even killed to expunge the shame that is perceived to have been brought on the family or community.

Political dimensions

The situations of Christian minorities and converts are often politically charged, and governments are under intense pressure from Muslim extremists to take a hard line against any activity that is seen as weakening, belittling or besmirching Islam. Sookhdeo observes that 'whenever tensions increase between the West and Islam there is a backlash against Christians in Muslim states' (2007: 371). On occasion, Muslim governments may use religious freedom issues for their own strategic purposes, and Western governments may intervene on behalf of Christian individuals or communities. However, some Evangelicals warn that such Western political intervention is a double-edged sword. It can signal to Muslims that a Christian minority or agency has Western political support and is a sort of Western fifth column in their midst, which is a danger to their security. Thus, there is an ambiguity for the world church in 'pursuing advocacy for suffering Christians in marginal situations while trying to avoid a repetition of perceived colonising interference that may exacerbate the insecurity' of local Christians (Sudworth, 2017: 76).

Such seemingly good intentions run the risk of sheer hypocrisy when the West then supports undemocratic, despotic regimes. President El-Sisi of Egypt is a case in point. Despite his 'unprecedented crackdown on freedom of expression', many Evangelicals view him positively because he overthrew an Islamist government and has since been relatively supportive of Christians in Egypt.[30] In November 2017, a group of American Christians, including well-known 'Evangelical advisors to Trump's White House', met with El-Sisi.[31] Talks included religious freedom, the rebuilding of churches and relations with Israel. *Barnabas Aid* has also commented positively on El-Sisi's government as being 'very supportive of the Christian minority'.[32] Likewise, it has been positive about President Assad, observing that 'the Assad regime in Syria had afforded considerable freedom and protection to Christians and other minorities; if it falls, there is some danger that the greater part of the church in Syria will be obliterated'.[33] These calculations clearly lead to a conflict in values.

Evangelical responses to persecution

In 2018, a report titled *Under Caesar's Sword* investigated how Christian communities react when their religious freedom is restricted, and it found three main types of responses: survival, association, confrontation. 'Survival' includes 'going underground, flight, and accommodation to or support for repressive regimes' such as those above. 'Association' involves building partnerships with other actors, Christian or not, who may support their cause. Finally, 'confrontation', the least common response, involves mobilizing to end injustice and, in very rare cases, violence.[34]

Advocacy and campaigning

For the first of these responses, as has been seen, there are many Evangelical groups seeking to support Christians who are trying to survive under pressure. They do so by publishing magazines, bulletins and e-mails to raise awareness, call to prayer and encourage petitions and letter-writing. Meral, himself an advocate, notes that these groups focus on three approaches: 'awareness raising, capacity building, and advocacy'. However, he believes the majority are only successful in two of these, with the least successful being advocacy. The reason he sees for this is that many are single-faith groups producing data that 'undermines their credibility, as the vast majority of the documents they produce are anecdotal and often hagiographical accounts of suffering and martyrdom' (Meral 2012: 29). Added to this, he admits that as Christians 'we perceive events through our own lenses, shaped by our questions, worries and limitations. We often find what we want to find and often choose a clear-cut and simple answer rather than allow the truth to remain patchy, complicated and much bigger than our particular concerns' (Meral 2011: 121–2).

Meral believes the most successful form of advocacy is 'quiet diplomacy' backed up by 'first rate research documents and briefings' focusing on 'international law rather than theology'. He sees the future lying not with single-faith groups but with 'robust non-sectarian organizations, especially those based in the non-Western world, with clear commitment for advancing religious freedom rights for everyone' of any religion or none (2012: 30–2). Writing in the *Cambridge Papers*, a quarterly Evangelical publication which 'help[s] Christians engage with a complex and changing world', Judd Birdsall agrees. He reports a lack of trust in 'religious freedom groups' within government and diplomatic circles, which prefer to work with 'the mainstream secular human rights organisations'. He highlights various pitfalls in Christian advocacy work, including the temptation to exaggerate for fund-raising purposes, uncritical partiality towards Christians and the neglect of the persecution of non-Christians (2018: 3).

Insistence on reciprocity

As another strategy to ameliorate the situation of Christian minorities in survival mode, some Evangelicals advocate a greater emphasis on reciprocity in Christian-Muslim relations. For instance, Cox and Marks want Muslims to 'acknowledge that there are few Muslim countries that offer Christians, Jews or those of other religions the freedom to practice their religion that Muslims enjoy in Western societies' (2006: 151). They feel Muslims should work to redress the balance. Likewise, Riddell reasons that 'it seems only fair that the effort extended by Western countries, home to nominally Christian majorities, to provide equal opportunity to Muslim minorities should be reciprocated by Muslim majority countries in relation to their Christian minorities'.[35] Citing the WCC, he is concerned that some Christians have rejected reciprocity in favour of 'reconciliation' and believes that this is detrimental to Christian minorities around the world who need the support of Western churches. He is concerned that they sense 'disloyalty and abandonment when Western Christian leaders refuse to speak out forcefully' on behalf of Christian minorities (Riddell, 2004: 180–1).

Nazir-Ali also believes that the concept of reciprocity is important but advises that it should not be a 'crude tit-for-tat' with the withdrawal of Muslim rights in the West. He observes that other Christian traditions agree, and he sees the need for personal freedoms to be 'held in tension with the good of the community' (2006: 154). He is also careful to stress that the lack of freedom for some Christians 'has to be set against other situations in the Muslim world where Christians do have the freedom to worship' and warns that we must not 'tar them all with the same brush' (2002: 89). In this spirit, there are Evangelicals who highlight the Golden Rule (e.g. Mt. 7.12) and feel that Christians cannot insist on reciprocity as a precondition for doing the right thing. Christians should treat Muslims as they themselves wish to be treated. Chapman reminds readers that 'Jesus encourages his followers to take the initiative … however the other party behaves' and feels that 'if Christians are sincere and follow the Golden Rule, they may be surprised to find that in time some Muslims may be willing to work on the same basis' (2007b: 48). These Evangelicals recommend that, as well as advocating for Christian rights and freedoms, Christians should demand economic and cultural justice for Muslims and the Palestinian people (Moucarry, 2007: 119; see also Chapter 10 in this volume). This would mean addressing what Muslims generally refer to as Islamophobia, seeing it as at least equivalent to the situation of Christians in Muslim-majority contexts. As Cumming (2011) puts it, 'Christians must outspokenly defend religious liberty for Muslims whether or not Muslims reciprocate'. If Christians fail to do this, then Birdsall notes that the 'hypocrisy does not go unnoticed' and 'we make life more difficult for Christian minorities when we mistreat minorities in the West. If we want religious freedom for ourselves and our fellow believers, we should reciprocate the same courtesy to others' (2018: 5). For these reasons, many Evangelical agencies are now focusing on FoRB for all and not just Christians. For instance, CSW insists that 'as Christians, we stand with everyone facing injustice because of their religion or belief'.[36]

Other Evangelicals, however, are critical of any stance which they feel does not present a strong face towards Islam. They are dismissive of complaints about Islamophobia as an attempt to shield Islam from criticism (see Chapter 7) and do not see the situation of Muslims in the West as in any way equivalent to the plight of the Christian minorities. They fear that a focus on Western guilt and culpability and especially Christian apologies for past transgressions, such as the Crusades, might be interpreted as weakness and would not be reciprocated by Muslims. In fact, Durie believes that 'Christian self-humbling' is 'another manifestation of dhimmitude'. While 'no doubt the Christians [believe] they [are] relating from a position of strength, by invoking Christian virtues of humility and self-examination, however, they appear not to have taken account of the dynamics of dhimmitude and the possibility that these statements could be understood by Muslims as a display of self-acknowledged inferiority' (2009c: 221–2).

Retaliation

Despite this tendency to humility, however, there are still occasionally violent Christian responses to oppression today. Some Evangelicals are honest enough to admit witnessing this, not just from those Western Christian politicians who have led their countries into war (see Chapter 9) but also from ordinary Christians, including Evangelicals, struggling to know how to react to the violence perpetrated against them. In the African context, Azumah observes:

> Some Nigerian Christians now strongly believe in what some term 'speaking the language the Muslims best understand' (i.e., use of violence). Some have even gone further to propound what is called the 'Third Cheek Theology', which argues that Jesus' teaching of turning the other cheek no longer applies in their context, since they have been slapped on both cheeks and have no third cheek to turn! (2011: 15)

Azumah in no way condones this violence and suggests that what is needed is to teach these Christians 'the history, witness and theology of the early church' which overcame the Roman Empire through suffering (2008b: 125).

Others have observed such violent retaliation at first hand. A newsletter from an Evangelical working in Plateau State, Nigeria, reported how their Muslim neighbours' houses had been burned down by some members of a local Evangelical church:

> Most of those who've been fighting are members of local Evangelical churches – these are *our* people, and you can't divorce yourself from your family! And this is what grieves me most. This is *not* a matter of 'the suffering church', but 'the church at war' – most of the violence *suffered* by 'Christians' has been in revenge for violence *done* by 'Christians'. And in the last 2 months, 'Christians' have killed and burned more than Muslims have.[37]

This is certainly a case of what the *Under Caesar's Sword* report calls a 'confrontational' response, and it mentions some other instances in which 'Christians have massacred civilians, including Muslims in Indonesia during the clashes in Maluku of 1999–2003' and, more recently, the Central African Republic. However, it finds that these cases are rare and that 'Christian responses to persecution are almost always nonviolent and, with very few exceptions, do not involve acts of terrorism'.[38]

Ojo, a university professor in Nigeria, does observe that when Nigerian Christians 'retaliate forcefully', attackers are 'more cautious'.[39] However, this is a response explored and rejected by Sunday Bobai Agang, a leading Nigerian Evangelical peacemaker. In his book *No More Cheeks to Turn?* he lists his family members and friends who have been killed by Muslims in the violence and recounts how he moved from hatred to forgiveness to advising his community to 'master the art of creative, non-violent self-defence'. He tells stories of Christians who have refused to retaliate after their churches were burned down but rather built a clinic for Muslims. In fact, he advocates non-violence as a strategy for converting Muslims and reports that 'there are former Muslims who testify that it was the Christians' refusal to retaliate for the violence done to them that eventually drew them to Christ' (Agang, 2017: 31, 84).

Partnership

Other Evangelicals in situations of pressure are taking the 'associational' approach. For instance, some Nigerian Evangelicals advocate partnering with moderate Muslims within civil society to combat the extremists. Josiah Idowu-Fearon, an Anglican bishop in Nigeria, insists that 'African Christians must advocate for individual freedom and liberty. In the same vein, they need to work with African Muslims against Islamist laws concerning blasphemy and apostasy within and outside the Islamic community' (2013: 189).

Johnson believes that there can be 'a partnership between Evangelical Christianity and Humanitarian Islam' which would offer a 'universal ethical compass for all' (2021: 10). Indeed, WEA is working together with Nahdlatul Ulama on some aspects of human rights.[40] Other organizations such as Peace Catalyst International (PCI) are likewise seeking to partner with Muslims.[41] Meral also sees hope in 'the increasing number of courageous Muslim men and women of deep faith who are standing up for human rights, tolerance, peace and reconciliation. This does not make problems disappear overnight, but it gives us a strong reason to believe in the possibility of a shared future together' (2011: 132).

Valorisation of the martyrs

The surprising thing is that, despite political opposition, religious persecution and social pressure, the Christian church is growing in Muslim-majority contexts (Chapter 13). Iran is a good example of this, and several books include the history (e.g. Safa, 2006).[42] One biographer remarks that 'given the hostility of the Islamic Republic to active Christians for the last 35 years resulting in the murder of at least six Evangelical pastors, the closure of churches, the banning of the Bible and Christian literature, and the arrests of hundreds, one might have expected the Iranian church to have withered away. The opposite has happened.' He observes that 'while the government persecutes for political reasons, the impact on the Christians is entirely spiritual. And that spiritual impact brings about church growth' (Bradley, 2014: 18, 200). Such perseverance and steadfastness in the face of adversity is often valorised by Evangelical authors and raised up as an example for all Christians. Omar Elisha, researching what he calls the 'martyrological media' of VOM, suggests that, for American Evangelicals, 'the casting of foreign Christians as martyrs adds meaning to their misery and inspires Evangelicals with an admiration verging on jealous longing.'[43]

As noted in Chapter 2, biographies of those who have converted from Islam to Christianity – and who have often suffered for it – remain very popular. Without singling out the Muslim context, Sookhdeo has published *Heroes of Our Faith* (2012), a devotional guide with the stories of 366 Christian martyrs throughout history into the twenty-first century. VOM has also produced books telling stories of martyrdom and suffering (DC Talk and Voice of the Martyrs, 2020; Voice of the Martyrs, 2016).

Nik Ripkin in a remarkable survey of Christian suffering around the world, much in Muslim-majority contexts, suggests that such pressure is actually the normal mode for all true followers of Jesus. As a Western Christian, he wonders whether 'perhaps the question should not be: "Why are others persecuted?" Perhaps the better question is: "Why are we not?"' He sees their example as a challenge and wonders whether 'God may actually want to use them to save us from the often debilitating, and sometimes spiritually fatal, effects of our watered-down, powerless Western faith' (Ripken, 2013: 311, 304). Another book title makes a similar point: *The Privilege of Persecution: And Other Things the Global Church Knows That We Don't* (Moeller and Hegg, 2011).[44] Indeed, some even believe it may happen in the West. A Muslim convert speaking to The Moody Church in Chicago in 2007 warned that 'just as hundreds of thousands of Christians have been killed for being Christians in Islamic countries, the same might happen here in years to come' (Lutzer, 2007).

Love and forgiveness

Of course, focusing on the persecution, suffering and martyrdom of Christians in Muslim contexts runs the very real risk that Evangelicals will become afraid of Muslims and see them solely in a negative light. Muslims will be seen as morally inferior. For example, 'to many Christians in Britain, the negative portrayal of the experiences for the Christian minority in Pakistan by campaigning groups such as the Barnabas Fund suggests the inability of Muslim-majority regimes to robustly entertain plurality' (Sudworth, 2017: 78). It can even lead to hatred and violence, as we saw above. Chapman shares these concerns:

> When stories of persecution are combined with the big political issues related to Muslims and Islam, it is only natural that Christians begin to feel afraid. They then find it harder to trust Muslims or to develop natural and meaningful relationships with them. If Christians find that they are responding to Muslims and Islam more out of fear than out of love, it becomes very much harder for them to obey the commands to 'Love your neighbour as yourself' (Mt. 19.19). (2007b: 42)

This is addressed in another remarkable book on the theme of Christian suffering in a Muslim context which seeks to strike that balance. Although Brother Andrew's *Secret Believers* is fictional, the story is based on real-life situations known to the author, and he recounts the challenges, persecution and eventual martyrdom sometimes faced by those who have converted out of Islam. Remarkably after such an account, the message of the remainder of the book is not that Christians should fear Muslims or be resentful, but rather it is a challenge 'to love all Muslims by giving them the Good News, to forgive when we are attacked, to live lives totally committed to Jesus Christ, and to engage in the real war – the spiritual war' (Brother Andrew and Janssen, 2007: 228).

Discussion: Minority treatment

In the previous chapter, we saw how Muslim minorities in the West are viewed by Evangelicals. This chapter has highlighted the mirror concerns of Evangelicals over the situation of Christian minorities in Muslim-majority contexts from which at least four things emerge. Firstly, given the global political context, the actions of extremists and continuing Muslim resistance to conversion, it seems likely that the pressure on Christian communities will continue, as it does for other minority groups such as the Ahmadiyya, Sufis and the Shi'a or Sunnis depending on which is in the minority. This is a reminder that mistreatment should not always be interpreted as opposition to the Christian faith per se – although that is undoubtedly an element – but that it is also part of a wider reaction to minorities, scapegoating, political expediency and the actions of Western governments. That said, no Christian of any tradition, nor indeed any person of faith, can ignore the suffering of their brothers and sisters elsewhere in the world. Neither should they be ignorant of or impervious to the suffering of other religious groups such as those mentioned. Evangelicals should certainly continue to campaign against prejudice and mistreatment and need to do that wisely in ways that will not cause more harm. This could include working with international groupings such as The Network for Religious and Traditional Peacemakers, to which several Muslim initiatives are affiliated, along with holding signatories to documents such as ACW and the Marrakesh Declaration accountable.

Secondly, Christian advocacy for FoRB obviously needs to tell stories of persecuted Christians, but it should neither do so in a way that gives the impression that all Muslims and all contexts are alike, nor do so to the exclusion of telling stories of those who suffer for other faiths or beliefs. This means dealing carefully with data and statistics, not oversensationalizing and telling the good news stories alongside the bad. This already occasionally happens, but there needs to be more consistency. For instance, one edition of *Barnabas Aid* had these three positive headlines on one page: 'Muslim Minibus Driver Saves Lives of Christian Passengers in Kenya'; 'World's Largest Islamic Organisation Drops Legal Category of "Infidel"'; and 'Church Registration Increases in Uzbekistan'.[45] This helps to put a more hopeful, human face to Muslims. Many other editions, however, have had no good news stories whatsoever.

Thirdly, the traditional Islamic ban on apostasy and the treatment of those who choose to leave Islam, whether for Christianity or any other faith, or none, is a matter of serious concern. Evangelicals will certainly be encouraged, if not convinced, by the work of those Muslims such as Abdullah Saeed, Abdullahi An-Na'im and Abdulaziz Sachedina who are seeking to reinterpret their tradition to account for human rights.[46] For instance, Saeed argues that the right to 'believe freely is central to the Quranic idea of true belief' and that 'Muslims need to find peace with religious freedom in light of both Islamic legal history and modern socio-political realities'.[47] However, while their ideas are gaining traction in the West, the situation is not so hopeful for the freedom of conscience elsewhere.

Finally, many Evangelicals might be surprised to learn that, despite believing that they, the Christians, are at the bottom of a 'rarely acknowledged hierarchy of victimhood',[48] Muslims in the West often think that *they* are the most persecuted religious group in the world. Muslims form a large proportion of the world's refugees and have suffered great numbers of civilian casualties both at the hands of Muslim terrorists and as the 'collateral damage' of Western armies. They see the world as being unfairly dominated by the governments and multinationals of Western 'Christian' countries. Meanwhile, in those countries, they often feel marginalized and disadvantaged. The word most often associated with this latter phenomenon is Islamophobia (see Chapter 2), and for many Muslims, this is the parallel concern to the situation of Christian minorities. Most Evangelicals do not see it this way. However, it is not helpful to get into a victimhood competition. It is important for Evangelicals to recognize the strength of Muslim concerns about Islamophobia, whether or not they feel the comparison is justified and whatever their fears of Islamization. Wherever there is genuine suffering and disadvantage – of Christians, Muslims or others – Evangelicals should engage in FoRB advocacy, seeking an end to religious discrimination, coercion and persecution for all. That is what the Golden Rule teaches.

9

Violence

One does not have to look far in the first two decades of the twenty-first century to see a sad litany of violence, terrorism and wars around the world, much of it associated with Muslim contexts. Terrorist groups such as Al-Qaeda, ISIS, Al-Shabab and Boko Haram have, at times, dominated Western news cycles. Attacks in New York (2001), Bali (2002), Madrid (2004), London (2005), Paris (2015) and Manchester (2017) were all claimed – and celebrated – by those calling themselves Muslim. At the same time, Western forces invaded and occupied Afghanistan (2001–21), Iraq (2003–11) and engaged in various other battles on Muslim soil, including Libya (2011) and Syria (2017–ongoing). This is without mentioning Western support for unsavoury, autocratic regimes in Muslim contexts with poor records regarding justice, freedom and human rights. Millions have been affected by the brutality; hundreds of thousands have been killed, the majority of them Muslims but also including minority Christian groups, Western civilians as well as armed combatants on both sides.

It would be fair to say that it has been a bloody two decades, and, as we saw in the Introduction, for many Evangelicals on both sides of the debate, 9/11 was 'the day the world changed' (compare Price, 2001: 7 and Wallis, 2013: 133). There is certainly no shortage of Evangelical books written since that date on subjects connected to violence, terrorism and war in the context of Islam, with titles such as *Unholy War* (Price, 2001), *Holy Warriors* (Orr-Ewing and Orr-Ewing, 2002), *Christians, Muslims and Islamic Rage* (Catherwood, 2003), *How America Can Win the War against Radical Islam* (Safa, 2004), *Journey inside the Mind of an Islamic Terrorist* (Gabriel, 2007) and *God's War on Terror* (Shoebat and Richardson, 2008). However, the causes and nature of such violence are complex and cannot be reduced to soundbites and book titles.

Moucarry suggests that 'violence' should be 'defined as the illegitimate use of force. Force exerted to apply the law, provided it is measured, is not violence. Violence defined as such can be carried out by individuals, organizations, or the state' (2022: 75). Cotterell highlights a similar distinction (2013: 43). This means that, whether we are talking about illegitimate violence or lawful force depends on one's viewpoint. Most Evangelicals subscribe to the legitimacy of a 'just war', although some, as will be seen, are pacifists. However, there are plenty who think that the actions of Western governments in the Middle East have been illegitimate and amount to state-sanctioned violence, especially where disturbing stories of 'extraordinary rendition', torture and the execution of civilians have come to light.

Few other issues connected with Islam have given rise to as much comment or rancour in the Evangelical micro-public sphere as the question of the root causes of this violence. Some lay the blame entirely at the door of Islam, believing it to be inherently and essentially violent with an agenda of world domination. Others accept that different Muslims interpret their texts and traditions in different ways and that many are non-violent while remaining authentically Islamic. These Evangelicals often feel that the West is also to blame for the war and violence unleashed since 9/11. This leads to different Evangelicals proposing an assortment of explanations for the events above, some internal to Islam, some external, some resting the blame solely on Islam, others seeing a more complex picture.

'Islam means peace'

It is not uncommon to hear politicians and Muslim leaders declaring that 'Islam means peace'. Indeed, in 2001, the day after announcing his 'crusade' on terror in retribution for 9/11 (see the Introduction), President Bush attempted to mend fences with Muslims after his poor choice of vocabulary.[1] He pronounced that 'the face of terror is not the true faith of Islam. That's not what Islam is all about. Islam is peace. These terrorists don't represent peace. They represent evil and war' (Bush, 2001a).

Most Evangelical writers, however, are careful to stress that semantically *islām* does not mean 'peace', which is the Arabic word *salām*. The two words do come from the same Arabic root (s-l-m), but the literal meaning of the Arabic word *islām* is 'submission' (e.g. Bell, 2006: 46).[2] The connection between the two words is the Islamic idea that peace is achieved when a person – or society – comes into submission to God's revealed will. The question then becomes how that submission is achieved – through freewill or through coercion? This sounds ominous to some Evangelicals as it appears that the Muslim goal is 'to bring the rest of mankind to such submission' through obedience to Islam (Musk, 2003a: 243). Indeed, Robinson, referencing Muslim reformer Bassam Tibi, fears that Muslims will only ever be at peace when Islam extends to the whole world (2003: 209).

Opinion is divided over the genuineness of Muslim explanations of Islam as a religion of peace. For instance, Nazir-Ali believes that 'it is quite possible to encourage Muslims to find the roots of tolerance within Islamic tradition itself' (2002: 71). There are places where Muslims have traditions of peaceful coexistence with others. For instance, Ferry Mamahit, an Indonesian Evangelical scholar, observes that the mainly Muslim 'Javanese people … embrace two life principles: *rukun* (living peacefully or harmoniously with others) and *hormat* (living respectfully toward others)' (2020: 38). Azumah notes a similar tradition in West Africa (Azumah, 2011).[3] In any case, Medearis believes that 'there is nothing to be gained by accusing a religion of brokering violence committed by a handful of its followers' (2008: 115, 9). Morey, however, takes a much harder line. He feels that 'Muslims who say that Islam is a religion of peace … are either ignorant of what Islam teaches or they are trying to deceive you' (2002b: 114). Likewise, Sookhdeo (2005) believes that 'the mantra "Islam is peace" is almost 1,400 years out of date. It was only for about 13 years that Islam was peace and nothing but peace. From 622 onwards it became increasingly aggressive'.

'Islam is violent'

Maybe rather more Evangelicals are convinced that Islam does not mean peace and that it is, in fact, essentially violent. This is confirmed for them by some converts from a Muslim background such as Shoebat, who baldly states that 'violent Islam is true Islam' – the crux of this controversial debate (2008: 137). Robinson quotes the Caner brothers as saying that 'Islam does in fact have an essential and indispensable tenet of militaristic conquest at its heart' (2003: 204). So, it is not surprising that many Evangelicals fear that Islam is seeking world domination, whether by peaceful or violent means (see Chapter 7 on Islamization). For instance, Randall Price, a prophecy watcher and archaeologist, says that 'Muslims see themselves as a "peacemaking force"' and that for them 'the world cannot be fully secure until people come under the protection of Islam'. To accomplish this, he suggests that Islam permits Muslims to use 'threats, terrorism, warfare, and every other means possible to secure Islam as the only religion on earth' (2001: 190). Other Evangelicals likewise suspect that Islam is particularly prone to sanctioning violence. For instance, Sookhdeo reflects that 'no other religious group in recent times have [*sic*] been shown to pose such a threat of violence and terrorism across the globe as consistently as Muslims do'. He wonders whether there is 'something distinctive about Islam as a religion that makes it more likely to justify violence than other religions?' (2007: 44). This is a question many Evangelicals answer in the affirmative.

Other Evangelicals, however, sharply disagree. One example of a public disagreement took place when Sookhdeo published a 2005 article titled 'The Myth of Moderate Islam' in *The Spectator*, a British magazine. Following the 7/7 bombings, it criticized a general reluctance to name the violence as 'Islamic' and argued that 'if [the bombers] say they do it in the name of Islam, we must believe them. Is it not the height of illiberalism and arrogance to deny them the right to define themselves?' Sookhdeo went on to wonder whether 'the young men who committed suicide were neither on the fringes of Muslim society in Britain, nor following an eccentric and extremist interpretation of their faith, but rather that they came from the very core of the Muslim community and were motivated by a mainstream interpretation of Islam'.

Chapman in a strong riposte published on *Fulcrum* pointed out that 'the majority of Muslim leaders [had] condemned the suicide bombings in the strongest possible language' and 'dissociate[d] themselves from extremist positions and from suicide bombings'. He felt that, in 'suggesting that the suicide bombers represent the true heart of Islam', Sookhdeo was being unfair in not allowing 'other Muslims the right to define themselves, because [he did not] accept their estimate of how contemporary Islamism stands in relation to traditional orthodox Islam' (Chapman, 2005b).

These two opposing interpretations of events underlie much of what is written in the Evangelical public sphere about violence in Muslim contexts. The question is whether or not Islam is essentially and inherently violent. Evangelicals, including the specialists, are sharply divided on the answer, although most recognize that reductionist 'statements such as, "Islam is a religion of peace", or "Islam is a religion of war" are too general to be meaningful' (Orr-Ewing and Orr-Ewing, 2002: 103). So, the following sections look at the various drivers of Muslim violence identified by the different sides. For the hawks, the roots of violence lie solely in the Islamic texts and their interpretation, in the historical example of Muhammad and early Islam and in the Islamic theology of jihad. For the doves, while all of these are, maybe, more or less important factors, there is also an emphasis on external causes, including the history of colonialism, Western foreign policy, the Israel-Palestine situation and Western double standards.

Internal causes

Historical precedent

We have seen in Chapter 4 how the life and example of Muhammad himself and his participation in warfare form part of some negative Evangelical assessments of him. It also colours how Evangelicals assess Islam's relationship to violence today. Of course, it is uncontroversial to say that Muhammad took part in warfare. In fact, Catherwood observes that 'Muhammad as an undoubted military leader and strategist ... is something of which Muslims today are proud, rather than being in denial' (2003: 98; also Azumah, 2008b: 41). So, Goldmann contrasts the ministries of Jesus and Muhammad and especially their different approaches to warfare (2008: 21). Cotterell draws a similar contrast between Jesus 'the man of peace' and Muhammad 'a man of war' (2011: 6). He details some of the twenty-six or so battles Muhammad was involved in according to the earliest Muslim biography of Muhammad written by Ibn Ishaq (see also Power, 2016c; Gabriel, 2004). Given this history, which is accepted by Muslims,[4] many feel that it is not surprising that some Muslims turn to violence as, in their assessment, 'Muhammad's own example shows clearly that he ... himself ordered massacre, assassination and torture' (P. Sookhdeo, 2005).

As seen in Chapter 4, some Evangelicals do have a more positive assessment of Muhammad as either a 'man of his time' or as someone who brought positive reform. In fact, rather than seeing Muhammad's example as a cause of Muslim violence, McLaren suggests that 'the face of [Byzantine] Christianity towards Mohammad was a hostile one' and that subsequently Islam 'mirrored that hostility'. Given this, McLaren hopes that 'we can interpret Mohammad's choices and convictions in a more sympathetic light' (2012b: 91).

However, the involvement in warfare did not end with Muhammad. Many Evangelicals are quick to point out that Muslims have had a long history of imperial conquest and have colonized other nations, just as Western Christians have. So, 'was Islam spread by the sword?' Chapman, while not denying the military expansion, argues that it is 'a misleading half-truth to say that "Islam was spread by the sword"' (2007b: 136). However, many do not see it this way. Qureshi suggests that 'the short answer [is] technically no, but indirectly yes' (2016a: 61). Gabriel insists that there was an 'unrelenting bloodbath' during the early imperial expansion under the caliphs and their successors (2007: chapter 15). Sookhdeo adds lists of 'violent sects', historical and contemporary, and believes that 'Islam has an inbuilt urge at its very core towards empire-building' (2007: 103, 12, 270). Even the more irenic Moucarry points out that 'the glorious and sometimes bloody history of successive Islamic empires remains vivid in the collective memory of Muslims. Islamists want, by the rigorous implementation of Sharī'a, to resuscitate an idealized and long gone past' (2022: 84). Thus, for some, it grates when Muslims today complain about the injustices of historical Western colonialism. Catherwood opines that 'if it was wrong for Westerners to have conquered large parts of the globe in the nineteenth century, surely it was equally wrong for the Arab armies to have done that in the seventh. Conquest is conquest!' (2003: 61–2).

The Islamic texts and their interpretation

In addition to the history, most Evangelical authors look at texts in connection with violence. In Chapter 5, it was noted that there are several principles which Muslim scholars use to interpret their texts, including abrogation, context and the universal versus the particular. Many Evangelicals, however, ignore these principles and jump straight into reading the Qur'an and the Hadith for themselves in English, reaching their own conclusions. They generally find the number of verses related to fighting in those texts deeply disturbing. With hyperbolic force, Don Richardson reckons that 'there are at least 109 identifiable war verses in the Qur'an. One out of every 55 verses in the Qur'an is a war verse. War verses are scattered throughout Muhammad's chapters like blood splatter at a crime scene' (2003: 28). It is easy to make a connection between such verses and the actions of Muslim terrorists. In a YouTube video, Jay Smith (2008b) says, 'I just open up the Qur'an and I read its pages and I try to find out where people are sourcing their material for what they are doing in the world today'. Indeed, Musk points out that the violent Islamists themselves claim that 'the Qur'an is the primary motivator and justifier of their extreme actions' (2008: xiv).

Given the seeming weight of war passages in the Qur'an, some Evangelicals find it difficult to accept the arguments Muslims put forward for peaceful interpretations of these texts. For instance, one booklet says, 'The problem with finding and promoting moderation within Islam is that the most "natural" reading of Islamic texts, as well as much influential historical interpretation of these, provide fuel for the radicals' (Pilcrow Press, 2007: 50). As Erwin Lutzer,[5] emeritus pastor of The Moody Church in Chicago, puts it, 'If you take the Qur'an literally, you should be a militant Muslim. Anything else is to avoid its clear teachings' (2013: KL233).

Some Evangelicals do acknowledge that Muslims have their own ways of interpreting their texts. However, the one highlighted most often is abrogation, in which verses revealed later replace earlier verses with which they differ (see Chapter 5). It is widely noted, including by Muslims, that the earlier revelations to Muhammad did not include fighting, but that this came later with the *hijra* from Mecca to Medina in 622 AD (Q.22.39). From then on, Muslims were not just permitted but required to fight, when necessary (Q.2.216), and finally commanded to fight (Q.9.29). This leads some Evangelical authors to note that the Qur'an seems to move chronologically from peace to violence. As Qureshi puts it, 'The Qur'anic revelations reflect the development in Muhammad's life as he moved from a peaceful trajectory to a violent one, culminating in Sura 9 of the Qur'an, chronologically the last major chapter of the Qur'an and its most expansively violent teaching' (2016a: 53; see also Cotterell, 2011: 74). Simply applied, the conclusion is that 'according to the rule of abrogation, it is the harsher and more violent Medinan passages that apply today because they are later, while the earlier conciliatory passages dating from Muhammad's days in Mecca are not applicable' (P. Sookhdeo, 2007: 63). Gabriel agrees and reckons that 'there are at least 114 verses in the Qur'an that speak of love, peace and forgiveness', but they are all cancelled out by Sura 9.5 (known as the Sword Verse) (2002: 30).

Nonetheless, not all participants are persuaded that abrogation is the dominant tool used by *all* Muslims to interpret and apply the Qur'an. Musk acknowledges that it 'features strongly in Islamists' arguments' to legitimate the use of violence, and he calls on Muslim scholars and leaders 'to address the issue of abrogation as part of their response to the Islamists' agenda' (2008: 56–7). However, whereas abrogation may be the main tool used by extremists, more moderate Muslims tend to use the other tools explored in Chapter 5, such as the occasions of revelation and universal principles (Accad, 2019: 55). Campolo recalls how a Muslim scholar explained to him that qur'anic texts must be read in context. The scholar believed that, far from supporting terrorism, a passage such as Sura 2.190–2 was 'a warning against terrorists' like the Meccan tribe which was attacking Muhammad at the time when the verses were revealed (2004: 139). In this way, some Evangelicals accept that many Muslims interpret the Sword Verse as only being applicable in times of war and not as a directive to all Muslims at all times in all contexts.

Chapman recognizes that these different exegetical tools 'can sometimes point in different directions', which may go a long way to explaining the sort of disagreement and diverging trajectories we see among Muslims today (2007b: 286). In other words, 'both sides can legitimately point to parts of the Qur'an and say – there you are! My interpretation is the correct one!' (Catherwood, 2003: 129). Or, as Lee Camp,[6] an American theologian and ethicist, describes it, the symphony orchestra is 'sticking more closely to the written notes', while the jazz band is loosely 'bounded by the melody' (2016: KL2814). This leads Accad to suggest that

> we must strive for an understanding of Qur'anic exegesis that takes seriously the complexities of hermeneutics. Should we not listen to the moderate voices of Islam, and encourage the school of thought that calls for a peaceful Islam, rather than succumb to the narrative of Muslim extremists who are always looking for ways that legitimate their violent interpretation of Islam? (2019: 56)

The reliance among some Evangelicals on the Islamic texts in order to explain violence – and other phenomena – has been labelled by Azumah and Chapman as 'textualism'. This occasioned another exchange, again illustrating the debate within the Evangelical public sphere. In 2017, Chapman published an article challenging the way that for some Evangelicals 'everything that Muslims do can be explained by referring to texts, and that history and politics have little or no relevance'. This approach 'absolves Westerners of all responsibility for the mess that has been unfolding in the Middle East in the last hundred years', something about which Chapman feels strongly, as will be seen in Chapter 10 (2017a: 121). However, he was severely criticized in two

Evangelical responses. Durie complained that Chapman 'consistently downplays and misrepresents the role of Islam in these conflicts'.[7] Jenny Taylor (2018) likewise believed that 'Chapman dismisses as "textualism" the attempt to take seriously Islam's own huge internal literary dynamic, rooted and justified in scripture and the traditions to a degree only now coming to wider notice'. Chapman and Azumah (2018) responded to Taylor's accusation saying:

> We must be willing to listen to Muslims and allow them to tell us what Islam is for them. We may well want to challenge them over the Qur'anic verses about jihad and warfare if they think that these justify violence today, but we have no right to think that we know better than they regarding what is 'real Islam' ... While texts are important, they cannot be taken in isolation from all the other factors.

These are arguments returned to below. However, there are obviously also verses about peace in the Qur'an, and some Evangelicals are careful to balance the above violent verses by referring to them. For instance, Andrews, referring to the work of Abdul Ghaffar Khan (d. 1988), a Pakistani Muslim political leader dedicated to non-violent opposition and pacifism, quotes the well-known verse saying that 'there is no compulsion in religion' (Q.2.256) (2015: 99). He also draws on the thought of Wahiduddin Khan (d. 2021), a Muslim Indian peace activist. Riddell quotes another well-known peaceable verse which says that 'if anyone kills a person – unless in retribution for murder or spreading corruption in the land – it is as if he kills all mankind, while if any saves a life it is as if he saves the lives of all mankind' (Q.5.32). However, Riddell points out that Muslims who use this verse to explain that Islam is peaceful do not usually quote the following verse which prescribes 'death, crucifixion, the amputation of an alternate hand and foot, or banishment from the land' for those who 'spread corruption in the land' (Q.5.33) (2004: 199–200).[8] Clearly much depends on which verses are chosen for emphasis and how they are interpreted.

The teaching of jihad

Up to this point, the concept of jihad has hardly been mentioned. However, for many Evangelicals, it is the first word that springs to mind when talking about violence in the Islamic context. Indeed, in the popular imagination, jihad is closely associated with war. However, in Islamic thought, it has a wider range of meanings, and jihad is not the Arabic word for war (*ḥarb*) or the verb for fight (*qātil*). Plenty of authors point out that the literal meaning of jihad is 'struggle', and it can be used in many contexts (e.g. Catherwood, 2003: 141; Chapman, 2007b: 193). Nonetheless, a few, usually not Arabic speakers, insist that it narrowly means 'holy war'. For instance, the Caners translate it as 'holy fighting' (2003: 249), and Morey reports simply looking in English-language dictionaries and finding that they all understand jihad to mean 'war' (2002b: 72). Such Evangelicals are inclined to see any other explanation as a deception. For example, Durie in a testy exchange with Chapman accused him of downplaying the martial aspect of jihad and being 'misleading and unbalanced' in the article posted online. He said that 'while it is true that the Arabic root j-h-d means to struggle or strive, nevertheless, in Islamic jurisprudence, the term jihad refers to warfare against non-Muslims to establish Islam'. Chapman responded that he was fully aware of this tradition. Indeed, in an earlier book, he made it clear that this is the tradition and critiqued Muslims today who try to sidestep it (2007b: 194). In the exchange, he argued that he had 'spelt out the basic Islamic conviction that [quoting Cragg] "Islam must rule", and jihad for many Muslims is obviously the way to achieve that goal'. He then pointed out that he was arguing for 'a mixture of both' texts and politics as the cause of Muslim violence.[9]

This is an approach taken by several specialists in the Evangelical public sphere who accept that there is a diversity of applications and interpretations of jihad within the Muslim community. Moucarry acknowledges that 'it is possible to understand jihad in the sense of a spiritual, moral, social, political and even economic commitment'. However, where it does mean literal fighting, then 'for most Muslim scholars a legitimate jihad is a defensive one intended to defend Muslims when they are oppressed or persecuted'. He points out that classically jihad can only be conducted according to certain rules which protect women, children and the elderly and observes that the 'jihadists tend to ignore' these rules (Moucarry, 2022: 78–9, 109). Nazir-Ali, likewise, acknowledges its multiple meanings, seeing jihad as 'an effort to remove social ills from society, as a way of subduing one's lower self, or as a way of armed struggle when Islam itself is in danger' (2002, 62).

Furthermore, some authors quote a hadith used by moderate Muslims to say that Muhammad distinguished between a 'greater' and a 'lesser' jihad, in which physical fighting takes second place to the inner struggle (e.g. Chapman, 2007b: 194; Kuhn, 2009: 119; D. Brown, 2004: 76). For instance, Campolo believes that 'Muhammad transformed the concept of jihad into a war against the sin and decadence that exist within the Muslim community itself. It was only in the earliest days of Islam that jihad had the militaristic dimensions some contemporary leaders of Islamic nations now assume' (2004: 144). Going further, Andrews believes Christians can join Muslims in 'the greater jihad of personal growth and the lesser jihad of social change that [God] is calling us to be involved with' (2015: 75). Others, however, suggest that the softer interpretations are a more recent innovation. For instance, David Zeidan, a researcher and former missionary, points out that not all Muslims accept this weak hadith as being authentic (2002: 271–2), and Azumah claims that 'the notion that jihad is a spiritual struggle or a last resort in self-defence is purely a post-modern apologia and is hardly borne out by mainstream Muslim scholarship' (2008b: 41).

Notwithstanding these discussions and nuances, plenty of Evangelicals, including some specialists, believe that Islamic teaching about jihad is a main driver of contemporary violence in the name of Islam. Gabriel defines jihad as 'military power and invasion in the name of Islam' and suggests, without further explanation, that 'sixty per cent of the Quranic verses talk about jihad, which [for him] stands to reason because Muhammad received most of the Quran after he left Mecca' (2002: 31). Others suggest that there is a rather lower number of '164 jihad verses' in the Qur'an.[10] These Evangelicals are convinced that jihad is not just defensive but also offensive. For instance, Ankerberg and Caner (2019) see jihad as the 'sixth pillar' of Islam and obligatory for all Muslims. Solomon and Maqdisi agree and present it pictorially as the foundation for all the other pillars and duties of Islam. They argue that 'as long as there are communities out there that are non-Muslim, where Islam is not regarded as a supreme system, then jihad must continue' (2009b: 11, 4). Sookhdeo in his 669-page book on the topic states that 'there is no doubt that in Islamic history jihad has normally been viewed, both in traditional Islamic law and in Islamic practice, as the armed conflict against non-Muslims permanently waged to ensure the victory of God's chosen community and religion, the umma, over all polytheistic powers, peoples and lands' (2007: 13). He goes on to give an overview of influential Islamic scholars, teachers and jurists, historical and contemporary, who have expounded these themes in the service of Islamic expansionism. In common with other writers, the names of Hassan al-Banna (d. 1949), Abul A'la Mawdudi (d. 1979) and Sayyid Qutb (d. 1966) are particularly identified as 'primary ideological source[s] of contemporary radical Islamic movements' (P. Sookhdeo, 2007: 282; see also Nazir-Ali, 2012: 78; Musk, 2003a: chapter 12).

Martyrdom and paradise

Closely associated with the idea of jihad in the popular imagination over the first two decades of the twenty-first century has been suicide bombing. Several participants in the sphere believe that suicide, or martyrdom missions, has a deeply theological motivation. Islam, they argue, offers no assurance of a place in paradise other than to die in jihad. Qureshi suggests that, according to the final sura of the Qur'an, 'Muslims must fight … and if they do not, then their faith is called into question and they are counted among the hypocrites. If they do fight, they are promised one of two rewards, either spoils of war or heaven through martyrdom' (2016a: 54). The Orr-Ewings play down the idea that suicide bombers are politically motivated, but rather stress that 'we cannot underestimate the theological motivation behind these martyrdoms. For extremely zealous individuals searching for assurance of salvation from the God they serve, an attractive option, giving a sense of purpose and destiny, is martyrdom' (2002: 33). Testimonies from some converts bear this out (e.g. Al Fadi, 2023). Several others make the same point: this is the 'ultimate motive' for the young Muslim warrior as 'the Qur'an promises Paradise to those who die in battle for Islam more certainly than it promises salvation to anyone else' (Caner and Caner, 2003: 36); 'the only way to know for sure that you will get into paradise is to die in jihad – to die while fighting the enemy of Islam' (Gabriel, 2002: 28); for Muslims desperate to escape hell, 'becoming a suicide bomber is the one sure way to avoid the torments of the grave' (P. Sookhdeo, 2010b: 17). Added to this, Price, along with others, believes that Islamic texts such as Sura 55.56 and certain hadiths promise the martyr 'a literal sexual orgy' with the virgins, or houris, who will be awaiting him in paradise. 'Just the kind of place adolescent, unmarried men, isolated through their lives from the opposite sex by rigid cultural standards, would die for' (Price, 2001: 189; see also Malone, 2002: 65; MacArthur, 2001: 59).[11]

Some feel this is unfair, however. Moucarry agrees that 'the promise of direct access to paradise, through martyrdom, is undoubtedly very attractive to committed believers who feel anxious about their eternal destiny' but argues that 'the suicide bomb as a combat weapon is not part of traditional Islamic teaching'. Rather, 'traditionally, suicide has been equated with murder against oneself [and] suicide bombings show how far extremist Muslims are from mainstream Islam' (2022: 81, 91–2). Cotterell concurs and says that 'the modern development of terrorism, which involves indiscriminate attacks on non-combatants, women and children, is un-Islamic and has no support in Qur'an or Tradition. Tradition explicitly condemns the motives of the suicide bombers' (2013: 53).

Locating the causes of the recent violence solely within the Islamic tradition, in the manner of some of those above, carries dangers which some Evangelicals recognize. Trying to bring balance, Qureshi says:

> Acknowledging violence built into the foundations of Islam could lead people to see Islam as a necessarily violent religion, and by uncritical extension, it might lead people to see all Muslims as inherently or latently violent people. We must boldly assert that these are false and dangerous conclusions … we must be careful not to slide down the slippery slope of assuming every Muslim is a threat. (2016a: 18)

Spiritual causes

Alongside, but not replacing, these internal causes, some Evangelicals find 'spiritual' explanations for the violence associated with Islam, whether in the Bible or in the spiritual realm. American pastor, teacher and author John MacArthur declares that 'the historical reason for the terrorist action is clear: It stems from tensions rooted in biblical history, dating back to the time of Abraham' (2001: 38). This argument, mentioned by many Evangelicals, is rooted in the Bible rather than the Qur'an and has to do with biblical prophecy (e.g. Garlow, 2005: 17; J. Richardson, 2012: 221). These Evangelicals believe, as do Muslims, that the Arabs are descended from Ishmael, the first-born son of Abraham by Hagar. However, it was Isaac, Abraham's son born to Sarah, who is the child of the covenant (Gen. 17.19). So, they hold that the prophecies about Ishmael, 'Abraham's wild child', made in Gen. 16.12 are where the 'hate begins' and are coming true today along with other prophecies (Lindsey, 2002: 53). They believe that Muhammad himself was 'a direct descendant of Ishmael' (J. Richardson, 2012: 289). So, for them, it is not surprising if Muslims are violent, as 'this family feud goes back for over four thousand years as God in His foreknowledge described the temperaments, dispositions, and entailments of this conflict' (Zacharias, 2002: 67).

However, Houssney, himself an Arab, points out that it is 'not completely true' that Arabs are descended from Ishmael and he thinks it is 'likely that few Arabs have any blood relationship with Ishmael', although he accepts 'a spiritual link between them' (2010: 29–30). Others reject such explanations for Arab violence and point out, alongside the covenant with Isaac, God promised to bless Ishmael and his descendants (Gen. 17.20) (Campolo and Claiborne, 2012: 210). Tony Maalouf (d. 2020), a Lebanese Baptist seminary professor, provides a rather different interpretation for the seemingly negative prophecies, noting that God promises to make Ishmael a great nation and that, in fact, the 'wild donkey' mentioned in Gen. 16.12 was a 'valued and admired animal in the Near East' (2003: 70). Consequently, Palestinian Muslim convert and former Fatah member Tass Saada finds the biblical account positively affirming of his Arab heritage and has set up a Christian ministry invoking Ishmael's name (2008: 115–18, 79).[12]

Other Evangelicals believe that the physical violence is actually the outworking of a demonic struggle with 'the spiritual forces of evil in the heavenly realms' (Eph. 6.12) (e.g. Solomon and Debs, 2016: 198; R. Sookhdeo, 2005: 100). Some see Islam as a uniquely evil religion (see Chapter 11) and anticipate an Antichrist role for Islam in the End Times (see Chapter 10). However, for others, Islam is no more evil than any other religion when it becomes controlling, including Christianity (Garrison, 2014: 233). They are more cautious in their language. Warwick Farah, an American missiologist living in the Middle East and writing under a pseudonym, agrees that 'a spiritual battle is always raging around us; it is clear our battle is not against "flesh and blood"'. Nonetheless, he counsels that 'in a world of globalization, pluralism and terrorism, we would do well to avoid this metaphor when speaking of our mission to Muslims' (2020a: 439–40).

External causes

Global injustice

For other Evangelicals, the violence perpetrated by some Muslims is not solely due to the nature of Islam, biblical prophecy or spiritual warfare. While not denying many of the factors above, these commentators are aware of other contributing factors and are often highly critical of the role of the West, in marked contrast to many above who appear to attach no blame whatsoever to Western actions or attitudes. These Evangelicals believe that global injustices created by the West are key to understanding the causes of Muslim anger and violence. Added to this, in *Why the Rest Hate the West*, Evangelical historian Meic Pearse explains how many Muslims – and others – view the West as 'barbarians' and 'the ultimate cultural imperialists' as they lack respect for the past, have no honour and have embraced a culture of triviality. At the same time, religion in the West is on the decline, family life has been eroded, and sexual promiscuity is rife (Pearse, 2004: 44, 24). It is little wonder that other societies feel threatened, seek to protect themselves and that some employ radical means to strike back.

Of course, these Evangelicals are very careful to stress that they do not in any way condone violence as a solution to injustice. Chapman in his booklet declares at the outset his 'condemnation of terrorism of every kind in the strongest possible terms'. However, he believes that 'a firm stand against terrorism needs to go hand in hand with serious reflection on the root causes of terrorism' because the actions of terrorists are often the angry response to 'violence that has been done to them' but which itself 'is often not called "terrorism" largely because it is carried out not by individuals but by governments and their armies' (2005a: 4). In the booklet he highlights what he believes are the 'major grievances' of the Islamists:

- The weakness and humiliation of the Muslim world
- New forms of Western imperialism – 'political, military, economic and religious'

- The failures of ideologies imported from the West – especially 'capitalism, communism/socialism, nationalism'
- The establishment of the Zionist State of Israel in the heartlands of Islam (see Chapter 10)
- The presence of foreign troops in Saudi Arabia – which is 'colluding with the West'
- Corrupt and autocratic governments in Islamic countries
- (Western) double standards – comparing sanctions on Iraq with the failure to enforce the UN Resolution calling on Israel to 'withdraw from occupied territory' (2005a: 9–10).

Others agree with him. Medearis catalogues ways in which the West has interfered in Iran, Afghanistan, Kuwait, Iraq and Israel. He warns that 'Western policies sometimes create tensions and add insult to injury regarding the Muslim sense of honour, which runs very deep' (2008: 124). Anthony McRoy, a British Evangelical researcher, writer and lecturer on Islam, sees it in similar terms. He notes of 9/11 that 'most hijackers were well educated, had not been to madrasas, and were not poor. The basis of their action is the defence of the honour of Islam, "defiled" by the "desecrating" presence of US troops in the Holy Land' (2006: 234). Nazir-Ali agrees and explicitly identifies Israel-Palestine, Kashmir, Chechnya, Bosnia and Kosovo as the 'flashpoints' which 'are the cause of [terrorism] and not only the location for it'. He recognizes that 'there is a sense of injustice, and the sharper it is, the more extreme the measures to counter it will be' (2002: 92). However, he tempers this in some of his later writing by emphasizing the Muslim 'worldview which expects "manifest victory" and resents the loss of land and power' (Nazir-Ali, 2012: 77). Aaron Taylor encountered this rage personally, when he met face to face with a Western convert to jihadism called Khalid:

> Hearing the rage and frustration of Khalid helped me to see the anger and frustration of millions of Muslims ... They see us as hypocritical when we preach non-proliferation for Iran but not for Israel ... Democracy is seen by many as the same kind of force [as former colonialism], one that comes in the name of peace and love and prosperity, but which will drop bombs on innocent civilians in the name of these virtues. (2009: KL655–62)[13]

Christian support for war

Taylor's comment concerning the force that is used – or, maybe, the violence that is perpetrated – in the attempt to establish democracy in places such as Somalia, Libya, Iraq and Afghanistan is a final important theme for some Evangelicals responding to the question of violence committed in the name of Islam. Many are aware of the high levels of Evangelical support for military action in the Middle East, especially in America, and believe it is antithetical to the teachings of Jesus. Wallis asks, 'When did Jesus become pro-war?' (2005: 85), and with heavy irony, Taylor remarks that for 'the beautiful people I've grown up with in the charismatic movement ... Sweet Sister Sally's Jesus may be harmless as a dove when it comes to loving sinners, but clearly he's a hawk when it comes to war' (2009: KL942–3). This leads Camp to decide that the 'mainstream of Christianity, when it comes to war-making and peacemaking, has been playing a tune that is more akin to Muhammad's tune than to that of Jesus' (2016: KL2827).

These Evangelicals look back over a long history of violence committed by those calling themselves Christians, or by nations seen as being Christian, and see it as a significant cause of the anger many Muslims (and others) harbour towards the West today. Several authors give accounts of this history. Andrews laments the Church's collusion with political power from the time of the fourth-century Roman emperor Constantine, through the Western colonial expansion, to more recent wars and genocide. He believes that 'predominantly Christian states have killed more Jews and Muslims than predominantly Muslim states have killed Christians or Jews' (2015: 26). Many writers recount the horror of the Crusades from the late eleventh to the thirteenth centuries and recognize that they were conducted in the name of Christ under the banner of the cross (Cumming, 2008: 322; Camp, 2016: chapter 10). Some even refer to them as Christian Jihad (Caner and Caner, 2004). Others recognize the damage that the Crusades do to the reputation of Christianity among Muslims, even today, although they feel that some Muslim leaders deliberately keep their memory alive in order to stoke ill-feeling against the West. Moucarry, having gone to a Syrian school as an Arab child, confirms that concerning the Crusades 'even today this glorious and somewhat mystified past continues to be taught systematically in public schools, and both nationalist governments and Islamists keep it in the forefront of their shared ideological struggle against Western countries' (2022: 4). Catherwood too sees the Crusades as a stain on Christian history but, in a reversal of McLaren's lament above, believes the crusade 'has to be seen as a medieval, Western version of the Muslim jihad, or Islamic holy war, of the kind that we saw sweep across so much of the world in the seventh century. Military jihad, sometimes called the lesser jihad, is a Muslim concept. It is certainly not anything Christian … The crusaders were using the Muslim tactic against their Islamic enemies – paying them back in their own kind' (2003: 46). Others also point out that the Crusades were partly responses to Muslim aggression (e.g. Barnabas Fund, 2008a).

However, Catherwood goes on to make a strong case for Christian non-violence today. Christians need to speak out when Muslims are suffering and being mistreated. Recalling the 1995 atrocities at Srebrenica, he wonders, 'Where were all the Evangelical leaders then who write so eloquently about the evils of 9/11?' He muses, 'How much better a witness we would have had to the Muslim world if thousands of Christians worldwide, and especially in the West, had led global protests at the atrocious mass murder of innocent Muslims by Serb soldiers who claimed to be Christians' (2003: 155).

The pivotal event of all these things is, of course, the destruction of the Twin Towers in 2001 (see Introduction). In terms of the impact it had on America first and foremost, MacArthur likens it to the attack on Pearl Harbour in 1941 and calls it 'the bloodiest day in our nation's history' (2001: 6). How America and her Western allies responded would be crucial for the two decades to come. In a searing analysis, Wallis describes it as a 'teachable moment' which opened up two paths before Western leaders. The first path was the 'spirit of justice', the 'rule of law' and bringing the perpetrators to account.

The second was the 'spirit of retribution' and 'vengeance'. They chose the latter, and Wallis regrets, along with many others in the Evangelical public sphere, that this led to 'indiscriminate retaliation and the "collateral damage" of even more loss of innocent life' along with 'glee among the Osama bin Ladens of the world, who finally are able to raise the armies of terror they've always dreamed of' (2005: 94–6). Cragg also believes that, as 'truly horrendous and catastrophic as the attack on the World Trade Center was ... it was wrong to proclaim forthwith a "war on terrorism" ... . It would have been saner to summon goodwill anywhere to a "World Order against Criminal Conspiracy"' (2005: 6).

All this causes Moucarry to admit that 'switching from force to violence is not too difficult when sinful people believe they carry out God's will', even for Christians and Western states (2022: 92). Aaron Taylor warns that 'power always comes at a price: faith becomes a servant of power and must bend to its criteria'. He reflects that, as much as he enjoys freedom and democracy, 'an agenda to democratize the world at the barrel of a gun is grounded in false presuppositions' (2009: KL726–7). This resonates with the peace churches and pacifist participants in the public sphere, such as Shenk and other Anabaptists. Others are not pacifists but remain ambivalent, inclining to peace. For instance, Qureshi says, 'I am not promoting pacifism, but neither am I advocating a violent response' (2016a: 147). Australian author Christine Mallouhi presciently responded to the violence by suggesting that Christians should be *Waging Peace on Islam* (2000).[14]

Unsurprisingly, those on the right completely reject any hint of pacifism or engagement with Muslim extremists. For them, the solution is military, as 'the advance of Islam has only ever been stopped by military defeat' (P. Sookhdeo, 2007: 401). MacArthur is convinced that 'our government backed by other nations ... ought to move forward boldly in the execution of the war, and we who are Christians ought to pray that our armed forces will be used both as God's instrument of judgment on those who have murdered innocent people, and as the power to restore peace' (2001: 127). Musk disagrees. He suggests that 'solving the Palestinian/Israeli issue is a far surer way to protect America and the West from Islamist suicide attackers than ratcheting up a possible pursuit of "evil" in countries such as Afghanistan and Iraq' (2008: 227). Wallis takes a similar line and, in 2003, wrote to a well-known Evangelical American army general, William Boykin, upbraiding him for engaging in 'Christian jihad' and having a faith that is 'more American than Christian'. For Evangelicals such as these, speaking out on these 'hard truths', however unpopular, is part of their 'prophetic religious vocation' and of 'being on God's side, rather than the other way around' (Wallis, 2005: 155–7, 96–7; Chapman, 2005a: 22).[15]

Discussion: Resolving the violence and injustice

This all leaves a feeling that 9/11 was an opportunity missed. The Western powers could have chosen to talk to Muslim-majority countries which were also suffering at the hands of extremists. They could have asked, *Why the Rest Hates the West* (Pearse, 2004), and honestly addressed issues of global injustice. Evangelicals could have united to protest the rush to arms, as a minority did. They could have insisted that, rather than spending money on bombs, Western governments explore more effective ways to aid and develop countries such as Afghanistan and Yemen, which became havens and breeding grounds for terrorists.[16] Later, they could have collectively raised their voices to question whether the war in Iraq was truly just. Again, some, mainly on the left, did and saw it as part of their prophetic commission to speak truth to power. Many others, however, were content to support the war cries.

Today, there are ongoing conflicts and tensions around the world, many of them involving Muslims and Christians in some way. While those in the Middle East are obviously significant, there are others in places rarely heard of. One such is the Philippines where Muslim separatists from the Moro people have been fighting for independence for many years. Yet, Aldrin Peñamora, director of the Christian-Muslim Research Center of the Philippine Council of Evangelical Churches, has been involved in peace talks with the Moro Islamic Liberation Front and admits that the 'Moro Problem' is 'really about the Christians being the problem of the Moros' through the injustice they have created (2016: 33). He leads a joint working group searching for peace.[17]

However, those that embrace such peacemaking approaches need to explain exactly what a pacific response looks like in the face of terror attacks. How can a securitized response be avoided? How can the terrorists be engaged in a process to redress injustice without rewarding violence? Some, such as Peñamora, have met and talked with extremist groups, as will be seen in Chapter 13. What impact has this had? How can Christians adopt a position of humility when those they encounter believe that, religiously and culturally, 'might is right'? Could humility lead to annihilation?

At the same time, Evangelicals on the right need to explain their strategy. How would Muslims ever come to the conclusion that the way of Jesus, the 'Prince of Peace', is indeed peaceable and just for as long as they see Evangelicals supporting nationalism, global inequality and war? At the very least, the Christian just war tradition needs to be rigorously applied and war only embarked on as a very last resort. Furthermore, if confrontationist Evangelicals insist that the jihadis are the 'true Muslims' and that 'real Islam' necessarily entails a struggle for world domination, then does this not reinforce the position of the extremists? How does it help the cause of peace and coexistence to undermine the moderate position? Do the hawks hope that so many Muslims will become disenchanted when they realize the 'true nature' of Islam, that they will abandon the faith entirely and Islam will eventually fade away? This seems an unlikely scenario, especially given the thwarting of similar hopes in a previous generation.[18] Maybe more likely Evangelicals of this persuasion, with an ear to the prophets of Armageddon and their many books, anticipate an inevitable, preordained apocalyptic conflict between Islam and the West which portends the beginning of The End. This mirrors the eschatology of groups such as ISIS which also anticipate an End-Times battle that will usher in their final vindication. This is a theme that is picked up in the next chapter as we turn to look at the place of Israel and Palestine in the Evangelical-Muslim encounter.

10

Israel-Palestine

No conflict has proved more intractable over the past century than that in Israel-Palestine. Against the background of anti-Jewish pogroms and the Holocaust in Europe, it stretches from the 1916 Sykes-Picot Agreement and the 1917 Balfour Declaration, through the 1948 Declaration of the Establishment of the State of Israel and five major Israeli-Arab wars, to the Intifadas, terrorist attacks and state military incursions of more recent years. A sporadic Middle East Peace Process, poorly brokered by the United States, has failed to bring resolution, with each side blaming the other. Jews, Muslims and Christians are all drawn into the conflict. The Bible, the church and, of course, Jesus himself have Jewish roots. Yet, at the same time, there is a shameful history of Christian antisemitism running from the early church fathers, through the medieval popes and the Reformation, to the time of the Nazis.[1] Nonetheless, through much of that time, there has been a Christian fascination with the 'Holy Land' resulting in the launching of crusades, support for the 'Jewish Return' (*Aliyah*) and speculation about 'End Times' events.

However, this chapter is not about the history, politics and rights or wrongs of this sensitive issue, as important and pressing as it is. Rather, it attempts to explore the profound impact the conflict has on contemporary Muslim-Christian relations. The majority of Palestinians, but by no means all, are Muslims, and Muslims around the world have adopted their plight as a *cause célèbre*. Events in Gaza can cause unrest in Jakarta, and Western political support for Israel is seen as biased, anti-Muslim – and Christian. Meanwhile, many Christians support the State of Israel, for reasons of theology, history or twentieth-century guilt, against what they see as threatening hordes of Arab Muslims. So, this chapter looks at how the Israel-Palestine issue affects the way Evangelicals see and interact with Islam and Muslims. As in other chapters, the quotations given are not exhaustive, and many other authors and books could have been included if it were not for space. The chapter looks at Evangelical attitudes to the people, the land and the politics before considering how Evangelicals respond in mission, prayer, prophetic speculation and peacemaking. However, we start with an all-too-brief look at some of the theology that underlies the various positions.

The theology

It is impossible to understand the attitudes of Evangelicals to the Israel-Palestine situation without some reference to 'Zionism'. This is the belief that there should be a homeland for the Jewish people and has a long history in both Christian and Jewish thoughts. From the time of the Protestant Reformation and the Puritan movement, some Christians became interested in the idea that God might restore the scattered Jewish people to 'The Land' in a literal fulfilment of how they understood biblical prophecies.[2] This enduring idea is called 'restorationism'. It became particularly important in the 'dispensationalist' teaching of John Darby (d. 1882), which drew a sharp distinction between Israel and the church, placing a great emphasis on the return of Jesus and the 'rapture' of true Christians into heaven either before or during a great End Times 'tribulation'. This teaching is still influential, especially among many American Evangelicals, and has been popularized by the Left Behind multimedia franchise.[3] However, not all 'Christian Zionists' subscribe to dispensationalism, and there are plenty of Evangelicals who reject its more extreme teachings while maintaining that 'the return of Jews from all over the world to their land, and their efforts to establish a nation-state after two millennia of being separated from controlling the land, is part of the fulfilment of biblical prophecy' (McDermott, 2016: 12).

On the other hand, there are Evangelicals who do not see the twentieth-century Jewish return as being a fulfilment of biblical prophecy. Some of these may hold a 'supersessionist' or 'replacement' theology which has a long history within Christianity. These Christians see the church as having replaced the Jewish people whom they claim God has rejected. In a very different approach, others teach that all the promises made to Israel under the Old Covenant have been fulfilled by Jesus in the New Covenant and are available to all peoples. This is often called 'fulfilment' theology, and it teaches that all Jews and non-Jews who follow Jesus are part of God's one supranational people. Its proponents reject the charge of replacement theology.

These two positions broadly parallel the polarization we have seen throughout the preceding chapters. The right-leaning, confrontational Evangelicals are more likely to be Zionist, and the left-leaning, conciliatory Evangelicals are more likely to embrace fulfilment theology. Added to these theological presuppositions, there are different ways of reading and understanding the history and politics of the situation, the details of which are beyond this chapter. However, Kuhn's descriptions of the two perspectives are, maybe, apt, noting that the first group tends to see things from a 'Western perspective' and the second from a non-Western, 'Muslim perspective' (2009: 162–70). The former Evangelicals tend to be motivated by a strong interest in the Jewish people, their customs and The Land and identify the Israeli state with the kingdom of Israel in the Bible. They often live or spend time in Israel and are inclined to see Israelis as victims while painting a negative picture of Palestinians and Muslims. The latter Evangelicals tend to see Palestinians – including both Muslims and Christians – as victims of an injustice and do not see contemporary events as a fulfilment of biblical prophecy. They are often critical of the Israeli state and its policies and are concerned that the issue creates an obstacle to Christian mission among Muslims.

The people

One of the recurring biblical texts used by confrontationists writing on the Israel-Palestine situation is Gen. 12.3, where God promises Abraham that he will bless those who bless him and curse those who curse him. This is taken to apply not just to Abraham but to all Jewish people as his offspring and hence to the modern Israeli state. 'The Word could not be plainer: if you want the blessing of God upon your life, you must *bless* Israel, not *curse* it' (Hagee, 2006: 63–4, original emphasis). This warning is sometimes presented with historical 'proof' of the danger of not blessing Israel. For instance, Pawson argues that British prime ministers Churchill, Chamberlain, Eden and Callaghan all left office shortly after 'letting God's ancient people down', whereas long-serving prime ministers Wilson, Thatcher and Blair all supported Israel in some way (2013: 152). For some it even explains why terrorist attacks happen. Evans declares that there is 'absolutely no question that God's hedge of protection was lifted from America. September 11 was a curse on our beloved nation' because of America's lack of support for Israel, and worse could follow (2005: 14).

There are many critiques of this approach. Some are concerned that it can become self-serving. For instance, Munther Isaac (2021), a Palestinian pastor and theologian, finds the 'idea that if you bless Israel, God will bless you' objectionable as it leads many people to 'support Israel simply because they want what's best for them[selves], not necessarily for Israel'. This is even the case in Africa where 'Christian Zionism combines perniciously with Prosperity Gospel preaching, interpreting Gen. 12.3 as a divine map to gain blessings – material and otherwise – through complete and uncritical support for the modern-day State of Israel'.[4] Added to this self-interest, there is a risk to associating the ancient peoples of the Bible with ethnic groups today. The promise of God's blessing is not seen to apply to Abraham's offspring through Ishmael, who is usually associated with the Arabs (see Chapter 9), despite God's words about him in Gen. 17.20. Rather, the Palestinian Arabs are often unfoundedly traced back to the Philistines of the Bible, leading to unfortunate conclusions (Price, 2001: 134).[5] Campolo overheard one Christian Zionist leader in New Zealand say, 'Were [the Jews] not called upon to exercise genocide back then? The God who ordered genocide back when Joshua invaded the Holy Land is the same God we have today' (2012: 215). The consequences of such interpretations are potentially horrific.[6]

While Christians are encouraged to bless the Jewish people and the Israeli state, Muslims are seen by antagonists as foremost among those who curse the Jews. This again is linked back to biblical themes. So Garlow suggests that 'the intense struggle in Israel and the surrounding Arab nations can only be understood historically as a struggle between the descendants of two brothers who lived 4,000 years ago: Ishmael (modern-day Arabs) and Isaac (the Jews)' (2005: 17). James Goll, an American prayer leader and writer on prophecy, sees 'the spirit of Haman' at work among Muslims today. 'It is as if the genocidal, specifically anti-Semitic spirit of Haman has stepped from the book of Esther into new death-dealing entities, not least of which is Hamas. The similar-sounding names are no accident' (Goll, 2009: 77).[7]

Such Muslim antisemitism is also found by confrontationists to be indelibly written into the Islamic texts, tradition and history. In their book *Al-Yahud: Eternal Islamic Enmity and the Jews*, Solomon and Al-Maqdisi find that 'the Islamic enmity towards the Jews, and thus to modern Israel, is profoundly Qur'anic, inspired by Allah as claimed by Mohammad' (2010: 120). Gabriel acknowledges that there are 'nice words about Jews' in the Qur'an, but points out that they are all early verses from Meccan suras and that once the Jews rejected Muhammad, he punished them. He claims from personal experience that even today Muslims are systematically taught in school, home and mosque that 'Jews hate Islam and want to destroy it' (Gabriel, 2003: 73–6, 159). Teplinsky denies that Muslim anger towards Israel is the result of the modern political situation. Rather, for her, 'hate for the Jews is embedded into fundamental Islam, beginning with the Quran. It forms an essential tenet of the ideology espoused by every Islamist state … Through the centuries, fundamental Islam has depicted the Jewish people as its greatest enemy. Fundamental Islam has generated furiously anti-Semitic rhetoric predating modern Israel by over 1,300 years' (2013: 142–3). Indeed, Lindsey traces this apparent hatred from 'the Arabian holocaust' when Muhammad was fighting Jewish tribes (a phrase also used by Gabriel (2003: 107)), through the 'institutionalized antisemitism' of the Islamic empires, to the 'admiration for Hitler' shown by some Muslims. He finishes by listing qur'anic verses which he believes 'nourish this hate' (including Q.5.51,82 and Q.4.46) (Lindsey, 2002: 120–43). Others quote the reported antisemitic comments of contemporary Muslim leaders such as Sheikh Tantawi (d. 2010), a former grand mufti of Egypt, who apparently said that the Jews are 'the enemies of Allah, descendants of pigs and apes' (P. Sookhdeo, 2007: 209).

The belief that Islam and Muslims are antisemitic is clearly a very significant factor in the way some Evangelicals view their relationship with Muslims. Irenic Evangelicals are concerned about the negative impact this has on Palestinians, both Muslim and Christian. Palestinian Christians are felt to suffer the 'double jeopardy of being a marginal presence within an already disenfranchised Arab community in Israel' (Sudworth, 2017: 81). They suffer the effects of living under Israeli control and at the same time are increasingly under pressure from extremists in the Muslim community, despite having 'fared well living with a Muslim majority and under Muslim rule' for many centuries (Awad, 2001: 70). Regardless of this, Zionists have long argued that historically 'there was no Palestinian state or people known as "Palestinians"' (Lindsey, 2002: 189). The argument is that Palestine was 'a land without a people' and that 'Palestinian' is a newly manufactured political identity. American theologian Gary Burge, however, refutes this and observes that many Evangelicals are now increasingly 'offended by Christian Zionism' and 'in surprising numbers are "crossing the line" and witnessing first hand the nature of life in the West Bank. Palestinian pastors are writing and speaking, and in the last few years, their voices have been heard' (2003: 246, 236). These include Alex Awad (2001), Yohanna Katanacho (2013), Salim Munayer (2011, 2013) and Isaac (2020), who are all both pastors and academics. Maybe surprisingly, many Palestinian Christians – although by no means all – do not have a negative view of all Muslims, being more concerned about what they see as the unjust Israeli occupation of their land.[8] For instance, 'Palestinian Evangelical theologians were instrumental in drafting' the 2011 ecumenical *Kairos Document* which makes clear their attitude to Muslims:

> 5.4.1 Our message to the Muslims is a message of love and of living together and a call to reject fanaticism and extremism. It is also a message to the world that Muslims are neither to be stereotyped as the enemy nor caricatured as terrorists but rather to be lived with in peace and engaged with in dialogue. (Kuttab, 2018: 77)[9]

The Land

Maybe even beyond their desire to bless Jewish people, many Evangelicals are fascinated by The Land itself and have a deep, emotional connection to it. It goes beyond the Jews' need for a place of security. They believe this is the very Land that God promised Abraham, Isaac and their descendants. Hagee remembers the 1948 announcement of the creation of the new Israeli state on the radio and hearing his father weeping as he said, 'Son, today is the most important day of the twentieth century. God's promise to bring the Jewish people back to Israel is being fulfilled before our eyes.' In 1978, Hagee and his wife visited Israel and experienced the 'thrill' of walking in The Land of the Bible. They 'went as tourists and came home as Zionists' (2007: chapter 2). The various twentieth-century battles that the Israelis fought and won against the surrounding Arabs over The Land became further proof that Israel is a 'miracle nation'. 'Superior training' of their army, maybe, played a part but 'God had to have been with us' (Lindsey, 2002: 213). During that time and especially after the 1967 war, lots of books were written about how prophecy was being miraculously fulfilled, and people wondered, 'Has history ever witnessed anything like the return of the Jews to the Promised Land?' (Zacharias, 2002: 72).[10] Now, there is a strong feeling that the whole of the West Bank, Gaza and the Golan Heights should all belong to Israel with Jerusalem as its capital. Consequently, confrontationists usually reject the idea of a two-state solution, whereby Palestinians would have their own state within those territories. If The Land is 'Promised', then it cannot be shared.

Palestinians, Arabs and Muslims, in general, are seen as a problem for Islam antagonists with respect to The Land. Not only do Palestinians want to establish their own state on some of The Land, but Islamic groups such as Hamas, Hezbollah and Islamic Jihad have Islamized the issue and are engaged in a jihad against Israel to throw off the occupation. So, Robertson (2003) warns that 'if God's chosen people turn over to Allah control of their most sacred sites ... Islam will have won the battle. Throughout the Muslim world the message will go forth "Allah is greater than Jehovah"' (see Chapter 3). There is a deep mistrust of Arab Muslim intentions. 'Islam will never accept Israel ... History shows clearly Israel will never be small enough for the Muslims. Their real quarrel with Israel has never been the size of its borders but its existence' (Lindsey, 2002: 218). In fact, they are convinced that 'the Muslim world recognized long ago that a two-state solution was not the real answer to the "Jewish problem". The only answer that would suffice would entail pushing the Jews into the

Mediterranean, or, as President Ahmadinejad would later opine, wiping Israel "off the map"' (Evans, 2007: 91).

However, more conciliatory Evangelicals acknowledge that The Land is also important for Muslims, who likewise 'base their claims … on their scriptures, tradition and history' (Chapman, 2015: 173; see his explanation in pp. 390–403). The Land is mentioned in the Qur'an; Muhammad is believed to have visited Jerusalem on his miraculous Night Journey; and prayer at the Al-Aqsa Mosque is highly recommended in the Hadith. Moreover, as Palestine was once under Islamic rule, many Muslims see it as a sacred waqf (endowment) which should always be governed by Muslims and believe it will feature in End Times events.

In contrast to both these positions, many Evangelicals who focus on fulfilment theology do not see the physical land of Israel-Palestine as central in God's future plans nor see the conflict as primarily religious. They believe that just as other promises in the Old Testament were fulfilled in Jesus, so too were promises concerning The Land. Chapman argues that 'there is no reason why we should be content with a *spiritual* interpretation of the Davidic monarchy, the temple and its sacrifices, but at the same time insist that teaching about the land has both a *spiritual* and a *literal* meaning' (2015: 431, original emphasis). So, while there may be an affection for the historic sites where biblical events took place, there is no expectation that it is crucially important for Christian faith today. The physical land today is simply not theologically significant. Cragg calls this 'Christian disenlandisement … absolving the mother-territory of any indispensable role for faith apart from that of memory and love'.[11] So, Burge can say, 'God does not dwell [in the Holy Land] in a manner that is uniquely different from his dwelling in other lands' (2010: chapter 8). World-renowned British Evangelical theologian John Stott (d. 2011) points out that 'the Old Testament promises about the land are nowhere repeated in the New Testament'.[12] Rather, Jesus's 'disregard for the territorial interests of his generation stands out. He does not value Jewish nationalism tied to divine claims for the land' (Burge, 2010: 53). In fact, he commissioned his followers to go to the whole world (Isaac, 2015). In this way, the idea of The Land has been both 'spiritualized' and 'universalized' (Chapman, 2021: 74). This does not mean to say that for these Evangelicals, the issue of land is not important or that they oppose the existence of the State of Israel. Rather, the land issue is seen as a sociopolitical justice issue to be resolved. If The Land is not 'Holy', then it can be shared by Israelis and Arabs, and an equitable political solution must be found.

The politics

Again, Chapman has been at the forefront of the argument and has written extensively on the issue (2004c, 2015, 2021). He believes that 'we are dealing here with one of the most important and the most bitter of all the complaints that Muslims direct towards the West' (2004a: 194) and suggests that 'if we want to understand the anger that has been building up within the Muslim world in recent decades, it is important that we try to understand what the creation of Israel has meant for Muslims' (2007b: 145). The political history is complex. Zionists see the 1948 creation of the State of Israel and its survival in the face of subsequent Arab aggression as a miraculous fulfilment of God's promises. Dissenters from this view see Israeli occupation of some of the territory as unjust and unlawful. Several of the Evangelical participants in the public sphere provide histories, although such accounts are always open to accusations of bias in both directions (Awad, 2001; Burge, 2003; Chapman, 2015; Ellisen and Dyer, 2003; Lambert, 2018; Merkley, 2011; Shannon, 2012).[13] However the story is told, the reality is that over seventy years after the creation of the State of Israel there is no peace for anyone. Israelis have no security, and Palestinians are marginalized, living with a sense of grievance over loss of land, homes, political power and basic rights.

We have already seen the emotional connection which some Evangelicals have with The Land. However, for many Western Christians, there is also a strong sense of guilt and needing to make amends for European antisemitism. American historian Arno Mayer says that, following the Second World War, 'because of the complex of guilt and horror over the Judeocide, much of the Christian world was in favour of a Jewish state'.[14] Burge recognizes the same phenomenon and says that Christians 'bear a subliminal sense of guilt for the horrors of the twentieth century that have been perpetrated on Judaism' (2003: 9). This guilt becomes a strong driver of Evangelical support for Zionism. It also becomes a strong driver of negative feelings towards Islam, as Arabs, who are mostly but not all Muslims, are resisting Israel's presence in The Land. Indeed, the resistance to the Israeli occupation of previously Arab-controlled lands has become significantly Islamized since the Six-Day War in 1967. This has caused confrontationists to increasingly see Muslims as in conflict with the State of Israel and thus, in their understanding, standing against the purposes of God. Coupled with this, Israel is seen as a bastion of democracy and minority rights in a sea of despotic Muslim lands which deny minority rights and even refuse to welcome Palestinian refugees but rather 'keep them in refugee camps to use as a propaganda tool against Israel' (McDermott, 2016: 327). So, any compromise with the Palestinians in political negotiations is strongly resisted as it is seen as giving in to God's enemies and signing the death warrant of democratic freedom in the Middle East.

On the contrary, for Islam-friendly Evangelicals, the problem is not primarily a Muslim-Jewish issue. It is first and foremost a Palestinian-Israeli issue. When former US president Jimmy Carter, a well-known Evangelical, published a book in 2006 suggesting that Israel's treatment of Palestinians amounted to 'apartheid', supporters of Israel were outraged and saw it as proof of both Carter's incompetence and also 'the belief system of the extreme Left' (Evans, 2007: 7). Many pro-Palestinian Evangelicals, however, agree with Carter in seeing Israel's policies as being discriminatory. For them, if Israel is to be regarded as having a special place in God's purposes, then it must be 'an exemplar of biblical righteousness among the nations ... Israel should be held to the same standards of justice we expect from countries such as South Africa, where our criticisms have been harsh' (Burge, 2003: 258). While they condemn Palestinian terrorism, unlike many Christian Zionists, they do not always support Israeli security policies. Chapman questions whether or not 'the building of [the security] wall, combined with the targeted assassinations, the confiscation of land, the uprooting of olive groves, the demolition of houses and the constant harassment and humiliation of old and young at check-points amounts to a kind of violence that is just as reprehensible as the more obvious terrorism of Palestinian suicide bombers' (2003: 2). Likewise, Wallis describes the Israeli response to Palestinian violence as 'massive, disproportionate retaliation' and sees a Palestinian state as non-viable as long as 'there is no contiguous Palestinian territory in the West Bank or Gaza … [as] there are only pieces of Palestinian territory with Israel controlling everything in between' (2005: 173–5). Cragg is despairing of violence on all sides asking, 'What did Palestinian suiciders [sic] gain from their self-immolation vested in the griefs of Israelis? … What did Israel gain from sundry invasions or incursions into Lebanon except a mounting of legitimate resentment?' (2008: 197).

Even so, some Israeli Christian Arabs are very pro-Israel, refusing to call themselves Palestinians. Some are even Zionists. However, the majority of Palestinian Christians share the sense of injustice felt by their Muslim compatriots over the abuses described above and often espouse 'liberation theology'.[15] For instance, the *Kairos Document*, mentioned above, as well as affirming love for Muslims, also clearly identifies the Israeli occupation as the main source of the problem:

> 4.2.1 The aggression against the Palestinian people which is the Israeli occupation, is an evil that must be resisted. It is an evil and a sin that must be resisted and removed. Primary responsibility for this rests with the Palestinians themselves suffering occupation. Christian love invites us to resist it. However, love puts an end to evil by walking in the ways of justice.[16]

However, combative Evangelicals are not at all persuaded by their arguments. As already seen, they believe that Muslim hatred of the Jews is not caused by land issues. To identify contemporary political situations as the cause of violence is 'to put the cart before the horse' (Solomon, 2006). As Brother Rachid,[17] a Moroccan convert from Islam, puts it, 'The Arab-Israeli conflict is not primarily a conflict over land, as some people think. It's an eternal struggle over religion … [Muslim] hatred towards Jews is part of Islam's doctrine before it even became political as well' (2019: KL377). In fact, in company with others, Evans believes that 'the Islamic world doesn't want the Palestinian crisis solved. The thugocracies and Islamofascists will do everything in their power to keep it from being resolved' because 'an enemy is needed in order to have an army' (2007: 9). The Palestinian issue in his thinking serves as an incentive for Islamists to maintain militias and wage jihad. Riddell, while tending to the centre – and not at all extreme – in his views, also thinks that 'while the conflict fuels the radical Islamist movement, it is not [the] root cause [of violence]', which lies within the traditions of Islam itself (2004: 171; see also Chapter 9).

Inevitably, there is always a flurry of interest whenever there is any development within the so-called Middle East Peace Process. For many years, American Evangelical organizations such as Christians United for Israel (CUFI) were vocal in their demands for the United States to recognize Jerusalem, rather than Tel Aviv, as the capital of Israel.[18] So, they were delighted in 2018 when President Trump announced that the American embassy would move there and Hagee, founder of CUFI, promised him 'blessing' and 'political immortality' as reward for his decision, personally attending the opening ceremony in Jerusalem.[19] He later described Trump's 2020 Middle East plan as 'the best peace proposal any American administration has ever put forth'.[20] Evangelicals concerned about justice strongly disagreed. Accad observed that the plan did not involve the Palestinians at all and 'only the Israelis consulted on it'. Munayer, founder of Musalaha (see below), said, 'No Palestinian leader can accept this deal, because it doesn't meet our basic needs', and Katanacho said, 'It doesn't take a "prophet" to know Trump's plan is "destined to failure" '.[21] It seems certain that the two camps will remain divided on the nature of any political settlement.

The mission

Against all this background, Evangelicals have varied responses, priorities and strategies towards both Muslims and Jews. Evangelism and mission are always high on the agenda, and the Israel-Palestine context is no exception. However, 'there are missional implications to the political affinities of Evangelicals' discussed above (Kuhn, 2009: 160), and many fear that, despite a desire to share the gospel with both Israeli Jews and Palestinian Arabs, support for one side or the other is an obstacle to the gospel.

Evangelism

For some Christian Zionists, there is often a particular concern to evangelize Jews. Sometimes this is because they see the conversion of Jews as connected to the return of Jesus, although others strongly reject this notion (Merkley, 2001: 177). Whatever the case, Muslims are not their priority. The Church's Ministry among Jewish People (CMJ) for over 200 years has been seeking to 'impact the Jewish people with the truth about Messiah Yeshua, until the day "all Israel will be saved" (Rom. 11.26)' – one of the signs of the End Times.[22] Jews for Jesus also 'relentlessly pursue God's plan for the salvation of the Jewish people'.[23] Such proselytizing organizations are very unpopular within the wider Jewish community, and converts to Christianity are often marginalized in the same way that Muslim converts are.

However, the greater concern for conciliatory Evangelicals is that Christian Zionist support for Israeli policies in the Middle East gives Muslims everywhere a negative view of the Christian gospel. Bell suggests that 'one of the biggest blockages to gaining the trust of Muslims is the fact that they perceive the West (i.e. including the Christian church) to be endorsing and financially supporting the political State of Israel' (2011: 32; also Chapman, 2021: 195). Campolo shares these concerns, recognizing that in America 'most Evangelicals support what the Zionists are doing, believing that they are acting out the will of God for the restoration of Israel ... Consequently, Arab peoples in particular, and Muslim people in general, regard Christians as being allied with their enemies' (2004: 143). This is particularly problematic in Christian broadcasting into the Middle East. Anton Deik, a Palestinian Christian lecturer and researcher, points out that Zionist programmes are broadcast on the same satellite channels as those which 'proclaim the gospel to the Arab world. Such intertwining of evangelism and Christian Zionism is a major stumbling block to the gospel'. He feels strongly that Christians 'simply cannot continue to preach the gospel while holding discriminatory and ethnocentric Christian Zionist theologies' (2020: 78, 80). This continues to fuel the rift in the Evangelical public sphere.

Prayer

There is more agreement when it comes to prayer. All sides agree that they 'should pray for the peace of Jerusalem and all of its inhabitants' (Katanacho, 2021).[24] The Day of Prayer for Jerusalem mobilizes thousands of Christians to pray annually for 'the wall of separation between Jew and Arab [to be] broken'.[25] Goll urges that 'if God is to prevail in the Middle East, He must first prevail in the hearts of Gentile Christians and their Messianic Jewish counterparts, inspiring concerted prayer, fasting and strategic action' (2009: 78). However, how that is done – and the focus, tone and content of that prayer – varies considerably. Some focus on praying for blessing on Israel and praying against Islam, while others focus on praying for the peace process and for the blessing and conversion of Muslims.

There are many Evangelical ministries focused on praying for Israel as a nation, often with the end goal of seeing Jews accepting the Messiah. Evans is the founder of the Jerusalem Prayer Team, which aims 'to build Friends of Zion to guard defend and protect the Jewish people'. It is aiming to enlist around a 100 million people to pray for the peace of Jerusalem.[26] Prayer for Israel was founded in 1969, and its 'first concern … is prayer for Messianic and other believers in the Biblical Land of Israel, and that many more may be saved'.[27] The International House of Prayer (IHOP) is also 'committed to seeing the nation of Israel walking in their full destiny at the end of the age. Our primary role is to pray … for the nation of Israel to receive their Jewish Messiah, Yeshua (Jesus)'.[28] This sort of prayer very often involves 'praying against' Islam, which is seen not only as the physical enemy of Israel and the church but also as a demonic spiritual power (see Chapter 11). As Evans explains, 'We have two opponents, the irreconcilable wing of Islam and the evil power that inspires it' (2007: 42). Farah reports being in a meeting where the leader said, 'Islam is not a religious system. It is an actual spiritual being that holds people in bondage. Pray with me to break the spirit of Islam!' (2020a: 430). In a further example, a *Christian Friends of Israel* newsletter urged its supporters to 'pray that the foundations of Islam would crumble'.[29]

Muslim-affirming Evangelicals are also committed to interceding, but tend to pray for justice and blessing for all in Israel-Palestine, including Muslims. The mission of Evangelicals for Middle East Understanding (EMEU) is 'to pray for and promote God's justice, peace, reconciliation, and religious freedom by building friendships with the people and churches of the Middle East and the West'.[30] Many Evangelicals engage with 30 Days of Prayer for the Muslim World which takes place annually during Ramadan and encourages Christians around the world to pray for Muslims. In 2022, this included a specific day of prayer for Palestinians.[31] Other groups praying for Muslims include Fellowship of Faith for Muslims and the Mahabba Network, which is 'helping to grow regular, persistent prayer for Muslims'.[32] While about more than just prayer, the National Prayer Breakfast, which takes place annually in Washington, DC, also has a positive attitude to both Muslims and Jews, and many Evangelical leaders have hosted influential Muslims from the Middle East at it, including Yasser Arafat (d. 2004), PLO leader and then archenemy of Israel, one time.[33] One observer notes that, although the Fellowship that hosts the breakfast is staunchly conservative Evangelical, 'unlike many Christian Zionists, the Fellowship's core members do not see Muslims as the enemy of God's plan for Israel'.[34] This is an example of how lines can sometimes become blurred in the public sphere.

The End Times

It is true that most Evangelicals with an interest in biblical prophecy see Muslims featuring as the enemy in God's future plans for Jews, Israel and The Land, especially in the End Times. Many of them would agree that 'one unique feature of the Bible is its predictive prophecies. No sacred book of any other world religion offers anything comparable to the Bible in this respect. Its prophets consistently predicted events of history – with amazing accuracy and descriptive detail – many centuries before they took place' (Prince, 2016: 1).[35] This includes 'learning' about Islam, as, according to End Times watcher Mark Hitchcock,[36] 'there is one book that tells us some amazing things about the future of Islam, and that book, of course, is the Bible' (2002: KL56). Thus, commentary on current affairs is often highlighted by constant reference to biblical texts, such as the use of Zech. 14 by Asher Intrater,[37] a Messianic Jew and founder of Revive Israel, to explain the Second Intifada (2011: 82). Consequently, there is an almost inexhaustible supply of books written by mainly American Evangelicals explaining their particular interpretation of these prophecies in connection with the End Times and what will happen in the Middle East. Many of them involve an explanation of Islam's supposed role (e.g. Hitchcock, 2002, 2010; Dyer, 2004; Hunt, 2005; Intrater, 2011; Jeffrey, 2010; Shade, 2014; Stice, 2014), and many are convinced that, as Jill Shannon,[38] a Messianic Jewish author, confidently declares, 'we are privileged to be living in the generation that will see the return of the Lord Yeshua (Jesus) the Messiah' (2012: KL114). However, these writers often disagree with one another, and this is sometimes a cause of acrimony within parts of the Evangelical public sphere. Some even write very specifically to refute dissenting positions, such as Joel Richardson,[39] an American author, teacher and filmmaker, who insists on a 'Muslim' rather than 'Roman' Antichrist (2012: 143ff). Of course, 'Muslims are just the latest victims in a long line of potential eschatological villains' (Aperlo, n.d.). This line stretches from Rome (ancient and modern) to communism, but the spotlight today is very much on Islam and Muslims. Some of the key recurring themes related to Islam in this writing include the future rebuilding of the Jewish temple, the identities of the Antichrist and the Beast and the Battle of Armageddon.

Following the return of the Jewish people to The Land in the twentieth century, attention turned to Jerusalem. In some dispensationalist understandings of biblical prophecy, the Second Temple which was destroyed in AD 70 will be rebuilt on Temple Mount in East Jerusalem as the prelude to the End Times. Price (2016) devotes three chapters of his 2001 book to discussing the contestation over Temple Mount and, in a video posted online, claims that the blueprints for the new temple have been drawn up and that a special red heifer is even being bred so that temple sacrifices can be resumed.[40] Youssef is also convinced that the temple will be rebuilt, but notes that 'Muslim Palestinians are angry about Jewish plans to build a third temple where the Dome of the Rock now stands ... The prophecies of Daniel and Jesus in Revelation make it clear that a third temple will be built. And it is equally clear that the temple cannot be built without enraging the Muslim world' (2016: 95–7). Such a project certainly would have huge implications for Muslim relations with Christians, not to mention Jews, and, unsurprisingly, conciliators reject the idea of a new temple. Critics such as Stephen Sizer,[41] a British clergyman and author, feel that 'to advocate the rebuilding of the temple is heresy' as no temple is needed now. 'What makes their plans even more bizarre is that they believe the temple must be rebuilt just so that it can be desecrated one more time by the Antichrist before Jesus returns' (2007: 130, 116).

Some Evangelicals believe all this will happen at the time of the great Battle of Armageddon which interpreters of prophecy believe will take place in the Last Days and involve the invasion of Israel by a huge army. Earlier books such as Lindsey's influential *Late Great Planet Earth* (1970) envisaged this being led by communist Russia, maybe along with China. By 1999, this had expanded to an unholy 'Russian/pan-Islamic' alliance (Lindsey, 1999) and later grew to a full-blown focus on Islam and its 'everlasting hatred' of the Jews (Lindsey, 2002; Hitchcock, 2002). According to Price, this will be 'a war to end all wars' as it must take place 'before a lasting peace can come to the Middle East' (2001: 365). Not all Evangelicals of this persuasion agree that this final battle will involve flesh-and-blood soldiers. Youssef leans 'toward the belief that the battle of Armageddon will be a spiritual battle rather than a military conflict' and will involve 'demonic forces' (2016: 142). However, most take it literally and believe that it will be the signal for Jesus's Second Coming. For instance, Richardson believes that Jesus himself will come back and physically wage war in the Middle East 'until the blood of slaughtered Muslim peoples will literally flow like a river', and his robes will be stained with the blood of his enemies (2012: 36; see also Aperlo, n.d.).

All these events are closely associated in the proposed eschatological timetable with the appearance of the Antichrist and the reign of the Beast described in the biblical *Book of Revelation*. The Antichrist is variously expected to become a world leader, deceive the nations and lead the above armies against Jerusalem, and any number of contemporary Evangelical writers expect this figure to be a Muslim. Islam, of course, has an eschatology of its own involving an Antichrist, called the *dajjāl*; the appearance of the Mahdi, a sort of Messiah figure; along with the return of *'Isa* (the qur'anic name for Jesus), war and a final judgement. So, the associations are easy. Richardson identifies Islam as the spirit of the Antichrist, as his 'sole driving goal will be to achieve complete world domination through his political-military-religious empire [and] Islam has this very same goal inherent in its most core doctrines'. He suggests that the biblical Antichrist could be the Islamic Mahdi figure and presents a comparison table of how the Mahdi in Islamic teaching mirrors the description of the Antichrist in the Bible (J. Richardson, 2015: 153, 75–9; see also 2012). Pawson leaves his options open and predicts that the Antichrist is likely to be either a Jew or an Arab, but that certainly at the second advent of Christ, 'the days of Islam are numbered' (2003: 185). Jack Smith, however, squarely equates the Islamic Mahdi with the Antichrist (2011) as does Teplinsky, who sees Islamic eschatology as 'an inverse parallel or mirror image of the End Times outlined in scripture. The Mahdi (Islamic Messiah) would fit the role of the Antichrist in the Bible. The Islamic Jesus would represent the Antichrist's false prophet (see Rev. 16.13, 19.20, 20.10). Islam's *dajjāl* appears to describe the true Messiah' (2013: 133). Martha Lucia,[42] an American writer on prophecy, picks up the theme of empire and sees the same evil spirit which underlies Islam as lying behind ancient empires, such as Assyria, freemasonry and the European Union, the last of which she warns will soon be taken over by Islam. In *The System of the Beast*, she says that God has revealed to her that Islam is 'the little horn in Daniel intent to bring the whole world under submission … the most heinous, sinister, anti-Christ system ever' (2008; see also Stice, 2005; Fortner, 2006).[43]

The major concern for the irenic Evangelicals is that such prophetic interpretations are not merely, according to them, poor biblical exegesis, but they create fear and hatred of Muslims among Christians. For instance, a Zwemer Center article observes that 'though Richardson intends for his work to inspire evangelism and love for Muslims, it has also played a role in the rise of Islamophobia in the church' (Aperlo, n.d.). For these Evangelicals, 'the Israeli/Palestinian conflict is more about justice than Islam' (Bell, 2006: 52), and the more important prophetic role of the Bible is to critique the injustice (e.g. D. Wagner and Davis, 2014). For Moucarry, this means 'recognising the right of the Palestinian people to a genuine and independent homeland' (2007: 119) and acknowledging that 'because of US backing, Israel has never been forced to implement UN resolutions … Israel continues to enjoy virtually unconditional support from the international community. No wonder the policies of Western countries are seen by many Arab and Muslim people as applying double standards' (2022: 87). Even Murray, who is normally a more confrontational voice on Islam, believes that 'the gospel of peace must trump the politics of prophecy in the Middle East' (2009: KL49).

Peacemaking

This all leads Isaac (2021) to ask: 'What about God's call for us to be peacemakers? It's missing completely from the Christian Zionist narrative. What is the vision for peace? What is the vision for Palestinians?' Certainly, for conciliators, the emphasis is on peacemaking and justice, and there are many Evangelical initiatives today seeking to address issues of peace in the Israel-Palestine context (e.g. D. Wagner, 2022: chapter 17). Telos is a 'pro-Israeli, pro-Palestinian, pro-Peace' movement founded by a Republican and a Democrat in the United States conducting influential people on tours to the Middle East. They 'believe that resolution to the Israeli-Palestinian conflict remains an essential moral and security imperative for the world'.[44] Musalaha, a non-profit organization based in Jerusalem, 'teaches, trains and facilitates reconciliation mainly between Israelis and Palestinians from diverse ethnic and religious backgrounds … based on biblical principles of reconciliation'.[45] The Holy Land Trust is another Christian Palestinian organization committed to non-violent resistance (NVR) that is seeking 'a peace founded on honoring the dignity and rights of all peoples and the sanctity of the Holy Land where all individuals and communities live in equality, justice, respect, and trust'.[46] This includes cooperating with Palestinian Muslims, some of whom are also involved in NVR.[47] Finally, Christ at the Checkpoint is an annual conference held at

Bethlehem Bible College that brings together a range of speakers on topics related to the conflict.[48] This latter initiative in particular is much disliked by Christian Zionists who see it as 'propagating a theological or spiritual form of anti-Semitism which is damaging the Church, demonizing Israel, and dishonouring' God (Wilkinson, 2012).

Discussion: The stakes

Arguably, the Israel-Palestine question generates more emotion, bitterness and division within the Evangelical public sphere than any other issue, with the exception of perhaps Insider Movements (see Chapter 13). As a Zionist Christian, Pawson makes the interesting comment that 'the Israel-Palestine issue has become inseparable from that of Islam in our thinking' (2003: 73). The quotations above seem to bear this out, and it has become central to both the intra-Evangelical conversation and the dialogue between Christians and Muslims as it is frequently raised by Muslims. So much so that Accad advises Christians that 'you cannot carry the gospel to the Muslim world today without having a clear and well-articulated opinion on the Palestinian tragedy' (2011: 180). Chapman goes further and suggests that 'a serious attempt on the part of the West (and especially the USA) to understand the anger of Palestinians, Arabs and Muslims and to deal with the Israeli-Palestinian conflict in a more even-handed way would go a long way – perhaps even a very long way – towards defusing the anger that many Muslims feel towards the West' (2005a: 22). Moreover, Nazir-Ali believes that 'if the Israel-Palestine situation were to be resolved in a just and peaceful way, this would remove a huge plank in the strategies of extremist leaders' (2006: 168). Certainly, some Evangelicals want to work towards such a settlement and are willing to cooperate with Muslims to bring it about. Others, however, have different priorities and seem set to continue opposing any settlement other than complete Jewish Israeli control of the whole Land.

Along with its strategic importance, the issue demonstrates the different motivations that Evangelicals have for being involved in the micro-public sphere discussing Islam. Some are not specialists in Islam at all but consider themselves to have other expertise. On the one hand, they contribute because of their study of biblical prophecy or, on the other hand, because of their knowledge of the history and theology of Zionism. They also have different anxieties and emphases. Some are driven by theological or ideological interest in the Jewish people and The Land, others by eschatology, and others still by anti-Islam security fears. For irenic Evangelicals, along with a concern for good biblical exegesis, motivation is usually more focused on justice, peacemaking and mission to Muslims.

At stake is more than just the human outcome for the various communities of the Middle East, as important as that is. For Evangelicals, the debate involves the very vision of who God is and his purposes for humankind. There are contrasting messages. One group of Evangelicals sees God as tribal and depicts the Palestinians, and Muslims more generally, as being – at one and the same time – God's enemies and yet the preordained pawns of God's End-Times purposes. Moreover, Jesus, the 'Prince of Peace', is going to return as a furious 'pride-fighter' slaying Muslims and laying waste to the lands of the Middle East.[49] This seems far removed from the Jesus of the gospels, who talked of being the servant of all (Mark 10.43–5), loving enemies (Matt. 5.44) and laying down the sword (John 18.11). In contrast, for other Evangelicals, the willingness to search for justice and a democratic political solution suggests that the Bible is not to be understood as a prophetic guidebook and that the future is open to be shaped. God's compassion, justice and love – for Jews, Muslims and others alike – are to be mediated and demonstrated through his people because they are to bear his image as it is revealed in Jesus (Col. 1.15). These two ways of thinking will inevitably have a significant impact on how Evangelicals think about Islam and relate to Muslims. To pursue the first casts Muslims as hateful, violent enemies to be defeated. To pursue the second casts Muslims as victims to be partnered with in the pursuit of peace and justice. The first risks Christians themselves becoming hateful and violent, thus alienating Muslims. The second risks Christians being abused and overpowered, should the first prophetic warnings of Muslim enmity prove to be the case.

11

So Islam is …

This chapter outlines the range of different answers that Evangelical writers give to the question 'What is Islam?' It should have become clear through the preceding chapters that Evangelicals around the world differ greatly. The answers they give determine how they react to Muslims they meet, how they relate to Muslim communities and how they talk about Islam among themselves in the Evangelical micro-public sphere. How Evangelicals think about Muhammad and the Qur'an shapes how they see Islam, its origins and nature. If Muhammad was a demon-possessed deceiver, then Islam is a diabolical existential threat. If the Qur'an was a later fabrication, then Islam is an empty man-made system designed for political power. If Muhammad was in relationship with Christians and just in error on certain points, then maybe Islam can be viewed more positively, and Muslims may be seen as cousins. If the Sharia is a draconian, unbending legal code being used as a tool to seize power and control nations, then it must be resisted at every turn. If it is an outdated expression of how Muslims should live their lives, which is open to fresh interpretation, then maybe it can be reformed and accommodated. If violent Muslims are true Muslims and all Muslims persecute Christians, then maybe Evangelicals should go to war against them. If violent Muslims are the exception, tarnishing the image of Islam, then Evangelicals should stand shoulder to shoulder with moderate Muslims and partner with them. Most importantly, if Christians and Muslims worship the same God and Allah is the God of the Bible, albeit described erroneously, then the two communities may be on the same page and God/Allah may be at work among Muslims. However, if Allah is a different being, even a demonic being, then Christians and Muslims are on different pages and are in permanent enmity.

… a religion

It is uncontroversial to say that Islam is a religion. Indeed, for many Evangelicals it is 'a *man-made* religious system', although not to be confused with 'Muslims [who] are people, made by God in his own image' (Houssney, 2010: 13, emphasis added). Riddell suggests that there is a 'glue' holding Islam together which is 'a compound of various factors, including regard for Muhammad as the final and greatest prophet; holding to the Qur'an and Hadith as sacred scripture; considering the Islamic *shariʿa* as divine law …

and recognizing the pillars of Islamic practice and the core doctrines as shared elements of the faith' (2004: 210). All Muslims – and Evangelicals – would recognize these elements, although they will certainly disagree over their interpretation and relative emphasis.

Beyond these things Evangelicals disagree over exactly what Islam is. Quosigk found in her research that, in the United States, traditionalists 'saw Islam as a false religion', but progressives looked at it 'more as a cultural form than a religion that was either right or wrong'.[1] This would seem to be more broadly true. Confrontationists see it as a heresy, discontinuous from Christianity, as a political ideology or as an anti-Christian, existential threat which has one true or 'essential' nature. Conciliators, on the other hand, tend to focus on the complexity of different traditions within Islam and the diversity of Muslims, often using a social science lens to ensure that they do not misrepresent Islam.

… a heresy

Those who see Islam as a 'false religion' (e.g. Youssef, 2017: 2) stand in the tradition of early writers such as John of Damascus and the later Reformers who saw Islam as a Christian heresy. For instance, Houssney says that Christians 'must love Muslims while hating the lies that keep them in captivity. That sounds extreme to post-modern ears, which have been taught to respect all religions. But Islam is a false gospel, and Muhammad was a false prophet who claimed that Jesus did not die on the cross to save us from our sins' (2010: 47). Sookhdeo agrees and suggests that Islam should 'not be viewed as a brother monotheistic faith like Judaism with which Christians have a special relationship. The idea of three sibling "Abrahamic" faiths is an Islamic concept, not a Christian one. Rather Islam should be viewed in the same bracket as Christian heresies' (2009a: 58).[2]

Some, however, see parallels between Islam and Judaism, not least because of their shared emphasis on law. Bell describes Islam as 'an Arabized reflection of ancient Judaism' and believes that 'watching Muslims trying to live out *shariʿa* is like flashing back to Old Testament times and what it might have been like to live among ancient Hebrews' (2006: 73). Moucarry agrees that 'Islamic law and Jewish law are not fundamentally different' (2022: 20). Glaser also thinks that 'a starting point for theologizing about Islam might be that Islam is a form of Judaism, albeit a form that differs from current rabbinic Judaism as well as from Judaism of the New Testament period in several important ways' (2020b: 323). This encourages some Evangelicals to see more continuity between the three religions. Nazir-Ali sees 'close historical and, whatever the differences, theological connections' between them, such as the belief in one God, the Creator, and a final destiny for humankind, none of which are shared with Hinduism, for example (2008c: 30).

… a political ideology

Other Evangelicals, however, do not primarily see Islam as a religion. It is something much broader – and more concerning. Joel Richardson sees Islam as 'the epitome of a totalitarian ideology' (2012: 68). For Solomon and Maqdisi, 'Islam is neither a religion nor a faith in a personal way, as defined and understood in the West. It is a whole encompassing political system, armed in religious outfit, addressing every aspect of the life of its adherents' (2009b: 93).

For these Evangelicals, Islam is intrinsically undemocratic. It is an existential threat. 'Islam is, in effect, the single most vital competitor to Western ideals of civilization on the world scene. The logic of Islam is to bring every square inch of this planet under submission to the rule of the Qur'an' (Mohler, 2013). The Oak Initiative, mentioned above, encourages its adherents to 'stand for America [and] for our God given Constitutional Republic and stand against those who seek to subvert it thru Marxism, Socialism, and Islamization'.[3] Some fear that such a stand is not taking place. For instance, Robinson complains that politicians seem oblivious and take an 'attitude of appeasement towards Muslims' like that of Chamberlain's response to Hitler (2010: 21).

... a conspiracy

Many Evangelicals who fear that Islam is anti-democratic believe that Muslims are part of an orchestrated conspiracy to destroy Christianity and their way of life in the West. Several writers report on such a plan to 'destroy Western civilization from within', reportedly discovered by the FBI in 2004 in 'a treasure trove of jihadist documents' written by the Muslim Brotherhood and Hamas (Youssef, 2015: 20; see also Cox and Marks, 2006: 93; P. Sookhdeo, 2008a: 225). Such plans are believed to be cloaked in an Islamic concept called *taqīya* (dissimulation), which allows Muslims to conceal their identity or true intent in certain situations.[4]

However, the fear is that this use of *taqīya* is not just limited to a few extremist Muslims but is widespread among Muslims. A report by the Institute for the Study of Islam and Christianity, linked to Sookhdeo, suggested that even 'seemingly moderate and liberal British Muslim leaders are supporters of the "global Islamic revival" ... Could it be that they have a hidden agenda of a staged Islamization of Western society, in which duplicity and deceit must play an important role at this stage?' (2005: 129). Sookhdeo believes that such deception or lying has 'in practice become the norm of public behaviour among all Muslims whenever there is a conflict between faith and expediency' (2007: 196). Solomon and Maqdisi put it more bluntly: '*Taqiyya* is practised by all Muslims.' Referring to the Hadith, they point out that 'Muhammad sanctioned lying by saying that Allah will not hold a Muslim accountable when he lies in three situations', namely, when in war or espionage, between a husband and wife, and when peacemaking (2007: 25; also J. Richardson, 2015: 156–65).[5]

Gauss claims that 'Muhammad gave his followers permission – with the apparent blessing of Allah – to lie whenever it was convenient or to their advantage' (2009: 123). Others are a little more nuanced. Durie acknowledges that 'lying is considered a very serious sin in Islam' but looks at 'situations where lying is permissible' and concludes that Islam promotes a 'utilitarian ethic, that in lying, the end justifies the means' (2009c: 57–60). Thus, some believe that Muslims say one thing in public to English speakers but something else in Arabic or Urdu to Muslims in the mosque. For instance,

Houssney recounts a visit to a mosque in South Africa where the imam prayed in Arabic for 'the destruction of America and Europe, even using the phrase "Christian nations"'. When challenged afterwards, the imam, not realizing that Houssney was an Arabic speaker, denied it. He was then very embarrassed to discover that he had been understood by a Christian and admitted 'sheepishly [that] "the Qur'an tells us that the Umma of Islam is to conquer the world"' (Houssney 2010: 143). Stories like this lead Rosemary Sookhdeo to believe that 'in Islam there is not such a condemnation of lying as there is in Western culture'. She is particularly concerned that it is common for a Muslim man to lie in order to marry a non-Muslim woman who will then be converted to Islam (2005: 65). There are even stories of Muslims infiltrating churches in order to entice Christians away from the faith (P. Sookhdeo, 2009a: 38).

However, *taqīya* has become a controversial topic in Evangelical circles. Conspiracy theories, while always popular, are dangerous and corrosive of relationships and trust. There are Evangelicals very concerned that the concept, while evidently being an Islamic principle, is being invoked too broadly and is damaging Christian-Muslim relations. Anglican bishop Toby Howarth explains the background of *taqīya* in both Sunni and Shia thought and sees it as being separate from the issue of general lying, which is forbidden in Islam. He compares it to the Christian ethics around lying and observes that Christians themselves sometimes conceal the truth, for instance, when engaged in mission to Muslims or in times of war (2011). Accad points out that the Qur'an strongly denounces hypocrisy and that *taqīya* is a disputed concept among Muslims – especially between Sunnis and Shia – only to be used in certain situations. He implores Christians not to 'fear your Muslim neighbors. Do not accuse them of hypocrisy, in false witness to the truth. Invite them into your households and communities of faith by practicing biblical hospitality' (2017: 23). Azumah too worries that Christians will begin to suspect Muslims who claim to have converted of, in fact, practising *taqīya* (2012: 136). These authors are all afraid that an emphasis on *taqīya* will paralyse Christians with fear, prevent them forming normal relationships with Muslims and 'undermine trust between Christians and Muslims' – in both directions (Howarth, 2011: 221).

… the enemy

For confrontationists, however, the concern is that this threat is not just a concealed political conspiracy, but it is also both a violent and theological threat directed specifically against Christians. We have already explored in depth in Chapter 9 the degree to which Evangelicals consider Islam to be violent. The point here is that, for some, Islam is a specific existential threat to Christianity. Sookhdeo warns that 'Christians must always bear in mind that Islam denies the heart of the Christian faith, and that its very creed was formulated to deny the deity of Christ and the finality of His revelation' (2009a: 59). He believes that 'the vast majority of contemporary Muslim scholars hold to [the] classical theory of war', which gives Muslims, when they are strong enough to do so, 'normative … permission to attack Jews and Christians' who do not submit to Islam (2007: 98–100). Jenny Taylor (2018) warns that, around the world today, 'where Islam is dominant, churches will burn', and Wagner believes that as Muslims build mosques 'they also seek the destruction of Christian churches' (2012: 93). In fact, American pastor Jeff Morton feels that 'everything about Islam is anti-Christian, anti-Trinity, anti-Father, anti-Son, anti-church, anti-cross and anti-Bible' (2012: 84). For some, this theological undermining of Christian doctrine is one of the main reasons for attacks by Muslims on Christians, and especially those who have converted from Islam (see Chapter 8).

Africa is an acute example, as Christian and Muslim groups in society are often constituted along tribal and ethnic lines with neither being in a clear majority, thus creating a potential for tension, especially in West and East Africa. Taylor reports on a visit by Durie to Ethiopia, a country with historically peaceful Christian-Muslim relations. Today, however, 'some regions of the country have very high percentages of Muslims, particularly those in the northeast, and in these regions, Christians can be persecuted'. She wryly notes that 'apparently the same does not happen to Muslims in Christian-majority areas' (J. Taylor, 2018). So, it is, maybe, not surprising Azumah (2011) observes in the African context that 'Islam is presented mainly as a challenge, a threat, and an enemy to Christians and Christianity'. However, he also comments that 'apart from instances of communal violence in places like Indonesia and Northern Nigeria, Christians are not the primary targets of jihadist Muslims ... The actual number of Christians killed in Islamist violence pales into insignificance when compared with the number of Muslims killed. In other words, Muslims are the main victims of Islamist violence' (2009: 3).

Of course, everyone should be concerned when there are those who challenge the rule of law, conceal their true intent and threaten the security of those around them. Accounts of what terrorist groups such as Al-Qaeda, ISIS and Boko Haram are doing are chilling (e.g. Moore and Cooper, 2020; Kendal, 2016). Even those who usually demonstrate a more positive view of Muslims are concerned at what some segments of the Muslim community are doing. Bell says, 'If we're going to avoid political naivety, we have to recognise the fact that not all Muslims are "ordinary" ... [some] work subversively in an effort to use democracy in order to destroy democracy.' However, he calls this 'the dark side of Islam' and is 'angry with such Muslims who are engaged in "politicised Islam"' but stops short of associating this with the totality of Islam and Muslims (2006: 2, 43).

... demonic

It is not surprising that the end result of the above views of Islam as heresy and anti-Christian political conspiracy is for many confrontationist Evangelicals to see Islam as being demonic. Jones's book title, *Islam Is of the Devil* (2010), is typically pungent. Pawson writes of a 'satanic imitation' with 'supernatural power' for 'deception', 'distraction' and 'destruction', although he insists that as individuals 'Muslims are not our enemies' and that 'physical "carnal" warfare is worse than useless against them' (2003: 82–6). Likewise, Morton employs a New Testament (2 Cor. 11.14) image of the devil when he says that 'the source of Islam is the angel of light ... [and] his very fertile imagination' (2012: 83). This view is also common in West Africa where Akinade comments that 'Nigerian Evangelicals and Pentecostals have demonized the theological credentials of Islam' (2014: 125).

However, Chapman is concerned that

> there's a real danger of getting things out of proportion … Attributing everything we dislike or disagree with in Islam to demonic forces … [is] a terrible oversimplification of complex issues … and allows us to ignore much of what has happened. The very existence of Islam can be seen as a judgement on the Christian church, and the record of the church over fourteen centuries in its relations with Islam should leave us with a sense of shame. (2007b: 270–1)

Others share this sense of shame. Musk tells a story of hearing a preacher say from the pulpit that the Qur'an is a counterfeit from the devil and comments that 'even if he were absolutely right, should not such a pronouncement be made with weeping and with acknowledgement that our historic Christian failure in mission had probably left the field open for the development of alternative, religious allegiances such as Islam?' (2005: 84). And Intrater admits, 'I am saddened to think that the pride and corruption of Jews and Christians may have pushed Muslims away from faith in the Bible. I am also saddened that throughout the centuries, the religion of Islam has turned into such a monster, when its origins in the Qur'an were more moderate' (2011: 190).

This suggests to some that if Islam is a challenge to the church, it is not necessarily all demonic. Maybe God is using Islam to bring judgement on the Western church. Pawson bemoans the state of Western Christianity and observes that 'whenever Islam has spread in strength, the Christian church has tended to disappear'. He warns that 'unless there is a radical change (which is what repentance is), much of the church could disappear', although he does believe 'a remnant will remain' (2003: 188–9). Sookhdeo also thinks that the rise of Islam may be seen as 'a possible warning of a coming judgement' while at the same time seeing it as 'an opportunity for mission' (2011a: 91).

… an essence

Through all the above definitions, there is a common thread in confrontational thinking. Islam always has been and always will be essentially the same. For these Evangelicals, there is only one 'true' Islam, which is the more politically oriented, violent form of Islamism. For instance, Sookhdeo explains that 'Islamism is simply the essence of classical Islam' (2007: 10). Former Muslim Gabriel defines 'fundamentalist Muslims' as 'the ones who perpetrate terrorism. They sometimes have the long beards and head coverings. Their goal is to practice Islam as Muhammad did. Though we call them radicals, they are practising *true* Islam' (2002: 39, emphasis added). The conclusion of these Evangelicals is that Islam cannot be peaceful. 'That there are many moderate Muslims, there can be no doubt, but as to the existence of historical, mainstream moderate Islam – where's the evidence?' (Pilcrow Press, 2007: 50).

Muslims then are judged against this essential standard. For instance, BMB and former Hamas member Yousef sees Islam akin to a malevolent secret order drawing people in deeper and deeper:

> Islamic life is like a ladder, with prayer and praising Allah as the bottom rung. The higher rungs represent helping the poor and needy, establishing schools, and supporting charities. The highest rung is jihad. The ladder is tall. Few look up to see what is at the top. And progress is usually gradual, almost imperceptible – like a barn cat stalking a swallow .... Traditional Muslims stand at the foot of the ladder, living in guilt for not really practising Islam. At the top are fundamentalists, the ones you see in the news killing women and children for the glory of the god of the Qur'an. (2010: 11–12)

Yousef goes on to suggest that 'a moderate Muslim is actually more dangerous than the fundamentalist ... because he appears to be harmless, and you can never tell when he has taken the next step towards the top. Most suicide bombers began as moderates' (2010: 12). Pawson holds a similar view and thinks that 'though it is undoubtedly true that there are many peace-loving, law-abiding, hardworking, freedom-enjoying Muslims living in the West, it has to be said that this is at the cost of being less than true to their own religion' (2003: 74). In other words, moderate, peace-loving Muslims are not being true to 'real' Islam.

This does not stop some of these Evangelicals supporting the intent of these moderates. While viewing the more puritanical as being 'true' Muslims, they want to encourage those they see as being more open to Western views. For instance, while bemoaning the ubiquity of quotations by writers such as al-Banna, Mawdudi and Qutb on the internet, Gabriel suggests that moderate Muslims should post the books of Egyptian Muslim Farag Foda who, in 1992, was 'assassinated by radicals for exposing the evil of radicalism' (2007: 171). Those supported are often Muslim liberal progressives, such as Tariq Ali, Irshad Manji and Abdullahi An-Na'im, who either grew up in the West or have had to flee to the West because of threats and intimidation. Sookhdeo notes that 'some progressive Muslim reformers ... face charges of apostasy and blasphemy as well as threats of violence and death, so many have emigrated to the West' (2013: 36). These reformers are seen as having little support in their own communities (Cox and Marks, 2006: 151, 96; P. Sookhdeo, 2008a: 77). Those who are called moderates yet remain closer to the Islamic tradition, such as Tariq Ramadan, tend to be viewed with more suspicion.

Other Evangelicals accept that there is a legitimate intra-Muslim debate on the nature of Islam, with various factions laying claim to the 'true' interpretation of Islam. Catherwood believes that when it comes to extremist and moderate versions of Islam, '*both* are fully legitimate versions, depending upon the interpretation of Islam you wish to follow' (2003: 135, original emphasis). However, as Azumah points out, 'The issue that concerns non-Muslims is Islam as it is understood and lived by their Muslim relations and neighbours. It is this Islam, and not the so-called "true" and "original" Islam in textbooks, that affects non-Muslims' (2001: 234). Wallis suggests that 'the best thing that moderate and progressive Christians can do in the struggle with fundamentalism in other faiths is to make powerful alliances with the moderate and progressive leaders and communities in those other faith communities' and highlights the work of Muslims such as Eboo Patel and Daisy Khan in the United States (2013: 145).

... diverse

There are plenty of Evangelicals who find the above essentialist definitions of Islam to be problematic, unfair and destructive. Stone, who as a former convert to Islam has more experience than most, says:

> Frankly, I find that most Christians who write about Muslims and Islam are just way off base and end up presenting a straw man and furthering the misunderstanding of Muslims and Islam. As a distortion of both, they fail to prepare Christians to see and experience real Muslims as those Muslims think and live. They fail to show the diversity of expressions of Islam and erroneously boil Islam down to an essence that just doesn't exist. (2016: 4)

In any case, Riddell feels it is not for Christians to decide who the real Muslims are. He says that 'Muslim radicals are often seen by Christian evangelicals (especially fundamentalists) as "real Muslims" because of their scriptural-literalist approach. This response, however, is really more of a window into the mind of the Christians concerned' (2004: 166). Rather, these Evangelicals observe that 'not all Muslims have the same religious orientation. Muslims are as diverse in religious practices, appearance, and lifestyle as are Christians' (Taber, 2009: 78). They point to the huge diversity of Islam around the world and find it impossible to reduce it to one simple essence. For instance, Reisacher says:

> Although I believe it is important to highlight the common denominators in Islam, if we don't mention the observable differences in Islam and Muslim societies, we run the risk of reductionism, essentialism, and a distortion of a religion that spans centuries and the globe. In claiming that Islam is either bad with nothing good in it or good with nothing bad in it, we become blind to the many manifestations and interpretations of Islam. (2017a: 223)

Nazir-Ali says something similar and points out that historically there has been 'no one monolithic Islamic civilization. Rather, there are a number of civilizations that arose because of the interaction of Islam with the local culture and tradition' (2002: 45). Some authors recognize that many, maybe even most, Muslims want to distance themselves from the violent and puritanical interpretations of Islam. Musk thinks that the majority of Muslims are peace-loving and genuinely believe that Islam is peaceful (2008: xvi).

So, the definition or description of Islam becomes much broader. For instance, Farah suggests that Islam is 'a multifarious set of interpretations and practices that

Muslims use in various ways in different contexts to meet diverse needs'. This shifts the focus away from texts and what he calls a 'top-down' approach, and, indeed, away from Islam, and onto Muslims. While he recognizes that 'there is such a thing as Islam, there are also many islams [*sic*] that draw from this heritage'. He pictures each Muslim society as a 'braided rope' in which Islam is but one thread along with strands of 'politics, culture, history, geography, rituals, values, language, etc' (Farah, 2018: 14–18).

Of course, those who are concerned about the textual and theological roots of violence in Islam also recognize this diversity. For them too, it is clear that 'any thoughtful response to Islamism must take Muslim diversity extremely seriously and avoid religious and socio-political reductionism' (Orr-Ewing and Orr-Ewing, 2002: 109). In the same vein, Sookhdeo admits:

> Although Islam is one, there is still an important distinction which must be drawn between Islam the ideology, and Muslims the people who follow it. While Islam the ideology may cause great hardship and suffering to non-Muslims, it also causes great hardship and suffering to many Muslims (particularly women). If an 'enemy' is to be identified, then the enemy is not Muslims but the classical interpretation of Islam. (2007: 431)

However, in these writings the texts and top-down approach still tend to be prioritized over other factors.

… Muslims

So, Chapman suggests that 'we may need to be thinking about "Muslims" as much as about "Islam"' (2007b: 27), or what Azumah calls 'the human face of Islam' (2008b: 5). A 'bottom-up' approach which focuses on Muslims as people rather than a reified, essential Islam helps do this. This is consistent with caring for and loving Muslims as people. 'A Christian perspective on Islam ought to be at the same time incarnational, sympathetic, and critical. It should be concerned more with Muslim people than with Islam. Muslims are first and foremost human beings, made in God's image and loved by God as much as we are' (Moucarry, 2010a).

Such concerns have for a long time been reflected in the study of and encounter with Sufism (e.g. Collins, 2021) and what is often called 'Folk Islam' (e.g. Parshall, 2006; R. Love, 2000). As Musk puts it in *The Unseen Face of Islam*, 'It is plain that the beliefs and practices of ordinary Muslims contradict many formal aspects of Islamic faith' (2003b: 202).[6] For instance, many Muslims pray at the shrine or tomb of a reputed holy man; use charms, amulets and potions; or engage in occult practices. In a case study of the Beja tribe in Sudan, an American pastor and missions professor, Robin Hadaway, explores how Folk Muslims blend 'pure Islam' with the influences of both African Traditional Religions and Sufism and quotes Parshall as saying that, maybe, 70 per cent of Muslims follow some sort of Folk Islam (2018: 70). In Pakistan, Larson observes that 'the line of separation between folk and traditional Islam is often thin. "People of the shrine" are usually also "people of the mosque"' (2018: 82).

These practices are not limited to remote rural areas among backward or uneducated people. Professional people may well use charms; university students might visit shrines; and teachers might carry a Qur'an for physical and spiritual protection (Daniels, 2018: 211). So, many Evangelicals feel it is important to describe such unorthodox beliefs and practices in order to properly understand 'lived Islam'. They also see these practices as a possible source of demonic oppression in people's lives. 'The Muslims involved are bound by a very real fear and Satan rules without resistance in their lives. There can be no doubt that occult practices in folk Islam have spiritual power over those who in some way have strayed into that arena' (Goldsmith, 2009: 69). Some Evangelicals who have lived in Muslim communities even report being involved in demonic power encounters and deliverance (e.g. R. Love, 2000).

Another important aspect of defining Islam and describing Muslims is paying attention to gender. Much of the discussion above revolves around male commentators considering largely patriarchal ideas of Islam. However, it is important to hear women's voices – both Christian and Muslim. Cathy Hine, an Australian missiologist who is part of the When Women Speak network, points out that 'Muslim women today are (re)negotiating what it means to be Muslim: challenging the male interpretations and the rules of tradition in order to live their faith with integrity; fighting the violences of discourse and practice that marginalize and isolate, that promote their subjectivity and deny their agency; and seeking to be "true Muslims"' (2017: 114). Dale (2021) too engages with Muslim female writers and explores issues related to women. Likewise, Adeney challenges the idea that Muslim women are all oppressed and need 'saving', seeing them as highly diverse. 'Muslim women are not primarily victims. In many spheres, they are active decision-makers who demonstrate competency and creativity' (2018: 109).

These sorts of descriptions of gendered and lived Islam are a major focus for some who want to make sure they speak honestly and fairly. Glaser says that the command 'you shall not give false testimony' (Ex. 20.16) is 'the basis of all my attempts to talk about other faiths. It has been the driving force for my study of Islam … I want to speak the truth about my neighbour' (2005: 235). Chapman concurs and says that 'if we are to avoid giving false testimony against our neighbour (Ex. 20.16), it is essential that Christians should allow Muslims to define themselves' (2007a: 1). In other words, Evangelicals have to listen to different Muslims and accept that they will all understand and interpret Islam in different ways.

… a social construct

Such an approach often draws on the social sciences as much as on theology for its descriptions of Islam. Reisacher believes that 'anthropology and sociology of Islam offer a much "thicker description" of Muslim societies than the study of Islam limited to the sacred texts … . Islam cannot be defined in one sentence. I believe that our task as missiologists is to expand the definition of Islam to make it reflect the realities of the people we encounter in mission' (2017: 233, 241). Certainly, quite a few who have spent time living and working with Muslims have either been engaged in or gone on to study and research in the social sciences (e.g. K. Kraft, 2013). Schlorff calls the 'explosion in missiological studies ... nothing short of phenomenal' (2006: 25).

However, other Evangelicals are suspicious of social science and the focus on 'bottom-up' understandings. They vehemently reject Chapman's idea that 'Islam is what Muslims say it is' (2007b: 59). Bill Nikides, an American pastor and church planter, sees this as part of a wider trend, 'a tug-of-war for influence in the church waged between the theologians on one side and the sociologists and anthropologists on the other' (2006: 3). Former Muslim Qureshi says, 'The sociologically inclined might say that Islam is simply the sum experience of all Muslims, but I would disagree, as would most Muslims. Islam is an entity beyond its people. Even if there were no one to experience it, we could still talk about Islam. Islam exists beyond experience' (2016a: 25). Morton is also concerned that some Evangelicals 'more often than not rely on social science for their conclusions' rather than looking in scripture (2012: 90). For him Islam is an all-encompassing religion, and the culture of Muslims is the Sunnah of Muhammad.

Nonetheless, Evangelicals seeking fairness and engaged in the social sciences are not unaware of this danger and advocate holding the two approaches in balance. Glaser (2016), for instance, is committed to *Thinking Biblically about Islam*. Accad (2019) engages seriously with the Islamic *tafsīr* tradition, a textual undertaking, as does Cumming.[7] Farah is supportive of 'the anthropological approach to Islam' but goes on to say that 'as we seek to interpret Islam, both of these perspectives are important. Top-down and bottom-up approaches are often competing, but instead they should complement and critique each other' (2020b: 196).

Summing up the situation, Riddell sees two approaches in play with some focusing on 'the human faces of Muslim people, which reflect the diversity of Islam' and others on 'a system of Islam, which provides its elements of unity'. He believes that 'engagement should be two pronged: engaging with people, and engaging with the system' and counsels that 'we should be wary of those Christians who take a blinkered approach, insisting that we should focus on only one or the other of these two dimensions of Islam' (2004: 210).

Discussion: Imagined futures

This tension between Evangelicals has been clearly seen throughout the previous chapters. Bell sums it up and makes his own centrist position clear when he says:

> I have friends who are becoming either *ultra*-conciliatory or *ultra*-combative; to do this they have to be increasingly impervious to any facts that do not affirm their prior conclusions ... . This closed-mindedness is present at each end of the spectrum of opinion on which we can all be placed. My own position is where I believe we all should be, namely somewhere in the middle. This is one fence we do well to sit on and is not a matter of indecision, or a lack of conviction; rather it is grasping the fact and the fiction about both views. The aim of [his book *Mountains*

> *Move*] is to show how we can achieve a balance between *naivety* and *hostility*, and between *complacency* and *panic*. (2021: 7, original emphasis)

However, it has also become obvious that Muslims too are diverse and even divided. They interpret their texts differently to one another, look to different histories and come from different cultures. The struggle between progressives and conservatives mirrors that among Christians. Some Evangelicals are more willing to admit this diversity among Muslims than others. For Evangelical doves, the future direction which Muslims globally take in response to this struggle really is an open question. They can imagine that it is entirely possible for moderate Muslims to interpret and apply their texts and traditions in such a way as to integrate Muslim cultures and polities into peaceable, fraternal global relations. They believe it is possible that moderate Muslims may win the day and take an overwhelming majority of Muslims with them in this battle.

For the hawks, this seems not just unlikely but to be against everything they believe Islam to be. They have read the texts and the history. There is no other way for them to be honestly interpreted. Animated by dark spiritual powers, they can only imagine Muslims on an inevitable collision course with all non-Muslims around them. For these Evangelicals, Huntingdon was right.[8] A clash of civilizations is already taking place and is unavoidable and irreversible. The only hope is to destroy Islam ideologically – or for some, if need be, militarily. For those Evangelicals focused on apocalypse and the End Times, none of this is surprising. They are expecting a Muslim Antichrist, and Islam is destined to be the Beast, the demonic being of the *Book of Revelation*, which challenges God's kingdom and is destroyed in the Lake of Fire (Rev. 19.19–21).

The approaches and strategies that these different responses lead to will be explored now in Part 3. For those of an open disposition, dialogue, partnership and peacemaking with Muslims are all worthwhile activities alongside proclamation of the gospel. For those with closed views, this proclamation is best done in more assertive ways that not only defend the truths of the gospel but also aim to undermine and destroy the lie that is Islam – before it destroys the church.

Part 3

Evangelicals engaging with Muslims

12

Talking strategies

The previous chapters have looked at key questions in the encounter between Evangelicals and Muslims. The answers to these questions shape the attitudes Evangelicals have towards Islam and how they talk *about* Muslims. Part 3 looks at how Evangelicals talk *to* or *with* Muslims and explores the strategies they adopt in *mission* to Muslims. Inevitably these strategies stem from the attitudes and beliefs discussed above and exhibit a similar tension within the Evangelical public sphere. This chapter discusses ways which Evangelicals talk to Muslims and examines evangelism and conversion, friendship and dialogue, and apologetics and polemics. It cannot provide an in-depth treatment of each topic or strategy but again provides sample quotations from Evangelicals representing different points of view and approaches which are suggestive of further reading.

Evangelism: A non-negotiable

For Christians of a pluralist, ecumenical disposition, often along with civil authorities, evangelism and mission among Muslims may seem divisive, unnecessary, undesirable, dangerous even. For Evangelicals who hold to the uniqueness of Christ, however, evangelism, or bearing witness, is an important aspect – probably even the primary aspect – of their approach towards Muslims. They want Muslims to believe their gospel and start to follow Jesus. For instance, among Evangelical leaders at the Third Lausanne Congress on World Evangelization in Cape Town in 2010, 59 per cent said it was a priority to 'evangelize Muslims', second only to the 'non-religious'.[1] If this urge is sometimes repressed among Christians in Western cultures, which are largely cool towards religion and unsure about conversion, in other parts of the world, evangelism is very much the norm. For instance, 'African Christians, almost without exception, agree on the need to share their faith with Muslims and, unlike their Western co-religionists, are neither apologetic nor secretive about that' (Azumah, 2011: 62).

Even those who engage in what are sometimes labelled 'inter-faith relations' affirm that witness is important. For instance, some who work as inter-faith advisors for the Church of England recognize that Christianity and Islam are both missionary faiths whose followers want to bear witness to one another. However, how that is done is important, and the stories that Christians share must be 'real and authentic'

(Sudworth, 2007: 62). Tom Wilson, director of the St Philip's Centre in Leicester, UK, explains it this way.[2] 'Rather than talk about mission or evangelism, I prefer to talk about intentional growth, as all faith communities do this, normally focusing on three distinct but interrelated areas of family expansion, recalling the lapsed faithful, and welcoming spiritual seekers' (2019: 15).

This is certainly true of Muslim communities, and most Evangelicals are aware that Muslims engage in *da'wa* (P. Sookhdeo, 2014a). Indeed, this is seen as a real threat in the West, and there are fears that their efforts are meeting with some success, especially in Black communities (Ellis, 2008; Reddie, 2009). William Wagner calls it 'the quiet revolution', presenting a table comparing it to Christian mission before exploring how Muslims engage in *da'wa* in education, academia, prisons and among minorities. His recommended antidote is for 'Christians to become more vocal in proclaiming their own faith' (2012: 248). Azumah observes something similar in Africa and Asia, noting that *da'wa* is funded by Muslim governments as well as organizations (2013a: 137). Indeed, there are organizations, such as the World Islamic Call Society and Muslim World League, which exist for global *da'wa*.

Conversion: A real possibility

The idea that Muslims may be seekers and even choose to convert to Christianity is a very important part of the discussion about Evangelical approaches to Islam and witness. Cragg, for instance, for all his intellect and respect for Islam, 'never abandoned the aim of "recruitment" to Christian understanding and loyalty' and always held that 'the Gospel is conversionist through and through'.[3] However, we have seen in Chapter 8 that, under most interpretations of traditional Sharia, apostasy is outlawed within Islam, punishable by death. This means that the whole concept of conversion is inevitably set on a collision course with traditional Muslims. Evangelicals see it as fundamentally unjust that the door to Islam is one way. Azumah recognizes this within the African context and criticizes 'the inconsistency of those who encourage the propagation of their own faith but forbid the conversion of their own members, [thus turning] religion into a prison whose followers become inmates condemned to a life sentence' (2008b: 154). Thus, for Phil Rawlings, a Church of England vicar and inter-faith advisor, conversion sits 'as an elephant in the room', although, when openly discussed, he finds it need not be such a problem (2014: 12).

In theory, it is possible for both sides to assent that 'it is the work of God ... to convert people' rather than that of human agents (Nazir-Ali, 2002: 82). In practice it is not so simple, and feelings are often raw. Andrew Smith, an Anglican inter-faith advisor in Birmingham, UK, believes that Muslims in the West are beginning to realize 'the hypocrisy of encouraging conversion in one direction and opposing it in the other'. He goes on to add that 'the way converts from Islam to Christianity are treated in the UK and in other parts of the world is a cause of pain and embarrassment for some Muslims [and that] there is a noticeable shift in attitudes from a few years ago' (2018: 56). However, what happens when a Muslim does convert is a difficult issue with severe consequences (Chapter 8). There are many books and other publications telling the stories of Muslims who have converted to Christianity (e.g. Husnain, 2016; Hussain, 2012; Qureshi, 2014; H. Shah, 2010; Yousef and Brackin, 2010).[4] There are even books for Christians to give to or read with Muslims to explain the gospel to them (e.g. Hicham, 2008; Jabbour, 2006). However, a full exploration of the care and discipleship of Muslims should they convert is beyond the scope of this book (see Greenlee, 2013; Little, 2015; Miller, 2020; Oksnevad, 2019).

Preaching: From the few to the many

The classic image of evangelism is of a preacher standing on a soap box shouting. At one end of the scale is the preacher on the street corner trying to gather a crowd. At the other end is the touring evangelist speaking to thousands in a stadium, or maybe even the TV evangelist with his own satellite channel. There are certainly Evangelicals who engage Muslims with all these styles of communication today. In the UK, several Evangelicals have been arrested for supposedly breaching the peace while preaching to Muslims on the streets or criticizing Islam in public. These include Hatun Tash, the director of Defend Christ Critique Islam,[5] who, in 2021, was stabbed by a radical Muslim at Speakers' Corner in London. She and the others arrested were later acquitted after protests over the restriction on free speech, and the police were forced to apologize.[6] In a mirror image case in the United States, Qureshi and three other evangelists were arrested for preaching outside the 2010 Arab International Festival. They were likewise charged with breaching the peace but later acquitted and, in 2013, also received an apology.[7] At the other end of the scale, one of the best known of the stadium preachers was German Pentecostal Reinhard Bonnke (d. 2019) whose slogan was 'From Cape Town to Cairo, Africa shall be saved'. Bonnke, who preached at his last African 'crusade' in 2017, never preached in Cairo, but did preach to millions, including many African Muslims, reportedly seeing many miracles.[8] Another well-known preacher who claims to see miracles among Muslims when she preaches is Heidi Baker, co-founder of Iris Ministries. She reports that, when her team first goes into a Mozambique village, 'the Muslims throw rocks. But once they see signs and wonders and practical love they can't resist'. In this way, hundreds of churches have apparently been planted in 'a nation overrun by Muslim gangs'.[9]

Preaching to large crowds in plural contexts, such as sub-Saharan Africa, is one thing, but, in Muslim-majority contexts, it is not possible for Christians to preach publicly to Muslims – a source of complaint among many evangelists when they see that Muslims have much greater freedom to preach in Western countries. However, it is more difficult for Muslim governments to stop Christians preaching on radio and satellite TV channels. One of the best-known preachers in the Arabic-speaking context is Father Zakaria Botross,[10] an Egyptian Coptic priest who led a revival in Cairo in the 1970s and is something of a hero to polemically minded Evangelicals. Now based abroad, he preaches to huge audiences on TV and YouTube, explaining Christianity and raising difficult questions for Muslims about Islam (see Robinson and Botross, 2008).

Reportedly Al-Jazeera TV has credited Botross with being responsible for millions of Muslims converting to Christianity, with Islamic religious scholars unable to answer his questions.[11] Brother Rachid, a convert from Islam, is a similar US-based preacher. His programme, *Daring Questions*, has been aired on Al Hayat TV, and he too often refutes Islam. His videos on YouTube attract many comments from Christians excited about his journey to faith in Christ, from former Muslims who have been persuaded by his arguments and from a few Muslims angry at his broadcasts, who cast doubt on his story and claim he was paid to convert by missionaries.[12] Another BMB TV evangelist, Reza Safa, originally from Iran but now a pastor in the United States, broadcasts into his homeland in Farsi on his Nejat TV channel.[13]

Such programming and broadcasting are obviously very costly. SAT-7, an ecumenical Christian satellite television channel with more than 20 million viewers, broadcasting to the Middle East and North Africa, had an income of almost $16 million in 2020.[14] It aims to support Christians in the region, but inevitably attracts Muslim viewers, and reported that the total number of viewers who contacted them by e-mail, social media or telephone across its three language platforms – Arabic, Turkish and Farsi – in that year was 329,000. Despite the huge expense, there is no denying the powerful reach and impact of such media in the Evangelical public sphere and beyond.

Friendship Evangelism: From the many to the many

Most Evangelicals, however, are not likely to ever preach to large crowds or appear on TV. For the majority, the most likely evangelism is with their friends, neighbours and colleagues. To help equip these everyday Evangelicals for the task of sharing the gospel with Muslims, a host of books have been produced (e.g. S. Allen, 2016; Chatrath, 2011; Gilchrist, 2009; S. Green, 2019; Hicham, 2011; Masri, 2022; Maurer, 2008; Scott, 2021; R. Sookhdeo, 2010; M. Stone, 2015) and courses developed (e.g. Bell, 2016; de Ruiter, 2016; Houssney and Yandell, 2014; Swartley, 2005). They include advice on how to make friends with Muslims, the do's and don'ts of evangelism and explanations of Muslim culture. They stress that Christians 'can most effectively share Christ with Muslims when [they] are genuinely friends with them' (Greear, 2010: chapter 1), although some research suggests that Evangelicals in North America at least do not tend to have Muslim friends.[15] In making friends, Australian philosopher Richard Shumack, director of the Centre for the Study of Islam, encourages Christians to go beyond the superficial, to do 'some hard thinking … [and] spend a long time first understanding' before then taking 'the longer road of exploring deep questions of life with Muslims'. He stresses the importance of Christians speaking with 'boldness' but also 'shrewdness', 'integrity' and their own 'style' and gives advice on how to talk about different topics (Shumack, 2011: 15–16).

Above all, almost all Evangelicals in their writing stress the need to 'share with Muslims in a loving manner' (Challen, 2006: 176). This is particularly important in the charged political atmosphere in some Western countries where there is fear, distrust and even hatred of immigrants and certain ethnic communities. De Ruiter identifies fear as 'the single greatest hindrance to Christian witness amongst

Muslims in Europe' and observes that 'Muslims are more willing to hear about the gospel than Christians are willing to share the gospel with Muslims' (2010: xiii, 1; see also De Ruiter, 2014). To counteract fear, Brother Andrew suggests that the word Islam should be an acrostic standing for 'I Sincerely Love All Muslims' (2007: 264). Houssney tells lots of stories about his witnessing to Muslims and says, 'Love, love, love. It's all about love' (2010: 185).[16] Similarly, Neighborly Faith is a US initiative that seeks to 'equip Evangelical Christians to love ALL our neighbors, no matter their religion', particularly using podcasts. It reminds its audience that 'you can be gospel centered and a terrific neighbor to people of other faiths' and produced a report on 'the promise of friendship between US Muslims and Evangelicals'.[17] And it seems that the simple strategy of friendship is successful. Shenk recalls asking some former Bosnian Muslims why they were now following Jesus. 'One woman responded with tears caressing her cheeks, "I became a Christian because a Christian became my friend"' (Shenk, 2010).

Motivation for Evangelism: Coming clean

Evangelism among Muslims and the motivations for it are not uncontroversial, however, and there are some important questions and checks that evangelists need to bear in mind. Andrew Smith suggests that the sharing of faith 'needs to be undertaken with wisdom, sensitivity and a great deal of patience' (2009: 17). He recommends that, as an extension of the Golden Rule, 'any evangelism we do to others we have to be happy for them to do to us'. After all, 'evangelism is not a sin but it can be done in sinful ways' (2018: 52, 60).

Even the very idea of what is often referred to as 'friendship evangelism' can be problematic in itself. Some Christian evangelists may be tempted to build relationships with the sole purpose of converting their new 'friend' and may distance themselves if this does not happen. This causes problems for some Muslims. Chapman tells the story of a Shia sheikh in Beirut who explained that he had no problem with evangelism – as long as the evangelist was willing to remain his friend if he did not accept the message (2004b: 115). In other words, the friendship must be genuine. Bell puts it this way. 'Grace relationships do not mean that I love Muslims *so that they will* follow Jesus; it means that I want Muslims to follow Jesus *because I love them*. Grace must remain grace' (2006: 166, original emphasis).

A document produced by the Christian-Muslim Forum in the UK suggests some 'Ethical Guidelines for Christian and Muslim Witness'. The ten points include a recognition that both faiths are missionary faiths and that people want to witness to their faith, but suggest that this needs to be done sensitively and respectfully without coercion or demeaning the other faith. Particular care is needed when dealing with children, young people and vulnerable adults, and believers should be honest about their motivations for witnessing.[18] However clear and careful Christians and Muslims are in their approach to evangelism or *da'wa*, Wagner observes that, given both are 'missionary religions' and 'both believe that the widespread propagation of their message is God's will', there is certain to be conflict (2012: 46).

Dialogue: Talking together

The 'Ethical Guidelines' were produced by Christians *and* Muslims working together. Such a transition often happens when people stop talking *at* each other and start talking *with* each other. This is the essence of 'dialogue'. Indeed, Muslims and Christians, often those in the established mainline churches, have been talking with each other for decades and, in some cases, centuries. However, dialogue with people of other faiths has not always been popular with Evangelicals committed to the uniqueness of Christ and has even become a 'dirty word' in some circles (Accad, 2012: 29). There is a fear that any serious dialogue may 'unwittingly place the gospel on equal footing with other religions' (Tennent, 2002: 11). Others avoid it because it seems to preclude evangelism. Nonetheless, more and more Evangelicals today are engaging in both formal and informal dialogue with Muslims in a variety of settings.

British Evangelicals began to engage with Muslims in the Faith and Society initiative of the 1990s which culminated in two conferences in 1997 with up to 200 Christians and Muslims looking together at topics such as law, education, media, family and sexuality against the backdrop of increasing secularism (Glaser, 2000a). Globally, a series of 'Evangelical Christian-Muslim Dialogues' took place in Chicago (2006), Tripoli (2008), Pasadena (2009) and Toronto (2010) (Sizer, 2010). In the United States, it was ACW which 'suddenly propelled dialogue with Islam to a central position in the Evangelical agenda' (Accad, 2010: 10). The 'Yale Response' was warm and fulsome in tone and led to a major international conference at Yale in July 2008 bringing together Christians, Muslims and Jews (Attridge et al., 2007). These positive responses led to an outcry among more confrontational Evangelicals, as will be seen below.

In Africa, the churches had been engaging with Muslims for some time and in 2003 the Programme for Christian-Muslim Relations in Africa (PROCMURA) was founded, with some Evangelical funding, to seek 'a constructive engagement with Muslims for peace and peaceful co-existence'.[19] It is a 'call for dialogue while at the same time insist[ing] on the need and freedom for Christians (and Muslims) to share their witness' (Azumah, 2011). In the Middle East, ABTS in Beirut has become increasingly engaged in dialogue and its Middle East Consultation has been addressed by a Muslim.[20] Dialogue has also taken place in South Asia, including India (Nickel, 2005) and a most unusual 2017 meeting initiated by some conservative Evangelical leaders from the United States who 'sat down with conservative Deobandi and Salafi Muslim leaders from Pakistan in an attempt to find common ground'.[21]

Such Evangelicals have clear convictions about why they are engaging in dialogue. They demonstrate a renewed Christian confidence and boldness. If 'fear eliminates dialogue' then 'dialogue eliminates fear' (Chalke, 2016: 93). It is about boldly 'speaking the truth in love' (Eph. 4.15) (Moucarry, 2010b). It is about 'arguments for the sake of reaching the truth' (Nazir-Ali, 2006: 110). While it might be about 'finding common ground, it will also be about facing up to disagreement and conflict' (Sudworth, 2007: 100). It must not be 'kissy-kissy' but rather must ask 'tough questions' and not involve inter-faith worship (Nazir-Ali, 2012: 80, 5). Inter-faith dialogue and conflict resolution go hand in hand (see Chapter 13). 'If religious dialogue does not carry any political and social implications, it should be rightly dismissed as futile', although it must never dilute 'the full message of the Bible about Christ' or else it 'will not yield much fruit in the long run' (Accad, 2019: 30, 186). Yet, it is to be conducted with a 'convicted civility' which seeks the common good and must have social implications (Mouw, 2010).

However, not all Evangelicals are so enamoured with this new engagement in Christian-Muslim dialogue. Some fear it can amount to 'syrupy sentimentality' (Garlow, 2005: 64). Others are even more negative and view it as deeply disturbing and believe that the Evangelicals engaging in it are walking a dangerous road. They are concerned that it is about 'a search for the lowest common denominator' and that 'Christians will do all the giving and Muslims all the taking' (P. Sookhdeo, 2009a: 88). The message of the gospel will inevitably be compromised, especially if the basis of the dialogue is an affirmation that Christians and Muslims worship the same God (Chapter 3). This would serve 'the supersessionist program of Islam' and be 'a profound denial of the work of Christ' (Durie, 2013: 148). There is concern that such dialogue puts Christians in a position of weakness. Durie believes that 'interfaith dialogue can be another domain for the manifestation of *dhimmitude*' with Christians 'self-humbling' and avoiding criticism of Muhammad out of a deference that is not reciprocated (see Chapter 4).[22] He is particularly critical of Moucarry by name for apparently doing this (Durie, 2009c: 221). The Yale response to ACW met with severe criticism in this regard. Sookhdeo believed that the Christians with their apologies and gratitude 'were behaving like dhimmi' and must have appeared 'ridiculous in the eyes of the Muslims they dialogued with' (2009a: 90).[23] Moreover, several commentators doubted the good intent of the Muslim authors. They pointed to the fact that some of the signatories were known to hold extreme Islamist views and suggested that this was a tactic to deceive Christians into accepting Islam (Barnabas Fund, 2007). Solomon and Maqdisi saw ACW as a Muslim conspiracy to undermine the church and published a booklet warning Christians against it. They suggested that, through partial quotations and subtle plays on words, ACW veiled the Muslims' true intentions and falsely created 'the illusion that we have the common ground of "love of God and love of neighbour"'. For them, this was an example of *taqīya* (2009a: 20) (see Chapter 11).

These Evangelicals do not completely disregard inter-faith dialogue which 'can be of value', but they doubt that, in the case of ACW and other twenty-first-century initiatives, the Muslims involved are being 'open and honest' (Durie, 2008b). They have a malign intent and do not truly respect Christians, ultimately wanting to subjugate them. According to Solomon and Maqdisi those who enter into such dialogues do not realize that they are being 'lavishly courted through polite erudite dialogue and fellowship – all the while they are being "cursed" and condemned by their hosts through the "coded" daily prayers and much more' (2010: 4).

Despite these objections, some Evangelicals remain optimistic. Cumming sees himself as 'a convert to interfaith dialogue', having 'come 180 degrees' from the common Evangelical position. He is now convinced that 'even though a dialogue might seem disappointing he can communicate two important things: an accurate picture of Christianity through the person of Jesus and issues of religious liberty'.[24] While recognizing the tension that has been created, Accad goes as far as to call this new engagement in dialogue 'a *kairos* moment, an appointed time of God' and he sees those such as Sookhdeo as 'standing against dialogue' (2010: 10; 2011: 181).

Of course, the question arises as to whether dialogue is compatible with the types of evangelism which were discussed above. Is it disingenuous of Christians to enter dialogue with others when they have a concern and a desire for them to become Christians? Bell believes that this is not a problem. While dialogue is about 'hearing' and 'understanding', it is important that it is also 'proclamatory' (2021: 152–4). From his experience in Ghana, Rahman Yakubu, himself a convert from Islam, is clear that it is not a problem. He recalls a Muslim speaker clearly using a dialogue event to preach about Islam to Christians and considers that 'witness without willingness to engage in dialogue is arrogance, while dialogue without willingness to witness to our faith is naivety … If our dialogue partners do not separate *dawa* and dialogue, why should we?' (Yakubu, 2014: 25, 7). Moucarry (2010b) concurs and suggests that 'unless we accept conversion as a possible outcome for dialogue our claim to be tolerant remains unproven'. What is more, Shenk (2010) believes that such conversions *are* happening through the dialogues he has initiated. 'Around the world we hear reports of many who have come to faith in Christ. This is a contextual dialogue that has caught the appreciative attention of thousand.'

Apologetics: Answering your friends

Part of any conversation or dialogue will be answering the many questions and objections that Muslims raise regarding Christianity. As seen in Chapter 3, Islam poses many theological questions around the Trinity, Jesus as the Son of God and the Bible, and Evangelicals believe they should be ready to give an answer (1 Pet. 3.15). Therefore, Tennent is 'convinced that the unique and normative claims of the Christian gospel must be defended at the table of dialogue' (2002: 239). Indeed, he writes his book, *Christianity at the Religious Roundtable,* in the form of apologetic dialogues with Hindus, Buddhists and Muslims around the doctrines of God and Christ.

A plethora of books have been written and training courses designed to help Christians in the task of apologetics (e.g. Hicham, 2008; Geisler and Saleeb, 2002; Lingel, 2016; van den Toren and Tan, 2022).[25] There are also websites dedicated to apologetics.[26] Although some churches in the West offer courses, speaking with Muslims is often seen as a minority activity for a few specialists. Some proponents complain that not even seminaries and Bible colleges are providing apologetics training in the context of Muslims and believe it should be more mainstream in Christian education (Jay Smith, 2011: 239).

Qureshi recounts in his autobiography, *Seeking Allah, Finding Jesus* (2014), how he became a Christian through a combination of friendship, dreams and apologetic argument with David Wood, now a well-known American apologist.[27] Murray too was influenced by intellectual reasoning in his conversion and he later wrote a book on apologetics titled *Grand Central Question: Answering the Critical Concerns of the Major Worldviews* (2014), which includes questions posed by Islam.[28] One of these perennial questions is around the trustworthiness of the Bible and Nickel has produced an apologetic book in which he replies and, in doing so, demonstrates a *Gentle Answer to the Muslim Accusation* (2016).²⁹ Shumack is another 'gentle' apologist who offers 'a defence of the reasonableness of [his] personal Christian belief in the face of thoughtful objections by Muslim thinkers whom [he] respect[s]'. In particular, he responds to the work of British Muslim philosopher Shabbir Akhtar – an example of two public spheres engaging – and he addresses common philosophical objections to Christianity made by Muslims (Shumack, 2014). Clearly, apologetics does not necessitate shouting.

Even so, not all Evangelicals are so enthusiastic about apologetics. While recognizing that positive proclamation of the gospel is important and conceding that, as with Qureshi and Murray, 'some Muslims will be convinced to become Christians under the influence of heavy apologetic demonstrations of the truth of Christianity', Accad believes that historically this approach has 'locked up the discourse of both Christians and Muslims in generally sterile arguments that were passed along over the centuries' (2012: 37, 6). It is also beyond the ability of many ordinary Christians to debate in public with a well-prepared Muslim. So Duane Miller, an American missionary, pastor and academic, suggests the more humble aim of giving a coherent answer while remembering that 'the purpose of the answer is to continue the relationship more than to convince the person that your answer is intellectually superior' (2020: 83).³⁰

In *Speaking of Jesus*, Medearis puts it even more simply. His concern is that Christians should simply speak about Jesus. Engaging in apologetics, 'your first inclination will be to defend Christianity, which … is the wrong thing to do. Once you attempt to defend Christian history, you will quickly find yourself in a very difficult place'. He admits that 'there is a place for doctrines and dogma and science and history and apologetics, but these things are not Jesus – they are humanly manufactured attempts to make people think that having the right ideas is the same thing as loving and following Jesus' (2011: 172, 26).

Debate: A robust argument

Formal apologetic dialogues between Christians and Muslims often take place in the form of a debate, with a motion and a moderator. In North America, well-known apologists Jay Smith, White and Wood have all debated Muslims on both Christian and Muslim topics.³¹ In Australia, Power has taken part in many debates, often at universities where there are always students eager to listen to an academic clash of ideas.³² And there is no shortage of Muslim apologists who are ready to debate them. Following in the tradition of Ahmed Deedat in the twentieth century, speakers such as Zakir Naik, Shabbir Ally and Jamal Badawi are popular with Muslim audiences.³³ In London the Hyde Park Christian Fellowship for many years engaged in impromptu debates at Speakers' Corner in London.³⁴ Their website explains that they make 'a careful distinction between *dialogue* and *debate*. While both are equally important … dialogue in itself is only a preparation for debate.'³⁵ Many videos can be found online and the debates are often loud and fiery. Even so, Tash, one of the regular speakers, says she has seen 1,000 Muslims 'convert to Christianity' since 2013.³⁶

Supporters of such robust debates point out that these Evangelicals are the only people 'responding directly to the Muslim radical minority and its anti-Christian polemic' (Riddell, 2013: 190). The argument is that polite dialogue only attracts modernist and traditionalist Muslims. Someone has to confront the radicals. Speakers such as Jay Smith (2011) point out that debates are part of the South Asian Muslim culture and so are entirely appropriate. Bell agrees and suggests that the objections of some Western Evangelicals to such debates are 'primarily a cultural discomfort'. In fact, he goes further and isolates this discomfort to British and European Christians, observing that the American psyche is naturally 'more adversarial' (2021: 165, 171).

Nonetheless, other Evangelicals are concerned that such debates are counterproductive. For instance, Andrews feels that many conversations 'deteriorate from dialogue into debate and from debate into dispute, generating more heat than light on the subject. Often this occurs because both sides want to impose their own particular view … and are unwilling to respect the other person's particular point of view' (2015: 105). This is especially true of arguments seeking to undermine Islam rather than merely to defend Christianity, which may be labelled 'polemics'.

Polemics: On the attack

While pretty much all Evangelicals agree that apologetics and debates are important in some form, there is sharp disagreement when it comes to attacking Islam and the Qur'an. This polemical form of engagement can be approached in different ways. Some attack Islam from a distance in their writings. Others engage in live debate as mentioned above. Still others raise questions which they think Muslims will find difficult to answer. Beth Peltola, CEO of the One Truth Project, and co-author Dieppe do this in book form in 'Questions to Ask your Muslim Friends' which raises awkward questions about Muhammad, violence and women among others (Peltola and Dieppe, 2022; see also Scot and Abdulhaq, 2009).[37] On a larger scale, Father Botross's approach, mentioned above, is to raise questions on TV about what he believes to be weak points and inconsistencies in Islam and challenge the ulama to reply to him. Hicham, a Moroccan BMB, explains that 'Botross's exposures of little-known but embarrassing aspects of Islamic law and tradition have become a thorn in the side of Islamic leaders … [and] more often than not, the response is deafening silence – which attracts even more Muslim viewers' and he has heard reports of Muslims 'who had been saved by watching' such programmes (Hicham, 2009). Garrison confirms this, saying that Botross's 'satellite broadcast television programs and daily internet chat rooms have led thousands of Arab Muslims to turn away from Islam and place their faith in Jesus Christ', although he admits that the numbers are disputed (2014: 208–9).

Some organizations are seeking to train more such Christian polemicists. i2 Ministries has an 'online ministry school' called the Mission Muslim World University.[38] Their course book aims at both apologetics and 'an introduction to polemics that undermine one's confidence in trusting the Islamic historical origins, philosophy or doctrines as true. This is the "offense"' (Lingel, 2016: blurb). Teachers include many of those mentioned in this book such as Durie, Lingel, Jay Smith and Joel Richardson among others. The Pfander Centre for Apologetics, which seems to be closely related through shared staff, also offers training which includes lessons on the historical, textual and theological critiques of Islam.[39] Finally, Veritas International University offers a similar programme titled Master of Arts in Polemics & Apologetics to Islam.[40]

All this leads Jay Smith to warn Muslims that 'you've had it so good for so long in Europe. No one ever refutes you in public. Now we're doing so and we're doing so in a big way. And you're realizing our refutations are pretty good … now you're getting the heat of what it's like to be on the other end.' For Smith (2007), Speakers' Corner is 'the only place on earth' where Christians and Muslims can have this sort of interaction face to face, and he clearly relishes the challenge.

Some Evangelicals committed to a more conciliatory approach towards Muslims, however, have grave misgivings about the use of polemics and feel that this approach does more harm than good. For them, the polemicists are failing to take into account 'the limitations of the polemical approaches that have been adopted by both sides over many centuries' (Chapman, 2007b: 247). In fact, Moucarry believes that:

> Taking a confrontational approach to Islam generates more heat than light. It tends to be counterproductive as it usually provokes a defensive response, with Muslims becoming more radical in their beliefs, and often also an offensive reaction, with Muslims attacking Christianity even more vehemently. Such an approach is incompatible with 'the gospel of peace' (Eph. 6.15) … A polemical engagement with Islam is misguided on all counts, particularly when it is adopted by Westerners who are perceived by many Muslims as Islam's traditional enemies. (2011b: 251)

From experience, Accad feels that the cost of, for example, Botross's approach 'in terms of intercommunal conflict' is high and points out that 'no one openly using the polemical approach will be able to maintain a transparent presence in the Muslim world' (2012: 34). Indeed, it is true that Botross himself no longer lives in Egypt, where he was sentenced to life imprisonment before being sent into exile (Bell, 2021: 168). Others point out that, in their opinion 'too many of these evangelical polemics are historically inaccurate, theologically misinformed, and missiologically misguided … When we critique Islam, we need to be fair and accurate … There is a place for "unveiling" Islam, provided we do it with sensitivity, understanding, and careful research' (Larson, 2006). For these Evangelicals, however, the emphasis should be on 'respectful witness'.

Discussion: Trust in debate

How Evangelicals and Muslims talk to one another is extremely important. It impacts not just those in the conversation but others listening in – Christian, Muslim and other. In this regard the discussion concerning *taqīya* and the trustworthiness of Muslims is particularly important (see Chapter 11). Some Evangelicals are creating the impression that lying is unconditionally sanctioned in Islam, that deceit and falsehood are the norm and that no Muslim can ever be trusted. This is just not true and is an extremely disturbing trend as it leads to a complete breakdown in trust. If one always suspects that one's interlocutor is lying or dissembling to gain an advantage, then it becomes impossible to have any meaningful shared life. It is imperative that Evangelicals research further the theology and tradition surrounding the Islamic principle of *taqīya* and that this becomes a topic of serious discussion between Christians and Muslims. Ultimately, of course, there are no guarantees against deception and betrayal. There never can be, as Jesus knew when he invited Judas – his eventual betrayer – to become one of his closest circle (Luke 6.12–16).

Finally, it seems inevitable that Christians and Muslims of different temperaments, attitudes, cultures and approaches will have different conversations together. There are times when robust questioning requires a robust response. However, the manner in which this is done is important. Character and behaviour are always part of the message, even when unspoken. The New Testament enjoins Christians to be ready to give an answer but to do so with 'gentleness and respect' (1 Pet. 3.15). This does not mean weakness but rather a firmness and, what Newbigin calls, 'a proper confidence'.[41] It should certainly include rigorous research into the topics of debate and careful listening to what one's antagonist is saying. It should also not compare 'their worst' with 'our best' as many authors point out. Even so, the use of polemics seems set to remain a controversial issue among Evangelicals in the West, although maybe not for Christians from the Global South, where cultures are often more confrontational. An attention to such cultural differences is very much the focus of the next chapter.

13

Mission strategies

Movement in the House of Islam

When Evangelicals travel to talk with Muslims, it is usually labelled 'mission'. Of course, mission is broader than this. It can take place anywhere, even in the backyard (Payne, 2012). Furthermore, mission does not have to be evangelistic preaching but can involve mercy ministries, development work and service in the community. However, in the popular imagination, mission has been something that happens overseas in someone else's backyard. Today this can even include 'reverse mission' as Christians from Africa and South America bring the gospel back to the former missionary-sending countries of Europe and North America.[1] So this chapter focuses on the Evangelical mission to Muslim-majority contexts and particularly explores contentious issues that arise in the Evangelical public sphere with regard to contextualization, Insider Movements, ethical integrity and peacemaking.

In the Introduction, we very briefly reviewed over 200 years of the modern Protestant missionary movement and its engagement with Islam. Intrepid pioneer missionaries devoted themselves to often lifelong service in the most challenging of conditions, yet 'very few Muslims converted to Christianity'.[2] However, while for almost fourteen centuries the Christian gospel made little impact in Muslim lands, during the closing decades of the twentieth century, an emphasis on what was called the '10/40 Window' and 'Unreached People Groups' (UPGs) saw new mission agencies spring up with the sole purpose of sending Christians to Muslim countries.[3] Along with the factors discussed below, this resulted from the 1960s onwards in 'a very significant increase in the number of known conversions from Islam to Christianity' (Miller, 2014). By the end of the century, although Islam was still the fastest-growing world religion, this was entirely due to biological growth. According to the *World Christian Encyclopaedia*, annual conversions from Islam to Christianity stood at around 2.7 million, almost three times the rate in the opposite direction (Woodberry and Shubin, 2001). New churches were springing up in Muslim contexts (Martin, 2010).

There are reports that the first two decades of the twenty-first century saw a significant increase in this rate. Some are anecdotal. For instance, writing in 2007, Lutzer believes that 'Muslims are turning to Christ in large numbers – in Afghanistan, and even in the Sudan and Iran. For example, in the Sudan it is estimated that one million Muslims have converted to Christianity since the year 2000.'[4] However, no evidence is given for this claim. Other stories mention 'hundreds of thousands' and are better substantiated (e.g. Trousdale, 2012). In his carefully researched and widely read report, *A Wind in the House of Islam*, Garrison finds that 'in only the first 12 years of the 21st century, an additional 69 movements to Christ of at least 1,000 baptized Muslim background believers or 100 new worshipping fellowships have appeared. These 21st-century movements are not isolated to one or two corners of the world. They are taking place throughout the house of Islam' (2014: 18).

The Pew Forum survey at Cape Town 2010 showed that 78 per cent of Evangelical leaders believe Christianity to be 'attracting more converts' than Islam.[5] William Wagner quotes research showing that, while Muslim numbers are growing by 1.82 per cent, Evangelicals are growing by 2.06 per cent and charismatics by 2.42 per cent (2012: 248). Bell suspects the claim to Islam being the fastest-growing religion is purely based on birth rates, not 'spectacular conversion rates'. In fact, in his opinion, 'The evidence suggests that Islam may now be the fastest-shrinking religion on earth, because the number of practising adherents has dropped, signs of nominalism have increased, and the biggest defection in Islamic history is taking place' (2021: 120–1). Ayman Ibrahim, an Egyptian-born Southern Baptist theologian, agrees that 'the growing number of Muslims is mainly due to higher birth rates in Muslim families, not new converts to Islam'. Drawing on various survey and polling data, he confirms that not only are 'droves of Iranians abandoning Islam', with, maybe, as few as 40 per cent of Iranians now identifying as Muslims, but there is an increase in the number of Arab Muslims leaving Islam. This means that the 'growth of disbelief and nonreligion is a serious concern for Islam' (Ibrahim, 2022). Such assessments are upbeat and bolster Evangelical confidence. Not everyone is getting carried away by such accounts and statistics, however. Jenkins cautions that in Europe he sees 'little convincing evidence of any serious growth of this kind. The Christian expansion that can be reliably observed is overwhelmed by the figures for Muslim evangelism among former Christians.'[6] For others the emphasis on statistics is misguided. Veteran missionary Brother Andrew says, 'I think we're on the wrong track with all of our statistics. We are too results-oriented. I aim to be destiny-oriented … It's our job to go. We don't judge evangelism by results' (2004: 229). Clearly the picture is not uniform, is open to interpretation and requires more research.

Many reasons are given for the large numbers of Muslim conversions to Christianity. Studies at the end of the twentieth century identified mainly the positive draw of Christian factors, such as the person of Jesus, assurance of salvation, Christian community and the power of love.[7] Martin Goldsmith (2009),[8] a writer, speaker and missiologist, likewise finds that in his experience Muslims who convert have three things in common: they have had a friendship with a Christian, have read some of the New Testament and have experienced something miraculous in their lives, such as a healing or a dream. Wagner puts the number involving a 'vision or a dream of Jesus' at 95 per cent (2012: 256). To these factors we should certainly add migration and the explosion of the internet and online social media. Houssney observes that 'globalization and the massive shuffling of peoples between continents are exposing Muslims to Christianity … satellite TV and the Internet are giving Muslims the opportunity to investigate Christianity in phenomenal numbers. One Christian website alone had over 100 million visitors in one year, and there are hundreds of similar websites' (2010: 197).

However, in the twenty-first century there also appear to be push factors. Garrison went very public with some of the causes he sees in a 2019 *Newsweek* opinion piece. This included the pull factors of increased Christian prayer for Muslims, intentional evangelization and translations of the Bible into Muslim languages alongside increased access to the internet.[9] However, from the Muslim side, he identifies the trauma and disillusionment brought about by war, the violence of Muslim extremists and, most surprisingly, the increased availability of the Qur'an in 'colloquial translations that are demystifying their holy book and leaving many of them yearning for something different' (Garrison, 2019). As noted in Chapter 5, this has led some Evangelicals to recommend encouraging Muslims to read the Qur'an in their own language as 'there are many Christians from Muslims backgrounds who can testify to the Qur'an being their starting point on the journey towards Jesus' (S. Allen, 2016: 234; see also Peltola and Dieppe, 2022: 70). In fact, some suggest that the Qur'an should be translated into even more languages to expose it to scrutiny in the hope that this will lead to disenchantment and conversions away from Islam. This has parallels with the translation of the Bible from Latin into vernacular languages from the fourteenth century on, which contributed to the proliferation of Protestant sects and the weakening of the institutional Western church.

Others too have observed the impact of turmoil and violence in Muslim contexts and believe that Muslim radicals are driving Muslims towards Christianity. Even before Garrison's study, Bell had observed that 'more Muslims have come to Christ in the past two decades than at any other point in history' and quoted Christian statistician Patrick Johnstone as claiming that 'Osama bin Laden is responsible for more Muslims following Jesus than anyone else alive today' (2006: 122–3). In 2016 in the context of the Syrian civil war, the Christian Aid Mission observed that 'one reason [ISIS is] killing is that they wish to stop the rapid spread of Christianity. There has never been a time when a greater percentage of Syrian Muslims, in-country and refugees, have believed in Christ than in the past three years of civil war.'[10] Others have given the Ayatollah Khomeini (d. 1989) similar credit for the growth of the church among Iranians following the Iranian Revolution (Bradley, 2014: 38). The Taliban in Afghanistan could be added to the list (Woodberry, 2011). In short, Larson observes that 'where Muslims are turning to Christ it has had something to do with suffering … [often] through Muslim-on-Muslim violence' (2012: 92).

Of course, whenever there is news of Muslim conversions to Christianity in any context, there are accusations from Muslims of coercion or material incentive.[11] However, from the stories recounted in Chapter 8, it seems that converts do not in fact gain materially. 'Much more common were the stories of converts who lost everything for the sake of following Christ. This is the normal way that the Muslim community treats apostates: they take everything away' (Garrison, 2014: 236).

Insider Movements or Chrislam?

This is often because Christian mission and Christianity are seen by Muslims as an extension of Western hegemony and so for a Muslim to change identities is an act of betrayal. However, many Evangelicals believe 'the gospel invites [a Muslim] to become an "eastern follower of Jesus" rather than a "western Christian" – with all the historic baggage attached to that term' (Bell, 2012: 13–14). This problem generates a fierce disagreement within the Evangelical public sphere on how mission to Muslims should be conducted.[12] There is not space for a full account of the different approaches to this question, partly as they are a question of what happens after a Muslim becomes a Christian which is not part of the focus of this book. However, the opinions of Evangelicals and missionaries on what should happen *afterwards* inevitably impacts the strategies that are used in the mission *before* conversion. The following section highlights the main controversaries and some of the central voices around the issues of contextualization and Insider Movements.

How should a faith practice and express its message in a particular context? What is essential and what is cultural? What did the Apostle Paul mean when he said that 'to those under the law I became like one under the law' (1 Cor. 9.20) or when he referred to an altar 'to an unknown god' (Acts 17.23)? Such questions of contextualization are a huge topic within Christian missiology (see Parsons, 2005)[13] and are becoming more of a talking point in Western Muslim communities too.[14] For Evangelicals in the Muslim context, it involves questions of: the degree to which Islamic forms can be used in communicating the gospel; whether the Qur'an can be used as a starting point for the Christian presentation of the gospel (see Chapter 5); how the Bible should be translated into Muslim languages; and the identity of new believers from a Muslim background.

The last of these questions in particular has ignited fierce debate within Evangelical mission circles in the early part of the twenty-first century and has produced sharp divisions. On the one hand, almost all of those who take a confrontational, polemical approach to Islam, while not denying the need to contextualize the gospel to some extent, believe that Muslims, on conversion, need to move decisively away from their old life in Islam and take on a new Christian identity. There is no possibility of continuity. On the other hand, some, but certainly not all, of those Evangelicals who engage in dialogue and take an irenic, conciliatory approach towards Muslims advocate a higher degree of contextualization and accept some continuity between the convert's life before and after conversion. This sometimes gives rise to what are called 'Insider Movements' (IM) in which new believers continue to call themselves Muslims and practice some Islamic rituals. Accad gives the analogy of two buildings and asks whether Christians need to knock down the one to build the other or whether they can ask 'the Spirit of Christ to indwell the building of Islam' (2019: 21)? However, the question for Parshall, one of the twentieth century pioneers of contextualization among Muslims, becomes 'how much Muslim context is too much for the gospel?' (Parshall, 2013).[15]

According to Rebecca Lewis, an American missionary and leading proponent, IMs are 'movements to obedient faith in Christ that remain integrated with or inside their natural community' (2009: 16). The new believers call themselves a variety of names and John Travis, a pseudonym for an American missionary and early IM practitioner, lists 'Muslim followers of Jesus', 'Holy Spirit Muslims' and 'Muslim believers' as examples. For him they all 'follow Jesus as Lord and Savior and the Bible as God's word without taking the step of leaving the religious community of their birth' (Travis, 2015). Other labels include 'Jesus Muslims', 'Muslim followers of the straight path' and 'Muslim disciples of Christ' (Miller, 2011: 229). Much has been written within the Evangelical public sphere on this phenomenon (e.g. Talman and Travis, 2016; Higgins, 2022; Dyrness, 2016) and Mazhar Mallouhi's story illustrates it in many ways (Chandler, 2007).

However, there has been vociferous opposition to IMs from Evangelicals concerned that they run the risk of encouraging syncretism – that is the blending together of Christian and Islamic ideas – resulting in what they term 'Chrislam'. A 2012 edited volume of that title included articles by twenty or so Evangelicals involved in mission to Muslims all trenchantly rebutting IMs and concerned about *How Missionaries Are Promoting an Islamized Gospel* (Lingel, Morton and Nikides, 2012).[16] Interestingly, in an example of how this public sphere can impact the more general Evangelical public sphere, this concern was quickly picked up among other American Evangelicals, and several pastors and authors with no specialist knowledge of Islam or mission to Muslims wrote pamphlets and books warning against the movement (G. D. Brown, 2014; D. Coleman, 2011; DeRuvo, 2012; Gwynn, 2013; Mike Oppenheimer, 2014). Other responses do not explicitly mention Chrislam but also critique IMs and their theology (Carson, 2012; Ibrahim and Greenham, 2018; Morton, 2012). The main concern in all cases is that the Christian gospel is being compromised in order to achieve results by lowering the bar for conversion. This sometimes leads to comparisons with the postmodern Emergent Church movement influenced by leaders such as McLaren and Rob Bell (Lingel, Morton and Nikides, 2012: 5–8).[17]

There is also concern that IMs will be seen by Muslims as being deceptive. Shumack feels that Christians using qur'anic language might miscommunicate and 'lack integrity', pointing out that Christians do not appreciate it when Muslims misappropriate the Bible (Shumack, 2011: 57). Some simply call it 'lying' and liken it to *taqīya*, advising that it is 'extremely dangerous and unwise' (Cook, 2012: 304). Nazir-Ali does not go quite as far but believes that, while the use of Islamic cultural norms, terminology and styles of worship may be acceptable, it must be done with integrity and 'without distorting the gospel or misrepresenting the other tradition'. Otherwise 'Muslims may see this as deception which "makes the apostasy worse" as orthodox Islam will not accept any deviation' (2008c: 124–5). Concerns have also been raised that harmful social and cultural norms may go unchallenged, and inequalities may be reinforced if new believers maintain Muslim cultural practices. This might be particularly true for women. 'The challenge of the Insider Movement for women followers of Islam is that it reifies culture and fails to accept that not every cultural expression of Islam is good for women' (Hine, 2018: 12). Finally, there is a concern that IMs ignore what some see as the spiritual forces behind Islam. Jay Smith warns that 'there is spiritual power in Islam which most of us do not understand' rendering it dangerous to compromise (2012: 295). An awareness of 'the kingdom of darkness attempting to subvert the Church, and offering a false gospel, all this is curiously absent' (Span, 2012).

One very specific manifestation of this debate is over how the Bible should be translated in Muslim contexts. The challenge for translators is always the tension between a literal translation of the original words or an equivalent translation of the original ideas.[18] For Muslims, the concepts of God as Father and Jesus as Son are perennially difficult. So, some translators look for other ways to represent these ideas. The best known of these recent texts is *The True Meaning of the Gospel of Christ*, associated with the work of Mazhar Mallouhi, which in certain places uses 'Messiah' or 'Beloved' for 'Son' (Mt. 3.17, 14.33) or 'God' in place of 'Father' (Mt. 6.15).[19]

However, critics worry about the outcomes of such an approach. Adam Simnowitz, an American Pentecostal pastor, warns, 'Let us not deceive ourselves; Bible translation is the foundation to all ministry. If these cracked foundations of Muslim-friendly translations are allowed to continue we should not be surprised at the coming collapse for everything built on it' (2012: 220). His chapter is an interesting example of a text in the public sphere which attacks others very personally and he targets Jabbour, Rick Brown and the Navigators along with a detailed refutation of the changes in Mallouhi's text above.[20]

A rather different approach is being taking in a series of *Bible Commentaries from Muslim Contexts*. These are serious theological reflections with Islam in mind specifically written by and for those living in Muslim contexts in different parts of the world. The first to be published was co-authored by Bangladeshi BMB Anwarul Azad (d. 2020) exploring *Genesis 1–11* (Azad and Glaser, 2022). Commentaries on the books of Jonah, John and others will follow written in other Muslim countries. Other theological texts are also taking the Islamic context seriously. *Reading the Bible in Islamic Context* (Crowther et al., 2017) was the output of a conference bringing the Bible into conversation with the Qur'an, which included some Evangelicals, and three volumes edited by missiologist David Singh (2008, 2011, 2014) explore Christology in that same context.

Much research is being conducted by proponents of the different positions to determine the impact and trajectory of IMs as well as to gather the stories and experiences of Muslims who have come to Christian faith (Greenlee, 2006, 2013; Woodberry, 2008; Prenger, 2017; Brotherson, 2022).[21] Feelings are so strong that Yancey and Quosigk suggest that 'these two terms [Insider and Chrislam] get at the heart of the divide between conservative and progressive Christians'.[22] Certainly, the debate seems set to continue in years to come and may have a decisive impact on intra-Evangelical relations, not to mention Christian-Muslim relations.

Integrity: One message to all

The concerns expressed above around how new movements are labelled and presented is reflected in the use of other mission language and strategies. Some have become uncomfortable with the use of military-sounding terms such as 'targeting', 'mobilization' or 'taking the land'. Rick Love, founder of PCI, in his book, *Glocal: Following Jesus in the 21st Century*, reflects how seeing people as 'targets or projects' had 'shrivelled' his heart. He suggests that Christians look for 'more appropriate metaphors for ministry in the third millennium' and he proposes terms such as 'blessing the nations', 'global engagement', 'peacemaking' and 'reconciliation' (2017: 26, 34, 117).

However, whatever you call it, the twenty-first-century mission to Muslim lands is still highly controversial, both with Muslims and among Christians. In many Muslim countries Christian proselytism is illegal and, as discussed in Chapter 8, changing religion may also be illegal. This raises a moral dilemma. On the one hand, Muslim nations do not allow Christians to freely share their faith with Muslims. Evangelicals see this as an infringement of fundamental freedoms of belief and conscience. On the other hand, Muslims connect Christian mission with power and colonialism, so seek to protect their societies from what they see as malign and destabilizing influences. So, Evangelicals wishing to share the gospel in Muslim countries often find regular employment, start companies or work in the development sector without officially or openly declaring their intent to evangelize. This can lead to awkward situations and Love tells the story of two Americans who were 'imprisoned by the Taliban in Afghanistan in 2001 for proselytizing. After a high-profile, dramatic release, they told a television reporter that they were aid workers who had not been proselytizing. Immediately, media worldwide broadcast a prayer card that identified them as missionaries ... Two worlds collided' (2017: 57).

Howarth recounts the similar dilemma faced by a British Christian couple going to a Muslim country to work as 'evangelistic missionaries'. At a leaving party thrown by their friends, who were 'Muslim immigrants living in Britain, happy that the couple were going to serve their home country', they were embarrassed and felt unable to reveal their true reason for going (2011: 233). Such stories raise questions about the integrity with which Christian mission is conducted. For Love, this came home to him after a malicious 2002 'exposé' by *Mother Jones*, an American magazine. A journalist attended one of Love's classes and reported on how new missionaries were being trained to be part of a 'stealth crusade' in Muslim contexts.[23] The skewed reporting provoked awkward conversations with high-profile Muslims who had read the article and led Love to reconsider what he said about his identity and communication in a 'glocalized' world where local events have global impact:

> Glocalization means that we can no longer have a different message or be a different person for each different audience. In the core of our being, we have to have the same message and personal identity for every audience [Christian, Muslim and secular] ... We need to clarify a core message worth dying for, a core identity worthy living for, and a core dream worth suffering for. (2017: 41, 23)

Integrity is also a strong theme for Shenk. The first two of his *Twelve Paths to Real Friendship* between Christians and Muslims are 'living with integrity' and 'keeping identity clear' (Shenk, 2014). For instance, when he was preparing 'a Bible study course for Muslims' in East Africa he openly sought advice from 'a polemical Muslim theologian who preached on the street' which helped to build trust. He says, 'We did nothing secretly' (Shenk, 2010). This openness is supported by Houssney who sees being secretive about Christian work in Muslim countries as 'counter-productive [as] most Muslim cultures value courage. Secrecy is viewed as weak and deceptive' (2010: 32).

Friendship: On an international scale

Such openness, honesty and friendship in relating to Muslims has been adopted by a few Evangelicals on an international scale. In 1992 Brother Andrew visited Hamas leaders who had been deported into no man's land between Israel and Lebanon to show them friendship. Following that, he had opportunities to meet with them again in Gaza and a relationship of trust was established that could support their robust conversations about faith (Brother Andrew and Janssen, 2004: 11–26). American Evangelical Mark Siljander is a controversial former conservative Republican congressman who used to see Islam as a violent threat to his country. However, after leaving office, re-evaluating the gospels and reading about Jesus in the Qur'an, he eventually founded Bridges to Common Ground in 2005.[24] He set out to rectify the lack of 'interpersonal relationships' in American diplomacy by meeting with high-profile Muslims around the world, including the president of the Saharawi, the Libyan foreign minister and Yasser Arafat among others. In several cases he claims that major diplomatic breakthroughs followed his meetings, a claim which is difficult to verify (2008: 21).[25]

Cumming is someone else who has had opportunities to interact with influential Muslims around the world. Since leading the Yale Reconciliation Program and spearheading Yale's response to ACW (Attridge et al., 2007), he has lectured at al-Azhar University in Cairo, met with leading Ayatollahs in Iran, and had an audience with Lebanese Ayatollah Sheikh Fadlallah (d. 2010) (Cumming, 2013: 47). These opportunities have all been built on openness and respect while in no way compromising his own faith which he clearly explains on his website.[26] Likewise, Medearis has met with leaders of various Islamic groups and has even had *Tea with Hezbollah* (2010). His approach is straightforwardly to talk about Jesus and avoid all debate and apologetics. He tells many stories in his books of Muslims who have been angry or dismissive of Christians and Christianity but are excited to talk about Jesus. This includes the story of a sheikh in Basra, Iraq, whom Medearis surprised with the question, 'I'm trying to follow Jesus, and we've come here looking for him. Have you seen him?' (2008: 164). Finally, high-profile American megachurch pastor Bob Roberts has hosted international Muslim leaders at the National Prayer Breakfast.[27] In a YouTube video he says, 'If we Evangelicals are going to love Muslims, then the most critical thing that we have to do is to love like Jesus to the degree that we're willing to put our life on the line for somebody's religious freedom even if it means that we totally disagree with their theology' (Roberts, 2019).

Peacemaking: In the way of Francis

The approach of these Evangelicals towards Muslims in the recent years has often been couched in terms of 'peacemaking', 'reconciliation' and 'conflict resolution' (e.g. Gushee, 2013; R. Love, 2014; Andrews, 2015; A. White, 2009). It came to the fore in the 1990s with the Reconciliation Walk, a high-profile enterprise, spearheaded by Youth with a Mission (YWAM), to coincide with the 900th anniversary of the Crusades. Hundreds of Christians walked the old Crusader routes from Europe to Jerusalem. 'Through an apology and thousands of face-to-face meetings between Western Christians and Muslims, Jews and Eastern Christians, [they] sought to erode the bitter legacy and mythologies of enmity that originated with the Crusades.'[28] This apology was reiterated by those Evangelicals involved in ACW (Volf, Cumming and Yarrington, 2010).

There is also a deep feeling of unease among some Evangelicals about the West's more recent military engagements among Muslims in the Middle East. Camp worries that American Christians are 'war addicts' and he does not see the wars as being conducted in accord with just war tradition (2016: KL1895). Wallis feels a 'deep sadness over the terrible cost of a war that was, from the beginning, wrong: intellectually, politically, strategically, theologically, and above all, morally. The war in Iraq was fundamentally a war of choice, and it was the wrong choice.' He too advocates peacemaking, although he does not 'advocate a bland interfaith pluralism that blurs the significant differences between religions'. Rather he believes that his 'religious tradition calls me to be a peacemaker and to love my neighbours, especially when I do not agree with them' (Wallis, 2013: 151, 142–3). In similar spirit, PCI has a vision for 'local movements of Christians and Muslims around the world living in peace and working together with their neighbors to create safe, just, and vibrant communities'.[29] Its founder Rick Love also sponsored a document titled *Grace and Truth: Toward Christlike Relationships with Muslims* (2013), an affirmation which was signed by over sixty prominent Christians and recommended biblical guidelines on combining 'words and witness'.

Christine Mallouhi captured this approach with her provocative book title, *Waging Peace on Islam* (2000), which takes Francis of Assisi as a model peacemaker who reached out to Muslims during the Crusades. She later calls it 'a multifaceted "third way" of responding to violence which is love of enemy, peacemaking as a journey of truth telling, reconciliation, and memory work', and advocates returning to Jesus's model by 'eating the way Jesus ate', opening up homes and 'sharing bread' with Muslims (Mallouhi, 2012: 260, 262). In the United States, Larson agrees and says that 'waging peace on Islam means reaching out to Muslim immigrants among us (nearly sixty percent of American Muslims are immigrants) and not hating them' (2005: 54). This is an idea which has been taken up by Peace Feasts in the United States and the UK which bring together people of different cultures to eat.[30] In Africa too, Evangelicals are among those involved in 'inter-religious peace building' initiatives in areas of conflict such as Nigeria.[31]

Some remain unconvinced and are uncomfortable with this emphasis on peace and reconciliation. Although they recognize that 'the twin themes of peace and reconciliation [are] central to the message of the gospels' and even recognize that 'irenic Muslim voices are open to bridge building around' them, they do not always agree with how it is being done and fear that 'traditional Christian mission has been one of the chief casualties' (Riddell, 2003). For instance, Musk critiqued the Reconciliation Walk as 'a pretty one-sided, non-costly kind of reconciliation', pointing out that there had been no Vatican representation and that local Christian communities had been ignored (2005: 265).[32] The Caners felt that 'an apology for events that came to pass nearly a millennium ago can deem [sic] hollow, especially in regards to granting or obtaining forgiveness' (2004: 211). Added to this, Sookhdeo worries that:

> Apologising for the crusades and for colonialism sends inappropriate cultural signals and can do more harm than good in that they reinforce the Muslims' sense of grievance against Christians ... The tragic result is often a backlash of Muslim violence against vulnerable Christian communities in the Muslim countries.

Reconciliation has no value if it is devoid of righteousness, justice and truth. (2009a: 101–2)

Furthermore, he believes that to 'argue for peace without a profound change in Islamic understanding of territory is not viable'. All this leads Dye to suggest that the peacemakers 'seem to be more attracted to the prize of a "delusional" peace than by their duty to confront error' (in his preface to Solomon and Al-Maqdisi, 2009a: xv). Others believe they have been deceived by *taqīya* (Solomon and Al-Maqdisi, 2007: 25; also Durie, 2009c: 56–62).

Perhaps the greatest concern that these Evangelicals have is that the peacemakers are inadvertently abandoning conversion as a goal and are on the road to syncretism. They point, for instance, to Hartford Seminary in the United States, 'an institution which a few generations ago was training Christians to evangelize Muslims' but now trains imams (P. Sookhdeo, 2009a: 100). Likewise, the Henry Martyn Institute in India evolved from being a centre of evangelism in the early twentieth century through a focus on dialogue to finally emphasizing reconciliation without evangelism.[33] This mirrors a wider concern that the church in the West has moved 'from mission clearly defined as worldwide evangelism to mission as the kingdom of God in the secular world' (Robinson, 2010: 26). In other words, they fear that the evangelistic task is being reduced to seeking the common good of all in society at the expense of a clear call to salvation and conversion.

Sookhdeo stresses that the ministry of reconciliation to which Christians are called is to reconcile people to God (2 Cor. 5.18–20). He can see 'no call in the Bible for Christians as a body to seek a reconciliation with other faiths' (2009a: 101) and his organization worries that 'watering down Christian fundamental doctrines and accepting Muslim claims to effect a hoped for reconciliation with Muslims can only lead to syncretism' (Barnabas Fund, 2008a: 10). Pawson spells out what for him seems an inevitable process: joint discussions lead to joint statements which in turn lead to joint action, joint intercession and finally joint worship. He warns that 'Islam and Christianity cannot be reconciled. We must not attempt such a futile task or even allow any impression that we consider it possible, much less desirable' (2003: 165).

The peacemakers seek to allay these fears. They strongly refute the idea that they are trying to reconcile the two religions but rather are seeking to build bridges of peace between Christians and Muslims as people. Cumming acknowledges the fear that 'building bridges with Muslims is part of a slippery slope toward one world religion' but insists that it is important 'to have constructive conversations with Muslims without being opposed by my brothers and sisters in Christ' and urges the church 'to learn to keep witness and peacemaking together' (2013: 49). Indeed, many of these Evangelicals see peacemaking as an important part of their witness to the gospel, which comes at a great cost. Bell recalls an imam friend asking him, '"Who are you leaving behind on your side in order to do what you're doing?" I was sad to admit that I have left quite a few Christian friends behind to become a peacemaker' (2006: 55). As Christine Mallouhi puts it, 'Witness as peacemaking is one's life offered or laid down as an act of love and worship, trusting that the glory of God will be revealed as God reconciles all through Christ' (2012: 270).

Cooperation: Together for the common good

All the above strategies have been focused on the relationship between Evangelicals and Muslims and the desire to communicate clearly. However, this final strategy is not so much about the message, although that is part of it, but rather it is about doing something – together. McLaren believes that 'words are good, but actions are better – especially actions that bring us together solving problems that affect everybody' (2012b: 246). Kaemingk points out that Christians have 'a lot in common with their Muslim neighbours' and suggests that Evangelicals should 'find Muslim cobelligerents' to work and campaign with (2018: 293). For many Evangelicals this makes sense as 'like Christianity, Islam teaches the importance of helping the poor and underprivileged, the orphaned and other disadvantaged groups. This shared concern should be explored to determine possible areas for cooperation' (Riddell, 2013: 189). Moucarry agrees and says that 'Christians and Muslims have in common a significant number of religious beliefs and ethical values that enable them to work hand in hand in the service of their society' (2022: xxii). So, in recent years, there has been an increase in joint initiatives between Christians, including Evangelicals, and Muslims around the world.

There are many examples. WEA has started to work with Nahdlatul Ulama in Indonesia to counter religious extremism (Johnson, 2020). Evangelical groups such as Sojourners and PCI are partners with the Shoulder-to-Shoulder campaign 'standing with American Muslims … committed to ending anti-Muslim hatred, discrimination, and violence in the United States of America'.[34] In the UK, The Feast sends Christian and Muslim youth workers into schools to 'bring together teenagers from different faiths and cultures to build friendships, explore faith and change lives', all without 'compromising what we believe but engaging with respect and honesty'.[35] The Centre for Muslim-Christian Studies in Oxford, while being a Christian institution, seeks to offer hospitality to both Christian and Muslim students and researchers,[36] and the Christian-Muslim Forum produces guidelines and reports on topics of shared concern for both communities such as mixed marriages and witnessing.[37] Despite these examples, statistics suggest that grassroots Evangelicals are still slow to engage in such cooperation. At Cape Town 2010, only 20 per cent of Evangelical leaders reported their churches working with other faiths on community projects.[38]

The issue of compromise is key here. There are many instances where the differences between Christianity and Islam are downplayed for the sake of partnership. Examples, such as those mentioned above, resist that tendency. However, some Evangelicals who wish to emphasize the uniqueness of Christ are still concerned. While conceding that 'cooperation' is a better word than 'reconciliation', Sookhdeo is suspicious of these sorts of initiatives. He points out that 'it is hard to find any warrant in the Bible for interfaith cooperation. In fact, it can be argued that cooperation with other faiths actually led to the decline of Israel and brought judgment upon the people of God' (2009a: 92). In similar fashion, 'joint action' is seen as one of the steps on the road to syncretism identified by Pawson above.

Discussion: Contested harvest

All Evangelicals have a commitment to mission and evangelism. It is axiomatic. They are the fulfilment of the two great gospel commands to 'love your neighbour' (Mk. 12.31) and to 'make disciples of all nations' (Mt. 28.19). However, within the Evangelical public sphere concerning Islam, there is a sharp disagreement about how these imperatives should be put into practice. As in previous chapters there is clearly a range of opinions and approaches. We have seen two poles. On the one hand, there are those who are more conciliatory and Islam-friendly and embrace friendship evangelism, dialogue and peacemaking. On the other hand, there are those who are confrontational and Islam-antagonistic, employing preaching, debate and polemics. Furthermore, there is profound disagreement over what should happen when a Muslim converts. Some are comfortable with a degree of continuity and even the development of IMs. Others trenchantly resist this and insist on complete discontinuity. There have also been those who occupy the middle ground and can see the merit in a variety of strategies, advocating different approaches for different Muslims in different contexts.

Clearly, something significant is happening in our interconnected, globalized, post-9/11 world. The number of Muslims in the West is growing, giving the impression of global strength and, for some, posing an apparent threat. Yet, at the same time, there is significant turmoil in Muslim-majority countries, and it seems that many Muslims are becoming disillusioned, even to the point of leaving Islam, suggesting significant weakness. Many leaving Islam reject religion altogether, but for those who decide to adopt Christianity the question is what type of Christianity it will be. Some, such as Sanneh, become Catholics or adopt various other traditions. This may include historical denominations which have coexisted with Muslims for many centuries. However, this is often problematic as it poses a security threat to those churches, which may be suspicious of the motives of new arrivals, who might attract the attention of – or even be from – the national security services. So, other converts become Evangelical Protestants, either joining existing churches or forming new 'underground' churches. They are most likely to take on the form, beliefs and traditions of those who have been instrumental in their conversion. If this is someone modelling IM, then they may retain much of their old identity. If it is someone more conservative, then they might make a complete break with their previous practice. Another possibility is that they might be influenced by global Christian media and the internet, in which case they might adopt any one of a host of forms. In fact, it is impossible for Evangelical mission workers to insulate the new believers from these outside media influences, and they may ultimately have no control over what path the new believers choose to follow in accordance with their own context, experience and preferences. The sorts of movements discussed by Garrison may prove to be spontaneous and uncontrollable.

What seems clearer is that the rift in the Evangelical mission community over IMs seems set to continue. The question is whether it will ultimately split the movement altogether over issues of contextualization. The twin dangers are that conservatives will remain entrenched, isolated and stoke hostility, while the progressives follow the path of a previous generation of Evangelical missionaries in focusing more on improving

Islam rather than seeking converts out of it and so cease to be Evangelical. The alternative is that the Evangelical public sphere will continue to facilitate a good quality of discussion and dialogue that might eventually facilitate, if not complete agreement, then at least a consensus among Evangelicals on how to maintain a minimal level of unity and goodwill towards one another.

14

Types of Evangelical response

The foregoing chapters have highlighted a range of opinions and approaches among Evangelicals which are caused and motivated by differing backgrounds, experiences, beliefs and priorities. Some of these factors can be represented by a series of dyads (Tables 14.1–14.4). As always, a spectrum is defined by its poles or extremes, but in real life, causes are more complex. People will be affected by a range of these factors and will often not be at all extreme, maybe occupying a middle ground that suggests either balance, uncertainty or even lack of courage.

The dyads do not always represent left/right. Neither do they all correspond to good/bad. For instance, a conciliator can be an idealist or a pragmatist. A confrontationist may or may not be informed or engaged with Muslims. However, they are useful as a diagnostic tool and may be used to construct types as suggested below.

Types of Evangelicals

Using these dyads as a diagnostic tool, here are some possible descriptions of the types of Evangelicals we have seen in this study. They are caricatures to illustrate a point. For that reason, I do not attempt to map names of participants onto these categories – not least because it is impossible to know from a person's public statements or writing all the details of their personal relations with Muslims and their unspoken attitudes. Some who might have a certain persona in the public sphere might behave quite differently in private and among friends. As seen, people also change over time. Even reading these descriptors may prompt changes in attitudes or approaches in the reader. Most types have been seen in this study, and, in fact, these are just a few of the possible combinations of the above pairings which could be used to describe Evangelical responses to Islam and Muslims.

Unengaged uninformed reactionaries[1]

These are often Evangelical religious or political leaders prone to making dogmatic public statements, often with an eye to their own domestic audience. They are not specialists or practitioners and know nothing or very little about Islam or Muslims, relying on others in the public sphere – Christian or secular – for their information.

Table 14.1 Motivations for Evangelical attitudes and actions

Party politics	Left	⟷	Right
Ideology	Liberal	⟷	Conservative
Activism	Progressive	⟷	Reactionary
Approach	Pragmatist	⟷	Idealist
Preference	Ambiguity	⟷	Certainty
Focus	Common good	⟷	Evangelism

Table 14.2 How Evangelicals view Islam

Diverse	⟷	Monolithic
People	⟷	Texts
Religious culture	⟷	Religious system
Of God	Human	Demonic
Continuous with Christianity	⟷	Discontinuous

Table 14.3 How Evangelicals view Muslims

Sincere	⟷	Deceptive
An opportunity	⟷	A threat
Victims	⟷	Troublemakers
Friends	⟷	Enemies

Table 14.4 Evangelical approaches to Islam and Muslims

Informed	⟷	Uninformed
Specialist	⟷	Non-specialist
Engaged	⟷	Unengaged
Dialogical	Apologetic	Polemical
Contextualist	⟷	Non-contextualist
Inclusive	⟷	Exclusive
Confident	⟷	Fearful
Self-critiquing	⟷	Muslim-critiquing

They only intervene in the public sphere when Islam is in the news. Their politics are to the right, and they may have a yearning to restore a Christendom model with Christianity at the centre of society.

Informed reactionaries

These Evangelicals see Islam as a religious system with an essential core and have studied the Islamic texts intensively. They see Islam as implacably opposed to Christianity and Muslims as a threat to societies – however mild and friendly they may appear. If they engage with Muslims, then it is usually in polemical debate, and they are suspicious of inter-faith activities, seldom having long-term Muslim friends. They may well have had negative experiences with Muslims in the past. Their politics are right-leaning, and they are very concerned with theology and salvation. They see progressive and conciliatory Evangelicals as naïve and dangerous.

Engaged informed pragmatists

These Evangelicals attempt to occupy the middle ground. They engage with Muslims and want them to become Christians. However, they are also concerned for the common good and so take part in inter-faith activities. They can see both sides of the debate. They see problematic aspects within Islamic texts, histories and traditions but also see Muslims as people and are interested in 'lived Islam'. They have a non-essentialist view of Islam and tend to talk of varieties of Islam or 'islams'. They believe that, where Muslims pose a threat, they should be challenged, but not all Muslims pose a threat, and the West is not blameless. They are concerned that Evangelicals on both sides of the debate are too extreme and that their words and actions are damaging the gospel in the eyes of Muslims – either by giving unwarranted offence or by devaluing the traditional Evangelical gospel.

Engaged informed progressives

These Evangelicals know a lot about Islam and culture and are frequently missionaries or former missionaries with many Muslim friends. For them Islam is not a threat, although certainly there are difficult topics to discuss and there is a small minority of atypical Muslims who are dangerous extremists who should be confronted. They see a continuity between Christianity and Islam, as Muslims are on a journey, as are we all. They engage in contextualization and often support Insider Movements (IMs). They are frustrated with reactionaries whom they find more problematic than they do most Muslims.

Engaged uninformed progressives

These Evangelicals know very little about Islam but prioritize relationships with Muslims whether in formal dialogue or in their personal lives. They have often had very positive experiences with moderate Muslims. They would rather avoid difficult topics and minimize awkward texts and histories, comparing them to the equivalent struggles they have faced in their Christian faith. Their politics lean to the left, and they are very concerned with social justice and the common good, blaming the West for much of Islamic extremism in the world today. They see the informed reactionaries as behaving in un-Christian ways towards Muslims.

Engaged evangelistic idealists

These evangelists focus on preaching the gospel to Muslims. They may or may not be informed about Islam but just want Muslims to become Christians – whether through friendship evangelism, preaching or supernatural miracles. They do not worry themselves with the debates going on in the public sphere.

And some not seen in this study …

Unengaged idealists

These Evangelicals hope, with their engaged cousins above, that Muslims will become Christians and that something good will happen in Christian-Muslim relations. However, they are not in any way involved with Muslims to bring that about.

Unengaged uniformed and fearful

This last category may well describe the majority of Evangelicals who do not live in proximity to Muslims. Informed only by the media – and, maybe, by the most reactionary of books – they would be afraid to approach or engage with Muslims, who might take on ogre-like qualities in their imaginations. It is this group that many of the participants in the Evangelical public sphere are seeking to influence – in one direction or the other.

Conclusion: The Evangelical micro-public sphere on Islam

At the outset of this book, I proposed that there is a transnational Evangelical micro-public sphere which is concerned with responding to Islam and Muslims. It is a long-standing sphere with a rich history of interaction stretching back over 200 years. In that time, it has debated many subtopics including the questions and issues that were a focus of Part 2, which in turn inform the practice and strategies of Part 3. This sphere clearly persists and is vibrant and active – if noticeably divided. Texts are constantly being published and exchanged in different forms, creating rational debate as participants react and respond to one another.

As far as possible, I have tried to allow these Evangelicals to tell the story in their own words. In doing so, we have seen a great range of responses. It should be clear that not all Evangelicals respond to Islam and Muslims in the same way. Although I have not attempted to assign individuals or organizations to specific categories, these quotations have created a map of Evangelical responses to Islam. These were depicted in terms of dyads and typological descriptions in the previous chapter. I hope that this will be a useful tool for practitioners, researchers and students – both insiders and outsiders – trying to understand the terrain. I also hope that it will be useful to theorists of the public sphere by way of being a case study of how to explore a micro-public sphere. It might even be suggestive of ways to approach similar study of a parallel Muslim public sphere. So, in concluding, I review the three essential elements of any public sphere (see Chapter 1). While the issue is often catalytic, I start by reviewing the diversity of Evangelical participants, how they are viewed by Muslims and how they change over time. I then briefly review the media and texts they circulate, before mentioning some important issues within this public sphere which have not been discussed.

Participants: People of a sphere

The names of over 200 Evangelical participants in this sphere have been mentioned. However, some names appear more than others and are clearly more influential – at least within the discourse of the micro-public sphere, if not necessarily among the grassroots and institutions with which the sphere is associated. Those who have written multiple books since 2001, such as Chapman, Durie, Moucarry, Musk and Sookhdeo, are clearly influential, although only to the degree that those books are read. Others, such as Accad, Azumah and Travis, are influential through the number of articles they have written in journals, magazines and online. A few are influential because they are converts from Islam, including Caner, Gabriel, Mallouhi, Qureshi and Solomon. Still others have held influential positions in denominations, organizations or movements, such as Rick Love, McLaren and Nazir-Ali. Those who engage in debates with Muslims are particularly visible through their online presence. Jay Smith and Pfander Films have hundreds of videos on YouTube, and there are videos of debates featuring Power, White, Wood and others. Still others are influential through their speaking and teaching, which has not featured so much in this book. For instance, in addition to their books and articles, participants such as Glaser, Reisacher, Tennent, Volf and Woodberry have all taught in universities, seminaries and also via innovative online courses.[1]

We have noted that important female voices are being heard, such as those of Cox, Dale, Glaser, Hine and Reisacher, sometimes on new platforms such as When Women Speak. Non-Western voices are also increasingly represented. There have been a number of Christian Arab voices, including Accad, Houssney, Jabbour, Masri and Shehadeh, along with some Asian voices, such as Azad, Nazir-Ali, Peñamora and Scot, and several Africans, chief among them Azumah. Furthermore, we have seen a cross-generational impact from the writings of Cragg and Newbigin, and some pre-9/11 books being republished. This is without considering those from earlier generations who still inspire Christians today, such as Gairdner, Pfander and Zwemer.

Moreover, on occasion, we have seen that the influence of this public sphere extends beyond the Evangelical community. It is, therefore, incumbent upon all who contribute to the public sphere to assess critically how their contribution will be understood by non-Evangelical audiences and whether or not it contributes constructively to the common good and to the greater cohesion of societies, in addition to the goals and ambitions of the Christian church. Evangelicals have to be aware that whatever they write, say or teach today will be heard and interpreted tomorrow by journalists, politicians, security services and ordinary citizens, including, maybe most importantly of all, Muslims.

Muslim perceptions

It is an interesting question as to whether Muslims perceive this diversity among Evangelicals. For some, there is a definite caricature of Evangelicals being right wing, anti-Muslim and politically motivated. A few years ago, I asked a British Muslim community leader what he thought of Evangelical Christians. His answer was immediate and strong:

> Evangelicalism is an aggressive brand of Christianity intent on conversion, especially of Muslims … particularly anti-Muslim in its outlook and strongly associated with George W. Bush … and a perception, in view of [Bush's] references to being 'born again', that the US invasion of Muslim Iraq and Afghanistan were at least in some part due to his religious beliefs.

These views are echoed by Abdal Hakim Murad, a Cambridge academic and convert to Islam, who recounts how:

> near Timbuktu, I listened to a wholly traditional Sufi leader expound the view that America's violence towards the Muslim world is the consequence of a *sahwa misihiyya*, a Christian revival. He was well-aware of the role of the *Christian Coalition* in the run-up to the Iraq war, despite living in a region where I saw no newspapers, and where internet access is almost impossible. Yet he was familiar with the names of Franklin Graham, Pat Robertson, and other icons of the Christian Right. For him … Bush and his team were crusaders, servants of Israel, and harbingers of the violent Second Coming of Christ.[2]

It seems that this caricature is deeply embedded in the minds of Muslims as much as it is in the Western media. However, some may have a more positive view. For instance, Cumming recalls a Muslim at a dialogue conference saying to him, 'We want to work with you Evangelicals, because we feel like we have something in common with you … we want to be talking with Christians who take their scriptures seriously' (2008: 314). It seems that some Muslims may be tired of engaging in politically correct pluralist dialogue. Undoubtedly, this book has shown that Muslims should not stereotype Evangelicals any more than Evangelicals should stereotype Muslims. As Quosigk puts it at the end of her research, 'For Muslims, it is important to recognize that not all Evangelicals conform to the stereotypical image of angry, hateful, Islamophobes … it should be helpful to the Muslim community to understand the different ways Evangelicals perceive Islam and the variety of ways they go about engaging Muslims.'[3]

A sphere divided

One thing that has become clear is that the Evangelical participants in this sphere are significantly divided in their attitudes and responses to Islam. This only confirms what others have noted before and reflects a wider divide within the Evangelical community. However, the interesting thing is that we have not seen this division fall neatly along geographic or denominational lines. There are American Evangelicals across the spectrum and so too Arabs and Africans, although perhaps a majority of converts are confrontationist. We have seen Baptists, Anglicans and Pentecostals taking contrasting stances within their own denominations. There are missionaries adopting different approaches and so too those working in political spaces. There is also no link to gender, and we have seen Evangelical women who are both Islam-friendly and Islam-antagonistic.

What is notable is that many – but not all – Evangelicals who hold the most exclusive beliefs about their own faith tend to essentialize Islam. For them, even other Christian traditions are suspected of being sub-Christian as there is only one way of practising faith which is according to their interpretation of the texts – usually to the exclusion of tradition. So, it is no surprise that these same Evangelicals believe that there is only one way for Muslims to be Muslims. On the other hand, open Evangelicals tend to have porous boundaries for their own communities and so are more willing to admit diversity within Islam. These groups then differ on a whole range of theological, historical and sociopolitical issues.

In the broader US context, Yancey and Quosigk question whether these two camps can remain together as one religion, although where a split would leave those who are clearly on middle ground is not clear.[4] Within the global Evangelical public sphere concerning Islam, the middle ground is more robust with many who appreciate both sides of the argument. Whether those in the centre can hold the extremes together in one space is uncertain.

A changing sphere

This study has presented a snapshot of the Evangelical public sphere over a relatively short time span (2001–22). Even during that period, participants have come and gone. Some write a book and then take little or no further part in the sphere. Others lose credibility such as the Caners, Shoebat or Zacharias. Still others have sadly passed away during this time, although their influence endures through their writing. However, views also change. This study suggests that Cimino is right that there has been a hardening of attitudes among some – but not all – Evangelicals since 9/11. At the same time, Evangelicals previously unengaged with dialogue engaged with ACW when it appeared in 2007, and since that time, several neighbourly, peacemaking Evangelical initiatives have been launched. Although I have not attempted a longitudinal study of how Evangelical views have changed over time, we have on occasion seen how this happens (see example of Qureshi in Chapter 3 and in Qureshi, 2016a: 112).

Others have noted how, in a previous generation, Zwemer's attitudes to Islam softened over time (Musk, 2005: 145). This is maybe reflected in the openness to dialogue and increased welcome over recent decades of Muslim Insider Movements among some Evangelicals and a greater emphasis on continuity between Christianity and Islam (see Chapter 13). However, for maybe rather more Evangelicals, attitudes have hardened since 2001. For instance, Sookhdeo's early writing was very welcoming and positive towards Asian migrants to Britain. He was positive about Muslims, suggesting that 'the Muslim's ethic is displayed in the character and life of Jesus', and was critical of polemics as 'we should not be negative in our approach, demolishing the other person's religion'. He went on to declare that 'our attitudes to the immigrant are very important. If they betray a hint of coolness, of prejudice, of superiority or patronage, then our work is nullified.'[5] Comparing this with his publications and quotations in this study, some of his views and approaches have clearly changed. This is almost certainly in response to global events, not least 9/11. He is now much more suspicious of Muslim migration and intentions, although he points out that his readers should be careful to 'distinguish Islam the religion', which causes many of the problems he perceives, from Muslims who are 'people loved by God and must be loved by Christians too' (2009a: 9).

Sookhdeo is not alone in changing emphases during a long career. Nazir-Ali's early books contained a strong emphasis on Christian-Muslim dialogue, an activity to which he is still committed today.[6] His 2002 book, written in the wake of 9/11, also sought to calm Christian fears and made clear that Christian-Muslim coexistence is perfectly possible. However, some of his later comments in the British press and his 2012 book reveal a growing concern about 'radical Islamism' against a backdrop of 'aggressive secularism' and what he sees as some of the failures of 'multiculturalism'. This in no way suggests a change in underlying attitudes to Muslims as individuals but demonstrates how events and changing global affairs mean that participants in the public sphere have to adapt and address new issues and re-examine their own positions. Such openness to change is critical to the health of any public sphere.

Media: Memory of a sphere

This study has principally focused on more than 300 books of different sorts published by Evangelicals since 2001. The majority of these have been published by Christian publishers but a few have been published by secular publishers or have been self-published. We have also seen almost 100 articles published in journals, magazines and newspapers. So, it is clear that formal publishing remains important for the Evangelical public sphere and many of the specialists and participants in this sphere interact with written texts and see publishing as an important vehicle for their ideas. However, not everyone reads books, and it is by no means certain that it is the best way to engage the target audience. So, we have seen other media being employed including articles on websites, blogs and especially online videos. A search of YouTube for 'Christian-Muslim debate', for instance, yields a large number of videos posted by both Christians and Muslims. Sometimes these media are combined in innovative ways, such as in the books of Dale (2021) and Garrison (2014) which link to websites and videos (see Chapter 1).

However, there must be questions as to the longevity of some of these new media. Websites come and go. Digital formats change. How many online articles and blogs have already been lost? For instance, articles on the Lapido Media website have already gone or become difficult to access.[7] Although there are internet archives, it is not certain that people will have the patience to delve into them. So, while formal publishing may be less influential than it once was, it remains very important for preserving the memory of a public sphere. The number of twentieth-century books being reprinted is testimony to the desire of a new generation to preserve and learn from the wisdom of previous generations. The fact that one can now search journals online means that past research is preserved and can readily resource new research and debate. It seems imperative that Evangelicals engaged in research and rational debate should organize and publish their work in such a way as to ensure that future generations can access it.

Issues: Concerns of a sphere

Finally, the core of any public sphere is the issue that is being discussed. Part 2 made it clear that, although this Evangelical micro-public sphere is responding to the challenge of Islam in general, it is also concerned about particular questions within that wider field. Some issues dealt with are enduring. Questions around Muhammad, the Qur'an, the Sharia and the other topics seen in Part 2 have always been points of debate and will continue to be so. Other issues are more ephemeral. For instance, certain events or sub-issues, such as ACW or Bible translation, spark a new spate of texts and interaction which may or may not endure. It is vital that as such issues and events arise the Evangelical micro-public sphere continues to process them together across their various divisions. Networks, conferences, publishing, exchange of texts and forums all discourage withdrawal and encourage rational debate. They might often seem like 'talking shops' – but they are important. Ignoring one another is not a good option.

However, the questions explored in Part 2 are clearly not exhaustive of the issues about which Evangelicals are concerned in their encounter with Muslims. Many more theological questions arise, including questions posed in both directions. There are undoubtedly social or ethical issues, such as drugs, alcohol, abortion and euthanasia along with those related to science, creation, genetics and artificial intelligence. These are, of course, all worthy of discussion in their own right, although space has not permitted their inclusion here. Nonetheless, some brief comments are in order about convert care, global demographic change, race, gender, sexual orientation and the environment as issues of outstanding import.

Convert care

For a long time, Christians were not able to talk publicly about caring for those who had come to Christian faith from a Muslim background. There was a reluctance to risk provoking Muslim anger, a desire to avoid publicity for the Christians who had led the converts to faith and most of all a concern to protect the identity of those who had converted lest they suffer a backlash from their families, communities or even state authorities. These all remain very real concerns (see Chapter 8). However, the situation in the West has changed considerably as Muslims are now talking very openly about conversion to Islam and the need to care for new converts. Indeed, initiatives have been started in different countries to help these new Muslims. In the UK the Convert Muslim Foundation was set up to offer 'a range of support, advice and services … so that everyone embracing Islam can feel comfortable as a Muslim in Britain'.[8] Something similar is offered by the Ta'leef Collective in the United States, Benevolence Australia and Mercy Mission Canada.[9] Obviously, if Muslims are openly talking about these things, then Christians should also feel confident in talking about the similar needs of converts in the opposite direction. As we have seen, there are now Muslims converting to Christianity both in Muslim-majority and Muslim-minority contexts. However, the public photographs on the Muslim websites are not found on Christian equivalents – even in the West. New converts still frequently face opposition and expulsion from their families and communities. So, churches welcoming them often have to provide temporary accommodation, emergency finance and advocacy, along with discipleship, friendship and a new community. This is forcing some churches in the West to re-examine their structures and programmes, as such converts clearly need more than a Sunday meeting with an occasional midweek Bible study (T. Green and Roxy, 2016).[10] It seems unlikely that such open support could be offered to converts in Muslim-majority contexts any time soon, despite initiatives such as the Marrakesh Declaration (see Chapter 8).[11]

Geography

Earlier chapters have already highlighted the different issues surrounding, on the one hand, the relatively new and increasing presence of Muslim minorities in Western countries (Chapter 7), and the situation of historical Christian minorities living among Muslim majorities (Chapter 8), on the other. This signals that geography is important in the Evangelical encounter with Muslims. Not every context is alike. Indeed, the global situation is changing rapidly. 'Over the past century the centre of gravity in the Christian world has shifted inexorably southward to Africa, Asia and Latin America. Already today, the largest Christian communities on the planet are to be found in Africa and Latin America.'[12] This means that the majority white Western voices mainly captured in this account of the Evangelical public sphere are rapidly going to change to at least include, if not be dominated by, those of Africans, Asians and Latinos. The few mentioned will be joined by many others.

In some places the church is waning. As in the West, some of the historical Christian churches of the Middle East will continue to decline due to demographic change, migration and war. Recalling past genocides of Armenian and Assyrian Christians, Jenkins even suggests that Christians need to develop 'a theology of extinction' to explain how and why churches die.[13] At the same time and in those same places, new churches are emerging and, in Africa and other parts of the world, Evangelical and Pentecostal churches are growing rapidly. Some of these are in zones of struggle with Muslims, such as West and East Africa and the Philippines, where numbers of Muslims are also growing rapidly. Likely Christian reactions to pressure have already been mentioned in Chapter 8 but there will be an increasing need to think carefully about Christian attitudes to war, violence and retaliation along with an imperative for conflict resolution and peacemaking on all sides, especially at these flashpoints (see the Philippine example of Peñamora in Chapter 9).

Race

This attention to geography is a reminder that race is another important and inextricable part of the encounter between Christians and Muslims with which both faith communities continue to struggle. As much as Christianity and Islam aspire to be universal faiths for all people, where people are born is still a huge factor in deciding what religion they start out with and there are strong geographic associations with religion – both at global and local level. This means that when an Anglo-Saxon Evangelical talks to an Asian Muslim there is not only a religious but also a racial dynamic at play – working both ways. It is visible, visceral and potentially discomfiting to both parties.

This is not to conflate religion and race. Obviously not all Arabs and South Asians are Muslims any more than all Anglo-Saxons are Christians. Clearly there are many Arab and Asian Christians (along with Hindus, Buddhists and Sikhs) and plenty of Anglo-Saxons who follow other faiths or none. In Africa the issue is even more complex and some tribes such as the Yoruba of West Africa are a mix of Christian, Muslim and African Traditional Religion. There are also increasing numbers of converts in both directions who remind us that faith is not entirely about birth or ethnic background but is also a matter of choice – and often a litmus test for freedom (see Chapter 8). This is one reason why definitions of Islamophobia that include a reference to race are unhelpful and controversial (see Chapter 2).

Any discussion of race inevitably raises questions of colonialism and slavery – for both Christians and Muslims. White Western Christians were complicit in the slavery visited on black Africans and other races. While Evangelicals, such as Wilberforce, were at the forefront of the abolition movement, many others owned slaves. Many Western churches and denominations which benefited financially from slave-owning benefactors and investments are now publicly repenting and are aware of the need to repair race relations. Muslims too have an imperial, slaving past. Muhammad himself owned slaves and Arab slavers were in Africa and other places long before the arrival of Westerners and continued after the Western abolition of slavery. Indeed, it was only abolished in Saudi Arabia in 1962 and in Mauritania in 1981. White convert to Islam, Medina Tenour Whiteman, candidly admits the contemporary 'ingrained' racism in the Muslim umma against both white converts and black communities.[14] So, neither Christians nor Muslims can take the moral high ground on their past involvement in slavery and present attitudes to race. As with so much from an imperial past, these are deeply rooted issues with complex contemporary implications and should be an open, honest, even-handed conversation between Christians and Muslims.

Gender

Gender has been discussed at various points (see Chapters 6 and 7). It is an issue for both communities as well as a topic of concern within this Evangelical public sphere. Although around 90 per cent of the voices heard in this study have been male, increasingly there is a recognition that it is vital to hear female Evangelical voices. There are many reasons for this, including the unique experiences and insights that Christian women have into the lives of Muslim women. Certainly, concerns persist over the place of women in Islam, but we have also seen indications of strong female Muslim voices with increasing agency. Furthermore, it is important for both Christians and Muslims to 'listen to the scriptures through the experiences of women' (Hine in Dale, 2021: 16). The presumption and privilege of patriarchal readings of scripture are not sufficient to sustain vibrant communal faith in the twenty-first century. Both communities need to hear female voices to understand what faith means and how it impacts just over half of their members.

Moreover, there are important questions surrounding the disparity between the numbers of female worshippers in many Western churches and the typically male worshippers in mosques. While Islam is usually regarded by Christians as being a male dominated faith, Muslims in some places see Christianity as becoming increasingly 'feminized' (Reddie, 2009). How will this affect relations in the future? Particularly, how does it affect the meeting of leaders? There are, of course, female leaders in Muslim public life. Bangladesh, Pakistan, Indonesia and Turkey have all had Muslim female prime ministers or presidents. Yet, internal religious roles have remained almost exclusively male.[15] At the same time, many Western denominations now have women in church leadership. The cultural dynamics when male Muslim leaders, many of them unused to interacting with women, meet female Christian leaders is something that will be interesting to watch and research.

Furthermore, none of this takes into consideration the massive cultural shifts happening in the West around gender more broadly. Virtually all Muslims and the majority of Evangelicals remain culturally conservative and are struggling to understand and respond to the redefinition of gender that is happening in Western societies. The scriptures in both religions appear to be clear on the binary nature of gender. 'Male and female he created them' (Gen. 1.27); 'We have created you male and female' (Q 49.13). Such verses seem to exclude the possibility of gender reassignment or the more than fifty gender options that are currently offered by Facebook. Yet there will be increasing cultural and legal pressure on faith communities in the West to accept gender fluidity. This also has implications for discussions of marriage and family. While conservatives in both camps might well make common cause that marriage should be between a man and a woman, Evangelicals would part company with many Muslims over views on the necessity of monogamy as opposed to polygamy. This suggests that, despite shared concerns, conservatives on both sides may find it difficult to make common cause on issues of family.

Sexual orientation

Both faith communities also have to face the issue of sexual orientation in the twenty-first century. The Christian community, including Evangelicals, is further down the road in this discussion than the Muslim community. Some Christian denominations now accept and offer same-sex marriages. This includes a small but growing number of Evangelicals who believe that Jesus's silence on such topics allows freedom, inclusiveness and the reinterpretation of scriptural prohibitions.[16] There is a much smaller number in Muslim communities campaigning for LGBTQ and gender rights.[17]

The progressive groups – Christian and Muslim – may well make common cause and join their voices to the overwhelming numbers in Western societies calling for full global recognition and rights for those of all sexual orientations. However, this will increasingly alienate more conservative Evangelicals and Muslims who do not believe such things are sanctioned by their scriptures and cannot in all conscience affirm this cultural shift. Ironically, this is one area in which Evangelical confrontationists would have common ground with Muslims, particularly in education, and yet it seems unlikely that the two will cooperate in their resistance. It is also important to note that this issue is exacerbating a deepening rift between Christians in the Global South and in the West. Christians in Africa, for instance, generally take a very conservative line on sexual orientation and this is one area in which Christians and Muslims in that region may be more closely aligned.

Climate and environment

Finally, the north–south divide is also a notable factor when it comes to climate change. Nowhere on earth is immune from the environmental crisis facing the planet in the twenty-first century. However, its effects are disproportionately felt by both Muslims and Christians in the Global South. This, on the one hand, fuels ill feeling towards the West, which has largely caused the problem, recalling grievances over the history of colonial exploitation. On the other hand, it may ignite conflict between communities in the Global South as they compete for increasingly scarce resources, chief among them being water.[18] This is already a reality in West Africa where nomadic Muslim Fulani tribes are moving further south driven by desertification to the north, bringing them into conflict with settled agrarian communities, both Muslim and Christian.[19] Jenkins notes that climate change and environmental factors from floods to famines and volcanoes to earthquakes have historically had religious consequences, triggering revivals and concerns of imminent apocalyptic judgement. For instance, the Little Ice Age, that extended for several hundred years up to the nineteenth century, impacted Christian-Muslim relations through not just competition for resources but also conspiracy theories, scapegoating and wars.[20] The backdrop of climate change is sure to affect the ongoing relationships between Christians and Muslims around the world. Whether it results in wars on the one hand or mutual action on the other remains to be seen.

The usefulness of a sphere

As the Evangelical micro-public sphere continues to debate these issues concerning Islam and Christian-Muslim relations, there is much that the wider public sphere can learn from its discourse. After all, as Davie observes, issues debated within the church are often those that society itself is struggling to come to terms with.[21] Firstly, the issue of faith needs to be taken seriously in public life. However much some countries and some secularists would like to exclude the religious voice, Habermas is right to insist on its inclusion, both for civility, but also for learning.[22] Those outside this sphere, whether other Christians, Muslims or policy makers, could learn a lot from both combative and irenic Evangelical readings of Islamic texts and histories. They might also learn from how the issues are being debated and from the various disagreements between Evangelicals.

Secondly, as Trigg advocates, 'Religious voices must be heard in the public life of every country' in order to expose them to 'public scrutiny and rational debate'.[23] This applies as much to Evangelical arguments as to those of Muslims. It is important that the Evangelical micro-public sphere remains open to outside critique. Hateful, racist, antisemitic and misogynistic teaching should be robustly countered and extremist ideologies rejected wherever they are found.

So, thirdly, paying attention to this Evangelical public sphere highlights the importance of rigorous, in-depth study of religions. The majority of people of faith have reasons for behaving the way they do. There is an internal logic based on religious texts, traditions and histories as well as on context and circumstance. It is not good enough to declaim that certain actors – Muslim or Christian – are not true believers or are unrepresentative of the faith. Trite platitudes will not suffice. For instance, when it was at its short-lived zenith of territorial power around 2014–16, ISIS produced a glossy magazine entitled *Dabiq* as part of its online recruiting campaign.[24] It was well produced, written in good English, replete with gruesome images of executions and pictures of apparently happy young fighters on the adventure of a lifetime. The allure – along with the horror – was clear. In March 2015, British imams, in an admirable attempt to counteract *Dabiq*'s appeal to young Muslims, launched a new magazine called *Haqiqah* with the first issue entitled 'What is the truth behind ISIS?' The imams argued that the authors of *Dabiq* had stopped 'consulting the Qur'an and the Sunnah' and were not true Muslims.[25] The trouble was that each of the fifteen editions of Dabiq was full of quotations from the Qur'an and Hadith. The ISIS writers had clearly not abandoned the Sunnah but were interpreting it literally. What was needed from the imams were rigorous, rational arguments as to why the Sunnah should be interpreted differently, in a manner likely to appeal to young Muslims.[26] Such clarity is incumbent on all faith communities. Finally, it is clear that in both the Christian and Muslim public spheres there are competing voices. The grassroots are not always being influenced by the specialist elites within those spheres but are prey to politicians and radicals as well as to broader media. This again highlights the importance of education and good quality public debate.

Education

All communities need to take education seriously. Both Christians and Muslims should educate their audiences, especially the young, honestly about their texts, traditions and histories including the good, the bad and the truly ugly. This includes Christians not ignoring difficult Old Testament war verses, as well as Muslims reading their texts in languages understood by all (see Chapter 9). In both cases, careful attention needs to be paid to explaining the hermeneutical process. It should also mean reporting good news stories as well as the bad. For instance, in one editorial Sookhdeo tells the story of the Grand Mufti of Syria, whom he describes as 'a man of peace'. His son was murdered by 'Islamist hit-men'. However, when the killers were arrested, rather than exacting revenge, the mufti forgave them. Sookhdeo (2014b) suggests that young Muslims in the West need to hear his voice. A willingness to tell such positive stories gives the reporting of disadvantage, persecution and killing added credibility and integrity, as does the admission of stories in which Christian violence against Muslims takes place (see Chapters 8 and 9). Such education should also involve reading texts written in the other community from multiple traditions and not just those which affirm previously held positions.

Research

This requires not just journalism but academic rigour. Both communities should engage in careful academic research of texts and histories. This should include studying the other tradition not solely for polemical purposes but in the cause of truth and integrity. Such research entails asking hard questions, both of the texts and one another. It is not intrinsically Orientalist – or Occidentalist – to ask one another difficult questions. It is not necessarily Islamophobic – or Christianophobic – to examine the other's tradition.

If it is motivated by hatred and the intention to cause violence, then it is wrong and should be condemned wherever it occurs. If it is driven by fear, then it is unhelpful and will thwart our shared life and the common good. If it results in mistreatment, socioeconomic disadvantage or denial of rights – whether of Christians in Muslim-majority countries or of Muslims in the West – then it must be resisted and wrongs should be set right. Rather, tough questions about texts, histories and contemporary practices should be motivated by the respectful search for truth and wisdom.

Both faiths have difficult histories to face up to. Christianity did not start as an imperial faith but was suborned by empire and went on to be implicated in Western colonialism. Its evangelistic mission to the world inevitably became associated with Western hegemony with all its injustices. Islam, after brief years as a minority in Mecca, quickly became a political power and was also involved in imperial expansion. Muslims have been no less colonial than Christians given the chance.[27] Researching and discussing these things requires honesty and courage. It is not good enough to have workshops where one side or the other does all the repenting, and the other admits no failings. This suggests that, where possible, both the educational and research tasks should be carried out by Christians and Muslims working together holding one another accountable while not denying the differences and passions which they hold so dearly. This requires extending and receiving hospitality.

Hospitality and humility

It is common in inter-faith and political circles to hear the argument that what is needed is tolerance. This sometimes seems to imply that anyone who criticizes the beliefs of others must be intolerant, or whoever believes something to be true, contrary to others, must be bigoted. Yet surely this is the supposedly tolerant being intolerant. Tolerance must be founded on something worth striving for. The danger is that so often 'we want tolerance but end up with relativism' (Payne, 2012: 88).[28] Trigg observes that 'a tolerant society is not one without any constitutive beliefs, since its tolerance may follow from those beliefs'.[29] Karl Popper, in his 1945 defence of democracy following the carnage of World War Two, commented on this 'paradox of tolerance'. He warned that 'unlimited tolerance must lead to the disappearance of tolerance. If we extend unlimited tolerance even to those who are intolerant, if we are not prepared to defend a tolerant society against the onslaught of the intolerant, then the tolerant will be destroyed, and tolerance with them.'[30] The global rise of dictatorship and authoritarianism in the early twenty-first century, even in the West, along with a weakening of the concept of truth, makes it all the more difficult to discern the limits of tolerance and the beliefs it is built on.

So, what are the alternatives? Martin Marty thinks that the concept of tolerance is weak and condescending and has 'no muscle' of its own but rather attempts to 'remake "the Other" into some manageable image'.[31] In the place of tolerance Marty advocates 'counter-intolerance', or what he calls 'risky hospitality', during which 'we greet, eat, gesture, listen, speak differently because of the presence of the Other, become sensitive to the changes we must make in our own outlook and community, and emerge as different beings than we were before the possibly tense but often enjoyable experience of mutual hospitality'.³² This might operate at different levels including between individuals, academic institutions, worshipping groups or whole communities. Kaemingk believes that, for Christians, such hospitality extends from the example of Christ (2018: 187). It is costly and disruptive, and can also be dangerous. Physically welcoming strangers into classrooms, offices, places of worship and homes risks being abused, robbed or even attacked. In the same way, academic hospitality risks being challenged, unsettled or misrepresented and societal hospitality risks loss of power, being taken advantage of or even being overrun.

Of course, hospitality poses a threat not just for the host but for the guest too. There is a power dynamic at work which risks what Jacques Derrida calls 'hostipitality', which is 'a reaffirmation of mastery and being oneself in one's own home'. This implies a conditionality to the hospitality which becomes coercive and verges on hostility.³³ In this case, hospitality is offered in order to subdue or subvert guests, to let them know who is in control. If this is to be avoided there must be openness and integrity. Polemical engagement, for all its failings, is admirably transparent. Undermine your opponent, win the argument, call to conversion. Unspoken motivations, on the other hand, whether in the form of subtle control, of *taqīya* or of unspoken hopes of conversion, subvert and undermine the practice of hospitality. Motivations, hopes and fears should be freely expressed, which requires courage and humility.

However, honesty and humility are also inherently risky virtues that open one up to exploitation. Employing the image of shared 'table politics', Kaemingk proposes that hosts need to be 'willing to vulnerably and humbly take a seat at the table next to their guests' (2018: 305). However, this is not without danger. Jenkins has some sober words of caution for those inviting Muslims to the table in their own 'home'. He suggests that military and political 'worldly success was a potent force in the growth of Islam, and in the shrivelling of Christianity. That fact may be troubling to Christians, whose faith so often extols the triumph of the meek and humble while rejecting worldly success, and who are so familiar with the concept of defeat as the root of long-term victory'.³⁴ He reminds Christians that nowhere in the Bible are they 'offered any assurance that they will hold political power'.³⁵ Academic, societal or any other sort of hospitality combined with humility is a double jeopardy – but for the Christian it is also the way of the cross.

The cross(roads)

Some Evangelicals suggest that, following 9/11, Islam is at a crossroads. They see that 'Muslims around the world are clearly divided ... there is a titanic struggle taking place between moderates and radicals for the hearts and minds of the Muslim masses in the middle' (Riddell and Cotterell, 2003: 192–4). Jabbour agrees. He points out that 'many people in the West assume that the biggest war in the world today is the war on terrorism'. However, he believes that there is 'a much bigger and more important war, with more dangerous consequences for the whole world ... this war is not against Muslims but within Islam itself ... Most Muslims are being pulled in one of two directions ... toward moderation and open-mindedness ... [or towards] fanatical Islam and/or Islamic fundamentalism' (2008: 80).

However, some Islam-antagonistic Evangelicals believe that the Christian church in the West is itself at a crossroads – and is in danger of extinction. In an article entitled 'The Church at the Crossroads: a global perspective', Nikides suggests that the church is 'balanced on the knife edge', as evangelicalism is 'changing dramatically and rapidly'. He mentions Chalke and McLaren, who have both featured in the foregoing chapters as Islam-friendly participants in the public sphere, as representatives of the Emergent Church who are 'spinning away from foundational definitions and restrictions'. This is weakening the church and leaving it prey to secularism and especially Islamization. He sees hope in the life and growth of the Bible-believing churches of the Global South, albeit with the inherent danger of 'their syncretistic practices', and he reflects that 'Christendom is only really dead as an idea in the West'. Meanwhile, in the West, 'We can see Islam coming; it is only a matter of time until it dominates.' He believes that 'Europe appears to be becoming a House of Islam. We have empirical data', and suggests that 'in such a case, perhaps the best we can do is strengthen our defenses before the onslaught begins. We bar the doors, stockpile the weapons and wait' (Nikides, 2006). It is not clear whether he means this to be taken literally. These are, of course, just one pastor's ideas but they resonate with many of the feelings of the confrontationists we have seen. The picture is clear. The Western church is at the crossroads of its own demise. It needs to awaken, strengthen what remains and resist the Muslim onslaught.

In total contrast, some open Evangelicals have identified a rather different struggle taking place within the global Evangelical community concerning the debate raging over the two views of Islam. Cumming says:

> There is a titanic struggle going on in the heavenly realms. It is a struggle that most Christians are completely unaware is taking place. It is not a struggle between Muslims and Christians or between Muslims and the West. Rather, I am talking about a struggle within Christianity itself, a struggle for the soul of the Christian faith … September 11 has set a question before the Christians of the world … Is the Christian faith primarily a tribal identity (we are the Christians, they are the Muslims)? Or is the Christian faith primarily costly discipleship to Jesus Christ the Crucified? (2008: 319)

Azumah supports Cumming in his assessment. He quotes the above text in an article of his own to suggest that 'Islam *per se* is not necessarily the greatest challenge facing Christians today but rather, how Christians choose to respond to Islam' (Azumah, 2009: 3). The challenge is for Christians to continue loving Muslims in a Christ-like way, whatever the cost.

The crossroads image conjures a sense of binary choice. Modernity/tradition, progress/regress, friendship/enmity, acceptance/rejection, love/hate. Indeed, I have set out dyads that suggest extremes and research has shown that Evangelical leaders tend to those extremes, although the grassroots are often found with 'hybrid identities' occupying the middle ground.[36] However, crossroads need not be binary choices. They can be complex places. Guinness offers us the example of Spaghetti Junction, a notorious motorway interchange in Birmingham, UK, a place confusing for the novice or unwary driver (Guinness, 2010: 164). I know a crossroads which has six roads leading into it!

Of course, it makes it more difficult to navigate but it means there are more options. This is a reminder to those consumed with the Christian-Muslim encounter that it is not the only site for a crossroads. There are encounters with other faiths, other political debates and other theological challenges. Nonetheless, even in the Christian-Muslim encounter the options are not binary. Choices are more nuanced. Dialogue need not entail abandoning uniqueness. Friendship need not imply agreement. Cooperation need not involve merger. Wisdom need not give way to naivety.

But choices there must be. Remaining at the crossroads is not an option. A driver stalled at Spaghetti Junction will cause a pile up. Decisions are inevitable, indecision disastrous. The middle ground is a place of great power and influence, and we need those who can see all sides of the debate and draw in opposing parties. We need those who can tread the line between hostility and naivety. However, the middle ground can also be a place of indecision and inactivity. Prevarication creates a void that other agendas will fill. Courage is required.

It is striking that the two passages about the Christian crossroads above both end by invoking the cross of Christ and the image of the Christian martyr taking up the cross to follow in his footsteps. Yet, the two authors, and the Evangelicals they represent, do not seem to agree on what that path looks like in the lived encounter with Muslims. This only reflects the wider fissures already observed in the global Evangelical movement. For the moment, the shared commitment to mission among Evangelicals engaged with Muslims may be enough to at least maintain a semblance of common identity, if not unity. If Evangelicals are to remain together, it seems essential that they hold together in tension the need for proclamation of the gospel message with the need to share societies with Muslims in Christ-like ways that enhance the common good. Paying attention to their shared religious micro-public sphere and continuing the hard work of circulating texts, reading, listening, meeting and engaging in rational debate will be essential to holding the tensions in balance.

Notes

Introduction: Evangelicals responding to Islam

1. Woodberry is quoting Todd Johnson, editor of the *Atlas of Global Christianity*.
2. Kidd, Thomas (2009), *American Christians and Islam: Evangelical Culture and Muslims from the Colonial Period to the Age of Terrorism*, Princeton, NJ: Princeton University Press, 144.
3. Slomp, Jan (1995), 'Calvin and the Turks', in Haddad and Haddad (eds), *Christian-Muslim Encounters*, Gainesville: University Press of Florida, 126–42, 129.
4. Basset, Jean-Claude (1998), 'New Wine in Old Wineskins: Changing Protestant Views of Islam', in Waardenburg (ed.), *Islam and Christianity: Mutual Perceptions since the Mid-20th Century*, Leuven: Peeters, 79–96, 79. See also Francisco, Adam (2007), *Martin Luther and Islam: A Study in Sixteenth-Century Polemics and Apologetics*, Leiden: Brill.
5. Khalaf, Samir (1997), 'Protestant Images of Islam: Disparaging Stereotypes Reconfirmed', *Islam and Christian-Muslim Relations*, 8 (2): 211–29, 217.
6. Goddard, Hugh (2020), *History of Christian-Muslim Relations*, Edinburgh: Edinburgh University Press, 112.
7. Smith, Jane (1998), 'Christian Missionary Views of Islam in the Nineteenth and Twentieth Centuries', *Islam and Christian-Muslim Relations*, 9 (3): 357–73, 360.
8. Ibid., 366.
9. Sharkey, Heather (2008), *American Evangelicals in Egypt: Missionary Encounters in an Age of Empire*, Princeton, NJ: Princeton University Press.
10. Watt, Montgomery (1991), *Muslim-Christian Encounters: Perceptions and Misperceptions*, London: Routledge, 364.
11. Basset, 'New Wine', 88.
12. Barth quoted in McDermott, Gerald (2000), *Can Evangelicals Learn from World Religions? Jesus, Revelation & Religious Traditions*, Downers Grove, IL: Inter-Varsity Press, 28.
13. Jenkins, Philip (2007), *The Next Christendom: The Coming of Global Christianity*, Oxford: Oxford University Press, 120.
14. See, for instance, Bebbington, David (1989), *Evangelicalism in Modern Britain: A History from the 1730s to the 1980s*, London: Routledge; Larsen, Timothy (2007), 'Defining and Locating Evangelicalism', in Larsen and Treier (eds), *The Cambridge Companion to Evangelical Theology*, Cambridge: Cambridge University Press, 1–14; and Noll, Mark (1986), *Between Faith and Criticism: Evangelicals, Scholarship and the Bible*, New York: Harper & Row.
15. Stackhouse, John (2011), 'Generic Evangelicalism', in Bauder, Naselli and Hansen (eds), *Four Views on the Spectrum of Evangelicalism*, Grand Rapids, MI: Zondervan, 116–42.
16. George Marsden quoted in Noll, *Between Faith and Criticism*, 5.

17. For instance, during the writing of this book, pastor Thabiti Anyabwile, mentioned below, announced on Twitter that he had left Evangelicalism (@ThabitiAnyabwil, 7 February 2022).
18. Buckeridge, John (2006), 'Drop the "e" Word', *Christianity*, May. In this editorial for *Christianity* magazine, Buckeridge refers to a survey conducted for the UK Evangelical Alliance which found that '87% of the sample describe themselves as evangelical but only 59% reveal their "evangelical" identity to others'.
19. See Bielo, James (2016), *Emerging Evangelicals: Faith, Modernity, and the Desire for Authenticity*, New York: New York University Press.
20. Hansen, Collin (2011), 'Introduction', in Bauder, Naselli and Hansen (eds), *Four Views on the Spectrum of Evangelicalism*, Grand Rapids, MI: Zondervan. The latter term has been coined by Tony Campolo and others, and it refers to certain editions of the Bible which have the words of Jesus printed in red ink.
21. Jenkins, *Next Christendom*.
22. See Taylor, Matthew (2023), *Scripture People: Salafi Muslims in Evangelical Christians' America*, Cambridge: Cambridge University Press. Also, for an example, see Hellyer, Hisham (2008), 'At Yale, We Muslims and Christians Found a Kind of Sincerity', *The National*, UAE, 2 August.
23. Berger, Peter (1992), *A Far Glory: The Quest for Faith in an Age of Credulity*, New York: Free Press, 32.
24. O'Mahony, Anthony, and Emma Loosley (eds) (2008), *Christian Responses to Islam: Muslim-Christian Relations in the Modern World*, Manchester: Manchester University Press.
25. Lindsay, Michael (2007), *Faith in the Halls of Power: How Evangelicals Joined the American Elite*, Oxford: Oxford University Press; and Swartz, David (2012), *Moral Minority: The Evangelical Left in an Age of Conservatism*, Philadelphia: University of Pennsylvania Press.
26. See, for instance, Smith, Christian (1998), *American Evangelicalism: Embattled and Thriving*, Chicago: University of Chicago Press; and Smith, Christian (2002), *Christian America? What Evangelicals Really Want*, Berkeley: University of California Press.
27. Kidd, *American Christians*, xiii.
28. Ibid., xiv.
29. Ibid., 165.
30. Ratliff, Walter (2011), *Christians and Muslims at the Epicenter: How the Sept. 11th Attacks Shook and Transformed American Evangelicalism*: Herndon, VA: Agilis Press, 185.
31. It is worth noting that prior to this, until the fall of the Berlin Wall in 1989, communism and the Soviet Union were viewed in much the same way as Islam and Muslims are viewed today.
32. Ratliff, *Christians and Muslims at the Epicenter*, 7.
33. Bhatia, Amit (2017), *Engaging Muslims and Islam: Lessons for 21st-Century American Evangelicals*, Skyforest, CA: Urban Loft, 345.
34. Ibid., 332.
35. Quosigk, Ashlee (2021), *American Evangelicals: Conflicted on Islam*, London: Bloomsbury, 5, 39.
36. Yancey, George, and Ashlee Quosigk (2021), *One Faith No Longer: The Transformation of Christianity in Red and Blue America*, New York: New York University Press, 93, 17.
37. Ibid., 92.
38. Ibid., 205.

39. Bebbington, David (2009), 'Evangelical Trends, 1959–2009', *Anvil*, 26 (2): 93–106, 104–5.
40. Cimino, Richard (2005), '"No God in Common": American Evangelical Discourse on Islam after 9/11', *Review of Religious Research*, 47 (2): 162–74, 165–7.
41. Casanova, José (2009), 'Immigration and the New Religious Pluralism: A European Union–United States Comparison', in Levey and Modood (eds), *Secularism, Religion and Multicultural Citizenship*, Cambridge: Cambridge University Press, 139–63, 161–2.
42. Hoover, Dennis (2004), 'Is Evangelicalism Itching for a Civilization Fight? A Media Study', *Brandywine Review of Faith and International Affairs*, Spring: 11–14, 14 (emphasis in original).
43. Meulenberg, Michal (2017), 'Attitudes and Behavior Intention of American Evangelicals in Faith Conversations with Muslims: An Analysis Using the Reasoned Action Approach', unpublished thesis, Fuller Theological Seminary, ii.
44. See www.multifaithmatters.org and an unpublished report sent to the Louisville Institute. See also an article based on the research by Sabates, Angela (2021), 'The ABC's of Christians' Anti-Muslim Attitudes: An Application of Eagly and Chaiken's Attitude Theory', *Journal of Psychology and Theology*, 50 (4): 387–403.
45. Atherstone, Andrew (2019), 'Evangelicals and Islam', in Atherstone and Jones (eds), *The Routledge Research Companion to the History of Evangelicalism*, Abingdon: Routledge, 127–45, 128.
46. Ibid., 144.
47. Ipgrave, Michael (2008), 'Ecumenical Christian Responses to Islam in Britain', in O'Mahony and Loosley (eds), *Christian Responses to Islam: Muslim-Christian Relations in the Modern World*, Manchester: Manchester University Press, 5–20, 7–9.
48. Lewis, Philip, and Sadek Hamid (2018), *British Muslims: New Directions in Islamic Thought, Creativity and Activism*, Edinburgh: Edinburgh University Press.
49. Lewis, Philip (2002), *Islamic Britain: Religion, Politics and Identity among British Muslims*, London: I.B. Tauris, and Lewis, Philip (2007), *Young, British and Muslim*, London: Continuum.
50. Mitchell, Barbara (2008), 'The Response of the Church of England to Islam and Muslim-Christian Relations in Contemporary Britain', in O'Mahony and Loosley (eds), *Christian Responses to Islam: Muslim-Christian Relations in the Modern World*, Manchester: Manchester University Press, 21–37, 30. Maybe Mitchell has in mind the caricature of 'happy-clappy simpletons' that Buckeridge refers to above.
51. Siddiqui, Ataullah (2005), 'Islam and Christian Theology', in Ford (ed.), *The Modern Theologians: An Introduction to Christian Theology since 1918*, Oxford: Blackwell, 663–81, 673.
52. Kidd, *American Christians*, 82–3.
53. Smith, Greg (2018), 'Evangelicals and the Encounter with Islam: Changing Christian Identity in Multi-faith Britain', *Entangled Religions*, 5: 154–209. Smith's sample, provided by the UK Evangelical Alliance, consisted of over one thousand 'self-defined evangelical Christians'.
54. See Ojo, Matthews (2007), 'Pentecostal Movements, Islam and the Contest for Public Space in Northern Nigeria', *Islam and Christian-Muslim Relations*, 18 (2): 175–88.
55. https://bertderuiter.eu.
56. More details of books and authors can be found at the website www.christianresponsestoislam.com.

1 Public spheres

1. Keane, John (1998), *Civil Society: Old Images, New Visions*, Cambridge: Polity Press.
2. Berger, *A Far Glory*, 32.
3. Habermas, Jürgen (1989), *The Structural Transformation of the Public Sphere: An Inquiry into a Category of Bourgeois Society*, Cambridge: Polity Press. The book first appeared in German in 1962 as *Strukturwandel der Öffentlichkeit* but was not translated into English until 1989.
4. Ibid., 14.
5. Habermas, Jürgen (1987), *The Theory of Communicative Action, Vol. 2: Lifeworld and System – A Critique of Functionalist Reason*, Cambridge: Polity Press.
6. Taylor, Charles (2007), *A Secular Age*, Cambridge, MA: Harvard University Press, 185.
7. Crossley, Nick, and John Roberts (eds) (2004), *After Habermas: New Perspectives on the Public Sphere*, Oxford: Blackwell, 2.
8. Calhoun, Craig (ed.) (1992), *Habermas and the Public Sphere*, Cambridge, MA: MIT Press, 39.
9. Fraser, Nancy (1992), 'Rethinking the Public Sphere: A Contribution to the Critique of Actually Existing Democracy', in Calhoun (ed.), *Habermas and the Public Sphere*, Cambridge, MA: MIT Press, 109–37, 116.
10. Habermas, Jürgen (1992), 'Further Reflections on the Public Sphere', in Calhoun (ed.), *Habermas and the Public Sphere*, Cambridge, MA: MIT Press, 421–57, 424.
11. Habermas, *Structural Transformation*, 175.
12. Ibid., 178.
13. Goode, Luke (2005), *Jürgen Habermas and the Public Sphere*, London: Pluto Press, 20.
14. Fraser, *Rethinking the Public Sphere*, 123.
15. Fraser, Nancy (2007), 'Transnationalizing the Public Sphere: On the Legitimacy and Efficacy of Public Opinion in a Post-Westphalian World', in Benhabib, Shapiro and Petranović (eds), *Identities, Affiliations and Allegiances*, Cambridge: Cambridge University Press, 45–66.
16. Keane, *Civil Society*.
17. Hauser, Gerard (1999), *Vernacular Voices: The Rhetoric of Publics and Public Spheres*, Columbia: University of South Carolina Press, 61.
18. Warner, Michael (2005), *Publics and Counterpublics*, New York: Zone Books, 16.
19. Hauser, *Vernacular Voices*, 77.
20. Rawls, John (1997), 'The Idea of Public Reason Revisited', *University of Chicago Law Review*, 64: 765–807.
21. Ibid., 807.
22. Habermas, Jürgen (2006), 'Religion in the Public Sphere', *European Journal of Philosophy*, 14 (1): 1–25.
23. Ibid., 10.
24. Ibid., 4.
25. Trigg, Roger (2007), *Religion in Public Life: Must Faith Be Privatized?* Oxford: Oxford University Press, 236.
26. Ibid., 235.
27. Habermas, Jürgen (1984), *The Theory of Communicative Action, Vol. 1: Reason and the Rationalization of Society*, Cambridge: Polity Press.
28. Plummer, Ken (2001), 'The Square of Intimate Citizenship: Some Preliminary Proposals', *Citizenship Studies*, 5 (3): 237–53, 243.

29. Salvatore, Armando, and Dale Eickelman (eds) (2004), *Public Islam and the Common Good*, Leiden: Brill.
30. Lynch, Cecelia (2005), 'Public Spheres Transnationalized: Comparisons within and beyond Muslim Majority Societies', in Salvatore and LeVine (eds), *Religion, Social Practice and Contested Hegemonies*, New York: Palgrave Macmillan, 231–41, 236.
31. Oloyede, Jonathan (2007), 'Catalyst of Unity!', *GoodNews*, May/June. www.ccr.org.uk/old/archive/gn0705/g03.htm.
32. Hauser, *Vernacular Voices*, 61.
33. Ibid., 77.
34. Fraser, *Rethinking the Public Sphere*, 123.
35. https://angelinanoblecentre.com.
36. https://whenwomenspeak.net.
37. For small-scale, qualitative studies of grassroots American Evangelical responses to Islam, see Quosigk, *American Evangelicals*; and Bhatia, *Engaging Muslims and Islam: Lessons for 21st-Century American Evangelicals*. In the UK, Greg Smith has conducted quantitative and qualitative research as part of a wider survey of grassroots British Evangelicals: in Smith, *Evangelicals*.
38. https://embracethetruth.org. Murray is also a former vice president of Ravi Zacharias International Ministries (RZIM) (see note 44).
39. Citations and references to Rosemary Sookhdeo are clearly marked throughout the book. Otherwise references to 'Sookhdeo' are to Patrick.
40. https://i2ministries.org/about.
41. www.pfander.uk/videos.
42. https://michaelnazirali.com.
43. www.archbishopofcanterbury.org.
44. Ravi Zacharias was a very well-known Christian apologist who founded the RZIM. However, its public ministry ceased following his death in 2020 when evidence of Zacharias's serious sexual misconduct came to light. Zacharias still features in this book as he was very influential in the Evangelical public sphere. Amy Orr-Ewing is a former RZIM vice-president and is now president of the Oxford Centre for Christian Apologetics (OCCA).
45. Warner, *Publics and Counterpublics*, 90.
46. Social media is, of course, another vast site of interactions, which is beyond the scope of this book. However, Evangelicals are certainly active in this domain. For example, in 2019 the fact-checking website *Snopes* published an article exposing a supposed Facebook network of Evangelicals with extreme anti-Muslim views, which it calls the 'Kullberg network'. See Kasprak, Alex (2019), 'Disguising Hate: How Radical Evangelicals Spread Anti-Islamic Vitriol on Facebook', *Snopes*, 10 June. www.snopes.com/news/2019/05/15/radical-evangelical-facebook.
47. https://isaac-publishing.com.
48. Interestingly, a 1996 article exploring how 'contemporary evangelicalism ha[d] embraced modern media of communication' focused on 'radio, cassettes, videos, satellite and cable television programmes' and made no mention of the internet or digital communication about to explode on the world; see Coleman, Simon (1996), 'Words as Things: Language, Aesthetics and the Objectification of Protestant Evangelicalism', *Journal of Material Culture*, 1 (1): 107–28, 109. Later developments have proved that Evangelicals remain adept at embracing new technology to further their cause.
49. https://brianmclaren.net.

50. www.zwemercenter.com/articles, www.mst.edu.au/ajc-publications and https://fullerstudio.fuller.edu/publication/evangelical-interfaith-dialogue.
51. www.answering-islam.org, https://debate.org.uk.
52. www.graceformuslims.org/blog, https://markdurie.com/blog, www.michaelfkuhn.com.
53. See @pfanderfilms at www.youtube.com, named for the nineteenth-century polemicist. Other examples include @TheJayShow, @ApologiaStudios and @DrOakley1689 (James White).
54. www.crescentproject.org/learn, www.onetruthproject.org/onlinecourses.
55. https://foclonline.org.
56. https://windinthehouse.org, https://hagarsheritage.com.
57. Where Evangelicals write as academics for academics, their works do not feature in this book.
58. www.btdnetwork.org.
59. www.commanetwork.com.
60. www.europeanea.org/networks/muslim-ministries.
61. https://tsinet.org.
62. The text is available at www.acommonword.com.
63. For more discussion, see Quosigk, *American Evangelicals*, 40; and McCallum, Richard (2012), 'Love: A Common Word between Evangelicals and Muslims?' *Journal of Political Theology*, 13 (4): 400–13.
64. https://jennytaylor.media.
65. Now at https://religiousliteracyinstitute.org. Note that the domain www.lapidomedia.com on which Taylor wrote many of her articles on Islam is no longer active.
66. 'Lost in Translation: Keep "Father" & "Son" in the Bible', *Journal of Biblical Missiology*. www.change.org/p/lost-in-translation-keep-father-son-in-the-bible.
67. 'Bible Translation Review', https://worldea.org/bible-translation-review.
68. Adams, Nicholas (2013), 'Interreligious Engagement in the Public Sphere', in Cheetham, Pratt and Thomas (eds), *Understanding Interreligious Relations*, Oxford: Oxford University Press, 281–305, 303–4.

2 Typologies of encounter

1. *ABC News*, 18 November 2002.
2. Goodstein, Laurie (2003), *New York Times*, 27 May.
3. Shellnutt, Kate (2017), *Christianity Today*, 26 July.
4. https://bobrobertsjr.com.
5. See Atherstone, 'Evangelicals and Islam'; Bhatia, *Engaging Muslims and Islam*; Kidd, *American Christians*; and Quosigk, *American Evangelicals* in Chapter 1.
6. Bennett, Clinton (2008), *Understanding Christian-Muslim Relations: Past and Present*, London: Continuum, 9.
7. https://abtslebanon.org/author/marzaatar.
8. See below for his second typology.
9. Smith, *Evangelicals*.
10. www.josephcumming.com.

11. Runnymede Trust (1997), *Islamophobia: A Challenge for Us All*, London: Commission on British Muslims and Islamophobia, 1; and Elahi, Farah and Omar Khan (2017), *Islamophobia: Still a Challenge for Us All*, London: Runnymede Trust.
12. All Party Parliamentary Group on British Muslims (APPG) (2018), *Islamophobia Defined: The Inquiry into a Working Definition of Islamophobia*, London: APPG. https://appgbritishmuslims.org/publications.
13. Note that Judaism and Sikhism are seen as being both religions and races, meaning that they have been protected under UK race laws in a way Islam and Muslims are not.
14. Runnymede Trust, *Islamophobia*, 4.
15. APPG, *Islamophobia Defined*, 11.
16. For instance, Allen, Chris (2010), *Islamophobia*, Farnham: Ashgate; Beydoun, Khaled (2018), *American Islamophobia: Understanding the Roots and Rise of Fear*, Oakland: University of California Press; and Green, Todd (2019), *The Fear of Islam: An Introduction to Islamophobia in the West*, Minneapolis, MN: Fortress Press.
17. Duffner, Jordan Denari (2021), *Islamophobia: What Christians Should Know (and Do) about Anti-Muslim Discrimination*, Maryknoll, NY: Orbis Books, 3.
18. Following the *OED*, I have chosen to use the spelling 'irenic', meaning 'non-polemic', rather than 'eirenic', meaning 'tending to peace', although the two spellings are obviously closely related and usually considered synonyms.
19. Berger, Peter (2010), 'Introduction: Between Relativism and Fundamentalism', in Berger (ed.), *Between Relativism and Fundamentalism: Religious Resources for a Middle Position*, Grand Rapids, MI: Eerdmans, 1–13, 1–7.
20. Quosigk, *American Evangelicals*, 143.
21. Ibid., 49.
22. Hunter, James (1991), *Culture Wars: The Struggle to Define America*, New York: Basic Books.
23. Hunter, James (2010), 'Fundamentalism and Relativism Together: Reflections on Genealogy', in Berger (ed.), *Between Relativism and Fundamentalism: Religious Resources for a Middle Position*, Grand Rapids: Eerdmans, 17–34, 34.
24. www.holylandtrust.org.
25. https://actionresearchassociates.org.
26. https://sojo.net.
27. www.redletterchristians.org/author/tony.
28. Pew Forum on Religion and Public Life (2017), 'In First Month, Views of Trump Are Already Strongly Felt, Deeply Polarized', 16 February. www.pewresearch.org/politics/wp-content/uploads/sites/4/2017/02/02-16-17-Political-release.pdf.
29. Smith, Greg, and Linda Woodhead (2018), 'Religion and Brexit: Populism and the Church of England', *Religion, State and Society*, 46 (3): 206–23.
30. www.matthewkaemingk.com.
31. Quoted in Shellnutt, Kate (2017), 'Missionaries Dreamed of This Muslim Moment: Trump's Travel Ban May End It', *Christianity Today*, 20 March.
32. According to the back cover of his 2007 book *Global Jihad*, Sookhdeo was at that time a 'senior visiting fellow at the Defence Academy of the UK' and 'served as cultural adviser for Iraq and Afghanistan'.
33. www.daveandrews.com.au.
34. Hahn, Gregory (2007), 'Sali Clarifies Comments on Faith, Colleague', *The Spokesman*, 11 August. www.spokesman.com/stories/2007/aug/11/sali-clarifies-comments-on-faith-colleague.

35. Pew Research Center (2021), 'Faith on the Hill', 4 January. www.pewresearch.org/religion/2021/01/04/faith-on-the-hill-2021.
36. See, for instance, www.christianheadlines.com/contributors/lori-arnold/ilhan-omar-trivializes-9-11-calls-it-a-day-when-some-people-did-something.html (accessed 5 December 2022).
37. See the Wikipedia's 'List of British Muslims'. There are a total of 650 MPs, so at 4 per cent this is only slightly less than the average number of Muslims in the population at large.
38. www.abc.net.au/news/2022-06-02/first-muslim-federal-ministers-anne-aly-ed-husic/101117106.
39. Casper, Jayson (2019), 'Evangelicals Who Distrust Muslims Likely Don't Know Muslims', *Christianity Today*, 12 September.
40. www.jerryvines.com.
41. https://drstuartrobinson.com/about.
42. https://uk.ltw.org.
43. Kidd, *American Christians*, 147.
44. Ibid. Nathan Lean (2017) claims the Caners' book sold over 200,000 copies, in *The Islamophobia Industry: How the Right Manufactures Fear of Muslims*, London: Pluto Press, 89.
45. Kennedy, John (2010), 'Ergun Caner Out as Seminary Dean', *Christianity Today*, 2 July. See also Kidd, *American Christians*, 149.
46. www.drmarkgabriel.com.
47. Kidd, *American Christians*, 149.
48. https://sonofhamas.wordpress.com.
49. Smith, Christopher (2014), '"Ex-Muslims", Bible Prophecy, and Islamophobia: Rhetoric and Reality in the Narratives of Walid Shoebat, Kamal Saleem, Ergun and Emir Caner', *Islamophobia Studies Journal*, 2 (2): 76–93. Shoebat rebuts these accusations on his website https://shoebat.com.
50. https://albertmohler.com.
51. www.desiringgod.org.
52. Race, Alan (1983), *Christians and Religious Pluralism: Patterns in the Christian Theology of Religions*, London: SCM Press.
53. Lamb, Christopher (2014), *A Policy of Hope: Kenneth Cragg and Islam*, London: Melisende, 220.

3 Allah

1. *ABC News* (2004), 'Bush on Religion and God', 26 October. https://abcnews.go.com/Politics/story?id=193746&page=1.
2. https://chuckbaldwinlive.com.
3. Smietana, Bob (2016), 'Wheaton College Suspends Hijab-Wearing Professor after "Same God" Comment', *Christianity Today*, 4 January. www.christianitytoday.com/news/2015/december/wheaton-college-hijab-professor-same-god-larycia-hawkins.html.
4. See Choong, Chong Eu (2014), 'The Christian Response to State-Led Islamization in Malaysia', in Platzdasch and Saravanamuttu (eds), *Areas of Toleration and Conflict*, Singapore: ISEAS Publishing, 290–320.

5. Smietana, *Wheaton College*.
6. https://timothytennent.com.
7. Note that the book by Nigerian pastor G. J. O. Moshay is a re-publication of a 1994 book reprinted by an American conservative Christian publishing house in 2008.
8. 'Messianic Jew' is a common term used to refer to a convert from Judaism to Christianity, emphasizing the fulfilment of Jewish hopes rather than a move to a new religion.
9. Sanneh, Lamin (2004), 'Do Christians and Muslims Worship the Same God? Part II', *Christian Century*, 121 (9): 35–7.
10. Gledhill, Ruth (2016), 'Franklin Graham on Wheaton Row: Muslims and Christians Do NOT Worship the Same God', *Christianity Today*, 25 January.
11. www.andybannister.net.
12. YHWH is a variant of Yahweh respecting Jewish reticence to pronounce the divine name.
13. Quosigk, *American Evangelicals*, 153.
14. https://berniepower.com.
15. For a discussion, see Griffith, Sidney (2013), *The Bible in Arabic: The Scriptures of the 'People of the Book' in the Language of Islam*, Princeton, NJ: Princeton University Press.
16. Thomas Schirrmacher, secretary general of WEA, discusses this issue in his article 'Is It Appropriate That Arab Christians Call God Allah?' (2010).
17. Power (2012) calls these two friends Theo, making 'two Theos (bad pun intended!)'.
18. Newton, P., and Rafiqul Haqq (1991), *Allah, Is He God?* West Midlands: Qawl-ul-Haq.
19. https://lightofzion.org.
20. https://jerrylwalls.com.

4 Muhammad

1. www.michaelfkuhn.com.
2. Akhtar, Shabbir (2020), *Be Careful with Muhammad! Salman Rushdie and the Battle for Free Speech*, Jakarta: BIJAK.
3. Such ideas echo Christian theology around the pre-existence of Christ.
4. St John of Damascus (~749), *Fount of Knowledge, Part 2: Heresies*. http://orthodoxinfo.com/general/stjohn_islam.aspx.
5. John Calvin's 'Second Sermon on the Eighteenth Chapter of Deuteronomy' in *Sermons on Deuteronomy* (www.moncrgism.com/sermons-deuteronomy-ebook) and Martin Luther's 'Appeal for Prayer against the Turks' in *The Works of Martin Luther, Volume 43: Devotional Writings II*, 238. Note that sixteenth-century Western Christian writers frequently used 'Turk' as a synonym for 'Muslim' due to their geopolitical proximity to the Ottoman Empire.
6. Sachs, Susan (2002), 'Baptist Pastor Attacks Islam, Inciting Cries of Intolerance', *New York Times*, 15 June.
7. *Houris* are mentioned in the Qur'an (e.g. Q.44:54, Q.52:20) with the word being variously translated. For a discussion of the *houris* and martyrdom in Islam, see Cook, David (2007), *Martyrdom in Islam*, Cambridge: Cambridge University Press, 32ff. For the controversial role of this issue in suicide bombing, see Chapter 9.
8. https://warrenlarson.wordpress.com.

9. McKay, Mary-Jayne (2003), 'Falwell Brands Mohammed a "Terrorist"', *CBS News*, 5 June. www.cbsnews.com/news/falwell-brands-mohammed-a-terrorist.
10. Guillaume, Alfred (1955), *The Life of Muhammad: A Translation of Ibn Ishaq's Sirat Rasul Allah*, Oxford: Oxford University Press.
11. Sahaja Carimokam seems to be a pen name for an American Evangelical academic.
12. See Chapter 10 for an Evangelical discussion of whether the future Antichrist will be a Muslim.
13. For an example of such revisionism, see Holland, Tom (2012), *In the Shadow of the Sword: The Battle for Global Empire and the End of the Ancient World*, London: Little, Brown. Holland's book drew on the work of John Wansbrough, Patricia Crone and Michael Cook. The academic debate over Islamic origins continues. For one leading scholar's defence of a more traditional approach to the Qur'an, see Sinai, Nicolai (2017), *The Qur'an: A Historical-Critical Introduction*, Edinburgh: Edinburgh University Press.
14. See the debate between Jay Smith and David Wood titled 'Did the Muhammad of Islam Exist?' (@pfanderfilms) and also Smith's 'Muhammad: A Historical Critique' (@ KTOnlineLearning) at www.youtube.com.
15. www.aomin.org/aoblog.
16. https://understandingislam.today.
17. Küng, Hans (2007), *Islam: Past, Present and Future*, Oxford: Oneworld. Note that this is not official Catholic teaching. *Nostra Aetate*, the document which defines the relation of the Catholic Church to non-Christian religions, and which admits to Muslims and Christians worshipping the same God, is silent on the role of Muhammad.
18. https://fouadmasri.com.
19. Marshall, David (2013), 'Muhammad in Contemporary Christian Theological Reflection', *Islam and Christian-Muslim Relations*, 24 (2): 161–72, 167–8.
20. All qur'anic quotations are taken from Abdel Haleem, Muhammad (2005), *The Qur'an*, Oxford: Oxford University Press.
21. This idea is similar to the book title *All Truth Is God's Truth*, a 1979 book by Arthur Holmes quoted by Glaser (2016: 210).
22. Akhtar, *Be Careful with Muhammad*, xxi, xxxvi.

5 Qur'an and Hadith

1. See Murad, Abdal-Hakim (2009), 'America as a Jihad State: Middle Eastern Perceptions of Modern American Theopolitics', *Faith and Public Policy Seminar*, Kings College, London, 21 April. www.acommonword.com/america-as-a-jihad-state-middle-eastern-perceptions-of-modern-american-theopolitics.
2. Pack posts content on his Facebook page aimed at Christian responses to Islam and at Muslims (www.facebook.com/darrellandkathy).
3. For a detailed discussion of early Muslim sources, see Ahmed, Shahab (2017), *Before Orthodoxy: The Satanic Verses in Early Islam*, Cambridge, MA: Harvard University Press.
4. See Reynolds, Gabriel Said (2010), *The Qur'an and Its Biblical Subtext*, London: Routledge.
5. www.danielbrubaker.com.

6. All at www.youtube.com/c/pfanderfilms (accessed 7 April 2022).
7. https://mateenelass.wordpress.com.
8. https://stevenmasood.org. His story is told in Masood, Steven (1992), *Into the Light*, Bromley: OM.
9. Linked to an app version (https://biblequranapp.com).
10. Bertaina, David (2017), 'Christians and the Qur'an', in Thomas (ed.), *Routledge Handbook on Christian-Muslim Relations*, New York: Routledge, 279–87, 281. See also Whittingham, Martin (2012), '"Deciding by the Gospel": Some Protestant Christian Responses to the Qur'an since the Nineteenth Century', *CMCS Oxford*. www.cmcsoxford.org.uk/s/M-Whittingham-Deciding-by-the-Gospel.pdf.
11. For more on SR, see www.scripturalreasoning.org; or Ford, David, and C. Pecknold (eds) (2006), *The Promise of Scriptural Reasoning*, Oxford: Blackwell.
12. The Qur'an itself mentions this, for example, in Q16:101: 'When We substitute one revelation for another – and God knows best what He reveals – they say, "You are just making it up", but most of them have no knowledge.'
13. Oppenheimer, Mark (2010), 'A Dispute on Using the Koran as a Path to Jesus', *New York Times*, 12 March.
14. See, for instance, Sahih Bukhari Vol 4, Book 56, Hadith 829.
15. Sahih Muslim Book 26, Hadith 5389.
16. For instance, Q5:60 and Sahih Bukhari Book 56, Hadith 139.
17. Jenkins, Philip (2011), *Laying Down the Sword: Why We Can't Ignore the Bible's Violent Verses*, New York: HarperOne, 73. Greggs makes a similar point. 'If evangelicalism is to take its claim to Biblicism seriously, there is a need to attend to *all* of the Bible, including those places in which one can identify some of the complexities found in the body of Scripture', in Greggs, Tom (2012), 'Peoples of the Covenants: Evangelical Theology and the Plurality of the Covenants in Scripture', *Journal of Scriptural Reasoning*, 11 (1): n.p.
18. A term that originally came to prominence in this field through the writing of Edward Said (1978), *Orientalism*, London: Routledge and Kegan Paul.
19. Adams, Nicholas (2006), 'Making Deep Reasonings Public', *Modern Theology*, 22 (3): 385–401; and Stone, Brad (2011), 'Making Religious Practices Intelligible in the Public Sphere: A Pragmatist Evaluation of Scriptural Reasoning', *Journal of Scriptural Reasoning*, 10 (2): n.p.
20. See McCallum, Richard (2018), 'Evaluating Inter-faith Initiatives: A Cambridge Case Study', *Studies in Interreligious Dialogue*, 27 (1): 83–103.

6 Sharia

1. Lewis and Hamid, *British Muslims*, 101.
2. For a discussion, see Pearse (2004: 45–58).
3. http://danieljanosik.com.
4. Brown, Jonathan (2014), *Misquoting Muhammad: The Challenge and Choices of Interpreting the Prophet's Legacy*, London: Oneworld, 23.
5. This article was later available at https://en.europenews.dk/Sam-Solomon-Shari-ah-79050.html (accessed 5 April 2017). Neither link is now available.
6. Rzepka, Marcin (2017), *Prayer and Protest: The Protestant Communities in Revolutionary Iran*, Krakow: Unum Press, 174–5.

7. www.elizabethkendal.com.
8. By 2020, the CDHRI no longer had the exact word *sharīʿa* in Arabic, and it had disappeared from the English translation. Article 24 (now 25.a) reads: 'Everyone has the right to exercise and enjoy the rights and freedoms set out in the present declaration, without prejudice to the principles of Islam and national legislation', where in Arabic the word for legislation is *tashrīʿāt*, a word derived from the same root as *sharīʿa*. Both English and Arabic versions can be found at www.oic-oci.org.
9. www.ziyameral.com.
10. He draws his data from Esposito, John, and Dalia Mogahed (2007), *Who Speaks for Islam? What a Billion Muslims Really Think*, New York: Gallup Press.
11. Pipes, Daniel (2009), 'Eurabia – Europe's Future?', in Claydon (ed.), *Islam, Human Rights and Public Policy*, Brunswick East: Acorn Press, 177–82.
12. Rivers quotes research suggesting as many as 80 per cent of British Muslim marriages are contracted this way.
13. Goddard, Andrew (2008), 'Prudence and Jurisprudence: Reflections on the Archbishop's Interview and Lecture'. www.fulcrum-anglican.org.uk/articles/prudence-and-jurisprudence-reflections-on-the-archbishops-interview-and-lecture.
14. Referencing Taha, Mahmoud (1987), *The Second Message of Islam*, Syracuse, NY: Syracuse University Press.
15. See, for instance, An-Na'im, Abdullahi (2008), *Islam and the Secular State*, Cambridge, MA: Harvard University Press.
16. Habermas, *Religion*, 10, 4.

7 Islamization

1. Volf, Miroslav (1996), *Exclusion and Embrace*, Nashville, TN: Abingdon, 143.
2. Vishanoff, David (2013), 'Boundaries and Encounters', in Cheetham, Pratt and Thomas (eds), *Understanding Interreligious Relations*, Oxford: Oxford University Press, 341–64.
3. Yancey and Quosigk, *One Faith*.
4. 'Parallel lives' was a phrase popularized by a report looking into riots that took place in UK northern cities in 2001, which found that the lives of Asian Muslims and the white working-class lives 'often do not seem to touch at any point' due to 'separate educational arrangements, community and voluntary bodies, employment, places of worship, language, social and cultural networks'. Cantle, Ted (2001), *Community Cohesion: A Report of the Independent Review Team*, London: Home Office, 5.
5. www.thegospelcoalition.org/blogs/thabiti-anyabwile.
6. Herbert, David (2003), *Religion and Civil Society: Rethinking Public Religion in the Contemporary World*, Aldershot: Ashgate, chapter 6.
7. For instance, the 2001 racist murder in Arizona of a Sikh man, Balbir Singh Sodhi, following 9/11. See Laughland, Oliver (2021), '"This Is My Country": How the Family of Balbir Singh Sodhi Resolved to Carry on His American Dream', *The Guardian*, 14 September.
8. Freidenreich, David (2011), *Foreigners and Their Food: Constructing Otherness in Jewish, Christian, and Islamic Law*, Berkeley: University of California Press, 56.
9. https://carlmedearis.com.
10. For a discussion, see Sanneh, Lamin (2009), *Translating the Message: The Missionary Impact on Culture*, Maryknoll, NY: Orbis Books.

11. There are Eastern churches, Orthodox and Catholic, that still use *koiné* Greek as well as other ancient languages such as Coptic for their liturgical worship.
12. Bardsley, Fran (2008), 'Bishop Backs Mosque's Call to Prayer', *Oxford Mail*, 11 January.
13. www.hallindsey.com.
14. Note that this booklet also appears online titled *The Mosque Exposed*, authored by Solomon and Al-Maqdisi. Belteshazzar and Abednego are pseudonyms, and it is interesting that they chose the names of two Jewish heroes in the Hebrew scriptures who survived being thrown into the fire because of their faith (Daniel 3).
15. Roach, David (2017), 'Platt Apologizes for "Divisive" IMB Amicus Brief', *Baptist Press*, 16 February. www.baptistpress.com/resource-library/news/platt-apologizes-for-divisive-imb-amicus-brief.
16. DeHanas, Daniel, and Zacharias Pieri (2011), 'Olympic Proportions: The Expanding Scalar Politics of the London "Olympics Mega-Mosque" Controversy', *Sociology*, 45 (5): 798–814.
17. Planning permission was eventually refused.
18. DeHanas and Pieri, *Olympic Proportions*, 810.
19. As of 2022, the Islamic centre had still not been built.
20. In the UK, the Church of England has sought to address this issue through its Presence and Engagement programme. See the reports at www.churchofengland.org/about/work-other-faiths/about-presence-engagement.
21. It is worth noting that, while some Muslim clothing items are obviously Islamic, there is sometimes confusion, and members of other faith groups such as Sikhs have been mistaken for Muslims.
22. See, for instance, www.staylitapparel.co.uk.
23. Cooke, Bernard, and Gary Macy (2005), *Christian Symbol and Ritual: An Introduction*, Oxford: Oxford University Press, 42.
24. Michael, Maggie (2003), 'Christian Fish, Muslim Shark Swimming through Cairo Traffic in War of Stickers', *The Day*, 30 November.
25. Dougherty, Kevin, and Jerome Koch (2019), 'Religious Tattoos at One Christian University', *Visual Studies*, 34 (4): 311–18, 311–12.
26. For instance, Bishop Tom Wright (2016) points out that 'some have found the sign of the cross to be a symbol of fear. The horrible dark history of "Christian" persecution of people of other faiths, particularly Jewish people, has left a stain on what should be a symbol of hope and welcome', in *The Day the Revolution Began*, London: SPCK.
27. On 'parallel lives', see Cantle, *Community Cohesion*.
28. See, for instance, Ye'or, Bat (2005), *Eurabia: The Euro-Arab Axis*, Madison, NJ: Fairleigh Dickinson; Phillips, Melanie (2006), *Londonistan: How Britain Is Creating a Terror State Within*, London: Gibson Square; or Spencer, Robert (2008), *Stealth Jihad: How Radical Islam Is Subverting America without Guns or Bombs*, Washington, DC: Regnery.
29. Ibid., 11. This was something Cantle made clear in his report with respect to white working-class communities also being isolated.
30. See, for instance, Ashworth, Pat (2008), 'Clergy Criticise Nazir-Ali's Talk of No-Go Areas', *Church Times*, 10 January.
31. Note that, in the UK, Ted Cantle also wrote a 2017 report *Understanding School Segregation in England: 2011 to 2016*, London: iCoCo Foundation, SchoolDash and The Challenge.
32. www.williamwagner.org.
33. www.morningstarministries.org, www.theoakinitiative.org.

34. Yancey and Quosigk discuss the idea of in-groups and out-groups extensively in *One Faith*.
35. Hiebert, Paul (1994), *Anthropological Reflections on Missiological Issues*, Grand Rapids, MI: Baker Books. For further discussion, see Bauder, Naselli and Hansen, *Four Views on the Spectrum of Evangelicalism*.
36. Newbigin, Lesslie (1989), *The Gospel in a Pluralist Society*, London: SPCK, 243.
37. See Duffner, *Islamophobia*.

8 Persecution

1. *World Watch Monitor* (n.d.), 'The Story of Asia Bibi'. www.worldwatchmonitor.org/the-aasiya-noreen-story.
2. http://news.bbc.co.uk/1/hi/world/south_asia/4841334.stm.
3. The phrase 'church under pressure' is preferred to the 'persecuted church' by, for example, the *World Watch Monitor*. The word 'persecution' is used in this chapter as that is the most common perception of the majority of Evangelicals with respect to the treatment of Christians in Muslim-majority contexts.
4. For examples of reports on the situation of Christians in Muslim contexts, see Shortt, Rupert (2013), *Christianophobia: A Faith under Attack*, London: Rider Books; Mounstephen, Philip (2019), 'Bishop of Truro's Independent Review for the Foreign Secretary of FCO Support for Persecuted Christians: Final Report and Recommendations' (https://christianpersecutionreview.org.uk/storage/2019/07/final-report-and-recommendations.pdf); and the Pew Forum on Religion and Public Life's 2013 report *Arab Spring Adds to Global Restrictions on Religion*.
5. www.thomasschirrmacher.net.
6. www.opendoors.org.
7. Dutchman Andrew van der Bijl came to prominence after the publication of his best-selling 1967 biography *God's Smuggler*. After starting his missionary career in communist countries, he later visited the Middle East, a story told in *Light Force* (Brother Andrew and Janssen, 2004).
8. The 'World Watch List' (www.opendoorsuk.org/persecution) is independently audited by the International Institute for Religious Freedom.
9. https://barnabasfund.org/en/about (accessed 22 August 2018).
10. For the CDI, see *Barnabas Aid*, November/December 2010.
11. Rippin, Andrew (2000), *Muslims: Their Religious Beliefs and Practices*, London: Routledge, 96.
12. The word dhimmitude was a neologism of the late twentieth century popularized by Bat Ye'or in her 1996 book *The Decline of Eastern Christianity under Islam: From Jihad to Dhimmitude*, London: Associated University Presses.
13. Sahih Bukhari Vol. 3, Hadith 881.
14. Some academics argue that it developed later in the ninth century. See, for instance, Levy-Reubin, Milka (2009), 'The Pact of 'Umar', in Thomas (ed.), *Christian-Muslim Relations. A Bibliographical History, Vol. 1: 600–900*, Leiden: Brill, 361.
15. www.opendoorsusa.org/take-action/pray/whats-threat-islamic-state-to-church-worldwide (accessed 22 August 2018).
16. *Open Doors Magazine*, May 2016, 11.
17. 'ba'd as-sabt bijī yawm al-aḥad'.

18. Note that medic Susan Adelman chose the same phrase for the title of her 2018 history of the region, *After Saturday Comes Sunday*, Piscataway, NJ: Gorgias Press.
19. Release International (2018), 'Pakistan Elections: Christians Likely Losers as Extremists Tilt Agenda', 25 July. https://releaseinternational.org/pakistan-elections-christians-likely-losers-as-extremists-tilt-agenda.
20. *Release* magazine, July/August 2016, 9.
21. 'Prisoner Profile – Basuki Tjahaja Purnama' (2018). https://releaseinternational.org/wp-content/uploads/2018/02/Prisoner-of-Faith-Alert-February-2018.pdf. He was later released in January 2019.
22. www.persecution.com.
23. 'Prisoner Alert – Abraham Ben Moses' (2018). www.prisoneralert.com/pprofiles/vp_prisoner_263_profile.html. He has since been released.
24. www.marrakeshdeclaration.org.
25. Love, Rick (2016), 'The Marrakesh Declaration'. www.peacecatalyst.org/blog/2016/2/1/the-marrakesh-declaration-a-game-changer-for-christian-muslim-relations.
26. For instance, Lewis and Hamid quote poll data showing that among Muslims in South Asia 'more than three quarters supported the execution of those who left Islam': Lewis and Hamid, *British Muslims*, 91.
27. Elam Ministries (n.d.), 'What We Do'. www.elam.com/what-we-do.
28. www.elam.com/page/advocacy-0 (accessed 18 February 2019).
29. CSW, an advocacy organization, was previously known as Christian Solidarity Worldwide but changed its name to CSW in 2018 to focus more inclusively on FoRB for all.
30. Amnesty International (2018), 'Egypt: Unprecedented Crackdown', 20 September. www.amnesty.org/en/latest/news/2018/09/egypt-unprecedented-crackdown-on-freedom-of-expression-under-alsisi-turns-egypt-into-openair-prison.
31. Casper, Jayson (2017), 'What Trump's Evangelical Advisers Took Out of Egypt', *Christianity Today*, 14 November.
32. *Barnabas Aid* (2021), September–October, 14.
33. *Barnabas Aid* (2013), November–December, iv.
34. Under Caesar's Sword Project (2018), *In Response to Persecution: Findings of the Under Caesar's Sword Project on Global Christian Communities*. Washington, DC: Religious Freedom Institute, 36.
35. Note the Marrakesh Declaration above as an example of this, although Riddell was cautious in his response.
36. www.csw.org.uk.
37. The name and identity of the worker has been withheld for their own safety. Emphasis in original.
38. Under Caesar's Sword Project, *In Response*, 39.
39. Ojo, Matthews (2013), 'Competition and Conflict: Pentecostals' and Charismatics' Engagement with Islam in Nigeria', in Azumah and Sanneh (eds), *The African Christian and Islam*, Carlisle: Langham, 147–76, 169.
40. Casper, Jayson (2021), 'Christian and Muslim Leaders Agree on Legitimacy of Evangelism', *Christianity Today*, 22 July.
41. www.peacecatalyst.org.
42. For a more detailed academic history, see Bradley, Mark (2011), *Iran and Christianity: Historical Identity and Present Relevance*, London: Bloomsbury; Rzepka, Marcin (2017), *Prayer and Protest: The Protestant Communities in Revolutionary Iran*, Kraków: Unum Press.

43. Elisha, Omar (2016), 'Saved by a Martyr: Evangelical Mediation, Sanctification, and the "Persecuted Church"', *Journal of the American Academy of Religion*, 84 (4): 1–25, 4.
44. www.drcarlmoeller.com.
45. *Barnabas Aid* (2020), January/February, 13.
46. See, for instance, An-Na'im, Abdullahi, and Mashood Baderin (2010), *Islam and Human Rights: Selected Essays of Abdullahi An-Na'im*, Farnham: Ashgate; and Sachedina, Abdulaziz (2014), *Islam and the Challenge of Human Rights*, Oxford: Oxford University Press.
47. Saeed, Abdullah (2017), *Islam and Belief: At Home with Religious Freedom*, Washington, DC: Center for Islam and Religious Freedom, 24.
48. Shortt, *Christianophobia*, ix.

9 Violence

1. Kuhn points out that the word 'crusade' in Arabic translates to 'cross-war', making it all about faith (Kuhn, 2009: 32).
2. It is interesting to note that, in Sookhdeo (2006: 13), it was wrongly stated that '"salam" (peace) and "Islam" may sound similar but they are unrelated and do not come from the same (Arabic) root'. This was corrected in a later edition to say, 'It is true that both "salam" (peace) and "Islam" (submission) come from the same root. But in Arabic a root can carry a variety of meanings' (Sookhdeo, 2009: 18).
3. See also Sanneh, Lamin (2016), *Beyond Jihad: The Pacifist Tradition in West African Islam*, New York: Oxford University Press.
4. See, for example, Lings, Martin (2006), *Muhammad: His Life Based on the Earliest Sources*, Rochester, VT: Inner Traditions.
5. www.moodymedia.org/blog.
6. www.leeccamp.com.
7. The exchange is all at Chapman (2017b). See also Chapman (2017a), a journal article of the original post.
8. The example he uses is of a 2001 statement on British radio by Zaki Badawi, a prominent British Muslim, immediately following 9/11, who quoted Q5:32 but not Q5:33.
9. Chapman (2017b).
10. Natan, Yoel (2004), '164 Jihad Verses in the Koran'. www.answering-islam.org/Quran/Themes/jihad_passages.html. This would equate to less than 3 per cent of the Qur'an. It is not at all clear how Gabriel reached his figure of 60 per cent.
11. For an explanation of houris, see Chapter 4.
12. www.hopeforishmael.org.
13. Taylor references Pearse (2004).
14. This book was reprinted in 2004 and is now available on demand from IVP.
15. 'On God's Side' became the title of Wallis' 2013 book.
16. While there is little evidence that economic aid to underdeveloped countries reduces terrorism, support for civil society and good governance may be more effective. See, for instance, Savun, Burcu, and Daniel Tirone (2017), 'Foreign Aid as a Counterterrorism Tool: More Liberty, Less Terror?' *Journal of Conflict Resolution*, 62 (8): 1607–35.

17. PBCI (2017), 'Inter-Faith "Joint Working Group for Peace" Is Established', 27 October. https://peacebuilderscommunity.org/2017/10/inter-faith-joint-working-group-for-peace-is-established.
18. For instance, Zwemer fully expected that, following the First World War, 'history was moving inexorably toward Islam's destruction'. Kidd, *American Christians*, 71.

10 Israel-Palestine

1. On the contested spelling of antisemitism, see www.holocaustremembrance.com/antisemitism/spelling-antisemitism.
2. 'The Land' is capitalized when it refers to the idea that the territory of Israel-Palestine is the 'Holy' or 'Promised Land'.
3. A series of twelve books published by Tyndale House in the United States and five full-length Hollywood films.
4. Holder Rich, Cynthia (ed.) (2020), *Christian Zionism in Africa*, Lanham, MD: Fortress Academic, abstract.
5. The only connection here is geography. There is undoubtedly a connection between the early biblical 'land of the Philistines' (Gen. 21.32) and the later toponym 'Palestine'. However, 'there is no clear ethnic or hereditary connection between modern Palestinians and the ancient Agean "Sea People" known as the Philistines': Bakan, Abigail (2020), *Israel, Palestine and the Politics of Race: Exploring Identity and Power in a Global Context*, London: I.B. Tauris, 46.
6. In a different context, one scholar points out how, during the colonial conquest of North America, 'many Puritan preachers were fond of referring to Native Americans as Amelkites and Canaanites – in other words, people who, if they would not be converted, were worthy of annihilation': Warrior, Robert (1989), 'Canaanites, Cowboys, and Indians: Deliverance, Conquest, and Liberation Theology Today', *Christianity and Crisis*, 49 (12): 261–5, 264.
7. For the story of Haman, see the *Book of Esther* chapters 3–7. HAMAS is an acronym for Ḥarakah al-Muqāwamah al-'Islāmiyyah, meaning 'Islamic resistance movement'.
8. For a discussion of different Arab Christian responses to Islam across the Middle East, see Sabra, George (2006), 'Two Ways of Being a Christian in the Muslim Context of the Middle East', *Islam and Christian-Muslim Relations*, 17 (1): 43–53.
9. See the document at www.kairospalestine.ps/index.php/about-kairos/kairos-palestine-document.
10. See, for example, Smith, Wilbur (1968), *Israeli/Arab Conflcit and the Bible*, Glendale, CA: G/L Publications; Lambert, Lance (1975), *Battle for Israel*, Wheaton, IL: Tyndale House; Lindsay, Gordon (1982), *The Miracle of Israel*, Dallas, TX: Christ for the Nations.
11. Cragg, Kenneth (1996), 'The Place of the Name', in Karmi (ed.), *Jerusalem Today: What Future for the Peace Process?* Reading: Ithaca, 145–72, 151.
12. In 'The Place of Israel', a sermon by John Stott at Langham Place, London, reproduced in Sizer (2007: 164–72). No date is given.
13. Note that Lance Lambert, a well-known Messianic Jewish Bible teacher, passed away in 2015, but this book authored in 1975 has been republished illustrating the enduring influence that some writers have on the public sphere. His eponymous 'Ministry'

continues at www.lancelambert.org. Dyer has also revised and updated an earlier 1991 version of Ellisen's book. Both illustrate generational influence in the public sphere.
14. Mayer, Arno (2008), *Plowshares into Swords: From Zionism to Israel*, London: Verso, 210.
15. See Sturm, Tristan, and Seth Frantzman (2015), 'Religious Geopolitics of Palestinian Christianity: Palestinian Christian Zionists, Palestinian Liberation Theologists, and American Missions to Palestine', *Middle Eastern Studies*, 51 (3): 433–51.
16. www.kairospalestine.ps/index.php/about-kairos/kairos-palestine-document.
17. https://en.brotherrachid.com.
18. www.cufi.org/learn/issues/jerusalem/page/5 (accessed 15 April 2019).
19. Korade, Matt, Kevin Bohn, and Daniel Burke (2018), 'Controversial US Pastors Take Part in Jerusalem Embassy Opening', *CNN*, 14 May. https://edition.cnn.com/2018/05/13/politics/hagee-jeffress-us-embassy-jerusalem/index.html. A *Rapture Ready* blog also believed that because of this decision 'Donald Trump will go down as one of America's greatest presidents'. See www.raptureready.com/category/israel-watch (accessed 26 March 2019).
20. Casper, Jayson (2020a), '13 Christian Takes on Trump's Peace Plan for Israel and Palestine', *Christianity Today*, 28 January.
21. Ibid.
22. www.cmj.org.uk/about-us.
23. www.jewsforjesus.org (accessed 12 April 2019).
24. 'Pray for the peace of Jerusalem' is a quotation from Ps. 122.6.
25. https://daytopray.com/about (accessed 12 April 2019).
26. www.jerusalemprayerteam.org.
27. www.prayer4i.org.
28. IHOP (n.d.), 'Israel Mandate'. www.ihopkc.org/israelmandate. Consider also Christians for Israel, One for Israel and International Fellowship of Christians and Jews, just a few of the bewildering array of Christian ministries dedicated to praying for Israel.
29. Carolyn Jacobson (2007), 'The Palestinian Authority Coalition Government', *Watchman's Prayer Letter*, 2 April, quoted in Spector, Stephen (2008), *Evangelicals and Israel: The Story of American Christian Zionism*, New York: Oxford Univeristy Press, 85.
30. http://emeu.net/resources/reading-list/ (accessed 17 April 2019).
31. 30 Days of Prayer (2022), 'History Hinders Church in Palestine', 8 April. https://30daysprayer.com/pages/history-hinders-church-in-palestine.
32. www.ffm.org.uk, www.mahabbanetwork.com.
33. See, for instance, Love, Rick (2012), 'Jesus in Washington D.C.'. www.peacecatalyst.org/blog/2012/2/9/jesus-in-washington-dc.
34. Spector, *Evangelicals and Israel*, 106.
35. First published in 1992. Derek Prince, a Christian Zionist Bible teacher, died in 2003, but, like Lambert, his influence lives on through his books being republished and the 'Ministry' named after him (www.derekprince.com).
36. www.marklhitchcock.com.
37. www.ritg.org.
38. https://coffeetalkswithmessiah.com.
39. https://joelstrumpet.com.
40. The heifer is a reference to the biblical ceremony mandated for cleansing priests (Num. 19.1–22).

41. www.stephensizer.com.
42. https://marthalucia.com.
43. Accessed in PowerPoint version uploaded to www.youtube.com/watch?v=A24r uKKQWiY.
44. www.telosgroup.org/who-we-are/#mission-vision.
45. www.musalaha.org. See Munayer (2020).
46. www.holylandtrust.org/about-us (accessed 16 April 2019).
47. See, for instance, the 2013 film *Five Broken Cameras* by Emad Burnat.
48. https://christatthecheckpoint.bethbc.edu.
49. This was an image conjured by American pastor Mark Driscoll, founder of Real Men, which drew a sharp rebuke from theologian Greg Boyd. Driscoll claimed that 'the guy' he could worship is the Jesus who is depicted in Revelation as 'a pride-fighter with a tattoo down His leg, a sword in His hand and the commitment to make someone bleed'. Boyd argues that this 'subverts the Jesus of the gospels who out of love chooses to die for enemies rather than use his power against them'. See Boyd, Greg (2010), 'Revelation and the Violent "Pride Fighting" Jesus', 28 September. www.reknew.org/2010/09/revelation-and-the-violent-prize-fighting-jesus.

11 So Islam is …

1. Quosigk, *American Evangelicals*, 148.
2. For a discussion of the nuances around the idea of three 'Abrahamic' faiths, see Sudworth (2017: 79–82).
3. Oak Initiative (n.d.), 'San Antonio Follow Up'. www.theoakinitiative.org/san-antonio-follow.
4. *Taqīya* can also mean caution or prudence and comes from an Arabic root meaning to guard, preserve, shield and protect. *The Hans Wehr Dictionary of Modern Written Arabic* (1976), New York: Spoken Languages Services.
5. See, for instance, Sahih Muslim Hadith 2605.
6. Musk's book was first published in 1989 but has been influential and was reprinted in 2003.
7. See, for instance, Cumming's 2020 doctoral thesis presented to Yale University, 'God, Word and Spirit: The Doctrine of the Trinity in the Qur'ān and Islamic Interpretation', which engages deeply with the Islamic textual tradition.
8. Huntington, Samuel (1996), *The Clash of Civilizations and the Remaking of World Order*, New York: Simon & Schuster.

12 Talking strategies

1. Pew Forum on Religion and Public Life, 'Global Survey of Evangelical Protestant Leaders', 28.
2. https://stphilipscentre.co.uk.
3. Lamb, *A Policy of Hope*, 218. Lamb takes the second quotation from Cragg, *The Christ and the Faiths*, 1986, 17.

4. See www.christianfrommuslim.com, a website dedicated to the topic. There are also many video testimonies on the internet, such as the YouTube channel @IFoundTheTruth.
5. www.dcciministries.com.
6. Reported in *Christianity* magazine (2022), 'Street Preachers Exonerated', December, 10.
7. American Freedom Law Center (n.d.), 'Acts 17 v. City of Dearborn'. www.americanfreedomlawcenter.org/case/acts-17-v-city-of-dearborn.
8. See stories on the *Christ for All Nations* website (www.cfan.org.uk).
9. Flinchbaugh, Hope (2006), 'Brave Hearts in a Desperate Land', *Charisma Magazine*, 28 February.
10. www.fatherzakaria.net.
11. Ibrahim, Raymond (2008), 'Islam's "Public Enemy #1"', *National Review*, 25 March. www.nationalreview.com/2008/03/islams-public-enemy-1-raymond-ibrahim.
12. YouTube @BrotherRachidTV.
13. https://nejattv.org.
14. The SAT7 annual reports can be found at https://sat7.org.
15. Casper, *Evangelicals Who Distrust*.
16. See also www.engagingislam.org.
17. www.neighborlyfaith.org.
18. Available at www.christianmuslimforum.org/resources.
19. Ojo, Matthews, and Folaranmi Lateju (2010), 'Christian–Muslim Conflicts and Interfaith Bridge-Building Efforts in Nigeria', *Review of Faith & International Affairs*, 8 (1): 31–8, 35.
20. https://abtslebanon.org.
21. Patton, James (2018), 'Including the Exclusivists in Interfaith', *Review of Faith & International Affairs*, 16 (3): 23–33, 23.
22. See Chapter 8 for a discussion of *dhimmitude*.
23. For the reactions of church leaders and the Evangelical grassroots to inter-faith dialogue and ACW, see Quosigk, *American Evangelicals*, 100–5, 36–9; and Bhatia, *Engaging Muslims and Islam*, 143.
24. Casper, Jayson (2020b), 'The Redemption of Interfaith Dialogue: Three Evangelicals Wrestle with Faithful Witness in Conversations with Muslims', *Christianity Today*, 22 June.
25. Geisler and Saleeb (2002) is another example of an older book (first edition 1993) being republished in a second edition following 9/11.
26. For instance, www.answeringislam.org, www.engagingwithislam.org.
27. https://community.acts17.com.
28. The testimonies of both men can be heard at 'Testimonies: Why Abdu Murray & Nabeel Qureshi Have Become Christians'. www.youtube.com/watch?v=ZsEEfyRIS0w.
29. See also Nickel's longer 2011 academic book on the topic.
30. https://duanemiller.wordpress.com.
31. White runs Alpha & Omega Ministries (www.aomin.org) and Wood maintains www.answeringmuslims.com.
32. https://berniepower.com/debates (accessed 2 March 2022).
33. See, for example, the debate between Qureshi and Shabbir Ali which has had over 3.5 million views on the RZIM YouTube channel @rzimmedia (www.youtube.com/watch?v=FWpqqqZn7Kg).
34. https://hydeparkcf.com.
35. Debate (n.d.), 'Mission: Purpose Statement'. www.debate.org.uk.

36. Reported in *Christianity* magazine (2022), January, 9.
37. www.onetruthproject.org.
38. www.mmwu.org.
39. www.pfander.uk/courses.
40. https://viu.ves.edu/mapi.
41. Newbigin, Lesslie (1995), *Proper Confidence: Faith, Doubt, and Certainty in Christian Discipleship*, London: SPCK.

13 Mission strategies

1. See, for instance, Adogame, Afeosemime (2013), *The African Christian Diaspora: New Currents and Emerging Trends in World Christianity*, London: Bloomsbury.
2. Kidd, *American Christians*, 46.
3. 'The 10/40 window is the geographic area between 10- and 40-degrees latitude stretching from North Africa on the west to Southeast Asia on the east. Missiologists have pointed out that the majority of the world's peoples who have yet to understand the gospel reside in this area' (Kuhn, 2009: 273n2). For instance, in 2023, the Joshua Project listed 4,057 Muslim people groups globally, 3,488 of which it described as 'unreached'. Curiously this was an increase on the 2020 figures (3,756 and 3,213, respectively) suggesting that identifying UPGs is an evolving 'science'; see https://joshuaproject.net/religions/6 (accessed 12 October 2020 and 11 May 2023).
4. Another article claims there are 12,000 Afghan Christians in Afghanistan as well as many more outside of the country. See Casper (2023), 'Afghan Christians Are Very Online', *Christianity Today*, 4 January.
5. Pew Forum, *Global Survey*.
6. Jenkins, Philip (2017), 'The Western Frontier: Euro-Islam and the Remaking of Global Faith', in Reisacher (ed.), *Dynamics of Muslim Worlds: Regional, Theological, and Missiological Perspectives*, Downers Grove, IL: Inter-Varsity Press Academic, 37–56, 38.
7. For instance, Gaudeul, Jean-Marie (1999), *Called from Islam to Christ: Why Muslims Become Christians*, Crowborough: Monarch. See also Woodberry and Shubin (2001).
8. https://martingoldsmith.wordpress.com.
9. For more on Christian prayer as a strategy for engaging with Islam, see Chapter 10 and Tucker (2005).
10. Christian Aid Mission (2014), 'Why Muslims Are Converting to Christ in the Face of ISIS Atrocities', 4 December. www.christianaid.org/News/2014/mir20141204.aspx (accessed 24 February 2016).
11. For examples see Zebiri, Kate (2001), 'Muslim Perceptions of Christianity and the West', in Ridgeon (ed.), *Islamic Perceptions of Christianity*, Richmond: Curzon Press, 179–203.
12. There is a large literature on mission to Muslims which is beyond the scope of this book. See, for instance, Farah and Daniels (2018), Schlorff (2006) and Woodberry (2008).
13. For further discussion, see Moreau, Scott (2012), *Contextualization in World Missions: Mapping and Assessing Evangelical Models*, Grand Rapids, MI: Kregel; and Kraft, Charles (2016), *Issues in Contextualization*, Pasadena, CA: William Carey.
14. See, for example, Ramadan, Tariq (1999), *To Be a European Muslim*, Leicester: The Islamic Foundation; Ramadan, Tariq (2004), *Western Muslims and the Future of Islam*,

Oxford: Oxford University Press; and Suleiman, Yasir. (2012), *Contextualising Islam in Britain II*, Cambridge: University of Cambridge in association with the Universities of Exeter and Westminster.
15. See Nehrbass and Williams (2021) for more on the life and work of Parshall.
16. Much of the early debate took place in journals such as *Evangelical Missions Quarterly*, the *International Journal of Frontier Missiology*, *Mission Frontiers* and *St Francis Magazine*. However, Quosigk believes that the edited volume titled *Chrislam* 'solidified a rift between Evangelicals on how to view Islam and Muslims': Quosigk, *American Evangelicals*, 42.
17. For interview responses of American leaders and grassroots to Chrislam, see ibid., 96–100, 130–5.
18. See Schlorff (2006) for a discussion.
19. *al-maʿnā al-ṣaḥīḥ li-injīl al-masīḥ*. For an explanation, see Al Kalima (n.d.), 'Questions and Answers about "The True Meaning of the Gospel of Christ"'. www.al-kalima.com/content/in-translation/questions-and-answers-about-brthe-true-meaning-of-the-gospel-of-christ.
20. The question of whether people, especially those working in sensitive environments, should be named publicly is an important aspect of the public sphere. In a later development, Simnowitz was controversially banned from an Evangelical conference for supposedly violating scholarly standards and putting people at risk by naming them publicly. See Dixon, Roger (2017), 'The Adam Simnowitz Case: About Harming the Debate', *Journal of Biblical Missiology*, 17 July. https://biblicalmissiology.org/blog/2017/07/17/the-adam-simnowitz-case-about-harming-the-debate.
21. Again, some of this research is appearing in journals. See, for instance, Farrokh (2015).
22. Yancey and Quosigk, *One Faith*, 92.
23. Yeoman, Barry (2002), 'The Stealth Crusade', *Mother Jones*, May/June.
24. https://bridgestocommonground.org.
25. In 2012, Siljander was found guilty and imprisoned in the United States for 'acting as an unregistered foreign agent' on behalf of the Islamic American Relief Agency (IARA) which was believed to have links to Islamic terror: Office of Inspector General (2012), 'Press Release', 12 January. https://oig.usaid.gov/sites/default/files/2018-03/pressrelease_islamicagency_011212.pdf.
26. www.josephcumming.com/bio/index.html.
27. Boorstein, Michelle (2018), 'How the National Prayer Breakfast Sparked an Unusual Meeting between Muslims and Evangelicals', *Washington Post*, 8 February.
28. Reconciliation Walk Community (2012), 'Building Peace through Relationships'. www.recwalk.net.
29. PCI (n.d.), 'Mission, Vision, Values'. www.peacecatalyst.org/vision (accessed 26 August 2020).
30. Run by PCI in the United States and Bridges for Communities in the UK. www.bridgesforcommunities.com/programmes/peace-feast.
31. See, for instance, Ojo and Lateju, *Christian-Muslim Conflicts*.
32. It is worth noting that the Reconciliation Walk explained that it was only descendants of Crusaders who went on the walk. 'Therefore, the organizers of this event do not represent any indigenous Christian movements within the Middle East and have not sought the participation of such groups in the Reconciliation Walk.' www.recwalk.net (accessed 20 October 2020).

33. D'Souza, Diane (2001), 'Evangelism, Dialogue, Reconciliation: A Case Study of the Growth and Transformation of the Henry Martyn Institute', *Muslim World*, 91 (1–2): 155–84, 177.
34. www.shouldertoshouldercampaign.org/national-partners.
35. https://thefeast.org.uk/about/what-we-do (accessed 20 October 2020).
36. www.cmcsoxford.org.uk.
37. http://www.christianmuslimforum.org/resources.
38. Pew Forum, *Global Survey*, 60.

14 Types of Evangelical response

1. Note that reactionary here is used not just to denote 'inclined to reaction' but also 'opposing political or social reform' (*OED*). Whether this is a positive or negative trait will depend on the reader's viewpoint.

Conclusion: The Evangelical micro-public sphere on Islam

1. See, for instance, www.cmcshouston.org/online-courses.
2. Murad, 'America as a Jihad State'.
3. Quosigk, *American Evangelicals*, 175.
4. Yancey and Quosigk, *One Faith*, 224.
5. Sookhdeo, Patrick (1977), *Asians in Britain: A Christian Understanding*, London: Paternoster, 5, 6, 58.
6. Nazir-Ali, Michael (1983), *Islam: A Christian Perspective*, Exeter: Paternoster; Nazir-Ali, Michael (1987), *Frontiers in Muslim-Christian Encounter*, Oxford: Regnum, and Nazir-Ali, Michael (1995), *Mission and Dialogue: Proclaiming the Gospel Afresh in Every Age*, London: SPCK.
7. www.lapidomedia.com became https://religiousliteracyinstitute.org but did not carry over the content.
8. www.convertmuslimfoundation.org.uk.
9. https://archive.taleefcollective.org/convert-care, https://benevolenceaustralia.org/converts/convert-care, https://mercymission.ca/new-muslim services (accessed 20 March 2022).
10. See www.joiningthefamily.org, www.bmbtraining.org.
11. For an example of covert safe houses in the Arab world, see https://advancingnativemissions.com/safe-houses-protect-new-muslim-to-christian-converts-from-persecution.
12. Jenkins, *Next Christendom*, 3.
13. Jenkins, Philip (2009), *The Lost History of Christianity: The Thousand-Year Golden Age of the Church in the Middle East, Africa, and Asia – And How It Died*, San Francisco, CA: Harper One, 249.
14. Whiteman, Medina Tenour (2020), *The Invisible Muslim: Journeys through Whiteness and Islam*, London: Hurst, 45.
15. For instance, Fatima Mernissi, a Muslim feminist writer, recalls Muslim men quoting a controversial hadith at her in which Muhammad is reported as saying, 'Those who

entrust their affairs to a woman will never know prosperity' (*Sunan an-Nasa'i* Book 49, Hadith 10), in Mernissi, Fatima (1991), *The Veil and the Male Elite: A Feminist Interpretation of Women's Rights in Islam*, Reading, MA: Addison-Wesley, 14.
16. See Gushee, David (2014), *Changing Our Mind*, Canton, MI: David Crumm Media.
17. See, for instance, www.mpvusa.org, https://imaanlondon.wordpress.com; and Shah, Shanon (2018), *The Making of a Gay Muslim: Religion, Sexuality and Identity in Malaysia and Britain*, Cham: Palgrave Macmillan.
18. For a discussion, see Wenzel, Jennifer (2020), *The Disposition of Nature: Environmental Crisis and World Literature*, New York: Fordham University Press; or Roberts, Timmons, Bradley Parks, Les Gasser, and Nazli Choucri (2006), *A Climate of Injustice*, Cambridge: MIT Press.
19. See Bello, Ismail, and Sophia Kazibwe (2022), 'Pastoralist, Farmers and Desertification Induced Conflict in North Central and Southern Nigeria', *Small Wars & Insurgencies*: 1–15.
20. Jenkins, Philip (2021), *Climate, Catastrophe, and Faith: How Changes in Climate Drive Religious Upheaval*, New York: Oxford University Press.
21. Davie, Grace (2007), 'Vicarious Religion: A Methodological Challenge', in Ammerman (ed.), *Everyday Religion: Observing Modern Religious Lives*, Oxford: Oxford University Press, 21–35.
22. Habermas, *Religion*.
23. Trigg, *Religion in Public Life*, 235–6.
24. The title refers to a town in Syria which, according to a hadith by Muslim (Book 54, Hadith 44), will be the site of a great apocalyptic battle (cf. Armageddon) between Rome and an army from Medina.
25. *Haqiqah*, 11. The title means 'truth' or 'reality' and the magazine can be downloaded from http://imamsonline.com/blog/haqiqah-what-is-the-truth-behind-isis.
26. For a fuller discussion, see McCallum, Richard (2015), 'The "Truth" about "Dabiq": Christian Reflections on Muslim Responses to Daesh ("Islamic State") Propaganda', *CMCS Research Briefings*, 5 (Autumn): 9–10. www.cmcsoxford.org.uk/resources/research-briefings.
27. Ramadan, Tariq (2017), *Islam: The Essentials*, Milton Keynes: Pelican, 163.
28. Pearse also launches a stinging attack on tolerance and its associated relativism in the West (2004: 173–8).
29. Trigg, *Religion in Public Life*, 19.
30. Popper, Karl (2020), *The Open Society and Its Enemies*, Princeton, NJ: Princeton University Press, 581.
31. Marty, Martin (2005), *When Faiths Collide*, Oxford: Blackwell, 124.
32. Ibid., 130.
33. Derrida, Jacques (2000), 'Hostipitality', *Journal of the Theoretical Humanities*, 5 (3): 3–18, 14.
34. Jenkins, *The Lost History of Christianity*, 223.
35. Ibid., 260. This is also a theme explored in Singh, David (2022), 'Christianity and Islam: Meekness-Servanthood and Faith as Polity-Majesty', *International Journal of Asian Christianity*, 5 (2): 163–79.
36. Quosigk, *American Evangelicals*, 143.

References

Books and pamphlets

Accad, Martin (2019), *Sacred Misinterpretation: Reaching across the Christian-Muslim Divide*, Grand Rapids, MI: Eerdmans.
Adeney, Miriam (2002), *Daughters of Islam: Building Bridges with Muslim Women*, Downers Grove, IL: Inter-Varsity Press.
Agang, Sunday Bobai (2017), *No More Cheeks to Turn?* Carlisle: Hippo.
Akinade, Akintunde (2014), *Christian Responses to Islam in Nigeria: A Contextual Study of Ambivalent Encounters*, New York: Palgrave Macmillan.
Al-Araby, Abdullah (2003), *The Islamization of America: The Islamic Strategies and the Christian Response*, Los Angeles,: Pen vs. the Sword.
Allen, Stafford (2016), *My Muslim Neighbour*, Malton: Gilead.
Anderson, Mark (2016b), *The Qur'an in Context: A Christian Exploration*, Downers Grove, IL: Inter-Varsity Press.
Andrews, Dave (2015), *The Jihad of Jesus: The Sacred Nonviolent Struggle for Justice*, Eugene, OR: Wipf & Stock.
Ankerberg, John, and Emir Caner (2019), *Islam and Jihad: Study Guide*, Chattanooga, TN: ATRI.
Azumah, John (2001), *The Legacy of Arab-Islam in Africa: A Quest for Inter-religious Dialogue*, Oxford: OneWorld.
Azumah, John (2006), *Let Your Light Shine: Christian Witnesses in a Muslim Context*, Cherrybrook, NSW: Horizons.
Azumah, John (2008b), *My Neighbour's Faith: Islam Explained for African Christians*, Lakewood, WA: Hippo.
Bannister, Andrew (2014), *An Oral-Formulaic Study of the Qur'an*, Lanham, MD: Lexington.
Bannister, Andy (2021), *Do Muslims and Christians Worship the Same God?* Nottingham: Inter-Varsity Press.
Barnabas Fund (2011b), *Unveiled: A Study Guide for Christians on Islam*, Pewsey: Barnabas Fund.
Bell, Steve (2006), *Grace for Muslims*, Milton Keynes: Authentic Media.
Bell, Steve (2011), *Friendship First: The Manual*, Market Rasen: Friendship First.
Bell, Steve (2012), *Gospel for Muslims: Learning to Read the Bible through Eastern Eyes*, Milton Keynes: Authentic Media.
Bell, Steve (2016), *Friendship First: Ordinary Christians Discussing Good News with Ordinary Muslims*, Milton Keynes: Kitab Interserve Resources.
Bell, Steve (2021), *Mountains Move: Shifting Obstacles as Muslims Make Choices*, Milton Keynes: Authentic Media.
Belteshazzar, A., and B. Abednego (2006), *The Mosque and Its Role in Society*, London: Pilcrow Press.

Bradley, Mark (2014), *Too Many to Jail: The Story of Iran's New Christians*, London: Monarch.
Bridger, Scott (2015), *Christian Exegesis of the Qur'an: A Critical Analysis of the Apologetic Use of the Qur'an in Select Medieval and Contemporary Arabic Texts*, Eugene, OR: Wipf & Stock.
Brother Andrew and Al Janssen (2004), *Light Force: The Only Hope for the Middle East*, London: Hodder & Stoughton.
Brother Andrew and Al Janssen (2007), *Secret Believers: What Happens When Muslims Turn to Christ?* London: Hodder & Stoughton.
Brother Rachid (2019), *The Ideology behind Islamic Terrorism*, Seattle, WA: Waterlife.
Brotherson, Derek (2022), *Contextualization or Syncretism? The Use of Other-Faith Worship Forms in the Bible and in Insider Movements*, Eugene, OR: Pickwick.
Brown, G. D. (2014), *Chrislam: A Dangerous Trend in Missions to Muslims*, self-published.
Brubaker, Daniel (2019), *Corrections in Early Qur'ān Manuscripts: Twenty Examples*, Lovettsville, VA: Think and Tell Press.
Camp, Lee (2016), *Who Is My Enemy? Questions American Christians Must Face about Islam and Themselves*, self-published.
Caner, Ergun, and Emir Caner (2003), *Unveiling Islam: An Insider's Look at Muslim Life and Beliefs*, London: Monarch.
Caner, Ergun, and Emir Caner (2004), *Christian Jihad: Two Former Muslims Look at the Crusades and Killing in the Name of Christ*, Grand Rapids, MI: Kregel.
Carimokam, Sahaja (2010), *Muhammad and the People of the Book*, self-published.
Catherwood, Christopher (2003), *Christians, Muslims and Islamic Rage: What Is Going On and Why It Happened*, Grand Rapids, MI: Zondervan.
Chalke, Steve (2016), *Radical: Exploring the Rise of Extremism and the Pathway to Peace*, London: Oasis Global.
Challen, Edward (2006), *Love Your Muslim Neighbour: Investigating the Impact of Islam in the World Today*, Leominster: Day One.
Chandler, Paul Gordon (2007), *Pilgrims of Christ on the Muslim Road: Exploring a New Path between Two Faiths*, Lanham, MD: Cowley.
Chapman, Colin (2005a), *'Islamic Terrorism': Is There a Christian Response?* Cambridge: Grove.
Chapman, Colin (2007b), *Cross and Crescent: Responding to the Challenges of Islam*, Nottingham: Inter-Varsity Press.
Chatrath, Nick (2011), *Reaching Muslims: A One Stop Guide for Christians*, Oxford: Monarch.
Chedid, Bassam (2004), *Islam: What Every Christian Should Know*, Darlington: EP.
Coleman, Doug (2011), *A Theological Analysis of the Insider Movement Paradigm from Four Perspectives*, Pasadena, CA: William Carey International University Press.
Collins, Ted (2021), *The Other Islam: Christian Witness to Mystical Muslims*, Manchester: The Higher Path.
Cotterell, Peter (2011), *Muhammad: The Man Who Transformed Arabia*, Brunswick East: Acorn Press.
Cox, Caroline, and John Marks (2006), *The West, Islam and Islamism: Is Ideological Islam Compatible with Liberal Democracy?* London: Civitas Institute.
Cragg, Kenneth (2000), *The Call of the Minaret*, 3rd ed., Oxford: OneWorld.
Cragg, Kenneth (2001), *Muhammad in the Qur'an: The Task and the Text*, London: Melisende.

Cragg, Kenneth (2005), *The Qur'an and the West*, Washington, DC: Georgetown University Press.
Cragg, Kenneth (2008), *A Christian-Muslim Inter-text Now: From Anathemata to Theme*, London: Melisende.
Crescent Project (n.d.), *Bridges Study Book*, Franklin, TN: Crescent Project.
Crimp, Susan, and Joel Richardson (2008), *Why We Left Islam: Former Muslims Speak Out*, Chicago, IL: WND.
Dale, Moyra (2021), *Islam and Women: Hagar's Heritage*, Oxford: Regnum.
de Ruiter, Bert (2010), *Sharing Lives: Overcoming Our Fear of Islam*, Linz: OM.
de Ruiter, Bert (2016), *Sharing Lives: Course Book*, Nürnberg: VTR.
DeRuvo, Fred (2012), *Chrislam*, Scotts Valley, CA: Study-Grow-Know.
Durie, Mark (2009c), *The Third Choice: Islam, Dhimmitude and Freedom*, Melbourne: Deror.
Durie, Mark (2010), *Revelation: Do We Worship the Same God?* Upper Mt Gavatt: City Harvest.
Durie, Mark (2013), *Which God? Jesus, Holy Spirit, God in Christianity and Islam*, Melbourne: Deror.
Durie, Mark (2018), *The Qur'an and Its Biblical Reflexes: Investigations into the Genesis of a Religion*, Lanham, MD: Lexingto.
Dyer, Charles (2004), *What's Next? God, Israel and the Future of Iraq*, Chicago, IL: Moody.
Dyer, Charles, and Mark Tobey (2015), *The ISIS Crisis: What You Really Need to Know*, Chicago, IL: Moody.
Dyrness, William (2016), *Insider Jesus: Theological Reflections on New Christian Movements*, Downers Grove, IL: Inter-Varsity Press Academic.
Elass, Mateen (2004), *Understanding the Koran: A Quick Christian Guide to the Muslim Holy Book*, Grand Rapids, MI: Zondervan.
Ellis, Carl (2008), *Saving Our Sons: Confronting the Lure of Islam with Truth, Faith & Courage*, Chicago, IL: Urban Ministries.
Evans, Mike (2007), *The Final Move beyond Iraq*, Lake Mary, FL: FrontLine.
Fortner, Michael (2006), *The Scarlet Beast: Islam and the Beast of Revelation*, Selah, WA: White Stone Press.
Gabriel, Mark (2002), *Islam and Terrorism: What the Qur'an Really Teaches about Christianity, Violence and the Goals of the Islamic Jihad*, Lake Mary, FL: Creation House.
Gabriel, Mark (2003), *Islam and the Jews: The Unfinished Battle*, Lake Mary, FL: FrontLine.
Gabriel, Mark (2004), *Jesus and Muhammad: Profound Differences and Surprising Similarities*, Lake Mary, FL: Charisma House.
Gabriel, Mark (2007), *Journey Inside the Mind of an Islamic Terrorist: Why They Hate Us and How We Can Change Their Minds*, Lake Mary, FL: Frontline.
Garlow, James (2005), *A Christian's Response to Islam*, Colorado Springs, CO: Victor.
Garrison, David (2014), *A Wind in the House of Islam*, Monument, CO: WIGTake Resources.
Gauss, James (2009), *Islam & Christianity: A Revealing Contrast*, Alachua, FL: Bridge-Logos.
Geisler, Norman, and Abdul Saleeb (2002), *Answering Islam: The Crescent in Light of the Cross*, Grand Rapids, MI: Baker.
George, Timothy (2002), *Is the Father of Jesus the God of Muhammad?* Grand Rapids, MI: Zondervan.

Ghattas, Raouf, and Carol Ghattas (2009), *A Christian Guide to the Qur'an: Building Bridges in Muslim Evangelism*, Grand Rapids, MI: Kregel.
Gilchrist, John (2009), *Sharing the Gospel with Muslims: A Handbook for Bible-Based Muslim Evangelism*, Nairobi: Life Challenge Assistance Network.
Glaser, Ida (2005), *The Bible and Other Faiths: What Does the Lord Require of Us?* Leicester: Inter-Varsity Press.
Glaser, Ida (2010), *Crusade Sermons, Francis of Assisi and Martin Luther: What Does It Mean to 'Take Up the Cross' in the Context of Islam?* Oxford: Church Mission Society.
Glaser, Ida (2016), *Thinking Biblically about Islam: Genesis, Transfiguration, Transformation*, Carlisle: Langham.
Goldmann, David (2008), *Islam and the Bible: Why Two Faiths Collide*, Chicago, IL: Moody.
Goldsmith, Martin (2009), *Beyond Beards and Burqas: Connecting with Muslims*, Nottingham: Inter-Varsity Press.
Greear, James (2010), *Breaking the Islam Code*, Eugene, OR: Harvest House.
Green, Samuel (2019), *Where to Start with Islam: A New Approach to Engaging with Muslim Friends*, Newtown: Matthias Media.
Green, Stephen (2005), *Understanding Islam*, Surbiton: Christian Voice.
Green, Tim, and Roxy (2016), *Joining the Family: Welcoming Christ's Followers of Muslim Background into His Community*, Milton Keynes: Interserve.
Greeson, Kevin (2010), *The Camel: How Muslims Are Coming to Faith in Christ*, Monument, CO: WIGTake Resources.
Gwynn, Murl (2013), *Chrislam: What Communion Hath Light with Darkness?* Reidsville, GA: MEG Enterprises.
Hicham, E. (2008), *Your Questions Answered: A Reply to Muslim Friends*, Darlington: EP.
Hicham, E. (2011), *How Shall They Hear? Sharing Your Christian Faith with Muslims*, Greenville, SC: Ambassadors International.
Higgins, Kevin (2022), *Insiders and Alongsiders: An Invitation to the Conversation*, Pasadena, CA: William Carey.
Hitchcock, Mark (2002), *The Coming Islamic Invasion of Israel*, Colorado Springs, CO: Multnomah.
Hitchcock, Mark (2010), *Iran: The Coming Crisis – Radical Islam, Oil, and the Nuclear Threat*, Colorado Springs, CO: Multnomah.
Houssney, Georges (2010), *Engaging Islam*, Boulder, CO: Treeline.
Houssney, Georges, and Barbara Yandell (2014), *Engage Muslims with Christ: A Source of Study*, Boulder, CO: Treeline.
Hunt, Dave (2005), *Judgment Day: Islam, Israel and the Nations*, Bend, OR: Berean Call.
Ibrahim, Ayman, and Ant Greenham (2018), *Muslim Conversions to Christ*, New York: Peter Lang.
Institute for the Study of Islam and Christianity (2005), *Islam in Britain: The British Muslim Community in February 2005*, Pewsey: Isaac.
Jabbour, Nabeel (2006), *Unshackled and Growing: Muslims and Christians on the Journey to Freedom*, Colorado Springs, CO: Dawdon Media.
Jabbour, Nabeel (2008), *The Crescent through the Eyes of the Cross: Insights from an Arab Christian*, Colorado Springs, CO: NAVPress.
Janosik, Daniel (2019), *The Guide to Answering Islam: What Every Christian Needs to Know about Islam and the Rise of Radical Islam*, Cambridge: Christian Publishing House.

Jardim, Georgina (2014), *Recovering the Female Voice in Islamic Scripture: Women and Silence*, Farnham: Ashgate.
Jeffrey, Grant (2010), *War on Terror: Unfolding Bible Prophecy*, Colorado Springs, CO: WaterBrook.
Johnson, Thomas (2021), *Humanitarian Islam, Evangelical Christianity, and the Clash of Civilizations: A New Partnership for Peace and Religious Freedom, Vol. 20*, Bonn: Culture and Science.
Jones, Terry (2010), *Islam Is of the Devil*, Lake Mary, FL: Creation House.
Kaemingk, Matthew (2018), *Christian Hospitality and Muslim Immigration in an Age of Fear*, Grand Rapids, MI: Eerdmans.
Kaskas, Safi, and David Hungerford (2016), *The Qur'an with References to the Bible: A Contemporary Understanding*, Fairfax, VA: Bridges of Reconciliation.
Kendal, Elizabeth (2016), *After Saturday Comes Sunday: Understanding the Christian Crisis in the Middle East*, Eugene, OR: Wipf & Stock.
Kraft, Kathryn (2013), *Searching for Heaven in the Real World: A Sociological Discussion of Conversion in the Arab World*, Eugene, OR: Wipf & Stock.
Kuhn, Mike (2009), *Fresh Vision for the Muslim World*, Downers Grove, IL: Inter-Varsity Press.
Kuhn, Mike (2019), *God Is One: A Christian Defence of Divine Unity in the Muslim Golden Age*, Carlisle: Langham.
Lindsey, Hal (2002), *The Everlasting Hatred: The Roots of Jihad*, Murrieta, CA: Oracle House.
Lingel, Joshua (2016a), *Christian Apologetics to Islam*, Scotts Valley, CA: CreateSpace.
Lingel, Joshua (2016b), *Islam's Issues, Agendas, and the Great Commission*, Scotts Valley, CA: CreateSpace.
Little, Don (2015), *Effective Discipling in Muslim Communities: Scripture, History and Seasoned Practices*, Downers Grove, IL: Inter-Varsity Press Academic.
Love, Rick (2000), *Muslims, Magic and the Kingdom of God: Church Planting among Folk Muslims*, Pasadena, CA: William Carey.
Love, Rick (2013), *Grace and Truth: Toward Christlike Relationships with Muslims*, Houston, TX: Peace Catalyst International.
Love, Rick (2014), *Peace Catalysts: Resolving Conflict in Our Families, Organizations and Communities*, Downers Grove, IL: Inter-Varsity Press.
Love, Rick (2017), *Glocal: Following Jesus in the 21st Century*, Eugene, OR: Cascade.
Lucia, Martha (2008), *The System of the Beast*, Santa Rosa Beach, FL: Christian International Publishers.
Lutzer, Erwin, and Steve Miller (2013), *The Cross in the Shadow of the Crescent: An Informed Response to Islam's War with Christianity*, Eugene, OR: Harvest House.
MacArthur, John (2001), *Terrorism, Jihad, and the Bible: A Response to the Terrorist Attacks*, Nashville, TN: Thomas Nelson.
Mallouhi, Christine (2000), *Waging Peace on Islam*, London: Monarch.
Mallouhi, Christine (2004), *Miniskirts, Mothers and Muslims: A Christian Woman in a Muslim Land*, London: Monarch.
Malone, Henry (2002), *Islam Unmasked*, Lewisville, TX: Vision Life Ministries.
Masood, Steven (2012), *The Bible and the Qur'an: A Question of Integrity*, Summerfield, FL: Jesus to Muslims.
Masri, Fouad (2014), *Connecting with Muslims: A Guide to Communicating Effectively*, Downers Grove, IL: Inter-Varsity Press.

Masri, Fouad (2022), *Sharing Jesus with Muslims: A Step-by-Step Guide*, Grand Rapids, MI: Zondervan.

Maurer, Andreas (2008), *Ask Your Muslim Friend: An Introduction to Islam and a Christian's Guide for Interaction with Muslims*, Kempton Park: AcadSA.

McLaren, Brian (2012b), *Why Did Jesus, Moses, the Buddha and Mohammed Cross the Road?* London: Hodder & Stoughton.

McRoy, Anthony (2006), *From Rushdie to 7/7: The Radicalisation of Islam in Britain*, London: The Social Affairs Unit.

Medearis, Carl (2008), *Muslims, Christians, and Jesus: Gaining Understanding and Building Relationships*, Bloomington, IN: Bethany House.

Medearis, Carl (2011), *Speaking of Jesus: The Art of Not-Evangelism*, Ontario: David C Cook.

Medearis, Carl (2012), *Simple Ways to Reach Out to Muslims: Understanding and Building Connections*, Bloomington, IN: Bethany House.

Medearis, Carl, and Ted Dekker (2010), *Tea with Hezbollah: Sitting at the Enemies' Table, Our Journey through the Middle East*, New York: Doubleday.

Miller, Duane (2020), *I Will Give Them an Everlasting Name: Pastoral Care for Christ's Converts from Islam*, Oxford: Regnum.

Moore, Johnnie, and Abraham Cooper (2020), *The Next Jihad: Stop the Christian Genocide in Africa*, Nashville, TN: Thomas Nelson.

Morey, Robert (2002b), *Winning the War against Radical Islam*, Orange, CA: Christian Scholars Press.

Morton, Jeff (2011), *Two Messiahs: The Jesus of Christianity and the Jesus of Islam*, Downers Grove, IL: Inter-Varsity Press.

Morton, Jeff (2012), *Insider Movements: Biblically Incredible or Incredibly Brilliant?* Eugene, OR: Wipf & Stock.

Moshay, G. J. O. (2008), *Who Is This Allah?* Ontario, CA: Chick.

Moucarry, Chawkat (2001), *Faith to Faith: Christianity and Islam in Dialogue*, Leicester: Inter-Varsity Press.

Moucarry, Chawkat (2007), *Two Prayers for Today: The Lord's Prayer and the Fatiha*, Tiruvalla: Christava Sahitya Samithi.

Moucarry, Chawkat (2022), *Islam on Trial: Globalization, Islamism and Christianity*, Carlisle: Langham.

Musk, Bill (2003a), *Holy War: Why Do Some Muslims Become Fundamentalists?* London: Monarch.

Musk, Bill (2003b), *The Unseen Face of Islam: Sharing the Gospel with Ordinary Muslims at Street Level*, London: Monarch.

Musk, Bill (2004), *Touching the Soul of Islam: Sharing the Gospel in Muslim Cultures*, Grand Rapids, MI: Monarch.

Musk, Bill (2005), *Kissing Cousins? Christians and Muslims Face to Face*, Oxford: Monarch.

Musk, Bill (2008), *The Certainty Trap: Can Christians and Muslims Afford the Luxury of Fundamentalism?* Pasadena, CA: William Carey.

Nazir-Ali, Michael (2002), *Understanding My Muslim Neighbour: Questions and Answers on Islam and Its Followers*, Norwich: Canterbury Press.

Nazir-Ali, Michael (2006), *Conviction and Conflict: Islam, Christianity and World Order*, London: Continuum.

Nazir-Ali, Michael (2012), *Triple Jeopardy for the West: Aggressive Secularism, Radical Islamism and Multiculturalism*, London: Bloomsbury.

Nickel, Gordon (2011), *Narratives of Tampering in the Earliest Commentaries on the Qur'ān*, Leiden: Brill.
Nickel, Gordon (2016), *The Gentle Answer to the Muslim Accusation of Biblical Falsification*, Calgary: Bruton Gate.
Nickel, Gordon (2020), *The Quran with Christian Commentary: A Guide to Understanding the Scripture of Islam*, Grand Rapids, MI: Zondervan Academic.
Oksnevad, Roy (2019), *The Burden of Baggage: First-Generation Issues in Coming to Christ*, Littleton, CO: William Carey.
Oppenheimer, Mike (2014), *Chrislam: The Blending together of Islam & Christianity*, Eureka, MT: Lighthouse Trails.
Orr-Ewing, Frog, and Amy Orr-Ewing (2002), *Holy Warriors: A Fresh Look at the Face of Extreme Islam*, Carlisle: Authentic Lifestyle.
Pack, Darrell (2013), *The Shari'ah Bomb: How Islamic Law Can Destroy American Freedom*, self-published.
Pack, Darrell (2014), *The Quranic Jesus: A Demonic Deception – An Evangelical Assessment of Jesus in the Quran*, self-published.
Parshall, Phil (2002), *Understanding Muslim Teachings and Traditions: A Guide for Christians*, Grand Rapids, MI: Baker.
Parshall, Phil (2006), *Bridges to Islam: A Christian Perspective on Folk Islam*, Grand Rapids, MI: Baker.
Parsons, Martin (2005), *Unveiling God: Contextualizing Christology for Islamic Culture*, Pasadena, CA: William Carey.
Pawson, David (2003), *The Challenge of Islam to Christians*, London: Hodder & Stoughton.
Payne, Tony (2012), *Islam in Our Backyard: A Novel Argument*, Kingsford: Matthias Media.
Peltola, Beth, and Tim Dieppe (2022), *Questions to Ask Your Muslim Friends: A Closer Look at Islamic Beliefs and Texts*, London: Wilberforce.
Pilcrow Press (2007), *The Islamisation of Britain: And What Must Be Done to Prevent It*, London: Pilcrow Press.
Power, Bernie (2016a), *Challenging Islamic Traditions: Searching Questions about the Hadith from a Christian Perspective*, Pasadena, CA: William Carey.
Power, Bernie (2016b), *Engaging Islamic Traditions: Using the Hadith in Christian Ministry to Muslims*, Pasadena, CA: William Carey.
Power, Bernie (2016c), *Understanding Jesus and Muhammad: What the Ancient Texts Say about Them*, Moreland: Acorn Press.
Prenger, Jan (2017), *Muslim Insider Christ Followers: Their Theological and Missional Frames*, Pasadena, CA: William Carey.
Price, Randall (2001), *Unholy War: America, Israel and Radical Islam*, Eugene, OR: Harvest House.
Qureshi, Nabeel (2016a), *Answering Jihad: A Better Way Forward*, Grand Rapids, MI: Zondervan.
Qureshi, Nabeel (2016b), *No God but One: Allah or Jesus?* Grand Rapids, MI: Zondervan.
Rawlings, Phil (2014), *Engaging with Muslims: Building Cohesion while Seeking Conversion*, Cambridge: Grove.
Reddie, Richard (2009), *Black Muslims in Britain: Why Are a Growing Number of Young Black Men Converting to Islam?* London: Lion.
Reisacher, Evelyne (2016), *Joyful Witness in the Muslim World: Sharing the Gospel in Everyday Encounters*, Grand Rapids, MI: Baker Academic.

Richardson, Don (2003), *Secrets of the Koran*, Ventura, CA: Regal.
Richardson, Joel (2012), *Mideast Beast: The Scriptural Case for an Islamic Antichrist*, Washington, DC: WND.
Richardson, Joel (2015), *The Islamic Antichrist*, Washington, DC: WND.
Riddell, Peter (2004), *Christians and Muslims: Pressures and Potential in a Post 9/11 World*, Leicester: Inter-Varsity Press.
Riddell, Peter, and Peter Cotterell (2003), *Islam in Conflict: Past, Present and Future*, Leicester: Inter-Varsity Press.
Robinson, Stuart (2003), *Mosques & Miracles: Revealing Islam and God's Grace*, Upper Mt Gavatt: City Harvest.
Robinson, Stuart (2010), *The Challenge of Islam: Calling the Church to Act*, Upper Mt Gavatt: Chi.
Robinson, Stuart (2017), *The Hidden Half: Women and Islam*, Upper Mt Gavatt: City Harvest.
Safa, Reza (2004), *The Rise and Fall of Islam: How America Can Win the War against Radical Islam and Terrorism*, Sevierville, TN: Insight Pub Group.
Safa, Reza (2006), *The Coming Fall of Islam in Iran*, Lake Mary, FL: Frontline.
Schlorff, Sam (2006), *Missiological Models in Ministry to Muslims*, Upper Darby, PA: Middle East Resources.
Scot, Daniel, and Michael Abdulhaq (2009), *Share the Gospel with Muslims*, Stafford: Ibrahim Ministries.
Scott, Robert (2011), *'Dear Abdullah': Eight Questions Muslim People Ask about Christianity*, Nottingham: Inter-Varsity Press.
Scott, Robert (2021), *Sharing the Gospel with a Muslim Neighbour*, Leyland: 10 Publishing.
Shade, Bill (2014), *The Prophetic Destiny of Israel and the Islamic Nations*, Scotts Valley, CA: CreateSpace.
Shehadeh, Imad (2020), *God with Us and without Us: The Beauty and Power of Oneness in Trinity versus Absolute Oneness, 1&2*, Carlisle: Langham.
Shenk, David (2003), *Journeys of the Muslim Nation and the Christian Church: Exploring the Mission of Two Communities*, Scottdale, PA: Herald Press.
Shenk, David (2014), *Christian. Muslim. Friend: Twelve Paths to Real Relationship*, Harrisonburg, VA: Herald Press.
Shoebat, Walid (2005), *Why I Left Jihad*, Newton, PA: Top Executive Media.
Shoebat, Walid, and Joel Richardson (2008), *God's War on Terror: Islam, Prophecy and the Bible*, Newton, PA: Top Executive Media.
Shumack, Richard (2011), *Witnessing to Western Muslims*, London: Milton Mill.
Shumack, Richard (2014), *The Wisdom of Islam and the Foolishness of Christianity*, Sydney: Island View.
Siljander, Mark, and John Mann (2008), *A Deadly Misunderstanding: A Congressman's Quest to Bridge the Muslim-Christian Divide*, New York: HarperOne.
Singh, David (2008), *Jesus and the Cross: Reflections of Christians from Islamic Contexts*, Oxford: Regnum.
Singh, David (2011), *Jesus and the Incarnation: Reflections of Christians from Islamic Contexts*, Oxford: Regnum.
Singh, David (2014), *Jesus and the Resurrection: Reflections of Christians from Islamic Contexts*, Oxford: Regnum
Small, Keith (2009), *Holy Books Have a History: Textual Histories of the New Testament and the Qur'an*, Wilkes-Barre, PA: Avant.

Small, Keith (2011), *Textual Criticism and Qur'an Manuscripts*, Lanham, MD: Lexington.
Smith, Andrew (2009), *My Friend Imran: Christian-Muslim friendship*, Cambridge: Grove.
Smith, Jack (2011), *Islam: The Cloak of Antichrist*, San Diego, CA: Last Mile.
Smith, Jay (2016), *Radical Evangelism to Muslims*, Scotts Valley, CA: CreateSpace.
Solomon, Sam, and Elias Al-Maqdisi (2007), *The Mosque Exposed*, Charlottesville, VA: Advancing Native Missions Press.
Solomon, Sam, and Elias Al-Maqdisi (2009a), *The Common Word: The Undermining of the Church*, Charlottesville, VA: Advancing Native Missions Press.
Solomon, Sam, and Elias Al-Maqdisi (2009b), *Modern Day Trojan Horse: The Islamic Doctrine of Immigration*, Charlottesville, VA: Advancing Native Missions.
Solomon, Sam, and Elias Al-Maqdisi (2010), *Al-Yahud: Eternal Islamic Enmity and the Jews*, Charlottesville, VA: Advancing Native Missions.
Solomon, Sam, and Atif Debs (2016), *Not the Same God: Is the Qur'anic Allah the Lord God of the Bible?* London: Wilberforce.
Sookhdeo, Patrick (2002), *A People Betrayed*, Pewsey: Isaac.
Sookhdeo, Patrick (2006), *Islam: The Challenge to the Church*, Pewsey: Isaac.
Sookhdeo, Patrick (2007), *Global Jihad: The Future in the Face of Militant Islam*, Pewsey: Isaac.
Sookhdeo, Patrick (2008a), *Faith, Power and Territory: A Handbook of British Islam*, Pewsey: Isaac.
Sookhdeo, Patrick (2008b), *Understanding Shariʿa Finance: The Muslim Challenge to Western Economics*, Pewsey: Isaac.
Sookhdeo, Patrick (2009a), *The Challenge of Islam to the Church and Its Mission*, McLean, VA: Isaac.
Sookhdeo, Patrick (2009b), *Freedom to Believe: Challenging Islam's Apostasy Law*, McLean, VA: Isaac.
Sookhdeo, Patrick (2010b), *A Christian's Pocket Guide to Islam*, Pewsey: Christian Focus.
Sookhdeo, Patrick (2011a), *Islam in Our Midst: The Challenge to Our Christian Heritage*, McLean, VA: Isaac.
Sookhdeo, Patrick (2011b), *Slippery Slope: The Islamisation of the UK*, Pewsey: Barnabas Fund.
Sookhdeo, Patrick (2013), *Understanding Islamic Theology*, McLean, VA: Isaac.
Sookhdeo, Patrick (2014a), *Dawa: The Islamic Strategy for Reshaping the Modern World*, McLean, VA: Isaac.
Sookhdeo, Patrick (2020), *Understanding Living Islam: Spirituality, Structures, Society and Sects*, Pewsey: Isaac.
Sookhdeo, Rosemary (2004), *Secrets behind the Burqa*, Pewsey: Isaac.
Sookhdeo, Rosemary (2005), *Stepping into the Shadows: Why Women Convert to Islam*, Pewsey: Isaac.
Sookhdeo, Rosemary (2010), *Breaking through the Barriers: Leading Muslims to Christ*, McLean, VA: Isaac.
Sookhdeo, Rosemary (2019), *Understanding Islam from a Christian Perspective*, McLean: Isaac.
Sproul, R. C., and Abdul Saleeb (2003), *The Dark Side of Islam*, Wheaton, IL: Crossway.
Stice, Ralph (2005), *From 9/11 to 666*, Chicago, IL: ACW Press.
Stice, Ralph (2014), *Arab Spring, Christian Winter: Islam Unleashed on the Church and the World*, Abbotsford, WI: Aneko Press.

Stone, Matthew (2015), *20 Reasons Christians Fail to Effectively Reach Muslims: With Helpful Recommendations to Become Effective*, self-published.
Stone, Matthew (2016), *Former Muslim Activist Reflects on Muslims, Islam, and Christians*, self-published.
Sudworth, Richard (2017), *Encountering Islam: Christian-Muslim Relations in the Public Sphere*, London: SCM Press.
Swartley, Keith (2005), *Encountering the World of Islam*, Milton Keynes: Authentic Media.
Taber, Shirin (2009), *Muslims Next Door: Uncovering Myths and Creating Friendships*, Grand Rapids, MI: Zondervan.
Tanagho, Samy (2003), *Glad News! God Loves You My Muslim Friend*, Waynesboro, GA: Authentic Media.
Tavassoli, Sasan (2011), *Christian Encounters with Iran: Engaging Muslim Thinkers after the Revolution*, London: I. B. Tauris.
Tavassoli, Sasan (2016), *Christian and Islamic Theological Issues*, Scotts Valley, CA: CreateSpace.
Taylor, Aaron (2009), *Alone with a Jihadist*, Manchester, CT: Foghorn.
Trousdale, Jerry (2012), *Miraculous Movements: How Hundreds of Thousands of Muslims Are Falling in Love with Jesus*, Nashville, TN: Thomas Nelson.
Volf, Miroslav (2011), *Allah: A Christian Response*, New York: Harper Collins.
Wagner, William (2012), *How Islam Plans to Change the World*, Grand Rapids, MI: Kregel.
Walker, Tanya (2017), *Shari'a Councils and Muslim Women in Britain: Rethinking the Role of Power and Authority*, Leiden: Brill.
White, James (2013), *What Every Christian Needs to Know about the Qur'an*, Bloomington, IN: Bethany House.
Whittingham, Martin (2021), *A History of Muslim Views of the Bible: The First Four Centuries*, Berlin: De Gruyter.
Womack, Deanna (2020), *Neighbors: Christians and Muslims Building Community*, Louisville, KY: Westminster John Knox Press.
Wood, Nicholas (2009), *Faiths and Faithfulness: Pluralism, Dialogue and Mission in the Work of Kenneth Cragg and Lesslie Newbigin*, Milton Keynes: Paternoster.
Youssef, Michael (2015), *Jesus, Jihad and Peace: What Bible Prophecy Says about World Events Today*, Brentwood, TN: Worthy.
Youssef, Michael (2016), *End Times and the Secret of the Mahdi: Unlocking the Mystery of Revelation and the Antichrist*, Franklin, TN: Worthy.
Youssef, Michael (2017), *The Barbarians Are Here: Preventing the Collapse of Western Civilization in Times of Terrorism*, Franklin, TN: Worthy.
Zacharias, Ravi (2002), *Light in the Shadow of Jihad*, Sisters, OR: Multnomah.
Zaka, Anees, and Diane Coleman (2004), *The Truth about Islam: The Noble Qur'an's Teachings in the Light of the Holy Bible*, Phillipsburg, NJ: P&R.
Zaka, Anees, and Diane Coleman (2006), *Cry of the Heart and Quest of the Mind: An Analysis of Muslim and Christian Women's Search for Truth and Honor*, Philadelphia, PA: Church without Walls.
Zeidan, David (2002), *The Resurgence of Religion: A Comparative Study of Selected Themes in Christian and Islamic Fundamentalist Discourses*, Leiden: Brill.
Zeidan, David (2003), *Sword of Allah: Islamic Fundamentalism from an Evangelical Perspective*, Waynesboro, GA: Gabriel.

Edited volumes

Accad, Martin, and Jonathan Andrews (eds.) (2020), *The Religious Other: A Biblical Understanding of Islam, the Qur'an and Muhammad*, Carlisle: Langham.

Azumah, John, and Peter Riddell (eds.) (2013), *Islam and Christianity on the Edge: Talking Points in Christian-Muslim Relations into the 21st Century*, Brunswick East: Acorn Press.

Azumah, John, and Lamin Sanneh (eds.) (2013), *The African Christian and Islam*, Carlisle: Langham.

Bell, Steve, and Colin Chapman (eds.) (2011), *Between Naivety and Hostility: How Should Christians Respond to Islam in Britain?* Milton Keynes: Authentic Media.

Campbell, Ronnie, and Christopher Gnanakan (eds.) (2019), *Do Christians, Muslims, and Jews Worship the Same God? Four Views*, Grand Rapids, MI: Counterpoints.

Claydon, David (ed.) (2009), *Islam, Human Rights and Public Policy*, Brunswick East: Acorn Press.

Crowther, Danny, Shirin Shafaie, Ida Glaser, and Shabbir Akhtar (eds.) (2017), *Reading the Bible in Islamic Context: Qur'anic Conversations*, New York: Routledge.

Dale, Moyra, Cathy Hine, and Carol Walker (eds.) (2018), *When Women Speak*, Oxford: Regnum.

de Ruiter, Bert (ed.) (2014), *Engaging with Muslims in Europe*, Nurnberg: VTR.

Farah, Warrick, and Gene Daniels (eds.) (2018), *Margins of Islam: Missiology in Diverse Muslim Contexts*, Littleton, CO: William Carey.

Greenlee, David (ed.) (2006), *From the Straight Path to the Narrow Way: Journeys of Faith*, Milton Keynes: Authentic Media.

Greenlee, David (ed.) (2013), *Longing for Community: Church, Ummah, or Somewhere in Between?* Pasadena, CA: William Carey.

Lingel, Joshua, Jeff Morton, and Bill Nikides (eds.) (2012), *Chrislam: How Missionaries Are Promoting an Islamized Gospel*, Garden Grove, CA: i2 Ministries.

Love, Fran, and Jeleta Eckheart (eds.) (2000), *Ministry to Muslim Women: Longing to Call Them Sisters*, Pasadena, CA: William Carey.

Martin, E. J. (ed.) (2010), *Where There Was No Church: Postcards from Followers of Jesus in the Muslim World*, n.p.: Fruitful Practice Research and Learning Together Press.

Nehrbass, Kenneth, and Mark Williams (eds.) (2021), *The Life and Impact of Phil Parshall: Connecting with Muslims – A Guide to Communicating Effectively*, Pasadena, CA: William Carey.

Newbigin, Lesslie, Lamin Sanneh, and Jenny Taylor (eds.) (2005), *Faith and Power: Christianity and Islam in 'Secular' Britain*, Eugene, OR: Wipf & Stock.

Reisacher, Evelyne (ed.) (2012b), *Toward Respectful Understanding and Witness among Muslims*, Pasadena, CA: William Carey.

Reisacher, Evelyne (ed.) (2017b), *Dynamics of Muslim Worlds: Regional, Theological, and Missiological Perspectives*, Downers Grove, IL: Inter-Varsity Press Academic.

Talman, Harley, and John Travis (eds.) (2016), *Understanding Insider Movements: Disciples of Jesus within Diverse Religious Communities*, Pasadena, CA: William Carey.

Volf, Miroslav (ed.) (2012), *Do We Worship the Same God? Jews, Christians, and Muslims in Dialogue*, Grand Rapids, MI: Eedermans.

Volf, Miroslav, Ghazi bin Muhammad, and Melissa Yarrington (eds.) (2010), *A Common Word: Muslims and Christians on Loving God and Neighbor*, Grand Rapids, MI: Eerdmans.

Woodberry, Dudley (ed.) (2008), *From Seed to Fruit: Global Trends, Fruitful Practices, and Emerging Issues among Muslims*, Pasadena, CA: William Carey.

Books partially relating to Islam

Awad, Alex (2001), *Through the Eyes of the Victims: The Story of the Arab-Israeli Conflict*, Bethlehem: Bethlehem Bible College.
Azad, Anwarul, and Ida Glaser (2022), *Genesis 1–11*, Carlisle: Langham.
Burge, Gary (2003), *Whose Land? Whose Promise? What Christians Are Not Being Told about Israel and the Palestinians*, Cleveland, OH: Pilgrim Press.
Burge, Gary (2010), *Jesus and the Land: The New Testament Challenge to 'Holy Land' Theology*, Grand Rapids, MI: Baker Academic.
Campolo, Tony (2004), *Speaking My Mind*, Nashville, TN: Thomas Nelson.
Campolo, Tony, and Shane Claiborne (2012), *Red Letter Christianity: Living the Words of Jesus No Matter the Cost*, London: Hodder & Stoughton.
Carson, Don (2012), *Jesus the Son of God: A Christological Title Often Overlooked, Sometimes Misunderstood, and Currently Disputed*, Wheaton, IL: Crossway.
Carter, Jimmy (2006), *Palestine Peace Not Apartheid*, New York: Simon & Schuster.
Chapman, Colin (2004c), *Whose Holy City?* Oxford: Lion.
Chapman, Colin (2015), *Whose Promised Land? The Continuing Conflict over Israel and Palestine*, Oxford: Lion.
Chapman, Colin (2021), *Christian Zionism and the Restoration of Israel: How Should We Interpret the Scriptures?* Eugene, OR: Cascade.
Cotterell, Peter (2006), *One God: The Deity Revealed in Jesus*, Milton Keynes: Authentic Media.
Ellisen, Stanley, and Charles Dyer (2003), *Who Owns the Land? The Arab-Israeli Conflict*, Wheaton, IL: Tyndale House.
Evans, Mike (2005), *The American Prophecies: Ancient Scriptures Reveal Our Nation's Future*, New York: Warner Faith.
Goll, James (2009), *The Coming Israel Awakening: Gazing into the Future of the Jewish People and the Church*, Ada, MI: Chosen.
Gushee, David (ed.) (2013), *Evangelical Peacemakers: Gospel Engagement in a War-Torn World*, Eugene, OR: Wipf & Stock.
Hagee, John (2006), *Jerusalem Countdown*, Lake Mary, FL: FrontLine.
Hagee, John (2007), *In Defense of Israel*, Lake Mary, FL: FrontLine.
Intrater, Asher (Keith) (2011), *From Iraq to Armageddon: The Endtimes Clock Is Ticking*, Shippensburg, PA: Destiny Image.
Isaac, Munther (2015), *From Land to Lands, from Eden to the Renewed Earth: A Christ-Centred Biblical Theology of the Promised Land*, Carlisle: Langham Monographs.
Isaac, Munther (2020), *The Other Side of the Wall: A Palestinian Narrative of Lament and Hope*, Downers Grove, IL: Inter-Varsity Press.
Katanacho, Yohanna (2013), *The Land of Christ: A Palestinian Cry*, Eugene, OR: Pickwick.
Lambert, Lance (2018), *Battle for Israel*, Richmond, VA: Lance Lambert Ministries.
Maalouf, Tony (2003), *Arabs in the Shadow of Israel: The Unfolding of God's Prophetic Plan for Ishmael's Line*, Grand Rapids, MI: Kregel.
McDermott, Gerald (2016), *The New Christian Zionism: Fresh Perspectives on Israel and the Land*, Downers Grove, IL: Inter-Varsity Press Academic.

Merkley, Paul (2001), *Christian Attitudes towards the State of Israel*, Montreal: McGill-Queen's University Press.
Merkley, Paul (2011), *Those That Bless You, I Will Bless: Christian Zionism in Historical Perspective*, n.p.: Mantua.
Moeller, Carl, and David Hegg (2011), *The Privilege of Persecution (and Other Things the Global Church Knows That We Don't)*, Chicago, IL: Moody.
Munayer, Salim (ed.) (2020), *Journey through the Storm: Musalaha and the Reconciliation Process*, Carlisle: Langham.
Munayer, Salim, and Lisa Loden (eds.) (2011), *The Land Cries Out: Theology of the Land in the Israeli-Palestinian Context*, Eugene, OR: Cascade.
Munayer, Salim, and Lisa Loden (2013), *Through My Enemies Eyes: Envisioning Reconciliation in Israel-Palestine*, Milton Keynes: Paternoster.
Murray, Abdu (2009), *Apocalypse Later: Why the Gospel of Peace Must Trump the Politics of Prophecy in the Middle East*, Grand Rapids, MI: Kregel.
Murray, Abdu (2014), *Grand Central Question: Answering the Critical Concerns of the Major Worldviews*, Downers Grove, IL: Inter-Varsity Press.
Nazir-Ali, Michael (2008c), *The Unique and Universal Christ: Jesus in a Plural World*, Milton Keynes: Paternoster.
Pawson, David (2013), *Defending Christian Zionism*, Ashford: Anchor Recordings.
Pearse, Meic (2004), *Why the Rest Hates the West: Understanding the Roots of Global Rage*, Downers Grove, IL: Inter-Varsity Press.
Prince, Derek (2016), *The Destiny of Israel and the Church: Understanding the Middle East through Biblical Prophecy*, Charlotte, NC: Derek Prince Ministries.
Ripken, Nik (2013), *The Insanity of God: A True Story of Faith Resurrected*, Nashville, TN: B&H.
Schirrmacher, Thomas (2018), *The Persecution of Christians Concerns Us All: Towards a Theology of Martyrdom, 14*, Bonn: Culture and Science.
Shannon, Jill (2012), *Israel's Prophetic Destiny: If I forget Jerusalem (Psalm 137)*, Shippensburg, PA: Destiny Image.
Sizer, Stephen (2007), *Zion's Christian Soldiers: The Bible, Israel and the Church*, Leicester: Inter-Varsity Press.
Smith, Andrew (2018), *Vibrant Christianity in Multifaith Britain: Equipping the Church for a Faithful Engagement with People of Different Faiths*, Abingdon: Bible Reading Fellowship.
Sookhdeo, Patrick (2010a), *A Call to Compassion*, Pewsey: Barnabus Fund.
Sookhdeo, Patrick (2012), *Heroes of Our Faith: Inspiration and Strength for Daily Living*, McLean, VA: Isaac.
Sookhdeo, Patrick (2019), *Hated without a Reason: The Remarkable Story of Christian Persecution over the Centuries*, McLean, VA: Isaac.
Sudworth, Richard (2007), *Distinctly Welcoming: Christian Presence in a Multifaith Society*, Bletchley: Scripture Union.
Tennent, Timothy (2002), *Christianity at the Religious Roundtable: Evangelicalism in Conversation with Hinduism, Buddhism, and Islam*, Grand Rapids, MI: Baker Academic.
Tennent, Timothy (2007), *Theology in the Context of World Christianity: How the Global Church Is Influencing the Way We Think about and Discuss Theology*, Grand Rapids, MI: Zondervan.
Teplinsky, Sandra (2013), *Why Still Care about Israel? The Sanctity of Covenant, Moral Justice, and Prophetic Blessing*, Minneapolis, MN: Chosen.

van den Toren, Benno, and Kang-San Tan (2022), *Humble Confidence: A Model for Interfaith Apologetics*, Leicester: Inter-Varsity Press.
Wagner, Donald (2022), *Glory to God in the Lowest: Journeys to an Unholy Land*, Northampton, MA: Olive Branch Press.
Wagner, Donald, and Walter Davis (2014), *Zionism and the Quest for Justice in the Holy Land*, Cambridge: Lutterworth Press.
Wallis, Jim (2005), *God's Politics: Why the American Right Gets It Wrong and the Left Doesn't Get It*, Oxford: Lion Hudson.
Wallis, Jim (2013), *On God's Side: What Religion Forgets and Politics Hasn't Learned about Serving the Common Good*, Grand Rapids, MI: Brazos Press.
Welby, Justin (2018), *Reimagining Britain: Foundations for Hope*, London: Bloomsbury Continuum.
Wilson, Tom (2019), *Hospitality, Service, Proclamation: Interfaith Engagement as Christian Discipleship*, London: SCM Press.

Biographies

Bibi, Asia (2020), *Free at Last: A Cup of Water, a Death Sentence, and an Inspiring Story of One Woman's Unwavering Faith*, Savage, MN: BroadStreet.
DC Talk and Voice of the Martyrs (2020), *Jesus Freaks: Stories of Those Who Stood for Jesus, the Ultimate Jesus Freaks*, Minneapolis, MN: Bethany House.
Haile, Ahmed Ali, and David Shenk (2011), *Teatime in Mogadishu: My Journey as a Peace Ambassador in the World of Islam*, Harrisonburg, VA: Herald Press.
Husnain, Ali (2016), *The Cost: My Life on a Terrorist Hit List*, Grand Rapids, MI: Zondervan.
Hussain, Khalad (2012), *Against the Grain*, self-published.
Livingstone, Greg (2014), *You've Got Libya: A Life Serving the Muslim World*, Oxford: Monarch.
Pieh Jones, Rachel (2019), *Stronger Than Death: How Annalena Tonelli Defied Terror and Tuberculosis in the Horn of Africa*, Walden, NY: Plough.
Qureshi, Nabeel (2014), *Seeking Allah, Finding Jesus: A Devout Muslim Encounters Christianity*, Grand Rapids, MI: Zondervan.
Robinson, Stuart, and Peter Botross (2008), *Defying Death: Zakaria Botross – Apostle to Islam*, Upper Mt Gravatt: City Harvest.
Rockness, Miriam Huffman (2003), *A Passion for the Impossible: The Life of Lilias Trotter*, Milnthorpe: Our Daily Bread.
Saada, Tass, and Dean Merrill (2008), *Once an Arafat Man*, Carol Stream, IL: Tyndale House.
Shah, Hannah (2010), *The Imam's Daughter: The Remarkable True Story of a Young Girl's Escape from Her Harrowing Past*, London: Rider.
Voice of the Martyrs (2016), *I Am N: Inspiring Stories of Christians Facing Islamic Extremists*, Colorado Springs, CO: David C Cook.
White, Andrew (2009), *The Vicar of Baghdad: Fighting for Peace in the Middle East*, Oxford: Monarch.
Yousef, Mosab Hassan, and Ron Brackin (2010), *Son of Hamas*, Milton Keynes: Authentic Media.

Book chapters

Accad, Martin (2012), 'Christian Attitudes toward Islam and Muslims: A Kerygmatic Approach', in Evelyne Reisacher (ed.), *Toward Respectful Understanding and Witness among Muslims*, Pasadena, CA: William Carey, 29–47.

Accad, Martin (2020), 'The Quest for the Historical Muhammad', in Martin Accad and Jonathan Andrews (eds.), *The Religious Other: A Biblical Understanding of Islam, the Qur'an and Muhammad*, Carlisle: Langham, 285–307.

Adeney, Miriam (2018), 'Do Muslim Women Need Saving? Cultural, Theological, and Missiological Perspectives', in Moyra Dale, Cathy Hine and Carol Walker (eds.), *When Women Speak*, Oxford: Regnum, 109–19.

Anyabwile, Thabiti (2011), 'Thinking for the Sake of Global Faithfulness: Encountering Islam with the Mind of Christ', in Rick Warren, Francis Chan and John Piper (eds.), *Thinking, Loving, Doing: Glorify God with Heart and Mind*, Wheaton, IL: Desiring God Ministries, 81–98.

Azumah, John (2008a), 'Different Models of Governance and Justice: A West African Christian Perspective', in Michael Ipgrave (ed.), *Building a Better Bridge: Muslims, Christians, and the Common Good*, Washington, DC: Georgetown University Press, 115–28.

Azumah, John (2013a), 'Fault Lines in African Christian Responses to Islam', in John Azumah and Lamin Sanneh (eds.), *The African Christian and Islam*, Carlisle: Langham, 125–46.

Azumah, John (2013b), 'Patterns of Christian-Muslim Encounters in Africa', in John Azumah and Lamin Sanneh (eds.), *The African Christian and Islam*, Carlisle: Langham, 41–64.

Azumah, John, and Abdullah Bahri (2009), 'The Sharia – Islamic Law', in David Claydon (ed.), *Islam: Human Rights and Public Policy*, Brunswick East: Acorn Press, 139–48.

Bahri, Abdallah (2009), 'Aspects of Sharia Introduced into Non-Islamic States', in David Claydon (ed.), *Islam, Human Rights and Public Policy*, Brunswick East: Acorn Press, 183–91.

Beaumont, Mark (2018), 'Christians, Prophethood, and Muhammad', in Charles Tieszen (ed.), *Theological Issues in Christian-Muslim Dialogue*, Eugene, OR: Pickwick, 26–41.

Bristow, George (2020), 'The Seal of the Prophets: Reflections on John the Baptist and Muhammad', in Martin Accad and Jonathan Andrews (eds.), *The Religious Other: A Biblical Understanding of Islam, the Qur'an and Muhammad*, Carlisle: Langham, 308–22.

Brown, Daniel (2020a), 'What We Don't Know about Islamic Origins', in Martin Accad and Jonathan Andrews (eds.), *The Religious Other: A Biblical Understanding of Islam, the Qur'an and Muhammad*, Carlisle: Langham, 173–88.

Brown, Daniel (2020b), 'Where Do Scriptures Come From?', in Martin Accad and Jonathan Andrews (eds.), *The Religious Other: A Biblical Understanding of Islam, the Qur'an and Muhammad*, Carlisle: Langham, 257–72.

Brown, Rick (2012), 'Who was "Allah" before Islam? Evidence That the Term "Allah" Originated with Jewish and Christian Arabs', in Evelyne Reisacher (ed.), *Toward Respectful Understanding and Witness among Muslims: Essays in Honour of J. Dudley Woodberry*, Pasadena, CA: William Carey, 147–78.

Chapman, Colin (2004a), 'Israel as a Focus for the Anger of Muslims against the West', in Ron Geaves, Theodore Gabriel, Yvonne Haddad and Jane Smith (eds.), *Islam and the West Post 9/11*, Aldershot: Ashgate, 194–209.

Cook, David (2012), 'Can Christians Be Muslims?', in Joshua Lingel, Jeff Morton and Bill Nikides (eds.), *Chrislam: How Missionaries Are Promoting an Islamized Gospel*, Garden Grove, CA: i2 Ministries, 297–305.

Cotterell, Peter (2013), 'War, Holy War and Islam', in John Azumah and Peter Riddell (eds.), *Islam and Christianity on the Edge: Talking Points in Christian-Muslim Relations into the 21st Century*, Brunswick East: Acorn Press, 40–53.

Cumming, Joseph (2008), 'Toward Respectful Witness', in Dudley Woodberry (ed.), *From Seed to Fruit: Global Trends, Fruitful Practices, and Emerging Issues among Muslims*, Pasadena, CA: William Carey, 311–23.

Cumming, Joseph (2012), 'Sifat al-Dhat in al-Ash'ari's Doctrine of God and Possible Christian Parallels', in Evelyne Reisacher (ed.), *Toward Respectful Understanding and Witness among Muslims: Essays in Honour of J. Dudley Woodberry*, Pasadena, CA: William Carey, 111–46.

Cumming, Joseph (2013), 'Christian Peacemaking and Witness with Muslims', in David Gushee (ed.), *Evangelical Peacemakers: Gospel Engagement in a War-Torn World*, Eugene, OR: Wipf & Stock, 46–50.

Cumming, Joseph (2019), 'Focus on Common Ground in Christian-Muslim Relationships: A Ministry Reflection', in Ronnie Campbell and Christopher Gnanakan (eds.), *Do Christians, Muslims, and Jews Worship the Same God? Four Views*, Grand Rapids, MI: Counterpoints, 208–23.

Dabbour Jaballah, Bassma (2018), 'A Feminine Reading of Christian Missions in the Middle Eastern Context: Views of Mission in North Africa and the Middle East as Seen by Christians from Muslim Background', in Moyra Dale, Cathy Hine and Carol Walker (eds.), *When Women Speak*, Oxford: Regnum, 50–7.

Dale, Moyra (2018), '(Re)forming Identities and Allegiances', in Moyra Dale, Cathy Hine and Carol Walker (eds.), *When Women Speak*, Oxford: Regnum, 67–88.

Daniels, Gene (2018), 'Conclusion: Learning from the Margins', in Warrick Farah and Gene Daniels (eds.), *Margins of Islam: Missiology in Diverse Muslim Contexts*, Littleton, CO: William Carey, 209–20.

Deik, Anton (2020), 'Christian Zionism and Mission: How Does Our Understanding of Christianity Impact Our Witness in the World?', in Martin Accad and Jonathan Andrews (eds.), *The Religious Other: A Biblical Understanding of Islam, the Qur'an and Muhammad*, Carlisle: Langham, 74–81.

Diab, Issa (2020), 'The Honorable Qur'an: From Revelation to the Book', in Martin Accad and Jonathan Andrews (eds.), *The Religious Other: A Biblical Understanding of Islam, the Qur'an and Muhammad*, Carlisle: Langham, 217–40.

Dieppe, Tim (2019b), 'Tim Dieppe', in Emma Webb (ed.), *Islamophobia: An Anthology of Concerns*, London: Civitas, 28–37.

Durie, Mark (2009a), 'Case Study: Amina Lawal and the Islamic Sharia', in David Claydon (ed.), *Islam: Human Rights and Public Policy*, Brunswick East: Acorn Press, 148–54.

Durie, Mark (2009b), 'The Hidden Currents of Western Responses to Islam', in David Claydon (ed.), *Islam: Human Rights and Public Policy*, Brunswick East: Acorn Press, 29–35.

Farah, Warrick (2018), 'How Muslims Shape and Use Islam: Towards a Missiological Understanding', in Warrick Farah and Gene Daniels (eds.), *Margins of Islam: Missiology in Diverse Muslim Contexts*, Littleton, CO: William Carey, 13–22.

Farah, Warrick (2020a), 'Discerning Spiritual Realities in Islamic Contexts: Missional Reflections of a Boring Charismatic', in Martin Accad and Jonathan Andrews (eds.),

The Religious Other: A Biblical Understanding of Islam, the Qur'an and Muhammad, Carlisle: Langham, 430–41.

Farah, Warrick (2020b), 'Hermeneutical Hinges: How Different Views of Religion and Culture Impact Interpretations of Islam', in Martin Accad and Jonathan Andrews (eds.), *The Religious Other: A Biblical Understanding of Islam, the Qur'an and Muhammad*, Carlisle: Langham, 189–203.

Glaser, Ida (2020a), 'Is There a Place for Islam in God's Salvation History?', in Martin Accad and Jonathan Andrews (eds.), *The Religious Other: A Biblical Understanding of Islam, the Qur'an and Muhammad*, Carlisle: Langham, 367–84.

Glaser, Ida (2020b), 'The Messengers and the Message: A Biblical Perspective on Qur'anic Prophethood', in Martin Accad and Jonathan Andrews (eds.), *The Religious Other: A Biblical Understanding of Islam, the Qur'an and Muhammad*, Carlisle: Langham, 323–30.

Green, Tim (2011), 'Conversion from Islam to Christianity in Britain', in Steve Bell and Colin Chapman (eds.), *Between Naivety and Hostility: How Should Christians Respond to Islam in Britain*, Milton Keynes: Authentic Media, 101–18.

Guinness, Os (2010), 'Pilgrim at Spaghetti Junction: An Evangelical Perspective on Relativism and Fundamentalism', in Peter Berger (ed.), *Between Relativism and Fundamentalism: Religious Resources for a Middle Position*, Grand Rapids, MI: Eedermans, 164–79.

Hadaway, Robin (2018), 'Magical Mystical Muslims: Sufi-Oriented Islam and African Traditional Religion – What It Is, How It Works, and Why It Matters', in Warrick Farah and Gene Daniels (eds.), *Margins of Islam: Missiology in Diverse Muslim Contexts*, Littleton, CO: William Carey, 69–80.

Harper, Lisa (2013), 'War, Terror, and Peace', in David Gushee (ed.), *Evangelical Peacemakers: Gospel Engagement in a War-Torn World*, Eugene, OR: Wipf & Stock, 9–13.

Hine, Cathy (2017), 'Negotiating from the Margins: Women's Voices (Re)imagining Islam', in Evelyne Reisacher (ed.), *Dynamics of Muslim Worlds: Regional, Theological, and Missiological Perspectives*, Downers Grove, IL: Inter-Varsity Press Academic, 113–34.

Hine, Cathy (2018), 'Veiled: Muslim Women in Modern Mission Strategies', in Moyra Dale, Cathy Hine and Carol Walker (eds.), *When Women Speak*, Oxford: Regnum, 7–18.

Hoover, Jon (2005), 'The Trinity: A Response to the Islamic Critique', in James Krabill, David Shenk and Lindford Stutzman (eds.), *Anabaptists Meeting Muslims: A Calling for Presence in the Way of Christ*, Scottdale, PA: Herald Press, 294–7.

Howarth, Toby (2011), '*Taqiyya* (Dissimulation) and Integrity', in Steve Bell and Colin Chapman (eds.), *Between Naivety and Hostility: How Should Christians Respond to Islam in Britain?* Milton Keynes: Authentic Media, 218–36.

Idowu-Fearon, Josiah (2013), 'The African Christian and Ideological Islam', in John Azumah and Lamin Sanneh (eds.), *The African Christian and Islam*, Carlisle: Langham, 177–92.

Johnston, David (2012), 'Squeezing Ethics Out of Law: What is Shari'a Anyway?', in Evelyne Reisacher (ed.), *Toward Respectful Understanding and Witness among Muslims: Essays in Honour of J. Dudley Woodberry*, Pasadena, CA: William Carey, 59–69.

Johnston, Douglas (2013), 'U.S. Foreign Policy and the Muslim World', in David Gushee (ed.), *Evangelical Peacemakers: Gospel Engagement in a War-Torn World*, Eugene, OR: Wipf & Stock, 51–9.

Kendal, Elizabeth (2009a), 'Case Study: Ontario and Quebec, Canada – Muslims Rally against Islamists to Defeat Sharia', in David Claydon (ed.), *Islam, Human Rights and Public Policy*, Brunswick East: Acorn Press, 192–6.

Kendal, Elizabeth (2009b), 'The Question of Islamic Freedom', in David Claydon (ed.), *Islam, Human Rights and Public Policy*, Brunswick East: Acorn Press, 81–94.

Knell, Bryan (2014), 'Engaging with Other Believers: Establishing Networks', in Bert de Ruiter (ed.), *Engaging with Muslims in Europe*, Nurnberg: VTR, 98–107.

Larson, Warren (2012), 'Current Trends in Islam and Christian Mission', in Evelyne Reisacher (ed.), *Toward Respectful Understanding and Witness among Muslims*, Pasadena, CA: William Carey, 87–94.

Larson, Warren (2018), 'Ordinary Muslims in Pakistan and the Gospel', in Warrick Farah and Gene Daniels (eds.), *Margins of Islam: Missiology in Diverse Muslim Contexts*, Littleton, CO: William Carey, 81–92.

Mallouhi, Christine (2012), 'Peacemaking as a Witness', in Evelyne Reisacher (ed.), *Toward Respectful Understanding and Witness among Muslims: Essays in Honour of J. Dudley Woodberry*, Pasadena, CA: William Carey, 259–70.

McDermott, Gerald (2019), 'Jews and Christians Worship the Same God: Shared Revelation View', in Ronnie Campbell and Christopher Gnanakan (eds.), *Do Christians, Muslims, and Jews Worship the Same God? Four Views*, Grand Rapids, MI: Counterpoints, 107–32.

Meral, Ziya (2011), 'Islam, Human Rights and "Our Way of Life"', in Steve Bell and Colin Chapman (eds.), *Between Naivety and Hostility: How Should Christians Respond to Islam in Britain?* Milton Keynes: Authentic Media, 119–32.

Moucarry, Chawkat (2011b), 'The Case for Dialogue', in Steve Bell and Colin Chapman (eds.), *Between Naivety and Hostility: How Should Christians Respond to Islam in Britain?* Milton Keynes: Authentic Media, 248–62.

Nickel, Gordon (2005), 'Peaceable Dialogue with Muslims', in James Krabill, David Shenk and Lindford Stutzman (eds.), *Anabaptists Meeting Muslims: A Calling for Presence in the Way of Christ*, Scottdale, PA: Herald Press, 334–8.

Reisacher, Evelyne (2012a), 'Portraying Muslim Women', in Evelyne Reisacher (ed.), *Toward Respectful Understanding and Witness among Muslims: Essays in Honour of J. Dudley Woodberry*, Pasadena, CA: William Carey, 71–86.

Reisacher, Evelyne (2017a), 'Defining Islam and Muslim Societies in Missiological Discourse', in Evelyne Reisacher (ed.), *Dynamics of Muslim Worlds: Regional, Theological, and Missiological Perspectives*, Downers Grove, IL: Inter-Varsity Press Academic, 219–41.

Riddell, Peter (2013), 'Christian-Muslim Dialogue into the 21st Century', in John Azumah and Peter Riddell (eds.), *Islam and Christianity on the Edge: Talking Points in Christian-Muslim Relations into the 21st Century*, Brunswick East: Acorn Press, 173–92.

Roberts, Bob (2013), 'Pastors and Peacemaking in a Glocalized World', in David Gushee (ed.), *Evangelical Peacemakers: Gospel Engagement in a War-Torn World*, Eugene, OR: Wipf & Stock, 86–92.

Shenk, David (2019), 'Focus on Respectfully Held Differences in Christian-Muslim Relationships: A Ministry Reflection', in Ronnie Campbell and Christopher Gnanakan (eds.), *Do Christians, Muslims, and Jews Worship the Same God? Four Views*, Grand Rapids, MI: Counterpoints, 224–36.

Simnowitz, Adam (2012), 'How Insider Movements Affect Ministry: Personal Reflection', in Joshua Lingel, Jeff Morton and Bill Nikides (eds.), *Chrislam: How Missionaries Are Promoting an Islamized Gospel*, Garden Grove, CA: i2 Ministries, 199–226.

Smith, Jay (2011), 'The Case for Polemics', in Steve Bell and Colin Chapman (eds.), *Between Naivety and Hostility: How Should Christians Respond to Islam in Britain?* Milton Keynes: Authentic Media, 237–47.

Smith, Jay (2012), 'An Assessment of IM's Principle Paradigms', in Joshua Lingel, Jeff Morton and Bill Nikides (eds.), *Chrislam: How Missionaries Are Promoting an Islamized Gospel*, Garden Grove, CA: i2 Ministries, 277–308.

Span, John (2012), 'The Confusion of Kingdom Circles: A Clarification', in Joshua Lingel, Jeff Morton and Bill Nikides (eds.), *Chrislam: How Missionaries Are Promoting an Islamized Gospel*, Garden Grove, CA: i2 Ministries, 77–86.

Taylor, Jenny (2005), 'The Multicultural Myth', in Lesslie Newbigin, Lamin Sanneh and Jenny Taylor (eds.), *Faith and Power: Christianity and Islam in 'Secular' Britain*, Eugene, OR: Wipf & Stock, 75–132.

Thorneycroft, Charlotte (2013), 'The Compatibility of Islamic Shariah Law with the Universal Declaration of Human Rights Charlotte', in John Azumah and Peter Riddell (eds.), *Islam and Christianity on the Edge: Talking Points in Christian-Muslim Relations into the 21st Century*, Brunswick East: Acorn Press, 95–112.

Tucker, Richard (2005), 'A Move of God in a Muslim Land', in David Greenlee (ed.), *From the Straight Path to the Narrow Way: Journeys of Faith*, Waynesboro, GA: Authentic Media, 255–64.

Volf, Miroslav, Joseph Cumming and Melissa Yarrington (2010), 'Loving God and Neighbor Together: A Christian Response to "A Common Word between Us and You"', in Miroslav Volf, Ghazi Bin Muhammad and Melissa Yarrington (eds.), *A Common Word: Muslims and Christians on Loving God and Neighbor*, Grand Rapids, MI: Eedermans, 51–75.

Walls, Jerry (2019), 'None Worship the Same God: Different Conceptions of God', in Ronnie Campbell and Christopher Gnanakan (eds.), *Do Christians, Muslims, and Jews Worship the Same God? Four Views*, Grand Rapids, MI: Counterpoints, 160–81.

Yousif, Ashoor (2020), 'Early Christian Views of Muslims, Muhammad and the Qur'an', in Martin Accad and Jonathan Andrews (eds.), *The Religious Other: A Biblical Understanding of Islam, the Qur'an and Muhammad*, Carlisle: Langham, 143–73.

Articles

Accad, Martin (2010), 'Interfaith Praxis: An Historic Moment in Muslim-Christian Dialogue', *Evangelical Interfaith Dialogue*, 1 (1): 10.

Accad, Martin (2011), 'Mission at the Intersection of Religion and Empire', *International Journal of Frontier Missiology*, 28 (4): 179–89.

Accad, Martin (2014), 'Towards a Theology of Islam: A Response to Harley Talman's "Is Muhammad also Among the Prophets?"', *International Journal of Frontier Missiology*, 31 (4): 191–3.

Accad, Martin (2017), 'Are Muslims Liars? A Missiological Reflection on Taqiyya', *Muslim-Christian Encounter*, 10 (1): 9–26.

Al Fadi (2023), 'I Wanted to Die for Allah. Now I Live for Jesus', *Christianity Today*, 3 January.

Azumah, John (2005), 'Theological Foundations of Shari'a in Islam: Concerns and Reservations', *Transformation*, 22 (4): 238–50.

Azumah, John (2009), 'Christian Response to Islam: A Struggle for the Soul of Christianity', *CIS Messenger*, Summer, 3–4.
Azumah, John (2011), 'The Church and Islam in Africa', *Evangelical Interfaith Dialogue*, 2 (3): 3–17.
Azumah, John (2012), 'Evangelical Christian Views and Attitudes towards Christian-Muslim Dialogue', *Transformation*, 29 (2): 128–38.
Azumah, John (2016), 'A Response to: "Is Muhammad also among the Prophets?"', *International Journal of Frontier Missiology*, 33 (3): 108–13.
Barnabas Fund (2008b), 'Islam and Love', *Barnabas Aid*, January/February insert, i–ii.
Barnabas Fund (2011a), 'Islam and Language', *Barnabas Aid*, November/December pullout supplement, i–iv.
Bell, Steve (2008), 'Christians Do Not Need to Fear Islamic Take-over in UK', *Christianity Today*, 18 July.
Birdsall, Judd (2018), 'Pitfalls in Combatting Persecution', *Cambridge Papers*, 27 (4): 1–6.
Brown, Daniel (2004), 'Clash of Cultures or Clash of Theologies? A Critique of Some Contemporary Evangelical Responses to Islam', *Journal for the Theology of Culture*, 1 (1): 69–84.
Brown, Rick (2006), 'Who Is "Allah"?', *International Journal of Frontier Missiology*, 23 (2): 79–82.
Chapman, Colin (2003), 'Apocalypse Now in Israel/Palestine?', *Bible in Transmission*, Autumn, 1–4.
Chapman, Colin (2004b), 'Time to Give Up the Idea of Christian Mission to Muslims? Some Reflections from the Middle East', *International Bulletin of Missionary Research*, 28 (3): 112–17.
Chapman, Colin (2007a), 'Christian Responses to Islam, Islamism and "Islamic Terrorism"', *Cambridge Papers*, 16 (2): 1–6.
Chapman, Colin (2008), 'An Islamic Understanding of Sin and Brokenness in Society', *Bible in Transmission*, Summer, 21–3.
Chapman, Colin (2017a), 'Christian Responses to Islamism and Violence in the Name of Islam', *Transformation*, 34 (2): 115–30.
Chapman, Colin, and John Azumah (2018), 'Islam through the Lens of the Golden Rule: Grace and Truth in Our Approach to Muslims and Islam', *Lausanne Global Analysis*, 7 (4): n.p.
Christianity (2022), 'Street Preachers Exonerated', *Christianity*, December, 10.
Cumming, Joseph (2011), 'Christians, Muslims and the Responsible Exercise of Freedom', *Christianity Today*, 8 July.
Farrokh, Fred (2015), 'Will the Umma Veto SITO? Assessing the Impact of Theological Deviation on Social Acceptability in Muslim Communities', *International Journal of Frontier Missiology*, 32 (2): 69–80.
Garrison, David (2019), 'Why More Muslims Are Turning to Jesus', *Newsweek*, 28 June.
Glaser, Ida (2000a), 'Faith and Society in the UK', *Transformation*, 17 (1): 26–9.
Glaser, Ida (2000b), 'Theological Questions: An Agenda for Study', *Transformation*, 17 (1): 44–8.
Hicham, E. (2009), 'Islam's New Enemy', *Evangelical Times*, February.
Ibrahim, Ayman (2015a), '"Is Muhammad also among the Prophets?" A Response to Harley Talman', *International Journal of Frontier Missiology*, 32 (4): 202–4.
Ibrahim, Ayman (2015b), '"Is Muhammad also among the Prophets?" A Second Response to Harley Talman', *International Journal of Frontier Missiology*, 33 (3): 116–20.

Johnston, David (2002), 'Are God and Allah the Same?', *Mission Frontiers*, January–February, 12–13.
Kuttab, Jonathan (2018), 'Palestinian Evangelicals and Christian Zionism', *Jerusalem Quarterly*, 76: 70–8.
Larson, Warren (2005), 'A Christian Response to Islam in America', *Evangelical Missions Quarterly*, 41 (1): 48–55.
Larson, Warren (2006), 'Unveiling the Truth about Islam: Too Many Christian Books Miss the Mark', *Christianity Today*, 1 June.
Lewis, Rebecca (2009), 'Insider Movements: Honoring God-Given Identity and Community', *International Journal of Frontier Missiology*, 26 (1): 16–19.
Mamahit, Ferry (2020), 'Abangan Muslims, Javanese Worldview, and Muslim–Christian Relations in Indonesia', *Transformation*, 38 (1): 31–45.
Meral, Ziya (2012), 'International Religious Freedom Advocacy in the Field: Challenges, Effective Strategies, and the Road Ahead', *Review of Faith & International Affairs*, 10 (3): 25–32.
Miller, Duane (2011), '"Your Swords Do Not Concern Me at All" The liberation Theology of Islamic Christianity', *St Francis Magazine*, 7 (2): 228–60.
Miller, Duane (2014), 'An Exploration of Christ's Converts from Islam: Reasons Given for Their Conversions', *Journal of Asian Mission*, 15 (2): 15–25.
Moore, Johnnie (2021), 'Africa's Silent Genocide', *Christianity*, Premier, 32–7.
Morey, Robert (2002a), 'Is "Allah" Just Another Name for God?', *Journal of Biblical Apologetics*, 5 (3): 61–7.
Moucarry, Chawkat (2010a), 'A Lifelong Journey with Islam', *Christianity Today*, 4 March.
Moucarry, Chawkat (2011a), 'Allah: A Christian Response', *Islam and Christian–Muslim Relations*, 22 (4): 503–4.
Mouw, Richard (2010), 'Convicted Civility & Interfaith Dialogue', *Evangelical Interfaith Dialogue*, 1 (3): 3–7.
Nazir-Ali, Michael (2008a), 'Extremism Flourished as UK Lost Christianity', *Daily Telegraph*, 6 January.
Nazir-Ali, Michael (2008b), 'Sharia Law Challenges British Justice', *Daily Telegraph*, 21 September.
Nikides, Bill (2006), 'The Church at the Crossroads: A Global Perspective', *St Francis Magazine*, II (4): n.p.
Parshall, Phil (2013), 'How Much Muslim Context Is Too Much for the Gospel?', *Christianity Today*, 16 January.
Peñamora, Aldrin (2016), 'Eucharistic Justice: A Christ-Centered Response to the Bangsamoro Question in the Philippines', *Asian Journal of Pentecostal Studies*, 19 (1): 31–44.
Peters, Duncan (2022), 'Questions about God: Overcoming Some Theological Barriers in Muslim-Christian Dialogue', *South Asian Journal of Religion and Philosophy*, 3 (2): 49–64.
Power, Bernie (2012), 'Do We Worship the Same God?', *Eternity Newspaper*, 4 August.
Riddell, Peter (2003), 'The Changing Face of Christian Engagement with Muslims', *Evangelicals Now*, May.
Riddell, Peter (2010), 'The Burqa Debate Reaches Australia', *Evangelicals Now*, August.
Rivers, Julian (2017), 'Could Marriage Be Disestablished?', *Tyndale Bulletin*, 68 (1): 121–51.
Schirrmacher, Thomas (2010), 'Is It Appropriate That Arab Christians Call God Allah?', *MBS Texte*, 142 (translation by Richard McClary of a chapter from

Thomas Schirrmacher (2003), *Feindbild Islam* (Islam: A Stereotypical Enemy), Nürnberg: Verlag für Theologie und Religionswissenschaft).
Shamoun, Sam (2002), 'Is Allah the God of the Bible?', *Journal of Biblical Apologetics*, 5 (3): 45–61.
Shehadeh, Imad (2004), 'Do Muslims and Christians Believe in the Same God?', *Bibliotheca Sacra*, 161: 14–26.
Shehadeh, Imad (2011), 'Book Reviews: *Allah: A Christian Response* by Miroslav Volf', *Themelios*, 36 (2): 374–6.
Singh, David (2022), 'Christianity and Islam: Meekness-Servanthood and Faith as Polity-Majesty', *International Journal of Asian Christianity*, 5 (2): 163–79.
Solomon, Sam (2006), 'When Will the Terrorism Stop?', *Evangelicals Now*, November.
Sookhdeo, Patrick (2005), 'The Myth of Moderate Islam', *The Spectator*, 30 July.
Sookhdeo, Patrick (2014b), 'The Two Faces of Islam', *BarnabasAid*, November/December, 14–15.
Talman, Harley (2014), 'Is Muhammad also among the Prophets?', *International Journal of Frontier Missiology*, 31 (4): 169–90.
Taylor, Jenny (2018), 'Why Grace Is Not Enough to Reach Muslims: Balancing Grace and Truth in Outreach', *Lausanne Global Analysis*, 7 (2): n.p.
Thomas, Kenneth (2001), 'Allah in Translations of the Bible', *Bible Translator*, 52 (3): 301–6.
Travis, John (2015), 'The C1-C6 Spectrum after Fifteen Years', *Evangelical Missions Quarterly*, 51 (4): 358–65.
Wagner, Peter (2002), 'Who Is Allah?', *Global Prayer News*, 3 (1): n.p.
Woodberry, Dudley (2004), 'Do Christians and Muslims Worship the Same God? Part III', *Christian Century*, 121 (10): 36–7.
Woodberry, Dudley (2007), 'To the Muslim I Became a Muslim? The Council of Jerusalem Applied', *International Journal of Frontier Missiology*, 24 (1): 23–8.
Woodberry, Dudley (2011), 'Muslim Missions Then & Now: How a Terrorist Attack Reshaped Efforts to Reach Muslims', *Christianity Today*, 8 September.
Woodberry, Dudley, and Russell Shubin (2001), 'Muslims Tell … "Why I Chose Jesus"', *Mission Frontiers*, March.
Yakubu, Rahman (2014), 'Dialogue and Witness "Through the Eye of the Other"', *Evangelical Interfaith Dialogue*, 5 (2): 25–7.

Reports and conferences

Chapman, Colin (2007c), 'Islam and Witness to Muslims', New Wine Conference, Shepton Mallet, UK.
Meral, Ziya (2008), 'No Place to Call Home: Experiences of Apostates from Islam, Failures of the International Community', New Malden: CSW.
Open Doors (2016), 'Crushed but Not Defeated: The Impact of Persistent Violence on the Church in Northern Nigeria', Witney: Open Doors.
Stark, William (2021), 'The Voiceless Victims of Pakistan's Blasphemy Laws', Silver Spring, MD: International Christian Concern.

Web articles

All articles accessed on 22 May 2023 unless otherwise stated.

Ajaj, Azar (2016), 'Is the God of the Bible the Same as the God of the Quran?', 20 January, www.nazcol.org/blog/303/is-the-god-of-the-bible-the-same-as-the-god-of-the-quran.

Anderson, Mark (2016a), 'The Chronology of the Qur'an', https://understandingislam.today/the-chronology-of-the-quran.

Anderson, Mark (n.d.), 'Is Mecca Really the Birthplace of Islam?', *Zwemer Institute*, www.zwemercenter.com/is-mecca-really-the-birthplace-of-islam.

Aperlo, Nathalie (n.d.), 'Joel Richardson and the Rise of Islamophobia', *Zwemer Institute*, www.zwemercenter.com/research?post_id=2435.

Attridge, Harold, Joseph Cumming, Emilie Townes and Miroslav Volf (2007), 'Loving God and Neighbor Together: A Christian Response to *A Common Word between Us and You*', 18 November, www.acommonword.com/loving-god-and-neighbor-together-a-christian-response-to-a-common-word-between-us-and-you.

Baldwin, Chuck (2007), 'Do Christians and Muslims Worship the Same God?', 23 October, https://chuckbaldwinlive.com/Articles/tabid/109/ID/491/Do-Christians-And-Muslims-Worship-The-Same-God.aspx.

Barnabas Fund (2007), 'Response to Open Letter and Call from Muslim Religious Leaders to Christian Leaders', 28 November, www.barnabasfund.org/news/archives/article.php?ID_news_items=342 (accessed 20 May 2008).

Barnabas Fund (2008a), 'Barnabas Fund Response to the Yale Center for Faith and Culture Statement', 24 January, http://docplayer.net/78300557-Western-protestant-christian-and-muslim-interfaith-relations-one-seminary-s-story.html.

Bush, George W. (2001a), '"Islam Is Peace" Says President', 17 September, https://georgewbush-whitehouse.archives.gov/news/releases/2001/09/20010917-11.html.

Bush, George W. (2001b), 'Remarks by the President upon Arrival: The South Lawn', 16 September, https://georgewbush-whitehouse.archives.gov/news/releases/2001/09/20010916-2.html.

Chapman, Colin (2005b), 'An Open Letter to Patrick Sookhdeo', *Fulcrum Forum*, www.fulcrum-anglican.org.uk/news/2005/200510chapman.cfm (accessed 14 June 2010).

Chapman, Colin (2017b), 'Christian Responses to Islamism and Violence in the Name of Islam', *Fulcrum Forum*, 26 May, www.fulcrum-anglican.org.uk/articles/christian-responses-to-islamism-and-violence-in-the-name-of-islam/.

Christian Concern (2010), 'Growing Concern as British Public Is "Misled" over Halal Meat', 22 September, https://archive.christianconcern.com/our-concerns/islam/growing-concern-british-public-"misled"-over-halal-meat.

Christian Concern (2021), 'Stopping the Newham Call to Prayer', 24 June, https://christianconcern.com/comment/stopping-the-newham-call-to-prayer.

Christian Voice (2005), 'Stop the Racial and Religious Hatred Bill', www.repentuk.com/hate.html.

Craig, Alan (2008), 'KICC: Church "Hung Out to Dry"', www.youtube.com/watch?v=Myq75L5eC58.

Dieppe, Tim (2019a), 'Open Letter to Home Secretary Rejects Islamophobia Definition', *Christian Concern*, 17 May, https://christianconcern.com/comment/open-letter-to-home-secretary-rejects-islamophobia-definition.

Dixon, Roger (2017), 'The Adam Simnowitz Case: About Harming the Debate', *Journal of Biblical Missiology*, 17 July, https://biblicalmissiology.org/blog/2017/07/17/the-adam-simnowitz-case-about-harming-the-debate.

Durie, Mark (2008a), 'Notes for Christians on Understanding "A Common Word between Us and You"', 4 February, http://acommonword.blogspot.com/2008/02/notes-for-christians-on-understanding.html.

Durie, Mark (2008b), 'Reflections upon "Loving God and Neighbor Together": The Yale Response to *A Common Word between Us and You*', 5 February, http://acommonword.blogspot.com/2008/02/reflections-upon-loving-god-and.html.

Ibrahim, Ayman (2022), 'Is Islam the World's Fastest-Growing Religion?', *Gospel Coalition*, 6 December, www.thegospelcoalition.org/article/islam-fastest-growing-religion.

Isaac, Munther (2021), 'Christian Zionism as Imperial Theology', *Balfour Project*, 24 March, https://balfourproject.org/christian-zionism.

Johnson, Thomas (2020), 'Evangelicals and Muslims: Not Brothers, but Best Friends', *Christianity Today*, 17 November, www.christianitytoday.com/ct/2020/november-web-only/christian-muslim-religious-freedom-wea-nahdlatul-ulama-nu.html.

Joyner, Rick (2010), 'The Rise of Islam Part 1 of 4 – The Threat of Islam to America', *MorningStar Ministries*, www.youtube.com/watch?v=fE4DxLeuxFQ&list=PLfpRySqe-6fdabZUYRsNscTzHmVBglVSo&index=1 (accessed 14 July 2021).

Katanacho, Yohanna (2021), 'How Should Followers of Christ Respond to the Current Situation in Israel/Palestine?', *Come and See*, 11 May, www.comeandsee.com/view.php?sid=1401.

Lutzer, Erwin (2007), 'The Resurgence of Islam', www.moodymedia.org/articles/resurgence-islam-response-church.

McLaren, Brian (2012a), 'My Take: It's Time for Islamophobic Evangelicals to Choose', *CNN*, 15 September, https://religion.blogs.cnn.com/2012/09/15/my-take-its-time-for-islamophobic-evangelicals-to-choose (accessed 30 November 2022).

Mohler, Albert (2013), 'Islam – The Great Challenge to Christian Evangelism of Our Times', 5 July, https://albertmohler.com/2013/07/05/islam-the-great-challenge-to-christian-evangelism-of-our-times.

Mohler, Albert (2015), 'Do Christians and Muslims Worship the Same God?', 18 December, https://albertmohler.com/2015/12/18/do-christians-and-muslims-worship-the-same-god.

Moucarry, Chawkat (2010b), 'A Plea for Dialogue between Christians and Muslims', *Lausanne Movement*, www.lausanne.org/content/a-plea-for-dialogue-between-christians-and-muslims.

Peters, Duncan (n.d.), '"Same God" for Muslims and Christians?', *Zwemer Institute*, www.zwemercenter.com/the-issue-of-same-god-for-muslims-and-christians.

Pfander Centre for Christian Apologetics (n.d.), 'About (Bible)', www.pfander.uk/tag/bible.

Piper, John (2013), 'Do Christians and Muslims Worship the Same Deity?', 17 April, www.desiringgod.org/interviews/do-christians-and-muslims-worship-the-same-deity.

Power, Bernie (n.d.), 'A Volf in Sheikh's Clothing? How "Allah: A Christian Response" May Deceive Both Christians and Muslims', www.mst.edu.au/faculty/bernie-power/.

Price, Randall (2016), 'Randall Price: Still Ready to Build (Part 1)', 20 June, www.worldofthebible.com/randall-price-still-ready-to-build-part-1-june-20-2016.

Qureshi, Nabeel (2015), 'Do Muslims and Christians Worship the Same God?', http://rzim.org/global-blog/do-muslims-and-christians-worship-the-same-god/ (accessed 21 November 2022).

Riddell, Peter (2016), 'The Marrakesh Declaration Avoids Hard Questions', *Lapido Media*, http://religiousliteracyinstitute.org/analysis-marrakesh-declaration-hard-questions (accessed 15 August 2018).

Roberts, Bob (2019), 'Why Evangelicals Hate Muslims: An Evangelical Minister's Perspective', www.youtube.com/watch?v=opcUsTBkIMA.

Robertson, Pat (2003), 'Why Evangelical Christians Support Israel', www.patrobertson.com/speeches/IsraelLauder.asp.

Shenk, David (2010), 'Experiencing Dialogue', *Lausanne Movement*, https://lausanne.org/content/experiencing-dialogue.

Sizer, Stephen (2010), 'Evangelical Christians and Muslims Engage in "Bridges of Faith" Conversation', 15 May, www.stephensizer.com/2010/05/evangelical-chritians-and-muslims-engage-in-bridges-of-faith-conversation.

Smith, Jay (2006), 'Is Allah God?', www.youtube.com/watch?v=gy_YrhJRYjA.

Smith, Jay (2007), 'Taqiyya: May Jay Smith Debate and Dialogue', *Pfander Films*, 4 June, www.pfander.uk/videos/041-taqiyya-may-jay-smith-debate-and-dialogue.

Smith, Jay (2008a), 'Challenging the Tablighi Jamaat's "Olympics" Mosque', *Pfander Films*, 14 March, www.pfander.uk/videos/061-challenging-the-tablighi-jamaats-olympics-mosque.

Smith, Jay (2008b), 'Fitna the Film: A Christian Response', 28 March, www.youtube.com/watch?v=I9MJIC238X0.

Smith, Jay (2020), '5) Quest: Where in the 7th Century Is That Elusive Islam?', *Pfander Films*, 17 October, www.youtube.com/watch?v=NuolerXrGx0.

Solomon, Sam (2009), 'Shari'ah', 3 February, http://pilcrowpress.com/shariah (accessed 28 July 2010).

Stone, Matthew (n.d.), 'A Messianic Jew and Former Muslim on the Allah vs God Debate', *Zwemer Institute*, www.zwemercenter.com/a-messianic-jew-and-former-muslim-on-the-allah-vs-god.

Whittingham, Martin (2012), '"Deciding by the Gospel": Some Protestant Christian Responses to the Qur'an since the Nineteenth Century', *CMCS Oxford*, www.cmcsoxford.org.uk/s/M-Whittingham-Deciding-by-the-Gospel.pdf.

Wilkinson, Paul (2012), 'The Church at Christ's Checkpoint', www.thebereancall.org/content/church-christs-checkpoint-free-booklet.

World Evangelical Alliance (2012), 'World Evangelical Alliance Condemns the Burning of the Qur'an', 28 April, https://worldea.org/news/14058/world-evangelical-alliance-condemns-the-burning-of-the-quran.

Index of public sphere participants and organizations

Bold – page number containing a short biographical description
† – former Muslim
* – pen name

Accad, Martin 23, 26, 28, 29, **34**, 36, 37, 38, 39, 41, 43, 44, 51, 52, 54, 57, 60, 70, 71, 73, 74, 82, 83, 84, 92, 100, 107, 140, 159, 164, 170, 177, 186, 187, 189, 191, 196, 212
Adeney, Miriam 23, **94**, 176
Agang, Bobai **129**
Ajaj, Azar **52**, 61
Akinade, Akintunde **9**, 43, 172
Al–Araby, Abdullah* 114
Allen, Stafford* 24, 29, 60, 77, 184, 195
Anderson, Mark 24, 29, **70**, 81, 82
Andrew, Brother 29, **120**, 131, 185, 194, 199
Andrews, Dave **39**, 49, 141, 142, 147, 190, 200
Angelina Noble Centre 22
Anyabwile, Thabiti† 26, **104**, 109, 110
Arab Baptist Theological Seminary 34, 186
Arthur Jeffrey Centre for the Study of Islam 27
Awad, Alex **154**, 157
Azad, Anwarul† **198**, 212
Azumah, John† 9, **24**, 26, 28, 31, 41, 43, 52, 53, 60, 66, 71, 74, 84, 85, 88, 92, 93, 94, 95, 97, 100, 112, 121, 124, 125, 129, 136, 138, 140, 141, 142, 170, 171, 173, 175, 181, 182, 186, 212, 224

Bahri, Abdallah† **95**, 97, 98, 124
Bannister, Andy 51, **53**, 54, 56, 57, 68, 79, 92
Barnabas Fund 24, 26, 30, 49, 59, 98, 106, 120, 122, 131, 147, 187, 202
Beaumont, Mark **73**

Bell, Steve 2, 23, 26, 28, 29, 35, **39**, 41, 50, 52, 92, 113, 115, 125, 136, 159, 163, 168, 171, 177, 184, 185, 188, 190, 191, 194, 195, 196, 197, 202
Birdsall, Judd 127, 128
Bridger, Scott **84**
Bridging the Divide 30
Bristow, George **74**
Brotherson, Derek 198
Brown, Dan 54, **56**, 59, 67, 70, 72, 79, 89, 142
Brown, Rick 55, **56**, 198
Brubaker, Daniel **80**
Burge, Gary 24, **154**, 156, 157

Camp, Lee 29, **140**, 147, 201
Campolo, Tony 25, 26, **38**, 58, 60, 140, 142, 144, 153, 159
Caner, Ergun and Emir† 29, **42**, 53, 61, 68, 78, 85, 86, 137, 142, 143, 147, 212, 234
Carimokam, Sahaja* 67, 95, 236 n.11
Carson, Don **25**, 197
Carter, Jimmy **157**
Cashin, David **39**
Catherwood, Christopher **108**, 121, 135, 138, 139, 140, 141, 147, 173
Chalke, Steve **39**, 186, 224
Challen, Edward 184
Chapman, Colin 6, 23, 24, 26, 28, **31**, 41, 50, 52, 54, 56, 66, 80, 83, 85, 86, 88, 91, 93, 96, 100, 112, 122, 128, 131, 137, 138, 140, 141, 142, 145, 148, 156, 157, 159, 164, 172, 175, 176, 177, 185, 191, 211
Chatrath, Nick 29, 55, 184
Chedid, Bassam 28
Christian Concern 35, 42, 105, 106, 109

Christian Voice 78, 88, 109
Claydon, David 26, 29, **98**
Coleman, Diane 29, 68, 121
Collins, Ted* 29, 59, 175
Cotterell, Peter 2, **56**, 67, 68, 72, 88, 121, 135, 138, 140, 144, 223
Cox, Caroline **25**, 29, 84, 95, 100, 127, 169, 173, 212
Cragg, Kenneth **9**, 11, 21, 29, 44, 45, 52, 66, 72, 81, 82, 83, 115, 142, 148, 156, 158, 182, 212
Craig, Alan **109**
Crescent Project 26, 28, 72
CSW 128, 241 n.29
Cumming, Joseph 23, 28, **34**, 41, 43, 44, 49, 50, 52, 57, 60, 61, 111, 128, 147, 177, 187, 200, 202, 213, 224

Dale, Moyra 23, 26, **28**, 29, 83, 87, 94, 176, 212, 215
De Ruiter, Bert **10**, 35, 115, 119, 184, 185
Deik, Anton **159**
Diab, Issa **80**
Dieppe, Tim 29, **35**, 40, 59, 66, 67, 79, 190, 195
Durie, Mark 26, 28, 29, 30, **31**, 42, 44, 49, 51, 53, 54, 57, 60, 79, 81, 94, 97, 98, 121, 122, 124, 128, 141, 169, 171, 187, 190, 202, 211
Dye, Colin **44**, 74, 202
Dyer, Charles 2, 157, 161
Dyrness, William 197

Elam Ministries 125
Elass, Mateen† 81, 88
Evans, Mike 2, 29, **39**, 153, 156, 157, 158, 160

Falwell, Jerry **25**, 38, 67, 236
Farah, Warwick* 24, **145**, 160, 174, 175, 177
Fortner, Michael 163
Fuller Theological Seminary 1, 8, 27, 39, 51

Gabriel, Mark†* 24, 29, **42**, 61, 67, 69, 83, 84, 93, 108, 114, 135, 138, 140, 142, 143, 154, 172, 173, 212
Garlow, James 1, **25**, 41, 107, 109, 113, 114, 144, 153, 187

Garrison, David 1, **27**, 28, 29, 145, 190, 194, 195, 204, 215
Gauss, James 29, **69**, 78, 107, 108, 113, 169
Geisler, Norman 55, 188
George, Timothy 25, 50, 51, **53**, 54, 57, 58, 59, 60
Ghattas, Raouf and Carol **85**
Gilchrist, John 29, 184
Glaser, Ida 23, 29, **52**, 55, 65, 68, 71, 73, 83, 92, 111, 168, 176, 177, 186, 198, 212
Goldmann, David 29, **52**, 57, 69, 138
Goldsmith, Martin 1, 176, **194**
Goll, James **153**, 160
Graham, Franklin **25**, 53, 213
Greear, James **25**, 184
Green, Stephen **78**, 184
Green, Tim 2, 216
Greenlee, David 26, 183, 198
Greeson, Kevin 85
Gushee, David 2, 29, 200

Hadaway, Robin **175**
Haddad, Elie **50**
Hagee, John **38**, 153, 155, 158
Hicham, E.† 29, 183, 184, 188, **190**
Hine, Cathy 23, 26, **176**, 197, 212, 218
Hitchcock, Mark 1, **161**, 162
Hoover, Jon **57**, 58
Houssney, George 23, 29, **43**, 59, 109, 144, 167, 168, 170, 184, 185, 194, 199, 212
Howarth, Toby **170**, 199, 267
Hungerford, David **81**
Hunt, Dave 29, 161

i2 Ministries 24, 190
Ibrahim, Ayman 74, **194**, 197
Idowu-Fearon, Josiah **130**
Institute for the Study of Islam and Christianity 169
International Christian Concern 123
Intrater, Asher (Keith) 2, **161**, 172, 262
Isaac, Munther 23, **153**, 154, 156, 163

Jabbour, Nabeel 1, 2, **23**, 29, 43, 107, 183, 198, 212, 223
Janosik, Daniel 25, **92**, 94, 98
Jardim, Georgina 23, 82
Jeffrey, Grant 161
Johnson, Thomas **100**, 130, 203

Johnston, David 54, **59**, 61, 97, 99
Johnston, Douglas **100**
Jones, Terry **78**, 171
Joyner, Rick **114**, 115

Kaemingk, Matthew **39**, 108, 203, 223
Katanacho, Yohanna **154**, 159, 160
Kendal, Elizabeth **96**, 123, 171
Knell, Bryan 30
Kuhn, Mike 1, 28, **65**, 68, 88, 142, 152, 159
Kuttab, Jonathan 155

Lambert, Lance 157, 243 **n.13**
Larson, Warren 1, 23, **67**, 85, 175, 191, 195, 201
Lewis, Rebecca **196**
Lindsey, Hal **107**, 144, 154, 155, 162
Lingel, Joshua **24**, 26, 188, 190, 197
Love, Fran 23
Love, Rick 29, 41, **124**, 175, 176, 198, 199, 200, 201, 212
Lucia, Martha **163**
Lutzer, Erwin 131, **139**, 193

Maalouf, Tony **144**
MacArthur, John 1, 143, **144**, 147, 148
Mallouhi, Christine 29, **148**, 201, 202
Mallouhi, Mazhar†* **43**, 197, 198, 212
Malone, Henry 29, 143
Mamahit, Ferry **136**
Masood, Steven† **81**
Masri, Fouad 23, 59, **72**, 184, 212
McDermott, Gerald 57, 58, 59, 152, 157
McLaren, Brian 25, **27**, 52, 54, 67, 72, 138, 147, 197, 203, 212, 224
McRoy, Anthony **146**
Medearis, Carl 23, 52, 55, **105**, 136, 146, 189, 200
Meral, Ziya **97**, 125, 126, 127, 130
Merkley, Paul 121, 157, 159
Miller, Duane 183, **189**, 193, 197
Moeller, Carl 131
Mohler, Albert **44**, 50, 53, 169
Moore, Johnnie **122**, 171
Morey, Robert 49, 53, 57, 114, 136, 141
Morton, Jeff 26, 29, **171**, 177, 197
Moucarry, Chawkat **23**, 29, 42, 43, 52, 53, 54, 66, 72, 73, 85, 88, 92, 94, 128, 135, 139, 142, 143, 147, 148, 163, 168, 175, 186, 187, 188, 191, 203, 211
Mouw, Richard 187
Munayer, Salim 44, **154**, **159**
Murray, Abdu†* **24**, 58, 163, 188, 189
Musk, Bill 23, 29, **41**, 50, 51, 52, 54, 55, 57, 61, 73, 74, 78, 83, 86, 92, 94, 96, 100, 105, 107, 109, 136, 139, 140, 143, 148, 172, 174, 175, 201, 211, 214

Nazir-Ali, Michael 4, **9**, **24**, 26, 28, 56, 93, 96, 98, 99, 106, 110, 112, 113, 122, 123, 125, 128, 136, 142, 143, 146, 164, 168, 174, 182, 186, 197, 212, 214
Newbigin, Lesslie **9**, 11, 112, 116, 192, 212
Nickel, Gordon 29, **81**, 186, 188
Nikides, Bill 26, **177**, 197, 224

Oksnevad, Roy 183
One Truth Project 28, 190
Open Doors 97, 120, 122
Orr-Ewing, Amy and Frog 29, 135, 137, 175

Pack, Darrell **78**, 98
Parshall, Phil 23, 29, **86**, 87, 175, 196
Pawson, David **8**, 24, 53, 68, 153, 162, 164, 171, 172, 173, 202, 203
Payne, Tony **75**, 193, 222
Peace Catalyst International 130, 198, 201, 203
Peltola, Beth 29, 59, 66, 67, 79, **190**, 195
Peñamora, Aldrin **149**, 212, 217
Peters, Duncan 52, **57**, 61
Pfander Films 24, 28, 51, 69, 80, 139, 212
Piper, John 25, **44**, 57, 58
Power, Bernie 23, 51, **54**, 57, 58, 69, 71, 85, 87, 138, 189, 212
Prenger, Jan 198
Price, Randall 1, 135, **137**, 143, 153, 161, 162
Prince, Derek 161, 244 n.35

Qureshi, Nabeel† 24, 29, 51, 54, **61**, 138, 139, 143, 144, 148, 177, 183, 188, 189, 212, 214

Rachid, Brother†* **158**, 184
Rawlings, Phil 23, **182**

Reisacher, Evelyne 23, 26, 29, **71**, 94, 174, 176, 212
Release International 123, 124
Richardson, Don 29, **41**, 66, 67, 69, 78, 114, 121, 139
Richardson, Joel 29, 125, 144, **161**, 162, 163, 168, 169, 190
Riddell, Peter 2, 26, 29, 67, **85**, 88, 107, 110, 121, 125, 127, 128, 141, 158, 167, 174, 177, 190, 201, 203, 223
Ripken, Nik* 24, 130–1
Rivers, Julian **99**
Roberts, Bob 25, **33**, 107, 124, 200
Robertson, Pat **25**, 38, 56, 155, 213
Robinson, Stuart 4, 23, 29, **41**, 93, 94, 98, 114, 115, 136, 137, 169, 183, 202

Safa, Reza† 130, 135, **184**
Saleeb, Abdul†* 29, **42**, 55, 188
Schirrmacher, Thomas **120**, 122, 123
Scot, Daniel†* 57, 67, 69, **75**, 121, 122, 190, 212
Scott, Rob 29, 59, 66, 184
Shade, Bill 161
Shamoun, Sam 55
Shannon, Jill 157, **161**
Shehadeh, Imed 29, 41, **50**, 51, 52, 54, 55, 56, 57, 58, 59, 71, 212
Shenk, David 29, 41, **44**, 52, 55, 56, 73, 74, 82, 84, 111, 148, 185, 188, 199
Shoebat, Walid† **42**, 135, 137, 214
Shumack, Richard 29, 59, 78, **184**, 189, 197
Siljander, Mark **200**
Simnowitz, Adam **198**
Singh, David **198**
Sizer, Stephen 24, **162**, 186
Small, Keith **24**, 28, 80
Smith, Andrew 23, 44, **182**, 185
Smith, Jack* 24, 162
Smith, Jay **24**, 41, 44, 51, 53, 55, 69, 70, 79, 80, 109, 139, 188, 189, 190, 191, 197, 212
Solomon, Sam†* 24, 29, 30, **42**, 49, 51, 53, 54, 57, 61, 66, 74, 94, 98, 105, 107, 110, 112, 114, 142, 145, 154, 158, 169, 187, 202, 212
Sookhdeo, Patrick 8, **24**, 26, 27, 29, 35, 39, 42, 59, 65, 71, 80, 83, 85, 86, 88, 92, 93, 94, 98, 99, 104, 105, 106, 107, 108, 110, 112, 113, 114, 115, 120, 123, 124, 125, 126, 130, 136, 137, 138, 140, 143, 148, 154, 168, 169, 170, 172, 173, 175, 182, 187, 188, 201, 202, 203, 211, 214, 221
Sookhdeo, Rosemary 1, 23, **24**, 26, 28, 57, 93, 145, 170, 184
Sproul, R. C. 29
Stice, Ralph 29, 161, 163
Stone, Matthew **51**, 52, 57, 58, 174, 184
Stott, John 156
Sudworth, Richard **113**, 126, 131, 154, 182, 186

Taber, Shirin 23, **41**, 174
Talman, Harley 26, 74, 197
Tanagho, Samy **92**
Tash, Hatun† **183**, 189
Tavassoli, Sasan† 28
Taylor, Aaron **92**, 93, 146, 148
Taylor, Jenny **31**, 112, 141, 170, 171
Tennent, Timothy 25, 26, 49, **50**, 51, 53, 54, 55, 73, 74, 186, 188, 212
Teplinsky, Sandra **58**, 154, 162
Thorneycroft, Charlotte **95**, 96
Travis, John 26, **196**, 197, 212

Vines, Jerry **41**, 66, 67
Voice of the Martyrs (VOM) 124, 130
Volf, Miroslav 30, **44**, 49, 50, 51, 52, 53, 54, 57, 59, 60, 62, 103, 125, 200, 212

Wagner, Donald 163
Wagner, Peter **56**
Wagner, William 1, 29, 108, **114**, 115, 122, 171, 182, 185, 194
Walker, Carol 23, 26
Walker, Tanya **99**
Wallis, Jim 1, 2, 25, **38**, 105, 108, 109, 135, 146, 147, 148, 158, 173, 201
Walls, Jerry **59**
Welby, Justin **25**, 26, 99
White, Andrew 200
White, James 25, 66, 69, **70**, 79, 82, 84, 85, 189, 212
Whittingham, Martin 24, 28
Wilson, Tom **182**
Womack, Deanna 23, **115**
Wood, David 25, **188**, 189, 212

Wood, Nicholas **9**
Woodberry, Dudley 1, 2, 29, **51**, 53, 73, 193, 195, 198, 212
World Evangelical Alliance (WEA) 30, 31, 78, 96, 100, 120, 123, 130, 203

Yakubu, Rahman† **188**
Yousef, Mosab Hassan† 29, 42, **173**, 183
Yousif, Ashoor 73

Youssef, Michael 29, **42**, 43, 56, 113, 162, 168, 169

Zacharias, Ravi 25, 115, 144, 155, 214, 231 **n.44**
Zaka, Anees 29, **68**, 121
Zeidan, David 114, **142**
Zwemer Center for Muslim Studies 27, 67, 163

Index of topics

A Common Word (ACW) 30, 49, 74, 132, 186, 200, 214
  suspicion of 53, 59, 107, 187
advocacy 119–20, 123, 125–7, 132–3, 216
Afghanistan 97, 120, 124, 146, 149, 199
  Christians in 119, 193, 195, 247 n.4
  Western invasion of 39, 135, 146, 148, 212
Africa 171, 183, 186, 201, 217, 218
  authors from 9, 20, 24
  Sharia in 97
  slavery. *See* slavery
Algeria 125
Allah. *See* God/Allah
Antichrist 29, 68, 145, 161–3, 178, 236
antisemitism 151, 154, 157
apocalypse. *See* End Times
apologetics 3, 29, 36–7, 51, 85, 188–9, 208
  apologists 25, 79, 84, 99, 188–9
  training for 190, 191
apostasy 125–6, 132, 173, 197
  laws of 86, 88, 119–20, 125, 130, 182
  treatment of apostates 24, 101, 125, 126, 195
Arabic 11, 73, 106, 136, 141, 184
  importance of 105
  speakers of 20, 24, 43, 52, 77, 170, 183
  word for God 55
Asia
  authors from 21, 212
Australia 11, 23, 27, 40, 75, 95, 98, 189, 216
  authors from 28, 31, 39, 41, 54, 75, 85, 95–6, 98, 148, 176

Baptist 9, 25, 39, 41, 44, 144
  Southern Baptist 25, 27, 41, 59, 85, 108, 114, 194
Bibi, Asia 119, 123
Bible 55, 92
  Evangelicals and 5, 60, 196
  interpretation of 8, 83, 91, 156, 163, 213
  Muslim views of 24, 37, 72, 188
  prophecy in 144, 161, 163, 165
  reading in Muslim context 198
  SR. *See* Scriptural Reasoning (SR)
  translation of. *See* translation
blasphemy laws 88, 119–20, 123–5, 130, 173
Botross, Father Zakaria 4, 183–4, 190–1
Brexit 39
burqa/niqab 109–10
Bush, George W. (US President) 2, 49, 136, 212–13

Calvin, John 3, 66
Canada 96, 119, 216
  authors from 70, 81, 94
Carter, Jimmy (US President) 157
charismatic movement 4, 7, 8, 146, 194
Chrislam 197–8
church buildings
  attacked 122, 129, 171
  closing 109, 130
  Muslims praying in 108, 112
  restrictions on 107, 120, 126
Church of England 9, 24, 27, 44, 181–2, 239 n.20
civil society 16–17, 116, 130
climate change 40, 219, 220
colonialism 3, 218
  complaints about 139, 220
  mission and 199
  Muslim 138, 218, 222
  Western 116, 145–7, 222
common good 19, 39, 62, 70, 101, 187, 202–3, 208, 210, 212, 222, 225
conferences 3, 26, 30, 163, 186, 198, 248 n.20
Constitution of Medina 124–5
contextualization 29, 196–8, 204, 209. *See also* Insider Movements

conversion 44, 63, 125, 182–3, 189, 196–8, 202
  BMBs 8, 24, 42–3, 60–1, 81, 94, 130–1, 173, 184, 194–5, 198, 204, 212
  convert care 183, 216
  dialogue and 188
  dreams 188, 194
  from Islam 120, 122, 132, 160, 184, 193, 195, 212
  to Islam 87, 106, 121–2, 146, 170, 213, 216, 218
  stories of 6, 29, 131, 143, 145, 188, 195, 246 n.4
  the work of God 45
cooperation 45, 203, 225. *See also* common good
cross 110, 111, 168, 223, 225
crossroads 2, 12, 223–5
crusade 34, 183, 199, 242 n.1
  the cross and 111
  medieval Crusades 3, 128, 147, 151
  peacemaking and 200–1, 248 n.42
  War on Terror as 2, 8, 136, 213

da'wa 5, 114, 117, 182, 185, 188
debate 28, 41, 79, 124, 189–92, 212
democracy 15, 19, 157, 222
  imposition of 146, 148
  Islam/Muslims and 19, 97, 169, 171
  Sharia and 97–8
  Western hypocrisy and 126
dhimmi 120–2, 124, 187
  dhimmitude 121, 128, 187, 240 n.12
dialogue 29, 44, 71, 186–8, 189, 208–9, 213–14, 225
  suspicion of 3, 187, 202
dispensationalism 152, 161
dreams. *See* conversion

education 114, 147, 203, 219, 221
  Christian 24–5, 107, 188, 190, 212
  Islamic 43, 105, 113, 154
  Islamization and 109, 112–14, 182
  madrasas 113, 146
  shared 222
Egypt 3, 97, 107, 110, 124, 125, 154
  authors from 4, 42, 92, 194
  President El-Sisi 38, 126
End Times 2, 8, 107, 152, 161–3
  Antichrist. *See* Antichrist
  Battle of Armageddon 149, 161, 162, 250, 262
  Beast 161–3, 178
  Israel and 151, 159–63
  Last Days 162
  Muslim views of 149, 156, 162–3
  role of Islam in 8, 29, 145, 161, 178
environment. *See* climate change
eschatology. See End Times
essentialism 34, 137, 168, 172–5, 209, 213
Eurabia 98
Europe 1–3, 10, 35, 105, 151, 185, 191, 194
  early public sphere in 16
  Evangelisch 4
  Islamization in 98, 108–9, 112, 114–15, 224
  secularism in 39
Evangelicals
  American 6–8, 103, 214
  British 8–9
  conservative 3, 7, 9, 25, 49, 161, 186, 219
  definition of 3–5
  Emergent Church 5, 27, 197, 224
  Evangelisch 4
  grassroots 7, 36, 203, 211, 221, 224
  Muslim views of 212–13
  open 7, 25, 213, 224
  post-Evangelicals 5, 44
  progressive 6–7, 36, 103, 173, 198, 209, 219
  Red Letter Christians 5, 58
evangelism 3, 181–5, 195
  evangelists 25, 43, 92, 183–5
  friendship 62, 184–5, 194, 199, 200, 210
  internet 124, 190, 194–5
  preaching 183, 210
  TV 159
exclusivism 44–5, 208, 213

fear 1, 3, 35, 41, 62, 115, 131, 208, 210, 239 n.26. *See also* Islamophobia
  causes of 40, 119, 164, 222
  of Islamization 98, 102, 109, 112–14, 133, 137, 169
  as motivation 6
  Muslim 96, 176
  as obstacle 170, 184

overcoming 8, 10, 115, 131, 185–6, 202, 214
   promotion of 34, 41, 113, 163
female voices 22–3, 176, 212, 218
FGM 94
folk Islam 29, 110, 175–6
France 23, 87, 112
freedom of religion 40, 96, 122, 125–7, 132, 160, 200
   and belief (FoRB) 120, 128, 132–3
fundamentalism 36, 122, 174
   Christian 83, 174
   Muslim 122, 172–3, 223

Gairdner, Temple 3, 212
gender 16, 94, 109, 176, 213, 219
   identity 218–19
genocide 122–3, 147, 153
globalization 17, 97, 145, 194, 204
God/Allah 49–63
   analogical reasoning 56–7
   attributes 52, 57–8
   creator 52–3, 56, 58, 72, 168
   experience of 60–1
   henotheism 60, 62
   names 53, 55–6, 155
   nature 57–60, 71
   philosophical reasoning 57–8
   Trinity 50–1, 57–9, 69, 171, 188
Golden Rule 128, 133, 185
grace responses 2, 81, 185, 201

Hadith 67, 71, 85–9, 142, 169, 221
halal food 104–5
hijab 49, 109–10
hijra 112, 139, 142
Holy/Promised Land 151–6, 163, 243
hospitality 41, 45, 105, 170, 222–3
   of Muhammad 71
   risky 222
houris 66, 143, 235 n.7
human rights 29, 93–7, 124, 130, 132
   campaigning 127
hypocrisy 126, 128, 138, 146, 163, 170

immigration 38–40, 106, 112–15, 184, 199, 201, 214
imperialism. *See* colonialism
inclusivism 44–5, 208

Indonesia 42, 100, 114, 124, 129, 171, 203, 218, 271
   authors from 136
Insider Movements 164, 195–8, 204–5, 209, 214
   Chrislam. *See* Chrislam
integrity 85, 184, 197–9, 221, 223
internet 17, 27, 124, 173, 194, 204, 215
   blogs 27–8, 215
   e-mails 25, 184
   social media 184, 231 n.46
   websites 27–8, 119, 194, 215–16
   YouTube 28, 183–4, 200, 215
Iran 108, 120, 122, 124–5, 146, 194, 200
   authors from 41, 184
   Christians in 125, 130, 193
   Iranian Revolution 96, 195
Iraq 146, 200
   ISIS in 2, 122
   Western invasion of 39, 123, 135, 146–9, 201, 212–13
irenic responses 3, 43, 84, 139, 154, 163, 196, 233 n.18
Ishmael 144–5, 153
ISIS 122–3, 135, 171, 195, 253
   Dabiq magazine 220–1
   eschatology and 2, 149
Islam 167–78
   a Christian heresy 168, 171
   compared to Judaism 71, 92, 168
   demonic 8, 145, 160, 171–2, 178, 208
   the enemy 1, 3, 34, 155, 160–1, 164, 170–1, 175
   essentially violent 8, 42, 136–7, 140, 172
   extremist 113, 122, 137, 155, 210
   Humanitarian 100, 130
   means peace 136
   moderate 27, 137, 172
   radical 108, 123, 135, 143, 158, 215
   Salafi 5, 99, 186, 228
   social science view of 168, 176–7
   Wahhabi 40, 108
Islamism 38, 67, 126, 130, 154, 158, 187, 215
   Evangelical response to 115
   violence 123, 148, 171, 221
Islamization 103–17
   conspiracy of 98, 169–70
   education and. *See* education

fear of 40, 91, 97. *See also* fear
identity markers 103, 111
mosque building. *See* mosques
parallel communities 98, 104, 112–13, 238
Saudi financing of 108, 113, 115
warnings of 29, 114
Islamophobia 34–6, 75, 100, 113, 133, 163
definition of 35, 40, 218
suspicion of 35, 117, 128
Israel-Palestine 24, 146, 151–65
authors from 52, 154
Palestinian Christians 154, 158

Jesus
incarnation of 58–9, 92
Muslim views of 72–3
Prince of Peace 149, 164
in the Qur'an 81, 85, 103
Second Coming 162–3, 213
Son of God 71, 81, 110, 188, 197
Word of God 88
Jewish people 152–5, 159–61
jihad 141–4
Christian 147–8
definition of 141–2
in Israel-Palestine 155, 158
offensive and violent 1, 42, 108, 112, 114, 142
spiritual struggle 142
Jordan 50, 69, 97
authors from 23

Kairos Document 155, 158

language 41, 43, 55, 77
as identity marker 105–6
religious language in public sphere 18–19
Lebanon 38, 158, 200
authors from 23
love 92, 108, 155, 158, 165, 186
concept in Islam 54, 59, 69, 140
of enemy 124, 165, 201, 245 n.49
God's love 175, 214
of God and neighbour 30, 59, 131, 187, 201, 204
as mission strategy 39, 41, 131, 183, 185
for Muslims 168, 185, 200
power and 58–9, 194

Luther, Martin 3, 66
lying. *See* taqīya

Mahdi 29, 162–3, 260
Malaysia 94, 100, 114, 124–5
use of Allah in 49
male dominance 94, 176, 218–9
Marrakesh Declaration 124–5, 132, 216, 241, 275
marriage 102, 122, 219
Islamic 93, 99, 169, 238
mixed 95, 203
polygamy 66–7, 99, 219
Martyn, Henry 3, 202
martyrdom
Christian 127, 130–1, 225
Muslim 66, 143–4, *See* terrorism, suicide bombing and
Mauritania 125, 218
Mecca 56, 69–70, 140, 222
Meccan suras. *See* Qur'an
Mennonite 44, 57, 148
Messianic Jews 51, 58, 161, 235
middle ground 36, 37, 204, 207, 209, 214, 224, 225
mission 2, 61, 159, 161, 193–205, 247
agencies 23, 108, 124, 200
contextualization. *See* contextualization
history of 3
IMs. *See* Insider Movements
obstacles to 152, 172, 198–9, 222
peacemaking. *See* peacemaking
stories of 6, 8, 29, 240
women and 22, 94
mosques 89, 107–9, 175, 218
building of 112, 114–15, 171
foreign funding of 108
Ground Zero Mosque 109, 115
learning in 83, 105, 154, 169
Olympic mega-mosque 108
positive views of 108
role of 108
size of 107
Muhammad 65–75
Allah and 66, 71, 78
battles and warfare 67–8, 138
in the Bible 72–3
compared to Jesus 68–9, 138
example of. *See* Sunnah

history of 69–70
insulting 24, 65–6, 74, 77, 119
Muslim love of 65–6
prophethood of 68, 70–1, 74
and slavery 95
wives of 66–7
multiculturalism 112, 116, 215
Muslims
   extremist 3, 83–4, 109, 122, 126, 130, 132, 139, 140, 144, 148–9, 154, 164, 169, 195, 209
   folk. *See* folk Islam
   fundamentalist 123, 172–3
   in the West 53, 113–17, 128, 132, 182, 196, 204, 216, 221–2
   moderate 84, 88, 109, 130, 140, 142, 167, 172–3, 178, 209
   Haqiqah magazine 221
   Sufi. *See* Sufism

Nahdlatul Ulama 100, 130, 203
nationalism 3, 38, 40, 111, 122, 146–7, 149, 156
Nigeria 38, 40, 97, 124, 130, 172, 201
   authors from 9, 129, 235
   Pentecostalism in 4, 9, 43, 229, 241
   violence in 43, 122, 129, 171
9/11 1–3, 6, 8, 11, 40, 49, 66, 109, 135–6, 146–7, 153, 214, 223–4
   an opportunity missed 148
non-violence 129, 136, 147
   NVR 163
   pacifism 44, 135, 141, 148–9

Orientalism 89–90, 221, 237

pacifism. *See* non-violence
Pact of Umar 121–2, 240
Pakistan 39, 97, 119–20, 122, 124, 131, 141, 175, 186, 218
   authors from 24, 61, 81, 119
   blasphemy laws in 123, 125
Palestine. *See* Israel-Palestine
peacemaking 9, 34, 37, 109, 129, 149, 163–4, 198, 200–2, 214, 217
Pentecostalism 4, 5, 44, 183, 198, 229
   in Africa 9, 43, 172, 217
   spiritual warfare 9, 44, 172
persecution 119–33

Pfander, Karl 3, 212, 232
Philippines 149, 217, 271
pluralism 19, 36, 60, 81, 201, 213
   plural society 38, 99–100, 116
   pluralist theology 36, 44, 63, 116, 181
polemics 3, 29, 36, 70, 80, 190–1, 209, 223
   criticism of 190–1, 214
   polemicists 24, 44, 78, 183
   training for 190–1
politics 37–40, 156–9, 209–10
postmodern 7, 142, 168, 197
prayer 114
   adhan (call to prayer) 106–7, 112
   for Christians 119–20, 124, 127
   for Israel 160
   for Muslims 160, 195
   National Prayer Breakfast 160, 200
public opinion 16, 19, 21
public sphere 15–31
   Christian 19, 22
   Habermas and 16–17
   micro-public spheres 17–19
   Muslim 19, 89, 211, 221

Qur'an 77–85
   compared to Bible 79, 80, 81, 88
   history and dating 79, 80
   interpretation of by Christians 82, 88, 178
   interpretation of by Muslims 78, 81, 83–5, 90, 99, 136, 139–41, 178. *See also* tafsir
   abrogation 83–4, 86, 139–40
   occasions of revelation 83
   universal and the particular 84
   Meccan suras 84, 99, 140, 154
   Satanic Verses 65, 79
   translations. *See* translation

racism 35, 217–18
radicalization 96, 108, 113–14
reactionary 208, 210, 249 n.1
reciprocity 107, 115, 127–8. *See also* Golden Rule
reconciliation 43, 127, 130, 160, 163, 198, 200–3
reform (Muslim) 88, 98–9, 101, 124, 138
   Muslim reformers 88, 136, 173–4, 219

Reformation/Reformers (Protestant) 2–4, 68, 151, 168
relativism 36, 44, 116, 222
replacement theology 152
retaliation 24, 39, 129, 148, 158, 217
   Third Cheek Theology 129
revisionism 69–70

Saudi Arabia 107–8, 120, 122, 146, 218
   Sharia in 97, 125
Scriptural Reasoning (SR) 82, 90
secularism 5–6, 39, 186, 215, 224
sexuality/LGBTQ 101, 186, 219
Sharia 91–102, 110
   apostasy. *See* apostasy
   countries incorporating 40, 96, 98, 120, 125
   finance 115
   human rights and 96–8
   women and 93–4
slavery 93–5, 101, 218
   abolition of 95, 218
social science 24, 33, 168, 176–7
   anthropology 94, 176–7
   distrust of 177
   sociology 4, 9, 15, 176–7
Speakers' Corner 183, 189, 191
spiritual warfare 8, 44, 145, 162, 171
Sufism 29, 59, 61, 66, 132, 175, 213
Sunnah 65, 77–8, 84–6, 99, 177, 221
syncretism 4, 36, 202–3
   Chrislam. *See* Chrislam
Syria 83, 122, 147, 195, 221, 250
   authors from 23, 43
   Christians in 40, 126
   President Assad 38, 126
   Western intervention in 39, 135

tafsīr 83–5, 177
taqīya 169–70, 187, 191–2, 197, 202, 223
tattoos 110–11
temple, Jewish 156, 161–2

terrorism 2, 6, 114, 122, 129, 135, 137, 140, 145–6, 149, 153, 157, 171–2
   former terrorists 42, 145, 173
   literature 6–7, 29
   suicide bombing and 1, 137, 143–4, 158, 173
   war on 2, 148, 223
tolerance 107, 188, 222
   in Islam 71, 119, 130, 136
translation 73
   of the Bible 31, 55, 105, 195–8
   misleading 96, 169
   of the Qur'an 89, 195
Trinity. *See* God/Allah
Trump, Donald (US President) 38, 126, 159
Tunisia 10
   authors from 94
Turkey 42, 74, 108, 126, 218

umma 1, 143, 218

violence 135–49
   terrorist. *See* terrorism
   war. *See* war

war 138–9, 146–8
   Crusade. *See* crusade
   jihad. *See* jihad
   just war 135, 149, 201
   pacifism. *See* non-violence
   Second Gulf War 123. *See also* country entries
   War on Terror. *See* terrorism
white flight 109, 113
women. *See* female voices
World Council of Churches (WCC) 3, 127

Yemen 80, 149

Zionism 8, 152–4, 157–9, 164
Zwemer, Samuel 3, 212, 214, 243 n.18

www.ingramcontent.com/pod-product-compliance
Lightning Source LLC
Chambersburg PA
CBHW071806300426
44116CB00009B/1220